THE CROWN *versus* CHAMBERLAIN

• 1980-1987 •

To my father,
who taught me more of justice
than all the lawyers in Christendom

THE CROWN *versus* CHAMBERLAIN

• 1980-1987 •

Ken Crispin

An Albatross Book

Published in Australia and New Zealand by
Albatross Books Pty Ltd
PO Box 320, Sutherland
NSW 2232, Australia

First edition 1987

National Library of Australia
Cataloguing-in-Publication data

Crispin, Kenneth John
The Crown versus Chamberlain: 1980-1987

ISBN 0 86760 088 8

1. Chamberlain, Lindy, 1948- — Trials, litigation, etc. 2. Chamberlain, Michael (Michael Leigh) — Trials, litigation, etc. 3. Chamberlain, Azaria, 1980-1980. 4. Trials (Infanticide) — Northern Territory — Darwin. I. Title.

345.9429'02523

Front cover photo: Kevin Goddard
Back cover photo: Michael Chamberlain
Typeset by Rochester Communications Group, Sydney
Printed by Australian Print Group, Maryborough

Contents

Acknowledgements

I AM ACUTELY CONSCIOUS of my debt of gratitude to a number of people who have assisted me in various ways.

First, I would like to thank Lindy and Michael Chamberlain without whose consent this book could not have been written. I am also indebted to the ACT Bar Association for its approval of this project. So far as I am aware, this is the first occasion upon which an Australian association of barristers has authorised one of its members to write a book about a case in which he appeared as counsel.

Second, Stuart Tipple, Dr Norm Young of Avondale College, Betty Hocking, Senator Bob Collins and others have proved a mine of valuable background information, whilst Mr Justice R.S. Watson has contributed not only an eagle-eye scrutiny of the manuscript, but the benefit of his vast experience in criminal law and procedure. The responsibility for any errors or opinions perceived as heretical must, of course, rest upon me alone.

Last, I would also like to thank my mother-in-law, Mrs N. Eagleton, who suggested the project, my wife Pam who endured countless barren evenings watching me pace up and down my study, muttering imprecations into a dictaphone, and Mrs Ann Charlton who transliterated these outbursts into a manuscript.

Ken Crispin
Canberra, ACT
7 August 1987

Introduction

THE PROSECUTION OF Michael and Lindy Chamberlain captured the public imagination in a manner unique in the annals of Australian legal history. It would take a social anthropologist to fully explore the reasons for this immense interest.

In some indefinable way, the incident seemed to strike at a number of basic beliefs. The very thought of an apparently loving mother brutally cutting the throat of her baby daughter was so abhorrent that it was bound to arouse strong emotions.

Some simply refused to believe it. Their faith in the bonds of motherhood was too strong. 'No mother would do that!' was an oft-repeated response to news of the tragedy. Others shared their abhorrence, but reacted differently. They were not incredulous, but outraged. This woman had betrayed the trust of motherhood and murdered the child she pretended to love.

The Chamberlains' religion was also a strong factor. Michael Chamberlain was a minister, Lindy a 'minister's wife'. Many believed that people with such a strong Christian faith could not have committed the horrific crimes with which they had been charged. But few Australians knew much about the tenets of Seventh Day Adventism. Many knew only that Adventists met on Saturday, a fact which suggested that their adherents were not among the mainstream of Christendom. The unfamiliarity of their religion and a spate of rumours suggesting that Azaria may have been killed in some sort of sacrificial rite led many to assume that the Chamberlains were members of some bizarre and dangerous cult.

Some, whether conservationists or simply dog-lovers, rallied strongly to the dingo's defence. Suddenly, it seemed, every office and workshop in the country boasted at least one dingo expert vociferously proclaiming that such creatures would never enter a tent and attack a child. As time went by, the scientific debate contributed to the growing polarisation.

Finally, when the Chamberlains were convicted, it became in the eyes of many people a question of trust in the Australian system of justice.

Whatever the reasons, the allegations against Michael and Lindy Chamberlain evoked strong emotions from many Australians. There were death threats, savage abuse and vicious rumours. Yet there were also staunch defenders, people who had never met the Chamberlains but were prepared to literally take to the streets to demonstrate their support for them.

This uniquely Australian drama, set against the backdrop of Ayers Rock rising like a colossus in a sea of red sand, was to create worldwide interest. In an endeavour to resolve the controversy, experts were to be brought from Britain, the United States, Canada, Japan, West Germany and Sweden. There seemed to be far more at stake than the guilt or innocence of these two people. There were scientific controversies, political disputes and, ultimately, serious questions about the adequacy of the legal safeguards to protect the innocent.

This was a case in which the Crown had been able to produce no eyewitnesses, no body, no confession and no motive. It had to overcome significant evidentiary obstacles, including an admittedly honest witness who claimed to have heard the baby cry when, on the Crown case, it must have been dead, and limited opportunity for the accused to have done what the Crown suggested. Yet it managed to secure convictions and, in Lindy's case, a mandatory sentence of life imprisonment.

What if they were not guilty? What if they were wrongly convicted on the basis of circumstantial evidence which ultimately proved to have been quite misleading? They had been able to rely upon undisputed evidence that they were people of impeccable character, that Lindy had loved the child that she was supposed to have murdered and that she had not exhibited any sign of postnatal depression or other mental abnormality. If, despite all that evidence in their favour, they could be convicted simply through coincidence and error, then how many others might have suffered a similar fate? Even now, are there other innocent people sitting dejectedly in prison cells and praying that some day their cases might also be reopened? Indeed, are we not all at risk?

By the time Mr Justice Morling's historic report was tabled, the matter had been the subject of two inquests, a trial, two appeals and a lengthy inquiry. To my knowledge no-one has ever added up the number of pages in the profusion of scientific reports, police running sheets and other documents tendered in evidence. However, the transcripts of the various proceedings run to more than 16,000 pages and the exhibits, perhaps, a further eight to ten thousand pages. As the Attorney-General told the Northern Territory parliament, 'the amount of evidence, exhibits, transcript and other items which were freighted from Darwin to Sydney, and back again, weighed an estimated five tonnes'. With such a vast store of material to draw upon, any discussion of the evidence must necessarily be selective. Any number of witnesses could fairly complain that I have failed to do justice to their evidence, but a complete exposition would require a multi-volume treatise. I have limited my account to what is necessary to explain how this strange saga unfolded and how it was that a jury's verdict, twice upheld on appeal, could now be discredited.

I have also taken the liberty of suggesting some changes to the law. Some may disagree, and if I achieve nothing more than to fan the spark of debate from which reform may ultimately emerge I will be well content. For in the end result, this case, perhaps more than any other in recent times, has demanded a reappraisal of the manner in which the law seeks to balance the rights of the individual against the interests of the community. In our understandable preoccupation with the need for protection from crime have we too readily dismissed the risk that our law might condemn the innocent?

PART I

THE INCIDENT

1

The devil dingo

AT THE HEART OF CENTRAL AUSTRALIA is a gigantic stone monolith. Uluru, or Ayers Rock as most of us know it, is an imposing sight. The sheer size is breathtaking. It is nearly nine kilometres around the base and towers 348 metres above the red, sandy plain. Yet even that is only the tip of the iceberg. It projects down into the ground some six kilometres. If some capricious giant were to dig it up and stand it on its base, it would be three-quarters the height of Mount Everest.

This mammoth stone dominates the surrounding plain absolutely, as though lesser stones had fled from its presence. To the Aborigines it is a place of deep religious significance, its perimeter dotted with sacred sites now closed to white tourists. It bears the scars of savage violence perpetrated by fearsome creatures and spirit people of the Dreamtime. The resulting features serve as a reminder of these events and of the ancestral beings who shaped them. They also contain the spiritual power of these beings some of whom were creatures of unsurpassed malevolence. The very names of these features evoke images of titanic conflicts.

Even the cynical white man finds it hard to dismiss the monolith as an interesting but random concatenation of atoms. It is too massive, too redolent of some mysterious brooding evil. This impression is heightened by the incredible variations in colour which make it seem as though it were pulsating with some inner life of its own. As John Williamson sings, 'Uluru has power!'

It was to see this awesome sight that the Chamberlains came to Ayers Rock in August, 1980.

Legend has it that the Mala or Hare wallaby people came from the north to an area on the northern side of Uluru known as Katjitilkil. There they formed two camps, one for the men and one for the women, and began to dance. Whilst they were dancing, Panpanpanala the bellbird brought an invitation from the Wintalka men to come to their dances at Kikingkura near the Docker River. The Mala refused to come and the Wintalka men decided to send a *mamu*, or evil spirit, to punish them for spurning their invitation. This being was the devil dingo, Kurrpanngu or Kulpunya as it is also known.

Kurrpanngu picked up the scent of the Mala people and followed them to Uluru. He came upon the Mala women dancing at a place called Tjukutjapinya, but the women were able to drive him off. It is said that the hair skirts of the women were transformed into cones of rock at Tjukutjapi, an area now set aside as a sacred site and restricted to women. Having been repulsed at Tjukutjapi, Kurrpanngu continued around the base of the rock to Inintitjara where the Mala men were sleeping. At the last moment, Lunpa the kingfisher woman called out a warning, but Kurrpanngu leapt into the camp and killed many of the Mala men. Lunpa is said to have been transformed into a boulder and the paw marks are said to be still visible in the side of the cliff. The surviving Mala fled from Uluru and Kurrpanngu pursued them into South Australia.

The Aborigines say that Kurrpanngu is one of the many Dreamtime creatures whose spirit lingers at Uluru. From time to time, his spirit inhabits the body of a living dingo, causing it to act with uncharacteristic malevolence and ferocity.

By August 1980, the rangers at Ayers Rock were worried men. Whilst Derek Roff, the chief ranger, had been on leave in June, there had been a number of attacks on children. His deputy, Ian Cawood, had investigated them and shot a number of the offending animals. One of these attacks had been particularly serious. On 23 June 1980, young Amanda Cranwell, then two years of age, had been dragged from the front seat of a motor car whilst her parents were talking to one of the rangers nearby. Her father returned to literally snatch his child from the dingo's jaws as it was in the process of dragging her away.

Dingoes are wild animals, and predators at that, and there had always been incidents in which overly friendly tourists had been reprimanded for their familiarity by abrupt snaps, but the attack on Amanda Cranwell seemed infinitely more serious. This was not the act of a dog demanding to be left alone, but the act of a predator intent on removing his prey. As if that were not enough, the other attacks raised the chilling possibility that this may not have been an isolated incident, but a newly emerging pattern of behaviour. As time went by there were more attacks, none of them serious, but their frequency and boldness were unprecedented. They heightened the rangers' fears.

In July, Derek Roff posted warning notices around the toilet blocks, visitors' centre office and the various motel and store leases warning people not to feed the dingoes. By that time the rangers were concerned that the local dingoes may have acquired an unusual degree of familiarity with man which had led them to lose their usual inhibitions about approaching humans. Not only were the attacks continuing, but the dingoes were doing things which wild animals would never do: boldly invading the camp and even entering tents in search of food. On 4 August, Derek Roff wrote to ranger headquarters in Alice Springs describing the problem and suggesting the need for a visitor education programme. At the same time he forwarded for consideration a more permanent poster design. He was later to report:

> I was still concerned that if no action on control was taken we could experience a more serious attack and, having discussed the matter with Ian Cawood and other staff members, I radioed on 6th August 1980 to our headquarters requesting the issue of six packets of 0.22 Hornet ammunition for dingo control. This request was made at 8.30 a.m. through Carol. At 9.00 a.m. Robbie Smith, the storekeeper, advised that bullets could not be supplied as we had not been issued with a high-powered rifle... With regard to the high-powered rifle issue perhaps I should mention that Ian Cawood owns a Hornet rifle that has recently been licensed in the name of the Director, Parks and Wildlife, which possibly could be read as being issued.
>
> After this refusal and still wishing to carry out some shooting as a control, I requested Bill Bickerton to buy some bullets for me. Bill tried, but none were available in Alice Springs.

In another report he made a comment which was to prove strikingly prophetic. The dingo, he said, 'is well able to take advantage of any laxity on the part of prey species and, of course, children and babies can be considered possible prey.'

In mid-August, a tourist named McGrath was woken by a dingo trying to force its way into his tent. Evidently no-one had taken the trouble to explain to the animal that dingoes always ran away when they were shouted at and it proved remarkably persistent. He was able to drive it off only by hitting it with the butt end of his rifle.

On 15 August another tourist, Mr Backhaus-Smith, reported that a wild dog had entered his tent, knocked over the central pole and picked through his belongings. A ranger told him that dingoes had been entering tents and stealing food. On the same day another tourist, Erica Letsch, was sleeping in her tent when a dingo literally snatched the pillow from under her head. Having successfully made off with that prize, the dingo waited until Miss Letsch settled down again and then returned in an attempt to remove her sleeping bag.

During the course of the next day there were three separate incidents involving dingoes. Ronald Billingham was snapped at, Catherine West had her elbow seized while she was sitting in a chair reading and Jason Hunter was bitten. Things were building to a crescendo.

It was on that evening, 16 August, that the Chamberlains arrived at Ayers Rock. They knew nothing of the recent attacks by dingoes and were given no warning that their children might be in danger. During the course of the next day they were to read one of Derek Roff's signs urging tourists not to feed the dingoes, but assumed that it was there for the dingoes' protection: to prevent them from being shot if they became a nuisance. The sign gave them no inkling of the tragedy to come.

Whilst there were no cartographers in the Dreamtime to record with precision the route followed by Kurrpanngu in his relentless pursuit of the Mala men, the marks on the northern face of Uluru are, to an Aborigine, eloquent of his passing. If one were to plot those positions on a map and follow his path to the south-east one would come to an area which, in 1980, was set aside as the 'top' tourist camping area. It was there that the Chamberlains chose to pitch their tent. During the course of the next evening a dingo was to take their daughter Azaria from the tent. She was never seen again.

Aboriginal tribal elders were later to say that this was the act of Kurrpanngu — presumably a shocking retaliation for the sacrilege of the white man who had heedlessly trespassed upon the sacred sites and invoked the wrath of the spirit beings. To the rangers, it was simply the act of a predator emboldened by his familiarity with man. Whatever the cause, it was left to a tourist bus proprietor, Richard Dare, to express the feelings of the locals. 'It had to happen,' he said simply.

2

The 'outback' pastor

Big galvanised rooves and monster pipes black,
pink and white clouds from a chimney stack,
red dust and hawks in the wind out back,
here I am at the Isa.

What do you do in a town like the Isa
retrenched at fifty, become an old miser
drink yourself blind so you're none the wiser,
sit at home with a race form and whinge.

Just over the hill in his own backyard
the landscape becomes a picture postcard,
where the colours are soft but the life is hard
on the stations here at the Isa.

Tonight's the night of the rodeo ball
before riders and bull and horses stand tall,
while out in the park some black people sprawl
and share their money on flagons.

There's so much more to be understood
before coming out here like Robin Hood.
The do-gooders do more harm than good
without really knowing the Isa.

'Back to the Isa'
John Williamson

Mount Isa is a mining town. It lies in north-west Queensland about 150 kilometres east of the Queensland/Northern Territory border and 330 kilometres south of the Gulf of Carpentaria. It is a hot dusty place where the temperatures frequently soar into the forties. A man can work up quite a thirst in a place like that and there have been no reports of hotels closing their doors for want of patronage. It can be a harsh and uncompromising town. As the song implies, the residents have little time for 'do-gooders'.

It was there that Michael Chamberlain was posted. He was a 'do-gooder', a minister of religion.

There was an innocence about the Chamberlains. Not a naivety born of lack of perception or understanding, but a guilelessness and a willingness to trust others. This latter quality was to be cruelly exploited in the months to come, but as they set off on their holiday there was no inkling of that — no premonition or sense of foreboding to inhibit their exuberance. For this was a happy time.

To understand the Chamberlains, one must first understand their religion. The Seventh Day Adventist Church is within the mainstream of Protestant denominations. It had its genesis in the worldwide interdenominational revival that occurred in the first half of the nineteenth century, though it did not formally become a church until 1863. Its adherents believe in the divinity of Christ, his virgin birth, his sinless life, his death as an atonement for sin, his bodily resurrection and his ascension to heaven. As the name implies, they stress a belief in the personal return of Christ or 'second advent' and observe the seventh day as the sabbath in accordance with the fourth commandment.

Their willingness to dissent particularly from some of the tenets of Roman Catholicism is sufficient to bring a grimace of distaste to the face of a zealous ecumenical, whilst their fundamentalism would distress those of a liberal outlook theologically. Yet their basic doctrines differ little, if at all, from those of their fellow Christians.

There is no hint of gnosticism about the Adventists. They believe that God is concerned with body, mind and spirit. They have a worldwide network of hospitals and clinics and employ literally thousands of doctors and other medical personnel. Many of their hospitals enjoy an international reputation for the excellence of their medical care. They are also concerned about the prevalence of tobacco and alcohol, each of which kill many times as many Australians each year as the so-called 'hard drugs' like heroin and other opiates.

When the Chamberlains married in November, 1969, Michael was twenty-five and Lindy four years younger. Their faith had been one of the things which had drawn them together. Michael was a pastor and Lindy was the daughter of a pastor. They were people who, in any denomination, would have been described as 'committed Christians'. To them, their faith was not a mere set of philosophical views to be grafted onto a lifestyle wherever the practical considerations of life permitted, but a personal relationship with God which had first priority. A Christian's duty was to serve others through some form of 'ministry'.

Both quickly found their niche in the role traditionally allocated to pastors and their wives. Both prided themselves on their fitness and encouraged others to look after their bodies which were, after all, 'the temple of the Holy Spirit'. By the mid '70s Michael had become involved in the conduct of anti-smoking classes. It was at this time that he decided that one needed a gimmick to drive home the perils of smoking. One particular gimmick was suggested by another pastor who had tried it himself. It sounded corny, but it seemed to work and he was willing to try anything that might save people from the lingering agony of lung cancer. It was for this reason that a cut-down varnished coffin came into existence. At the next anti-smoking rally Michael was to finish his address and with a dramatic flourish exclaim: 'Throw your butts in before they throw you in!' Some time later he established a radio programme in Mount Isa, becoming something of a local identity.

Michael had long been a fanatical photographer and would pursue a good shot with the kind of ardour another man might display in pursuit of a new mistress. By 1978 others had noticed that he had adopted the peculiar habit of driving with a camera bag under his knees. Car trips became stop/start affairs punctuated by sudden braking and numerous clicks from the shutter of the camera which was never far away.

By this time Lindy had developed a passion for clothes which almost matched her husband's passion for photography. This brought her some criticism. After all, a pastor's wife was expected to set an example and there was a feeling that a woman should dress soberly in recognition that her 'crowning glory' was gentleness of spirit. Yet Lindy had a passion for the dramatic — blacks, reds and other bold colours. To her, Christianity was a source of joy. There was no need to bury oneself in the drab and the dowdy.

With this penchant for colour came a passion for neatness which Michael also shared. Their car, a canary yellow Torana hatchback purchased in December 1977, when it was four months old, was washed every week.

Lindy Chamberlain was a woman with few ambitions, but there was one unfulfilled longing in her life. She desperately wanted a little girl. She had two sons, Aidan (six years) and Reagan (four), and she loved them both deeply, but as her pregnancy approached its culmination her thoughts turned frequently to little girls in satins and laces, pigtails and ribbons, tiny pink booties and other badges of femininity. They had been praying for a daughter and as her confinement grew imminent Lindy's friends began to pray too. If God had withheld this blessing, the disappointment would have been hard to bear.

On 11 June 1980, Azaria Chantal Chamberlain was born. To say that Lindy was pleased would have been an understatement of the kind which only the English or her New Zealand countrymen are prone to make. Friends were later to use words like 'thrilled', 'delighted' and 'ecstatic' to describe her reaction. There were many excited phone calls and effusive letters. To her mother, Avis Murchison, she sent a cassette tape bubbling over with the joy of it all.

Whilst still in hospital there was a difference of opinion with a nursing sister over Lindy's preference for demand feeding. In other places this might have been described as contretemps, but in Mount Isa it was simply a 'bit of a kerfuffle'. In the end, Azaria was allowed to sleep through until the next feed. The treating doctor, Dr Irene Milne, confirmed that she was adequately cared for and was gaining weight at the normal rate, but this trivial incident was to form the background for a police report attributing to Dr Milne the statement that 'Mrs Chamberlain did not love her baby' — an assertion which Dr Milne was to reject as completely untrue.

Upon her discharge from hospital, Lindy revelled in her new-found role as the mother of a little daughter. The nursery was extensively refurbished and in the next few weeks little Azaria acquired a collection of some thirty little dresses, most of them pink. When Liz Hickson, a grandmotherly reporter from *Woman's Day,* was permitted to examine the nursery she was to say that Lindy had obviously 'indulged herself' in the joy of having a little girl. Lindy's friends and family would have agreed.

When Azaria was about six weeks old, there was a minor accident in a Woolworths supermarket. Young Reagan, then aged four, attempted to climb up the side of a trolley which tipped over, spilling the baby onto the floor. A panic-stricken Lindy rushed her to the doctor's surgery but, to her intense relief, found that she had suffered no injury. However, staff at the medical clinic noticed that the baby was wearing a black dress. In fact the dress was a hand-me-down from Reagan's babyhood and had been hanging in the wardrobe for four years. It was also trimmed with bright red ribbon. Liz Hickson was later to describe the dress as 'perfectly ordinary' and the sort of dress she would have been happy to buy for her own child. Yet in the months to come it was to provide further fuel for gossips and rumour-mongers.

On 13 August 1980, the Chamberlains picked up their drycleaning from Mrs Hansell, taking the time to show off their new baby to the ladies in the drycleaning shop and drove off to start their holiday. They were seasoned campers who had taken away young babies before and had no qualms about their ability to look after Azaria in a tent. The last few weeks had been exciting, but Michael worked long hours as a pastor. Now they would be able to spend some time together as a family. Lindy was going to take up jogging again and get her figure back into shape. Michael and the boys were eager to climb Ayers Rock and they were all looking forward to seeing the mighty Olgas. This was going to be the best holiday they had ever had.

3

Kurrpanngu strikes

SINCE 1980, ABORIGINAL CLAIMS TO ULURU and surrounding areas have been recognised. Tribal Aborigines regard themselves as bound to the land in a manner beyond the understanding of white men. It has been said that the land does not belong to the Aborigine; the Aborigine belongs to the land. But that is a white man's cliche, repeated because it has the ring of pithy profundity about it rather than for any real insight into the nature of the relationship. Uluru has been leased back to the Commonwealth and the entry of white visitors is still unimpeded once they have purchased their ticket from the uniformed white ranger on duty. But the camping areas and motel near the rock have been bulldozed. In time to come they will be reclaimed by desert and scrub, leaving only the Aboriginal encampment to provide shelter in the lee of the greatest rock on earth.

In 1980, the new tourist village of Yulara had not been built and facilities at the camping areas could scarcely have been described as luxurious. A hundred metres or so to the east of the top camping area was a sand dune known as 'Sunrise Hill'. It was not a classic yellow sand dune of the kind which evokes romantic images of sheiks dragging damsels onto camels and galloping boldly away! The sand consisted largely of ferric oxide and was a deep dull red. Sparse bushes fought for survival on its shallow slopes. But it offered spectacular views of Ayers Rock at sunrise.

It was dark when the Chamberlains arrived and Azaria was hungry. She was crying while the Chamberlains laboriously heated her bottle. They fed her, pitched camp and put the children to bed. It was 16 August, 1980. The Chamberlains were not informed that three people had been attacked by dingoes that day. It is unlikely that the rangers knew.

The next morning was a fine sunny day and the whole family was in good spirits. Life is meant to be lived with enthusiasm and this was the first day of their holiday at Ayers Rock. Much of the afternoon was devoted to Michael's ascent of the rock with Aidan and Reagan. As it happened, the boys became separated and he had to climb the rock twice. That is no mean feat even for a man as fit as Michael Chamberlain and the whole exercise took some time. During the course of the afternoon a number of women saw Lindy with Azaria and noted her 'new mum glow'. At the trial, Mrs Wilkin was to describe her as a 'perfect little mother'. Mrs Eccles agreed that she was a 'true mother' and added that she had been 'very caring', 'affectionate', and 'concerned'.

On the southern side of the rock there is an interesting geological phenomen: a cave with strange undulations in the rock walls and ceiling and smooth protuberances from the floor. There are faded shapes on the walls, legacies of Aboriginal artists of an earlier age. In places, the stone has been worn smooth by the hands of generations of women seeking the blessing of children. It is called the Fertility Cave. Lindy explored it, quietly cradling Azaria in her arms.

Outside she had the uneasy sensation of feeling that she was being watched. She looked up and saw a dingo standing on a large boulder and staring down at her. 'Is that your dog?' she asked John McCombe, but though she tried to brush it aside with a joke there was something vaguely disturbing about its implacable stare. She was later to tell Inspector Gilroy that it was almost as though it had been 'casing the baby'.

Later in the afternoon they observed the usual tradition of going to the Sunset Strip to see the incredible phenomenon of Ayers Rock changing colour in the setting sun. It is a striking sight to see this huge edifice turn from orange to blood red.

The warmth of the day was fading quickly now that dusk was giving way to nightfall. The nights at Ayers Rock are crisp and clear as though designed to show off the canopy of stars like myriads of tiny diamonds strewn negligently across black velvet by some titanic jeweller. The temperature was later to drop to below freezing point, but it was not yet 8.00 p.m. and there was a warm ambience about the barbecue area. Perhaps it was the sight of the flames and the promise of food to come. Perhaps it was the gentle glow from the amber floodlight which bathed the whole area or, perhaps, it was just a feeling of contentment. There is something very satisfying about standing around the barbecue preparing dinner after a day's sightseeing. The boys were tired and Reagan was already fast asleep in the tent some twenty metres distant.

The Chamberlains were gregarious people. With a pastor's knack of getting to know people quickly, he and Lindy had spent half the morning talking to Bill and Judith West and their daughter Catherine. Now, as they prepared their dinner, they struck up a conversation with a young couple from Tasmania. Greg Lowe was a friendly affable man who had been known to knock off a 'tinnie' or two and was quick to offer one to Michael Chamberlain. Michael was a teetotaller, but he was happy enough to accept the friendliness that went with the offer. Sally Lowe quickly found that Azaria's middle name was Chantal. The spelling was different, but it was the same name as her own daughter Chantelle, then seventeen months old. Sally was a bright personable girl and Lindy enjoyed talking to her while she nursed Azaria off to sleep.

In real life tragedy strikes its victims without warning. There is no build-up in the dramatic content of a musical score, no measured drum beat to set the pulses racing with apprehension. When she was satisfied Azaria was asleep, Lindy interrupted the conversation with Sally Lowe. 'I'll just put bubby down,' she said. As she turned to leave the barbecue, she remembered that Aidan had had a long day and was obviously tired. 'You can come too,' she told him.

The tent was a little four-man affair about seven feet square. It had been erected beside the car, a yellow Torana hatchback. It was so close that when a door was opened fully it would brush against the canvas. Aidan held the baby whilst his mother smoothed out the bunny rugs and mattress in the bassinette. When Azaria was snugly tucked in, Aidan kissed her goodnight. His recollection of this simple incident was later to be used as a means of denigrating the value of his evidence. It was said to be an obvious reconstruction: something he thought he remembered because he had heard his mother mention it. The submission was made with great conviction as if it were advancing some self-evident truth, but no attempt was made to explain why a little boy approaching seven should not have retained the mental image of this kiss. It was to be the last time he would ever see his baby sister.

It is the experience of mothers the world over that small boys have appetites that would do credit to a shoal of piranhas and, by the time Lindy had got Aidan to bed, he was hungry again. She offered him a tin of baked beans and went to get it from the car whilst he wriggled out of his sleeping bag. They had a half-hearted race back, but slowed as they neared the barbecue area. Lindy picked up the conversation with Sally Lowe at the point where she had interrupted it.

In their tent nearby, the Wests heard the low menacing growl of a dog. It reminded Bill of the dogs on his sheep station near Esperance in Western Australia. When he slaughtered a sheep, he would throw pieces of offal to the dogs. One would seize a piece in his jaws and growl in just that fashion to warn off any other dog displaying an interest in his prize.

It was then that Sally heard the baby cry. It was a short distressed cry and stopped abruptly as if cut off. Lindy didn't hear it, but Aidan said, 'I think that is bubby crying.' Michael said, 'Yes, I think it was bubby too.' The area between the barbecue area and the tent was dotted with low straggly shrubs providing pools of shadow. In front of the tent there was a low railing of treated pine logs. As Lindy approached the tent, she saw a dingo emerge from its flap. It was shaking its head vigorously as a puppy might shake a shoe, but she could not see what was in its mouth because it was below the level of the railing. She shouted at it in the hope that it would drop whatever it was carrying.

It was then that she remembered the cry and something turned cold inside her. A quick glance through the flap told her that the bassinette was empty, but her mind refused to accept it. 'She must be there; she must have just fallen out of the bassinette or got caught up in the blankets.' She scrambled feverishly inside. The centre pole had been knocked askew and the baby's blankets were strewn across the floor of the tent. She rummaged through them desperately, her mind still refusing to accept what reason told her must be so. She emerged from the tent with her heart pounding. There was a dingo standing nearby behind the car. It looked vaguely different, but reason told her it had to be the same one. She gave chase but it ran off into the dark, leaving her alone with her panic.

'My God,' she thought, 'they'll never believe me. No-one will come.' But when her scream rang out, it was so full of anguish and despair that it carried conviction to all who heard it.

'A dingo has got my baby!' she cried.

4

In the wilderness

THE STREAM OF HUMAN THOUGHT can be alarmingly turgid, and it was a moment or two before those at the barbecue could assimilate the implications of Lindy's stricken cry. Then Michael and Greg Lowe ran, weaving around the straggly bushes. They caught up with Lindy at the back of the tent. Michael was still having trouble trying to grasp what had actually happened. 'What?' he asked incredulously. There was no time for explanations: a dog was making off with her baby and Lindy's response was half command, half plea: 'Will somebody please stop that dog?'

They were towards the periphery of the light cast from the amber floodlight and the area further back from the tent was ominously black. There was no sign of either the dingo or the baby. 'Where?' Greg Lowe barked. 'That way,' Lindy replied, pointing across the road and east towards Sunrise Hill. Michael took off in that direction, running frantically into the bush. He could barely see a hand in front of his face and was quickly reduced to searching as much by feel as by sight. But the dingo might have dropped the baby if it took flight at Lindy's shout. His child might be lying on the ground just another few feet further on. Perhaps he might hear her.

'Has anybody got a torch?' Lindy shouted. This produced a flurry of activity as Sally Lowe, Aidan and Judy West all sought to fill the need. Greg took a torch from Sally and ran into the bush. The light was a help but the spinifex and wattle which seemed so spindly in the daytime now seemed capable of casting the most impenetrable shadows. The softness of the sand beneath his feet was slowing him down. It was like running through treacle. He just couldn't seem to move quickly enough. Not that there was any hint of which direction to take anyway.

It is when 'the chips are down' that Australians are at their best and other campers were already hurrying to help. Word was to spread like wildfire and within thirty or forty minutes there were three hundred searchers who were to tramp the bush until the early hours of the morning trying to find this little girl. Greg Lowe was heard to shout, 'Get the police here'. About that time Michael came back. He had realised the futility of searching in the dark and come back for a torch. Judy West offered him a lantern with a fluorescent tube but he wasn't happy with it and returned it. He said there was a lamp in his car but he could not find his keys. Aidan gave him his own torch but the batteries were low and the beam pitifully weak. Eventually Bill West provided a more powerful torch and Michael ran back into the bush. It was about ten past eight.

At about 8.15 p.m. Constable Morris arrived in the police Toyota. He left the headlights on so they would shine out into the bush while he spoke to Lindy. She gave him a brief description of what had happened and he went to the entrance of the tent and shone his torch inside. As Lindy had told him, the baby was gone.

At a time which was probably between 8.15 and 8.20 p.m. Lindy spoke to Murray Haby. She told him what had happened and asked if he had a torch that she could borrow. He was a former Queen's Scout and had been an amateur naturalist for many years. Whilst he did not pretend to be in the same league as Aboriginal trackers he had long been interested in the tracks of animals and thought that he might have some chance of picking up the path of the dingo in the sand. He got a torch from his Kombi van and asked her which way the dingo went. She pointed slightly north of east, towards Sunrise Hill. 'It is better if I go,' he told her and headed off into the bush.

At about 8.20 p.m. Derek Roff was informed that the baby had been taken. He ran for his vehicle.

Out in the bush Michael and Greg Lowe were searching together. Michael's initial panic had been overcome and he was searching in a logical grid pattern. He pressed on hoping against hope that the next bush or the one beyond it might be concealing his little daughter. Greg Lowe had been thinking along a different line. The baby had obviously been taken for food and there was no reason to suppose that the animal would not have commenced to eat it as soon as it was a safe distance from the tent. At any moment they might stumble upon the horrific sight of a half- eaten corpse. He had to warn Michael, but how do you say that to a father? 'Whatever we find there is no joy for you, mate,' he finally blurted out. Michael stopped as the full import sank in. 'I should see to Lindy,' he said and turned back to the barbecue.

At about 8.25 p.m.Derek Roff arrived at the tent. He noted that Lindy was distressed and that Michael had his hands on her shoulders in an obvious attempt to comfort her. She told him what had happened and went into the tent moving some of the bedding to show him that the child was gone. 'She's not here,' she said plaintively and then repeated it.

The Whittakers were listening to hymns on the radio when Michael Chamberlain appeared at the entrance to their tent. 'You are playing Christian music. What does that mean?' Michael asked. Amy Whittaker was a qualified nurse who had later obtained a degree in social work. She was accustomed to dealing with people under stress and could see at a glance that Michael was maintaining self-control with great difficulty.

'It means we are Christian people,' she said quietly.

'Then pray, please pray,' he implored her. 'A dingo has taken our baby. She is probably dead by now.' He put his hands over his face. Vernon and their daughter Rosalie obtained torches and went out to investigate. Michael showed them the way. Amy stayed behind and prayed. Then she left the tent and went to find Lindy. She noticed that it was 8.32 p.m.

A few minutes later Mr and Mrs Demaine brought their dog over to the Chamberlains' car. Lindy had been told that it was a good tracker and asked them if they would be willing to help. She led them to the vehicle and threw open the passenger's side door, leaving them standing beside the car looking down at the passenger's seat and carpet, presumably illuminated by the courtesy light, whilst Lindy tried to find some clothing which might give the dog the baby's scent.

This was crucial evidence. The case brought against the Chamberlains at their trial was that Lindy had taken the baby to the car, sat in the front passenger seat and cut her throat. The Crown was to assert that there had been copious bleeding and that the floor of the car must have been virtually awash with blood. Later in the evening one or both of the Chamberlains had cleaned up the blood. In the interim, the Crown suggested, the Chamberlains had kept everyone away from the vehicle. The evidence of the Demaines established that the car was not awash with blood at that early stage in the evening. Any suggestion that it had been cleaned up earlier encountered obvious difficulties. When was there time for such an extensive and thorough clean-up? And with so many people flocking to the scene to take part in the search or comfort Lindy and the boys, how did they accomplish it without being seen? Furthermore, it seemed wildly improbable that Lindy would actually invite people to a recently cleaned-up car and run the risk of one of them noticing damp patches or the smell of blood or, for that matter, the risk of the dog picking up the scent of blood in the car. Unhappily the jury did not hear this evidence. The Demaines were not called as witnesses.

Whilst Derek Roff was organising people who had volunteered to search he was approached by Michael Chamberlain. Michael had been mulling over what Greg Lowe had said and now he knew that there was blood in the tent. He told Derek Roff that he fully realised that he would never see his child again, then he paused and asked: 'It would be probable that the dingo would kill the child immediately, wouldn't it?' At the time Derek Roff thought this was a strange comment to make, but Michael was simply seeking reassurance that death would have been mercifully quick.

Amy Whittaker reached Lindy shortly before 8.40 p.m. She didn't have to ask who was the mother whose baby had been taken. One look at Lindy's face was enough. She was later to describe her as being 'emotionally numb'. She had seen many such cases in her long nursing experience. Lindy was suffering from shock. Words of comfort are of little use at a time like that. The hurt is too great, too all-absorbing to be eased by the anodyne of reason. Sometimes all you can do is hold someone. Amy put her arms around her and drew the trembling body close. 'God is good,' she said. Lindy's voice as much as her words conveyed the measure of her struggle against despair. 'Whatever happens is his will. And it says, doesn't it, that at the second coming "Babes will be restored to their mothers' breasts?"' Amy was dubious about the theology but wasn't about to snatch away the last piece of driftwood to which this distraught woman was clinging.

Sally Lowe had taken on the role of comforting Aidan. He had come to her with tears streaming down his cheeks. His voice had been broken and pitiful. 'That dog has got bubby in its tummy,' he had said. She held him tight until the crying had gradually subsided, but now there was a new fear and the child's grief seemed to be more than he could bear. 'Reagan's dead,' he sobbed. His little brother had not moved since the dingo emerged from the tent and his mind told him that the dingo must have killed him, too. She tried to assure him that the boy was only sleeping, but he was inconsolable. Finally she took him to the tent and shook Reagan to wake him up. The boy was in a very deep sleep, but eventually he stirred sufficiently for Aidan to see that he was still alive.

A number of women were now clustered around Lindy endeavouring to comfort her. Journalists were later to suggest that she displayed little emotion and to draw sinister inferences from this so-called fact. These suggestions were to bring a sense of bewilderment to all who saw her that night. Evidence of her obvious distress was later to be given, not only by the women who had sought to comfort her, but by Derek Roff and the two policemen, Morris and Noble.

By this stage the searchers were in full swing. Derek Roff had called in his deputy, Ian Cawood, and a number of other rangers and they were being assisted by the two policemen, a number of Aboriginal trackers and the hundreds of campers and local residents who had flocked to the scene. Michael Chamberlain remained near the tent. The Crown was to use this seemingly innocuous decision as another thread in the tapestry of speculation and suspicion. It was suggested that he did not search because he knew there was nothing to find. By then, the Crown contended, he 'must have' been told that his wife had killed the child and concealed its body nearby. Why else would he have stayed behind?

From Michael's point of view there were many answers to that question. In the first place he was resigned to the fact that Azaria was already dead. The fact that she had been taken by a predator for consumption was all too obvious. The blood in the tent indicated that she had been seized in the animal's jaws and at least injured even before Lindy gave the alarm. The first frantic searches suggested that she had not been dropped when the animal was disturbed. That seemed to leave only one alternative. In the second place there were now hundreds of searchers led by experienced rangers and assisted by both Aboriginal trackers and dogs. There was no reason to suppose that his presence would make any difference to the effectiveness of the search. If they found the body, he would be promptly informed. He had no ambition to be the one to come across the grisly remains of the little baby girl for whom he had prayed so ardently. In addition, his pastor's training and experience told him that he should be with his wife and sons. It is a pastor's role to provide spiritual and emotional succour to the distressed. How could he now desert his family?

He was also to give evidence that Frank Morris had told him to stay at the tent so that the police would know where to contact him if the searchers found something. Frank Morris was unable to remember telling him that. He thought that he had allocated Constable Noble to stay with him throughout the evening, but Noble's evidence did not support that. He said that after Morris informed him of what had happened, he went back to the police station, contacted police in Alice Springs and then returned to Sunrise Hill and took part in a search organised by Morris.

It was apparent that Michael was also very distressed. The dominant impression gained by observers was that he was a man who was trying to maintain rigid self-control to avoid going to pieces. Perhaps it was James McComb who described his condition with the most perception. He said that he was a man who seemed to be trying to find strength in his religion, 'but that in the end his human emotions got the better of him'.

At one stage Amy Whittaker took the initiative of sending Lindy and Michael out to search the bush at the periphery of the camping area. Lindy had been concerned that the baby might have been dropped when Michael and Greg Lowe came running and that the searchers may have missed it in the dark. Michael knew it was pointless. He and Greg Lowe had searched that area systematically, but Amy thought it was important to put Lindy's mind at rest. They were gone about ten minutes and when they returned Amy noted that Lindy seemed more willing to entertain the possibility that Azaria was dead.

At about 9.15 p.m. Frank Morris returned and searched the tent. Five minutes later Mrs Whittaker brought over a gas light and set it up nearby. At about twenty to ten Lindy and Michael again walked away, this time to pray and to have some time alone with their grief. Again, they were gone about ten minutes.

At another stage Amy overheard Michael ask Lindy whether it was possible that something other than a dog — 'perhaps a person' — had come into the tent and taken the baby.

'What about the blood?' Lindy had asked sadly.

'Oh yes,' Michael said in a lost voice.

At about ten o'clock Morris returned and searched the tent again. By this time it was becoming quite cold and Lindy put on her tracksuit. The tracksuit pants were to be the subject of great attention at the trial, for when they were subsequently delivered to Mrs Hansell for cleaning she found marks upon them which appeared to her to be bloodstains. But for the balance of the evening Lindy was to wear them in front of the women comforting her, the police, the nursing sister, and others.

At about this time the Lowes packed up and moved into a motel. Others were to refer derisively to 'the dingo theory', but the Lowes had been there. They had no doubt about what had happened and saw no reason to leave another Chantelle in a tent for the next hungry dingo.

Some time before 11.00 p.m. Bobbie Downs, the nursing sister, arrived. It was obvious to her that the Chamberlains could not remain where they were. It was bitterly cold and she could see that they were both distressed. They needed warmth and proper shelter. She urged them to move into the motel. Michael expressed some initial reluctance, but finally agreed to go provided the police were notified so they could be contacted if there were any news. John Noble arrived and helped them unload the contents of the tent into the police vehicle. At this stage Bobbie Downs saw Lindy come out of the tent carrying a plastic ice-cream container which had held the baby's sterilising solution.

At the trial the Crown was to suggest that Lindy may have washed copious quantities of blood from her hands in this solution. Regrettably no-one thought to ask Bobbie Downs about this hypothesis. If they had they would have discovered that she had seen the liquid before it was poured out. It was quite clear.

Lindy poured the solution out on the ground and burst into tears.

They carried the sleeping boys into the police vehicle while Lindy and Noble set off for the motel. Michael offered Bobbie Downs a lift back into town. She was a qualified nursing sister with experience in operating theatres. Yet she neither saw nor smelt any blood. On the way into the motel she noted the camera bag under Michael's legs. The Crown was later to suggest that she had been sitting in that part of the car that had been awash with blood, though there may have been some hasty attempt at a clean-up earlier in the evening, and that either the body or Azaria's bloodstained clothing were hidden in the camera bag. Bobbie Downs, however, did not have a mind like Edgar Alan Poe. It did not occur to her that she was being invited to sit on the seat upon which a murder had been committed and, possibly, to ride into town with the corpse of the victim. She gave evidence that she simply saw Mr Chamberlain as a man trying to put on a brave face for his family and that there had been nothing to arouse any suspicion. They arrived at the Uluru Motel shortly after midnight. It had been a hell of an evening.

5

Marks of passage

DEREK ROFF HAD HAD AN INTERESTING CAREER. He had been Chief Ranger of the Uluru National Park for sixteen-and-a-half years. Prior to that he had been a policeman in Kenya. He had been there at the time of the Mau Mau uprising and had worked with the local native trackers. He had been eager to learn all that they could teach him about tracking and had later put his new-found skills to good use tracking poachers and terrorists as well as animals. At Uluru he continued his interest in tracking. He had learnt more from Nipper Winmatti and other tribal elders, yet despite almost three decades of experience in tracking he did not regard himself as a 'superb tracker' like the more skilled Aborigines. He was to single out Barbara Tjikadu, wife of the tribal elder Nipper Winmatti, as the best of the Aboriginal trackers.

Another outstanding tracker was Nui Minyintiri. The Pitjantjatjara language contains no numbers beyond five and ages can only be guessed at, but Nui was probably approaching seventy. He was reputed to have joined the Navy during World War II, though at the time he volunteered he had never seen a more expansive body of water than a billabong. He was an impressive man with grey hair and beard. In 1986 he was to arrive to give evidence before the Commission of Inquiry wearing old battered clothes and a colourful beanie. A white man would have been ridiculed for wearing such incongruous clothing in those august surroundings, but Nui exhibited a quiet dignity which transcended the cultural boundaries. One knew instinctively that this was a man who did not need to find security in clothing nor in the approval of others.

Among the Pitjantjatjara people there is a veneration for the elderly and for the wisdom and knowledge they possess. The adjective 'old' is sometimes added to the name of a person less advanced in years as a mark of particular respect. It was for this reason that Derek Roff had long been known to the Aborigines as 'Old Derek'. He and Nui had been friends for years. They communicated quite well despite Nui's limited grasp of English. The chief ranger found his English easier to understand than most. He was to explain that it seemed to be 'a matter of familiarity and feeling of comfort'. He also knew some words of Pitjantjatjara.

On the night of 17 August 1980 'Old Derek' and 'Old Nui' together searched for tracks as they had done so many times in the past. Yet this time was different. It was dark and they were trying to pick up the tracks of a predator with a human prey. Each searched in his own way, Derek Roff with a torch and Nui using burning spinifex or other shrubs.

When they finally came across the track, there was immediate agreement. Aborigines do not stress the obvious and none of them made the explicit statements that a white man might have made in the circumstances. Nui said simply: 'This is the one. This is the right track.' Derek Roff did not require elaboration. He was later to explain to the Commission that 'Everybody was convinced that we were following the right track, the track of the baby.'

What they had found was a shallow drag mark about eight to ten inches in width which meandered along the ridge of the sand dune. There were pieces of broken-off vegetation within the track which was associated with dingo tracks, although it was not until the next day when he was able to examine them in the daylight that Derek Roff was able to realise the full extent of their correlation. They followed it until the track petered out in an area where the ground was more hardly packed and then began to backtrack. It was almost but not quite continuous and went back down the dune to a point seventeen metres due east from the Chamberlains' tent.

The drag mark appeared to have been made by something with very little weight. Derek Roff was to express the view that it was probably the matinee jacket hanging down from the baby's body. But in three places the dingo had apparently put down its burden. In those places they were able to recognise depressions in the sand. The depth of those depressions was consistent with the weight of a nine-and-a-half pound baby. Within them was a pattern like the impression left by a crepe bandage. During the course of the Commission of Inquiry he was to be shown the matinee jacket and the jumpsuit. The fabric in each garment seemed reasonably consistent with the type of mark he saw but he tended to favour the matinee jacket, not only because it was the external garment but because the 'holes in the design' seemed likely to give the impression which he saw.

Though he was not to know it at the time Murray Haby had also found a depression with a cloth imprint in the sand. It, too, had been associated with dingo tracks.

Whilst he did not have a degree in zoology, Derek Roff had made a particular study of the fauna at Ayers Rock. In addition to the familiarity built up over years of experience, he had read widely on the topic and was able to indulge the curiosity of people like Chester Porter QC about such esoteric irrelevancies as when a particular marsupial became extinct in the region surrounding the Olgas. He was emphatic that even if one put aside the cloth impression, there was no game in the area which would have had the weight and shape to account for the depressions. Kangaroos do not frequent the sand dunes and had never been seen near that camping area. It was the wrong time of the year for goannas. Furthermore, both joeys and goannas leave very distinctive prints in the sand. Rabbits were too light to have accounted for the impressions. The matter was later taken up again by Mr Justice Morling, but after further discussion Roff concluded: 'There is just no animal in that area that fits in with that track in my estimation.'

As if that were not sufficient, Roff went on to say that the tracks were very fresh and had certainly been made that night. He explained that one can tell the freshness of the tracks by 'the consistency of the soil ridging'. As time passes 'you can see the movement of the sand grains, as it were, along the edging . . .' He had been back to see them again the next day and noted the deterioration in the quality of the print. Even at that stage it was possible to form an opinion as to its age, but it was obviously no longer fresh.

The next day Nipper Winmatti and Barbara Tjikadu were enlisted to assist in the search. Nipper was a wonderful character of a similar age to Nui. He was also a man of great dignity but was known to be 'a bit of a showman'. His position as tribal elder gave him a real measure of authority and he had a better grasp of English than the other Aboriginal trackers. Consequently, when he was present it was usually left to him to act as spokesman. This caused some confusion due to their strong corporate identity. Sometimes when Nipper would say that he had seen something he would mean that another tracker had seen it. He and the other tracker were members of the one tribal group. If one had seen it, the knowledge gained was the knowledge of them all. Consequently, one could speak of one's own knowledge. Pedantic quibbles about hearsay may have been of interest to white men, but they had no place in Nipper's thinking.

When that semantic difficulty was resolved, it emerged that Nipper had followed the tracks personally and was adamant that the dingo was carrying the baby.

Unlike Derek Roff, Nipper started at the Chamberlains' tent. He found that 'the dingo came from the north, then he went around the tent to the front entrance, and from there he backtracked around the tent'. He was asked to demonstrate the path taken by the dingo with his hand and traced around the tent clockwise to the entrance and then anti-clockwise again to the back. From there he said he tracked the dingo going east towards Sunrise Hill. Derek Roff later confirmed that this evidence was consistent with what he had seen.

Some effort was made to denigrate the value of Nipper's evidence by suggesting that he may not have been wearing his glasses. He said that he was and, when the matter was raised with Derek Roff, he said he thought that Nipper had been wearing them when he saw him. A photograph was later produced showing Nipper without his glasses and, it may be, that he removed them at some stage during the search. However, the matter proved to be of little importance when Nipper was shown a number of photographs and demonstrated his ability to pick out fine details without glasses.

Barbara Tjikadu, whom Roff had described as 'the best of the

Aboriginal trackers', was to prove even more emphatic. She had followed the tracks with Nipper and was to say emphatically, 'I know it was the child'. During cross-examination she was to exhibit some frustration at the apparent inability of white lawyers to understand what was to her a perfectly straightforward matter. She had followed the tracks round the tent to the entrance, back around the side and then up the hill and she knew that the dingo had been carrying the baby. Finally, when the Crown persisted with a suggestion that it may have been carrying a joey, the frustration proved too much. 'Was there a kangaroo living in the tent?' she demanded.

Marlene Cousens, the interpreter, was to share her frustration. Barbara was being asked how she knew that the tracks at the place where the baby's clothes were found were made by the same dingo as the tracks found at the tent, when she interrupted with a comment of her own.

'I would like to tell you something first before you ask questions like that. When Aboriginal people see tracks, they know who it belongs to, what person went there, because they know the tracks, whereas if all these people got out of the courtroom now and walked barefooted, you can't tell, can you?'

A startled prosecutor duly admitted his ineptitude.

'Aboriginal people can,' said Marlene with obvious feeling.

Strangely enough, it was the police who were to provide corroboration for the evidence given by the Aborigines concerning the tracks at the tent. Between 3.30 and 4.00 p.m. that day, Inspector Gilroy and Sergeant Lincoln inspected the area surrounding the tent. They had been sent out from Alice Springs to investigate the matter. They found large pug marks right up against the tent wall at the rear right-hand corner. Significantly, that was immediately outside the position occupied by the baby's bassinette. The prints appeared to suggest that the dingo had stopped there, presumably having caught the baby's scent. They found further marks along the tent wall on the southern side. These marks were so close that they were initially obscured by the billowing of the tent wall and it was only when the canvas was held back that they could be clearly seen. A further set of prints were found about two feet out from the southern wall of the tent heading in an easterly direction towards the sandhill.

Frank Morris also saw these prints. Wally Goodwin was later to give evidence that Morris had told him that an Aboriginal tracker had found paw prints going in and out of the tent.

To the trackers, both black and white, these tracks provided as clear a record of the incident as a video tape. There was only one question which left them confused: Why wouldn't people listen?

6

'A dingo took my baby'

THE MORNING OF 18 AUGUST 1980 brought no reprieve. There had been no last minute discovery, no Hollywood finish. It had been a bitterly cold night. If there had been not much hope the evening before, there was none now.

That was underlined with terrible finality when Frank Morris called at their motel room with a 'Notification of Death' form for the inevitable coronial inquiry. The Chamberlains were to give evidence that this occurred at about 7.30 a.m. Morris initially said that the form was completed in the motel office shortly after 8.00 a.m., but later confirmed that he had gone to their room at some time during the morning. He thought it was later but he did not know when. The Chamberlains' counsel were to make the obvious suggestion that their clients' recollection was far more likely to be accurate. For Frank Morris it was a routine task and it related to an incident in which there were no suspicious circumstances. As he said himself, he accepted the Chamberlains' account at face value. For the Chamberlains it was the final extinction of hope, like the last peal of the death knell for their only daughter.

Whatever the time, Morris recalled that it was Michael Chamberlain who provided the information and signed the form. He then said that he would like to have the baby returned to him irrespective of the condition in which it was found. The Seventh Day Adventists emphasise that the dead are raised at the second coming of Christ. They do not pass into the next life immediately, but sleep until Christ wakens them to new life and a resurrection body free from sickness or deformity. In the meantime, if the Chamberlains could do nothing else for Azaria, they hoped to at least offer her a decent Christian burial.

At about 8.00 a.m. Michael made his way to the motel office. He had to ring his parents in New Zealand and break the news to them. He also had to contact church headquarters in Townsville. It was there that the first call from the press came in. The Chamberlains had been advised that it was wise to speak to the press. It was better to 'get it over and done with' than to run the risk of being hounded by journalists desperate for a story. Besides, they felt they had a duty to warn others. If there was enough publicity concerning the danger at Ayers Rock, perhaps some other little baby's life might be saved. Michael emphasised the dangers to the caller from the *Melbourne Herald*.

Shortly thereafter Trevor Scadden from the *Adelaide News* rang. There was some discussion about what had occurred and then Scadden asked Michael if he would be willing to speak to a journalist from the *Adelaide Advertiser.* Michael was non-committal. Scadden then asked him if he would be willing to take some black-and-white photographs and send them down to him. He was quite insistent and eventually Michael agreed.

At about 9.00 a.m. Bobbie Downs came. The beds were still unmade and she began to clean up. She noticed that Lindy was sniffing as if she had been crying and that she was wearing dark glasses. Despite her own distress, she was 'very loving' toward the boys.

Bobbie finished tidying the room and then obtained paper and crayons from the office for the boys. When they were fully occupied, she went outside and found Lindy sitting in the car. The passenger's side door of the hatchback was open and Lindy was sitting on the passenger's seat with her legs out the door and her feet on the ground. She was crying. When Bobbie approached, she could see that Lindy had a book of Azaria's baby photos in her hands.

Later in the morning the Chamberlain family went for a ride on Lytle Dickinson's bus. Michael had bought some monochrome film and was going out to honour his undertaking to the *Advertiser.* It was a quiet trip. Lytle had worked in the bar until 2.00 a.m. and been up again at 6.00 a.m. He had been present in the office at 8.00 a.m. whilst Michael was on the phone but could not recall whether

Frank Morris had come to the office at that time. Michael completed his photographs, posing the boys in front of the tent.

Geoff De Luca from the *Adelaide Advertiser* arrived at the motel some time between 2.30 and 3.00 p.m. He found the Chamberlains calm and co-operative, although Lindy sobbed on one occasion and appeared to genuinely suffer distress in recalling events. They gave him a lengthy interview. He was later to quote the rangers as referring to the 'killer dingo' which had snatched the baby. Yet, though he did not tell the Chamberlains, he apparently harboured some concern that the police investigation had not been sufficiently thorough and that the police had accepted the 'dingo theory'.

Later he was to approach Inspector Gilroy and tell him that Mr Chamberlain had sent photographs to his paper and that he and Lindy had displayed a degree of eagerness to be interviewed which he felt was not consistent with what they said had occurred. When cross-examined in 1986, he conceded that he was aware that the *Adelaide News* had asked for the photographs and for the interview, but did not know if he had stressed that to Inspector Gilroy. He did however remember that Mr Chamberlain had wanted to warn others of the danger. So far as can be determined, De Luca's comments to Inspector Gilroy constituted the first stirrings of the storm of suspicion which was to erupt within the next few days.

At about 4.00 p.m. Pastor Cozens and his wife Norma arrived from Alice Springs. Lindy told them what had happened and started to sob. The Chamberlains had been quite emotional, but seemed more controlled after the Cozens arrived. They all prayed together in the motel room. Later they had dinner together.

Inspector Gilroy and Sergeant Lincoln arrived at the Chamberlains' motel room later in the evening. Michael Seamus Gilroy had an Irish brogue that would have charmed the leprechauns out from under their toadstools. He was a kindly, sympathetic man, but a skilled observer would have noted the underlying shrewdness of the investigator.

This case looked fairly straightforward. He had seen the pug marks at the tent himself and had spoken to Constable Morris who had relayed to him his own observations and the opinions of the rangers and the Aboriginal trackers. That impression was confirmed when Lindy opened the door. No-one as perceptive as Gilroy could have missed the grief etched in her face. He apologised for the need to interview her. 'It's all right,' she replied, 'it will probably help me to talk about it.'

John Lincoln had a tape recorder. Neither officer wanted the ebb and flow of conversation interrupted by the need to take notes. He set it up while Lindy explained that Michael was at the clinic with Aidan and would be back shortly.

Gilroy began with a series of questions designed to extract a detailed account in chronological sequence, but the recent events had had too great an impact and Lindy had obvious difficulty in remembering precisely when the family left Mount Isa. She became confused and upset at her confusion. The tape of this conversation was later to be played to the Commission of Inquiry in Darwin. It was at once moving, but vaguely inappropriate: almost indelicate. There was a strange feeling that this courtroom full of barristers, solicitors, court officials and members of the public had somehow been able to turn back the clock six years and to retrospectively trespass upon the intimacy of this woman's grief. The court hushed as fifty silent eavesdroppers listened whilst the woman infinitely younger than the Lindy Chamberlain who sat among them struggled to stifle her sobbing in a town fifteen hundred kilometres away.

Gilroy decided to try another tack. He would let her tell her own story. He asked: 'Can you tell me when you decided to bed down for the night? Or prior to that? Or when you had a meal?' This was more productive. She was able to build up confidence and momentum recounting these relatively painless memories. Then the whole incident came tumbling out. She spoke quickly as if wanting to get it over and done with before she broke down:

> And my husband said to me, 'Is that bubby crying? Didn't she go to sleep?' and I said, 'I don't know, I can't hear her,' and I walked back up, and I said I would go and see anyway, and I walked back towards the tent, and got halfway there, and it wouldn't be any more than the length of this room away from the tent, and I saw the dingo come out of the tent, and the light didn't show on the lower part of the tent because the bushes blocked it, and I saw the dingo from about, oh, shoulder up, and he sort of, he looked as if he'd got

> a fright and he heard me coming. He was having trouble getting out of the tent flaps, he sort of moved his head to get out, and I didn't realise he was in there, and the cry, the baby, he might have savaged it. The thought went through my mind because I had heard that they bite, they had been biting around here, and then I, oh, I yelled at it to get out of the road, and it took fright, and ran in front of our car, which was parked next to the tent, but I didn't sort of keep looking at it, I dived straight for the tent, to see what had made the baby cry, and when I got in the tent the bunny rug and the two thick blankets she had around were scattered from one end of the tent to the other. Some of them were on Reagan, so the dingo must have walked on his feet, at least walked right past him. The baby was sleeping at his feet, in her carry basket, and it must have walked right past him to get to the baby and taken the baby out. It was empty, there was nothing there, and I called my husband straightaway. I came straight out of the tent and called him, and to next door, that the dingo had taken the baby and, and to chase it. I chased it into the bush and followed it, and I got to the edge of the road. The light didn't carry any further than that. I was aware that it went into the bush, and oh, I realised it was no good, unless . . .

Gilroy found Michael Chamberlain harder to assess. He came in with Aidan during the course of the interview. Gilroy was struck by the fact that he displayed none of the distress exhibited so obviously by Lindy. He found that 'strange'. Of course, people react to grief differently. Had he known Michael better he might have found a hint of the emotional impact in the disjointed sentences. Lindy had explained that the dingo appeared to be 'a youngish dog'. 'It struck me as perhaps not being the one that was by the campfire earlier, because that looked mangy, and this one was very young and very strong,' she added.

'I thought it was the same dog,' Michael volunteered. 'But it may not have been the same dog, now that I think about it.' He paused as if puzzled by what he had already said. 'Not that I saw the dog.'

There was obviously nothing glib or rehearsed about a statement like that.

The interview was interrupted by Bobbie Downs who had brought a breast pump. 'My wife is in some pain from the milk,' Michael explained.

At the end of the interview Michael volunteered an observation. 'I have listened very carefully to a lot of people about this incident. I wouldn't be so unkind as to say that some of them would try to defend the dingo, and consider you are a bit daft for suggesting it. But I have noticed it that some of the more authoritative people have been the ones who try to knock the idea. Not openly. Through innuendo. Well, not innuendo, but questioning. Whereas, when you talk to people who live here and know the dingo, none of them have been at all surprised.'

Despite his observations of Michael Chamberlain's apparent lack of distress, it appears that Gilroy, like Morris and Roff, accepted what the Chamberlains had said, at least at that stage. He was later to tell the Commission of Inquiry that he interviewed them in 'an entirely unsuspicious and sympathetic fashion'.

It was later that evening that Gilroy was approached by De Luca. He echoed Gilroy's feelings about Michael Chamberlain's failure to exhibit obvious signs of distress and said that it was strange that a recently bereaved parent would be sending photographs to a southern newspaper. This was probably the first time in Australia's forensic history that the press had invited the police to draw sinister inferences from the fact that a tragically bereaved man had complied with their requests.

An experienced grief counsellor would have readily understood Michael's apparent lack of distress. Over the years many parents who had lost children in tragic circumstances were to protest that they too had exhibited little emotional distress in the first few days. If someone nurses a member of the family through a long terminal illness, the day-to-day contact brings home to him the harsh reality of the situation. He may hope and pray for a miracle, but his mind has had time to adjust to the extremity of the condition. In those circumstances there is usually an acceptance of the death when it occurs and an immediate emotional response. When a child is killed in an accident, the parent is taken by surprise. There has been no series of experiences to prepare him for it. In a very real sense the mind simply refuses to accept that it has happened. The immediate response is frequently 'No, it can't be . . .' The intellect accepts it, but the emotions take some time to catch up. During this time a parent may find himself saying, 'It all seems so unreal.'

There may be a feeling of seeing a tragedy enacted, but not really being a part of it, like watching a play on television. Psychiatrists refer to this phenomenon as dissociation. The emotional storm is still to come.

Unhappily, few of those who saw Michael Chamberlain in the forty-eight hours following his daughter's disappearance had the necessary training or experience to understand his emotional state. In normal circumstances police become acutely aware of the fact that people in shock frequently act in an incongruous manner, but such considerations were to be swamped by the tide of suspicion and rumour to come.

On Tuesday morning the Chamberlains decided it was time to go home. They were to be trenchantly criticised for this decision, but in reality there was little they could do. Teams of people were still searching the surrounding countryside and there were hopes of finding the clothing and perhaps remnants of the body, but there was no longer any hope that their daughter might be found alive. They were strangers in a strange environment and their children needed the security of home.

They had a discussion with the Cozens outside the Uluru Motel at about 9.00 a.m. and made arrangements to stay overnight at their home in Alice Springs. Later in the morning they drove out to the Aboriginal camp. There was a brief discussion with Derek Roff. Michael had heard that he had shot some dingoes and wanted to photograph the jaws. Roff declined permission. The Chamberlains were also anxious to erect a plaque as a memorial for Azaria. Roff was sympathetic to this request, but lacked the necessary authority. He referred them to the Conservation Commission.

After leaving the Aboriginal camp, the Chamberlains stopped at the Ininti store and bought some souvenirs for their nephews. Lindy was later to explain that 'When you make a promise to a kid, you keep it no matter what.' Before leaving the store she wrote her name and address in the visitors' book and added, 'A dingo took my baby.'

At about noon Michael turned the yellow hatchback onto Petermann Road and headed towards Alice Springs. Their holiday was over.

PART II

JUDGMENT BY RUMOUR

7

Home

THE CHAMBERLAINS ARRIVED HOME on Thursday 21 August 1980. It was about 10.00 p.m. when Lindy rang her friend, Jenny Ransom. It was an emotional reunion.

It was natural that Lindy should turn to Jenny. They had been members of the same church and had become close friends. They spent a lot of time together and had been away together on earlier camping trips. From time to time they had looked after each other's children. Though none of the male barristers was to be unchivalrous enough to ask her age, if one had taken the trouble to explain that he was using the term as it applied to fine wines rather than old cars he could have suggested that she was about the same vintage as Lindy.

There was a feeling of catharsis involved in speaking to Jenny. This was someone who understood, someone who had the empathy of one mother for another. She had been part of it all: Lindy's longing for a little girl, the prayers of faith and, ultimately, the joy of it all. She had visited her in hospital when Lindy was 'really over the moon' with her delight in her new little daughter. She had bought clothes for Azaria and had seen the nursery with its abundance of little dresses that so obviously reflected Lindy's pride and joy in having a little girl. She had heard the news but, as Lindy spoke it, it was as though the incident was recreated in front of her eyes. She had stood around camp site barbecues with Lindy cooking dinner for the children and knew well that little tent with the peaked roof.

They spoke until almost 2.00 in the morning. Lindy broke down and wept on four or five occasions. Parts of the conversation were to indelibly imprint themselves in Jenny's mind. There was a tremulous but brave affirmation of faith. 'If I am true to the Lord, then I know that baby will be placed back in my arms just as beautiful as what she was on that day that she was taken.'

Jenny had been a Christian for many years, but the tragedy was too fresh, her friend's pain too real. How could her God of compassion without whose leave not even a sparrow falls to the ground have permitted such a thing to happen? Even six years later she was to recall this vividly:

> I just said to her that it just seemed — Why? — I guess I questioned so much why, and Lindy said, 'Jenny, nothing can bring my baby back to me' and 'but so many of us put so much importance onto the three score years and ten that we have on this earth, and nothing into eternity; and that if through this, if one person could just realise and turn their life to God, that her baby wouldn't have died in vain.'

It was as though the roles were for a time reversed. The consoler was receiving consolation.

Jenny recalled them discussing Lindy's strong faith 'which I certainly didn't have at that time'. Lindy had said that 'if people can just see that with faith in God this earth is worth nothing but eternity is forever'.

This made a great impression on Jenny and, when Lindy mentioned that a reporter from *Woman's Day* was coming to see her the next day, she had an idea. If Lindy was seeking to find a purpose in Azaria's death through the eternal salvation of others then why not use the media? Why not demonstrate to the world the strength and reality of the faith that was so palpable to Jenny?

'If you feel so strongly about your faith and the way you feel about it, surely you will get to more people by going to something like *Today Tonight*?'

On Friday morning Jenny rang and asked, 'How do you feel about speaking to *Today Tonight*?' Lindy said quietly, 'I will'. There was some further discussion about it before Jenny rang off to contact the producers of the programme and make the necessary arrangements.

Later in the morning Jenny and another friend, June Simpson, dropped in to see if there was anything they could do to help. They were doing some washing for her when Lindy came down with a number of items she wanted drycleaned. There was a little cardigan of Reagan's, Lindy's tracksuit and a travelling rug or blanket. Lindy drew her attention to the tracksuit pants. 'Jenny, there's marks on these slacks. Will you make sure you show them to the cleaners so that they can get them out?' Jenny thought they may have been blood.

It was later to be suggested that these marks were caused by droplets of blood which had dripped down onto Lindy's slacks as she sat in the car with Azaria held out in front of her under the dashboard and brutally cut her throat. But these were early days and there was no inkling of such grisly conjecture when Jenny handed them to the drycleaners.

The interview with Liz Hickson commenced shortly before lunch. She had gone to Mount Isa to obtain 'a bit of a scoop' for *Woman's Day*. The Chamberlains had spoken to a number of journalists including Geoff De Luca whilst at Ayers Rock, but she hoped to be the first person to have a full interview with them since the tragedy. Michael had told her that he was doubtful whether Lindy would be available, but when she got there she found Lindy willing to discuss the matter with her, despite her evident distress. It was an emotional interview. For a time Lindy seemed to 'try to detach herself from the conversation' by talking about 'all sorts of irrelevancies'. When she did become involved in discussing the events of the evening, there was obvious distress. Liz Hickson was to tell the Commission of Inquiry that 'there were two occasions when she was clearly holding onto herself very hard indeed; and there was one time when she again was holding over, and I crossed the room, and she broke down, then... I think I put my arm around her shoulder.' They suspended the interview for two or three minutes while Lindy cried, the tears flowing down her cheeks while Liz held her. When asked about her attitude to the Chamberlains, she said, 'I started off with a completely detached attitude and I became sort of increasingly sympathetic, as a human being, to Lindy's very clear state of grief.'

She was also struck by Michael's rueful comment: 'I have had to comfort people many times when they have lost children. Now I know that my words were a little empty. You cannot possibly know unless it has happened to you. There are things you can never get rid of.'

Liz Hickson's article was to appear in the *Woman's Day* on 1 October 1980. Despite Miss Hickson's sympathy, some passages of it were to add fuel to the growing conflagration of suspicion and hostility towards the Chamberlains. The Crown was to seize upon it and endeavour to suggest that the Chamberlains were lying, by pointing to inconsistencies between quotes attributed to them in the article and portions of the account which they had given to the police. The Chamberlains were to protest that the article contained inaccuracies, but their protestations were to fall upon the deaf ears of an increasingly sceptical public.

Liz had tried to be accurate — to make the article 'factionalised rather than fictionalised' as she was later to put it. But it was an article for a magazine, not a police report and, as she was to tell the Commission of Inquiry, 'it's written partly from notes, and very incomplete notes, and partly from memory. I don't regard that as verbatim.' Its accuracy was further put in question by some 'updating' carried out by sub-editors whilst she was on holidays. She explained, 'I wasn't aware that all that was going to go in until I actually saw it in print. . .' She took strong exception to some of the updating. '. . .There are about four paragraphs there that I specifically objected to at the time with my sub-editors — I specifically and quite strongly objected to — which was updating from published material published by people other than myself, based on what I just don't know.'

The problem was to be further compounded when the police interviewed Miss Hickson on 14 February 1981. They came to her home on a Saturday afternoon. Her memory was 'influenced by the fact that I had just spent two months in hospital having a very serious operation' and she protested to the police that she had 'a very poor recollection' of the matters in the article. She was also without her notes. The police, however, produced her article and took her through it. She agreed that it was correct and they typed a statement for her to sign.

She was later to tell the Commission of Inquiry: 'I am very

uncomfortable about the whole of the police statement, frankly, because it was an attempt to get rid of the police, quite frankly. I did not want to be involved with the police. I was reading quite blatantly from my story and saying, "she said this and she said that".' She was later to say that although she had read it through 'rather cursorily', she had missed a few points that she really should have picked up. The final paragraph she said was 'totally inaccurate' and added, 'I don't know how I signed it certainly.' She was also to complain that some qualifications had been omitted and that 'they picked out certain things that I had said and left out others'.

One portion of the article which was to assume sinister connotations in the minds of many people was a reference to a 'thousand word thesis on dingoes' which Lindy was said to have written. This document was finally produced before the Commission of Inquiry in 1986. It turned out to be a project on dogs written when Lindy was eleven years old. The characteristics of a number of breeds had been discussed, but the passage dealing with dingoes was limited to one paragraph.

8

The seeds of suspicion

ON THE OPPOSITE SIDE OF THE ROCK to the scene of Kurrpanngu's savage attack on the Mala men lies the site of another legendary incident from the Dreamtime.

Two bellbird brothers had been hunting in a region known as Wangka Arrkal near the border between the Northern Territory and South Australia. They came across an emu but it caught their scent and fled north towards Uluru. There it was intercepted by two blue-tongue lizard men named Mita and Lungkata. The lizard men killed the emu and cut up the body with a stone axe. On the southern side of Uluru are two features which remind the Pitjantjatjara people of the lizard men's kill. Towards the eastern end there is a spur of rock named Kalaya Tjunta which is said to be a buried thigh of the emu. About one-and-a-half kilometres to the west lies a fractured slab of sandstone adjacent to a fissure in the rock known as Mutitjulu. The pieces are said to be large joints of meat from the emu transmogrified into stone.

The bellbird brothers had been outdistanced by the emu, but in due course they, too, arrived at the rock. They were met there by the lizard men who handed them a small portion of the emu meat and told them that nothing else was left. Infuriated by the loss of their quarry, the bellbird brothers set fire to the shelter of the lizard men who were forced to climb the side of the rock. It was to no avail. They fell back and were burnt to death. About two-thirds of a kilometre further west from Mutitjulu is the site of this legendary catastrophe, Mita Kampantja. There are two boulders half buried in the red sand, which are said to be the lizard men. Above them lichen on the rock soars hundreds of feet above the plain. There are two separate sections of lichen, but if viewed from the right angle, they merge forming a giant arrow.

It was near the base of this arrow that Wally Goodwin found Azaria's clothing on 24 August 1980.

Running down beside the two sections of lichen is a depression in the rock which becomes a natural watercourse when it rains. The watercourse runs down into a gully adjacent to the rock. Wally had been sightseeing with his wife and children when he came across an animal track. He followed it into the gully. Whatever had left the clothes there had travelled more than four kilometres from the Chamberlains' tent, passing Kalaya Tjunta and Mutitjulu on the way.

He stood looking at them for a moment. Then his son came running up behind him for a look and he pushed him away. His wife Margo also wanted to look, but one glance was enough for his daughter. She became hysterical and he got his wife to take both children back to the car.

The disposable nappy had been torn and there were fluffy white pieces of cotton wool strewn over the jumpsuit and the ground nearby, but it was the jumpsuit itself which caught his attention. There was heavy staining of what appeared to be blood around the neckline and it was open, the press studs unclipped down the front and the right leg. The feet were not flat like the rest of the jumpsuit; they stuck up into the air. He wondered whether the feet of the baby might still be inside. He thought that the singlet was still inside the jumpsuit, though this was later to be disputed by Constable Morris. He also thought that it might have been inside out, though some manufacturers apparently put the labels on the outside of babies' singlets and it can be difficult to tell which is the correct side out. He studied them for several minutes and then left to get the police.

He returned with Morris some time later and led him along the track into the narrow gully. On the way in he asked Morris for his opinion. He was later to give evidence that Morris told him that the trackers had picked up paw prints going in and out of the tent and that they could tell the difference between the paw print of a dingo, a camp dog and a normal dog. When they reached the clothes he was surprised to see Morris simply pick up the jumpsuit. There had been no photographs or detailed examination of the clothing in situ. He was still wondering about the wisdom of that when he noticed the tremor in Morris' hands. He assumed that he shared his apprehension at the prospect of finding the baby's feet still in the jumpsuit. Morris felt gingerly inside, but to the relief of both men there was nothing there.

Later, Morris put the jumpsuit back on the ground and attempted to reconstruct the position of the clothing at the time that it was found. The clothing was then photographed, but there was to be a disagreement between Goodwin and Morris as to the extent to which the photograph reflected the position of the clothing when it was found.

The discovery of the clothing was to spark off a series of disputes spanning a number of scientific disciplines. Ultimately, the controversy was to embroil dozens of scientists, many of them among the most eminent in the world in their respective fields. Of all the countless millions of garments manufactured throughout the centuries since man first wrapped the skin of an animal around himself for warmth, only the Turin shroud has excited more scientific debate than this tiny terry towelling jumpsuit.

Stirrings of suspicion had already begun among some members of the Northern Territory police. There was a feeling that this was out of character, that dingoes didn't enter tents let alone make away with children. Others confidently asserted that no dingo could have carried the weight of a baby for any distance. Those suspicions seemed confirmed by the discovery of the clothing. It was too far from the camp site and the clothes were grouped too closely together. A dingo would have been expected to scatter them over a wide area. Furthermore, some of the damage to the jumpsuit did not appear to have been caused by the tearing action one would expect from a dingo's teeth. It looked as though it had been cut by a sharp instrument. From this time onward the police were no longer concerned with making routine inquiries into a tragic accident. This was a murder investigation.

The police did not inform the Chamberlains of the discovery of the clothes. They found out the next day when they turned on the 7.00 p.m. news to find Sergeant Sandry displaying the jumpsuit for the television cameras.

Cliff and Avis Murchison had arrived in Mount Isa on 22 August 1980, but several days passed before Avis saw the marks on one of the green and silver space blankets which had been in the tent. She was ultimately to give evidence that:

> I was in the kitchen in the Chamberlain home and Lindy came out and she had a space blanket folded over her arm and she stopped there to talk to me. She was on her way downstairs and just stopped in the kitchen to talk. While she was talking, she noticed a little nick in the blanket and she seemed disappointed about it. I took it that it might have been a new blanket and then she noticed another one and, for some reason, I suggested she hold it up to the light so that she might see better, and there appeared to be a little trail of nicks across the blanket. She was looking at it and then she exclaimed, 'that thing' meaning the dingo 'must have walked right over Reagan to get to bubby'. The space blanket apparently was covering Reagan who was asleep alongside Azaria's cot. With that I went around to have a look, too. We were looking at that and then I noticed down underneath there were two large paw prints, muddy looking paw prints, and that was how we found them there. When we realised what they were, Lindy went and rang Alice Springs and told them what she had found and asked would they like to have it for the inquest, and they said yes, that they would send someone around to get it.

Lindy's brother and sister-in-law were also shown the marks. Later there was to be considerable controversy about who had actually collected the blanket from the Chamberlains' home. Detective Sergeant Brown from the Mount Isa CIB gave evidence at the trial that he had picked up the blanket from Michael Chamberlain, but that there had been no marks on it. He repeated that evidence before the Commission of Inquiry in 1986. On the other hand, Lindy and her mother gave evidence that the blanket was collected by a young fair-haired uniformed policeman. Lindy had pointed out the marks to him and he had exclaimed,'Oh, yes there's no d. . .', before realising that it may be inappropriate for him to make any comment and cutting himself off in mid sentence. In 1984 Avis Murchison was to write to the Premier of Queensland, Sir Johannes Bjelke Petersen, who in due course interviewed Sergeant Brown personally.

Brown claimed that he had made notes of the conversation with Michael when he collected the blanket but that his notebook had been lost since the trial. He was accused of lying.

'Was there some young constable that you wanted to keep away from the inquiry because he had a distressing streak of honesty?' he was asked.

'That's rubbish,' he replied.

In the end result, the controversy was probably of little significance since the marks could easily have been abraded from the smooth surface of the blanket between the time they were first seen and the time it was collected.

Shortly after the discovery of the paw prints, two of Lindy's friends arrived to take her jogging. Avis had encouraged her to go. It would do her good to get out of the house, she thought. Lindy had been changing when, abruptly, she 'just burst into uncontrollable sobbing' as Avis later recalled. The door opened and she came out holding her running shoes. 'Even my runners have blood on them,' she said.

Meanwhile, rumour and speculation were continuing to mount. At first most people were sympathetic. It was only the odd crank who was willing to assert that he knew what 'really happened'. But the rumours quickly became more widespread, more imaginative and more vicious.

On 29 August 1980, Michael and Lindy Chamberlain appeared on a television programme in Mount Isa. To their way of thinking the way to deal with rumour and suspicion was to tell people exactly what had happened. Surely if people could see and hear them, they would understand. They also had in mind Lindy's conversation with Jenny Ransom. Perhaps God was giving them the opportunity to demonstrate the reality of their faith, to demonstrate to a cynical world that no matter how great the adversity a Christian can always turn to God and draw new strength and comfort. As Michael Chamberlain was to explain, even in the midst of tragedy one can know 'the peace that passes all understanding'.

Many found the interview deeply moving, but others reacted negatively. As Edward St John pointed out in *A Time to Speak*, there is a larrikinism in the Australian psyche. It is characterised by a 'nose thumbing' attitude toward authority and an affection for those with the effrontery to kick over the traces. It has its positive aspects. There is an abhorrence of hypocrisy and an abundance of sympathy for the underdog. But Australians find the sanctimonious insufferable and anyone who appears to be 'too good' is likely to be relegated to that category. Perhaps we all feel a little uncomfortable around saints. It is less threatening if we can pull them down to our level. There were many who saw the Chamberlains' demeanour not as a triumph of faith but as evidence of callousness, the callousness of a couple who may well have murdered their child.

On 30 August 1980, Inspector Gilroy received the report from police at Mount Isa. The report included a number of serious allegations:

> It is reported that she appeared not to have cared for the baby, and at one stage did not feed it for over eight hours. Registration of the baby was never completed.
>
> When bringing the baby in for a check up she astounded the sisters by having the baby dressed completely in black. A doctor who treated the baby said she did not react like a normal mother.
>
> The same doctor said that he looked up the name Azaria in a dictionary of names and meanings and found that it means: 'Sacrifice in the wilderness'.

Doctor Irene Milne was eventually to deny having made the comment that Lindy Chamberlain did not care for her baby or that she did not react like a normal mother. The reference to the name meaning 'Sacrifice in the wilderness' did not emanate from her, but from another medical practitioner who had not looked it up but simply relied upon what he had overheard. In fact the rumour was completely misconceived. Azaria means 'Blessed of God'. Yet the rumour swept through the community like wildfire.

In late September a task force of police arrived in Mount Isa. A youthful Detective Sergeant Graeme Charlwood had taken over from Inspector Gilroy as the officer in charge of the investigation. He had approached the matter with characteristic thoroughness, immersing himself in the statements of various witnesses and the available scientific reports. He had replayed the tape of Lindy's interview with Inspector Gilroy and had listened intently. He had examined each of the items of clothing and camping gear taken from the Chamberlains and had spent some time at Ayers Rock studying the camping area and the area where the clothes had been found. He had arranged for the Chamberlains' sleeping bag to be seized from the drycleaners. All in all, he had learnt a great deal about the matter and what he had learnt left him with grave suspicions. He was at pains to keep those suspicions from the Chamberlains. He was, as he later explained, 'a secretive person'.

Upon his arrival at Mount Isa he had gone to the television station to watch the video tape of the Chamberlains' interview on *Today Tonight*.

Part of 29 September 1980 was occupied in interviewing doctors and other medical personnel. The information received by Gilroy had been taken seriously and any information which might cast light on a possible motive for murder had to be pursued. The Chamberlains gave no authority for any disclosures concerning their medical history. They were not told of the inquiries.

Later that day Charlwood called to introduce himself to Lindy. There was an informal discussion, which continued after Michael arrived home. The Chamberlains did not know that every word was being surreptitiously recorded. Charlwood asked for and was given various items of bedding in the tent at the time the baby disappeared. He left after making arrangements for Lindy to be interviewed more formally at the Mount Isa police station on the following day.

The interview covered most of the next afternoon with Charlwood seeking to explore each detail in the narrative of events. As the hours rolled by, the strain began to take its toll on Lindy and at about 5.30 p.m. Charlwood broke off for the night and asked her to return the next day.

The day that Liz Hickson's article was published was to prove a busy one for Charlwood and his team.

Lindy returned to the police station to complete the interview. Towards the end of the interview Charlwood referred to the results of 'certain forensic tests' and asked for Lindy's comments. There was no dingo or dog saliva present and the holes were not made by either a dingo's or a dog's teeth, he said.

'Are you trying to say that somebody murdered her?' Lindy demanded.

'I am just putting to you the facts I have. I am looking for answers,' Charlwood replied.

'What about the space blanket?' Lindy asked.

'It's still being tested at the moment,' Charlwood told her, though the evidence later established that that had not been the case.

Charlwood referred her to a report from Dr Andrew Scott on his analysis of some bloodstains found in the Fertility Cave, several hundred metres from where the clothes were found. Scott found that the blood was of the same grouping as Lindy, a grouping confined to fourteen per cent of the population. Subsequent testing was to show that it was not her blood, but as she sat across the table from Charlwood she found the combination of scientific conclusions deeply disturbing.

'The findings almost seem incredible to me. I am to consider that it was done by something other than a dingo. That brings in such a range of coincidences with split second timing, that it seems impossible. Reading about the blood group on Ayers Rock, the same as mine, almost sounds like a well planned, well-thought-out, fantastic plan to set me up.'

'If that is the case,' Charlwood asked, 'do you know who would want to do such a thing?'

'I have no idea,' Lindy replied.

The interview with Michael followed a similar course. Late in the evening Charlwood asked, 'Do you know what happened to Azaria?'

'No,' Michael said. He was now as puzzled as Lindy. 'Except on the evidence we have given you, I do not know.'

'Is there anything at all that you would want to tell me in relation to the disappearance of your child?' Charlwood persisted.

'No,' Michael answered, 'except for my continuing observation, and strong feeling, that she was killed by a dingo or wild animal. What other alternatives? God only knows.'

Whilst Charlwood was interviewing Michael, Detective Sergeant Scott was interviewing Aidan. Reagan had been asleep, but Aidan had been awake and with his mother during the most crucial moments of the incident. The police were anxious to obtain a statement from him. His mother was permitted to be in the room during the course of the interview, but both Scott and Senior Constable Graham who was also present were later to confirm that most of his answers had been spontaneous and that he had been confident and clear in his answers. On one or two occasions he had consulted with his mother about some point of detail, but she did not seek to influence him and Aidan did not ask his mother about the crucial portion of his account. Scott concluded that there was nothing to cause him to entertain any doubt as to the veracity of his answers. The answers were recorded in the form of a statement:

> Daddy went to the barbecue and got some tea. There was a man, a lady and a little girl there, too. Me and Reagan were watching Daddy cook tea and Mummy was there holding bubby in her arms. I think Reagan had some tea and then he went to bed in the tent. I think Mummy took him to bed. After I finished my tea I said that I wanted to go to bed and Mummy said that she would take me and bubby up to bed. I went up to the tent with Mummy and bubby and I said to Mummy, is that all the tea that I get. Mummy said that I could have some more tea. While we were in the tent Mummy put bubby down in the cot and I went to the car with Mummy and she got some baked beans and I followed her down to the barbecue area. When we got to the barbecue area Mummy opened the tin of baked beans and Daddy said, 'Is that bubby crying' and Mummy said, 'I don't think so'. Mummy went back to the tent and said, 'The dingo has got my baby'. Mummy shouted, 'Has anyone got a torch?' and Daddy went around and asked if anybody has got a torch. When Mummy saw the dingo come out of the tent I was behind her, but I didn't see the dingo come out of the tent. I went back to the barbecue and got Daddy's torch and I gave it to Mummy or Daddy. After I gave him the torch, I stayed with a lady and then I went to bed. Before I went to bed, there was lots of people there searching.

Senior Constable Graham had also been allocated the task of searching the Chamberlains' car. There was to be some confusion over just when he carried out that search. He maintained that he started to examine the car late in the evening, but the police running sheets which offered a reasonably contemporaneous record of events listed the search before the interview with Aidan, apparently commencing somewhere between 6.00 and 6.30 p.m.

Whatever the availability of natural light, Graham used a 'Big Jim' torch. This is an advantage even in the daylight. The interior of a car is full of shadows and the beam provides a circle of brightness which stands out in sharp contrast to the surrounding area even on the sunniest day. The added clarity is of great assistance if one is conducting a meticulous examination. Graham's examination occupied two to two-and-a-half hours. Despite the thoroughness of his search, he found no trace of any blood.

Throughout this period, the background noise of whispering and gossip had been steadily building. The black dress assumed sacrificial connotations. The varnished wooden coffin in the garage which had been used as a prop for smoking classes now became a small white coffin in Azaria's bedroom. It was rumoured that the clothes had been found neatly folded, that Azaria had been hideously deformed, that the Chamberlains had a history of child battering, that they belonged to a bizarre sect which believed in human sacrifices and even that a four-year-old child had disappeared mysteriously whilst in the care of Lindy's sister some years before.

With these commenced a rash of dingo jokes. Many of them were told simply for their amusement value, but a message was being subtly conveyed. The dingo 'story' was ridiculous.

The tone of the articles in the press also changed. Initially it was largely a matter of phraseology. The Chamberlains' account of what had happened was no longer reported as fact, but as 'allegations'. The involvement of the dingo began to be described as 'the dingo theory' or 'the dingo story'. Various experts were quoted, but their views always seemed to point to the unlikelihood of a dingo having taken the child. By the time Liz Hickson's article appeared on 1 October 1980, the climate of opinion had swung against the Chamberlains.

The Chamberlains themselves were besieged by crank phone calls and letters. It reached a stage where people openly spoke of Lindy as the woman who had murdered her child. Even the boys were harassed on the street. Aidan was taunted at school. 'Dingoes don't come into our house and steal babies,' he was told. There had been other cases which had aroused great public indignation and anger. The kidnap and murder of young Graeme Thorne in the sixties, for example, had created a storm of outrage which was to lead to an amendment to the New South Wales Crimes Act to provide heavier penalties for kidnapping. Yet none of those cases had produced the spate of rumours that was to bedevil the Chamberlains. The climate of hate which built up against this family was unique in Australia's history.

9

The first inquest

THE NORTHERN TERRITORY is a vast sparsely populated area. Australians are accustomed to the wide open spaces and both Western Australia and Queensland are larger still. But by European standards it is immense. Its area is almost exactly the same as that of France, Great Britain, East and West Germany, Austria, Belgium and Hungary added together. Yet this immense area contains only one hundred and forty thousand people. There are ten square kilometres of land area for every man, woman and child. Nearly half the population live in the capital city Darwin, hub of the 'Top End'.

Alice Springs is located 1,550 kilometres to the south. The town became immortalised in Nevil Shute's famous novel, *A Town Like Alice*, which spawned a film and later a television mini series of the same name. It is set in the midst of arid red desert. The town itself is surrounded by low knobby hills, with rocky protuberances and sparse scrubby vegetation. The isolation of this place is unbelievable. Yulara, the new tourist village at Ayers Rock, is a mere 450 kilometres away, the old gold-mining town of Tennant Creek 507, the opal mining settlement of Coober Pedy 752, but there is not a major town for well over a thousand kilometres in any direction.

Perhaps because of its isolation, there is a unique frontier flavour about Alice. There is the flying doctor service and the School of the Air, which provides an education service to children in far-flung stations. Aborigines, mining engineers, anthropologists, croupiers from the casino and Bible translators all rub shoulders. One can go to the camel races and barrack for bewhiskered 'Yosemite Sam' types almost as colourful as their steeds. In September, one can attend the Alice Springs Regatta.

The Todd River only flows through the town after periods of heavy rain and the annual rainfall in Alice Springs is a scant 200 to 250 millimetres. Consequently, there are few tacking duels of the kind one sees at the America's Cup. Some of the boats sail on wheels, others are pushed with broomsticks, but most skippers' instructions to their crews are typically laconic: 'When the gun goes ya pick 'er up and run like the clappers!'

It was here that the Chamberlains had stopped overnight at the Cozens' home before continuing their journey back to Mount Isa.

The Northern Territory police force is probably the only law enforcement body in Australia which would have allocated an officer with the name of Buzzard to the Coroner's Office and given him the task of calling on the relatives of people who had died in tragic circumstances. When off duty, Constable Peter Buzzard was a member of Pastor Cozens' Bible-study group and his visit on the evening of 19 August 1980, was in part a social call. The Chamberlains had been in bed, exhausted from the long drive and the strain of the last two days. But his visit was not entirely social. He had not known that Constable Morris had already had them complete an Information of Death form and he had brought another one. The Chamberlains got up and discussed the matter with him at some length.

He was later to give evidence that he found them both lacking in emotion and 'almost clinical' about their daughter's death. He was also to claim that Lindy had told him that she turned around 'on instinct' and saw the dingo. Pastor Cozens and his wife had lengthy experience in counselling bereaved people and they had lost a child of their own in tragic circumstances many years earlier. In contrast to Constable Buzzard, they were to describe the emotional reaction of the Chamberlains as perfectly normal. Pastor Cozens was also to say that the account which he heard Lindy give Constable Buzzard had been entirely consistent with the account that she had given him at Ayers Rock. Lindy was to suggest that the constable had confused two incidents. There had been an earlier incident when she had turned as if on instinct and seen a dingo, but that had nothing to do with the taking of Azaria.

It was here, too, that the Chamberlains returned for the inquest due to commence on 16 December 1980. They had not sought any legal advice until a few days earlier when, at the insistence of some friends, they had reluctantly agreed to engage a solicitor to represent them at the inquest. Despite the community's vitriol the Chamberlains felt they had little to fear from the Coroner. If you had nothing to hide, surely you didn't need a lawyer. After all, it was the court's function to see that the truth came out. Besides, the police had not suggested that they were treating them as murder suspects. The Chamberlains accepted their apparent friendliness and sympathy at face value. Surely, they felt, we can trust the police.

The opening of the inquest was heralded by a flurry of activity from journalists, camera operators and others associated with television news teams. The public gallery was packed and an overflow of potential spectators spilled out into the foyer. The Coroner, Dennis Barritt S.M., noted the appearances, Ashley Macknay as counsel assisting the Coroner and Peter Dean to appear on behalf of Mr and Mrs Chamberlain.

Macknay's first task was to establish that the court had jurisdiction to hear the matter. He began with a preliminary submission adverting to scientific deductions from the amount of blood found on the jumpsuit which suggested that Azaria must have lost at least twenty per cent of her normal blood volume and other evidence pointing inexorably to her death. He went on to refer to reports by Dr Andrew Scott, a forensic biologist, Dr Harding, an expert on hairs and Mr Rex Kuchel, a botanist. That evidence, he suggested, justified a number of conclusions:

> Firstly, the deceased was removed from her clothing by a person rather than by a dog or a dingo. Secondly, the damage to the clothing was more consistent with having been caused by a person rather than a dingo. Thirdly, the state of the clothes suggests that the clothes were put in the place in which they were found by a person rather than being dragged there by a dog or a dingo.

At that stage Barritt was concerned only with the tentative findings of fact necessary to establish jurisdiction. He made the formal finding that death had occurred and continued:

> I agree that because of the nature of the damage to the clothing and the manner in which the clothing was found, it would indicate that there has, at some stage, been human intervention in the disposal of the body, and that the body cannot now be found. I find that the body is in a place from which it presently cannot be recovered. On those grounds I find that I have jurisdiction.

No witnesses had given evidence at that stage and the magistrate had reached no firm conclusions about anything except his jurisdiction to hear the case, but his remarks were to be widely misinterpreted.

Lindy was the first witness. She confirmed that her name was Alice Lynne Chamberlain and that she resided at Avondale College, Cooranbong, the Seventh Day Adventist stronghold in which she and her family had sought refuge from the unceasing barbs of an increasingly hostile community. Macknay obtained from her an account of the events leading up to the disappearance of Azaria. The flow of the narrative was interrupted from time to time by her evident distress, but she choked down the sobs and went on. The dictates of fairness demanded that she be given the opportunity to comment on the scientific reports and to offer any explanation that may spring to mind. But it was, in the main, a barren exercise. Lindy was a pastor's wife not a walking compendium of science. She was scarcely in a position to challenge the views of a team of men with doctorates in various disciplines.

On the other hand, she and her family had suffered much as a result of unfounded speculation and she was not about to allow more speculation to go unquestioned simply because it was dressed up in scientific jargon.

Macknay described to her the experiment conducted by a forensic dentist, Kenneth Brown, of the Adelaide Zoo. He had dressed a decapitated goat kid in a jumpsuit and placed it in a dingo pen in the Adelaide Zoo. The results had surprised the experts in two respects. Firstly, the dingo had been able to extract the body without undoing any more than two studs and, secondly, it had proceeded to bury the jumpsuit. However, the nature of the damage to the jumpsuit was quite different from that evident on the suit worn by Azaria Chamberlain at the time of her disappearance.

This led Macknay to ask, 'If it were the case that the clothing located at Ayers Rock did not have any consistent features with those taken from the zoo, would you then accept that the damage to the clothing at Ayers Rock was not caused by a dog or dingo?' There were, of course, obvious differences between the two situations. Brown's experiment had consisted of offering a tame dingo confined by a pen an inert piece of meat in circumstances which were clearly non-threatening. It seemed a dubious means of comparison with the act of a wild predator, venturing into a human encampment to take a live baby and then transporting it four or five kilometres across country.

The leap of logic was not lost on Lindy. 'I would like to question what differences there are between domesticated dingoes and wild dingoes,' she replied.

'If the forensic dentist told you there were no significant differences between wild dingoes, tame dingoes and dogs, insofar as the present purposes are concerned?' Macknay persisted, but Lindy could also be persistent.

'Have tests been done on wild dingoes?'

Macknay tried again, 'If we hypothesise that the forensic dentist knows what he is talking about . . .'

Lindy cut him off: 'You are still hypothesising. I was just asking, "Have there been any tests done on wild dingoes?" ' There was no answer to that question, but the point was not lost on Barritt.

Later Macknay raised with her Brown's conclusion that a purple blanket which the Chamberlains had thought had been damaged by dingo teeth was in fact cut by a sharp implement. 'The fact that the forensic dentist has concluded there was no evidence of tooth marks on that blanket does not cause you any concern at all?' Macknay asked.

'It does cause me concern. The fact is they cannot tell what it was done by. And if they can be so accurate, why can they not be so accurate in stating what it is?'

Macknay assumed that she was simply trying to deprecate Brown's report. 'I see. So you are not prepared to accept the fact that he may be able to exclude some cause, but not necessarily pinpoint a particular cause?'

'I am prepared to accept that he knows, in a certain field, what has happened, yes,' Lindy replied.

'You are not prepared to accept his expertise in saying that there were no teeth marks?'

'I am not saying that at all,' Lindy explained. 'I am saying that I would like a full answer not a partial answer. I would like to know more perhaps than anyone else what happened to my daughter.'

Michael was the next witness. He spoke more slowly and deliberately, as if determined to maintain his composure. Macknay went over substantially the same ground with him.

During the course of the inquest the court office received a number of crank phone calls. One of them caused an interruption to the proceedings, whilst two worried lawyers and an equally concerned magistrate tried to devise some adequate means of protecting the Chamberlains. The call had apparently come from somebody who had been sitting in the public gallery. He had said, 'I am going to blow that bitch away.'

The evidence continued, Macknay running through the Lowes, the Wests, Wally Goodwin, Bobbie Downs and Derek Roff.

Nipper Winmatti was to cause something of a stir when he gave evidence of the Aboriginal tradition of keeping the stronger twin and leaving the weaker one out in the bush 'for the dingoes'. It was a part of the dreaming of Kurrpanngu, the dingo spirit, and the interpreter was affronted that it should have been raised in public.

Dr Scott gave evidence that he had not been able to find saliva on the garments, though he added that he had had to devise a test from scratch and it was very much a hit-and-miss-affair. He could easily have missed it.

When the inquiry resumed after the Christmas vacation the Chamberlains were represented by Phil Rice QC in addition to Peter Dean. Rice was an Adelaide barrister who specialised in criminal cases. He had the stamp of a tough and wily campaigner. Shortly after the resumption, the Coroner decided to issue a public appeal for information concerning any instances of dingoes attacking children. Among the heterogeneous assortment of replies were four letters from people who asserted that dingoes did not attack human beings and twenty-seven reports of dingoes doing just that.

Dr Newsome, a zoologist with extensive experience with

dingoes, suggested that the growl heard by the Wests was probably a warning signal to another dingo. That gave rise to the likelihood that there were two dingoes at the tent, a view shared by Roff. He was asked, 'But you consider there was some significance in the growl and the fact that a dingo was seen so close to the tent, but standing still and not fleeing?'

He replied, 'That it was not the animal which came out of the tent was my first response on reading it.' When it came down to the likelihood of a dingo having taken the child he concluded: 'The odds must be very long on such an event happening, but I do not see how its possibility could be dismissed.'

Kuchel expressed the view that the baby's clothing had apparently been rubbed in a relatively rare plant known as *parietaria debilis* which grew only in the lee of the rock.

Dr Harding gave evidence that there were animal hairs on the jumpsuit, but that any hairs on the blankets were too old to be relevant. During the course of his evidence, he discovered that hairs had been removed from them by vacuuming. Among them were facial hairs from a dog or cat, but the vacuuming had been too harsh and he could not tell whether or not they were fresh.

On Friday 13 February 1981, the Chamberlains were asked to leave their motel. Someone had called and threatened to blow it to pieces with a bomb. The police evacuated them to other accommodation, the identity of which remained secret.

In his address, Macknay was to invite the Coroner to accept the Lowes and the Wests as honest and reliable witnesses. It would have been difficult to have regarded them in any other light. That really highlighted the problem. On the one hand there was a compelling body of evidence from people present on the night in question which pointed to the Chamberlains' innocence. On the other hand there was a body of scientific evidence which appeared to indicate that the clothing had been interfered with by a human being.

When the time came for his judgment, Barritt made a controversial decision. He agreed to permit the press to set up cameras in court and televise its delivery. It was a step which had never been taken before in the Territory, but he wanted to lay the rumours to rest. On 20 February 1981, Australians in all parts of the country tuned in to a live programme to hear the Coroner announce his finding.

> I doth find that Azaria Chantel Loren Chamberlain, a child then of nine weeks of age and formerly of Mount Isa, Queensland, met her death when attacked by a wild dingo whilst asleep in the family's tent at the top camping area, Ayers Rock, shortly after 8.00 p.m. on 17 August 1980.
>
> I further find that neither the parents of the child, nor either of their remaining children, were in any degree whatsoever responsible for this death.
>
> I find that the name Azaria does not mean, and never has meant 'sacrifice in the wilderness'.
>
> I find that, after her death, the body of Azaria was taken from the possession of the dingo and disposed of by an unknown method, by a person or persons unknown.

The conservation authorites were publicly castigated.

> Prior to August 17 1980, the conservation authorities had received reports of several instances of dingoes attacking children. The significance of a dingo's range and a dingo's territory was known and understood by the rangers. The existence and whereabouts of a number of their lairs were known and known to be in areas where children might be expected to wander whilst exploring the many areas of interest around the base of the rock. The conduct of dingoes around campsites, together with their propensity to enter tents was known or ought to have been known. The propensity of a dingo reared by Homo Sapiens and treated as a pet in a domestic environment to violently attack children was known; yet in the face of this knowledge dingoes have been retained and indeed allowed to virtually infest the area as a tourist attraction.
>
> I would hope that as a moral responsibility to protect children visiting national parks would appear to have been avoided in the past, the legal consequences of such conduct in the future ought to lead to the elimination of any species dangerous to man from such parks, or at least from those areas frequented by tourists . . . If those charged with the protection of wild life within national parks would rely on laws forbidding the destruction of such creatures then they ought to be made to publicise the inherent dangers . . .

He also made trenchant criticisms of the police.

Once again during this inquisition I have had occasion to criticise the work performed by the Northern Territory Police Force Forensic Science Section. It was not only the examination of the tent but also the transcript of the interview of Dr Corbett by Sergeant Saudry that caused me great apprehension, concerning the bona fides of this section. An examination of the transcript reveals that when Dr Corbett made a statement in any way supporting the Chamberlains' account of this tragedy, the topic was immediately changed, obviously to avoid any further evidence emerging that might support the 'Dingo Theory'.

Police forces must realise, or be made to realise, that courts will not tolerate any standard less than complete objectivity from anyone claiming to make scientific observations. . . Any standard less than the highest attainable, where the rights and interests of suspect and prosecutor alike are protected, negates the credit of such a section, and renders the probitive value of its conclusions useless. . . I agree with Mr Macknay that supervision within the (Forensic Science) section must be negligent in the extreme.

He concluded his remarks with a real crie de coeur:

To you, Pastor and Mrs Chamberlain, and through you to Aidan and Reagan, may I extend my deepest sympathy. You have not only suffered the loss of your beloved child in the most tragic circumstances, but you have all been subjected to months of innuendos, suspicion and probably the most malicious gossip ever witnessed in this country.

I have taken the unusual step of permitting these proceedings to be televised today in the hope that by direct and accurate communication, such innuendos, suspicion and gossip may cease.

10

Operation Ochre

BARRITT'S HISTORIC JUDGMENT and the dramatic way it was announced to a sceptical public had brought relief and new hope to the Chamberlains. They were both New Zealanders, but they had spent enough time in Australia to soak up its ethos. They knew that there was more to the Australian character than the shallow vulgarity reflected in such celluloid creations as Bazza Mackenzie and Les Patterson. One could see pale reflections of such characters scattered around the down market pubs and clubs, but to the average Australian they were merely the 'ockers' or 'yobbos'.

The caricatures of film and television frequently reflect little more than the Australian penchant for self-deprecation or 'knocking'. There is a down-to-earth pragmatism reflected in their wartime reputation as being the best scroungers in the world. This is accompanied by a wariness of those who too overtly espouse lofty ideals or are 'airy fairy'. Perhaps this explains why many Australians are wary of 'parsons'. Yet buried beneath the banter and apparently irredeemable cynicism, there are tenets of faith. There is the concept of mateship which a sociologist might articulate as a fierce loyalty, especially in times of adversity. A man may neglect his children, observe his marriage vows only whilst his wife is watching and 'rip off' the taxman but if he doesn't 'stand by his mate in a fight', then by Australian standards he's not really a man at all.

It was a Frenchman, Voltaire, who came out with the immortal line: 'I may disagree with every word that you say, but I will defend to the death your right to say it.' Your archetypal 'Aussie' would not have put it in those terms. They are too dramatic. A man would have to be 'a bit of a show-off' to say a thing like that. But the sentiment is encompassed within a somewhat broader concept which constitutes another Australian article of faith. You have to 'give a bloke a fair go'.

The hostility had been too intense, the hurts too fresh for the Chamberlains to expect sympathy from all quarters. They knew that bigotry can be well nigh ineradicable, that some people seem to prefer to believe the worst of their fellows and that there would always be the risk of some hostile reaction from one crank or another. But the legal proceedings were over and the truth exposed for anyone fair-minded enough to see it. Surely now the overwhelming majority of Australians would give them 'a fair go'.

It was a relief tinged with sadness. Barritt had done what he could for them, but he could not bring back the little girl who had been a source of such delight. Perhaps now they would be free to work through the normal process of grieving.

There were other losses, too. They had been driven from their home, their church and their friends. The ministry which Michael had built up so painstakingly in Mount Isa had been torn from him. They had been uprooted and, to a degree, dispossessed. For the time being, at least, another parish seemed out of the question. There was too much chance that Michael would find himself preaching to a congregation of journalists and those whose only interest was one of morbid curiosity. Besides, the death threats still echoed in their minds and they had young children to think of. For the time being, they decided, they would remain within the Adventist community where time and the warm acceptance of fellow Christians might bring healing. The Adventist college was also at Cooranbong and they could use the opportunity to further their studies.

In June 1981 Kenneth Brown, the forensic dentist, arrived in London. He had obtained permission to collect the clothing which had been worn by Azaria at the time of her disappearance and to show it to Professor James Cameron, an internationally renowned forensic pathologist. Cameron's interest was immediately aroused. He arranged for a medical photographer from the London Medical School to photograph the jumpsuit using ultraviolet fluorescence as an aid to distinguishing blood from other stains.

As a result of his examination, Cameron formed a number of conclusions. The bleeding had occurred when the jumpsuit was fully buttoned up. The neck had been cut not by dingo teeth, but a cutting instrument such as scissors or a knife. The jumpsuit had been buried with the body still in it. There were impressions of an adult female hand on the back and shoulder of the jumpsuit, apparently caused by somebody holding the baby upright with bloodstained hands. He was to report:

> As to the possible causes of death, in the absence of a body, one must assume an unascertainable cause of death. Having said that, however, in the presence of the bleeding on the jumpsuit, and from its amount and various other findings at that moment in time, it would be reasonable to assume that she met her death by unnatural causes, and that the mode of death had been caused by a cutting instrument, possibly encircling the neck, certainly cutting the vital blood vessels.

Ten months after Azaria had disappeared, a man on the other side of the world had examined some clothing and decided that she had been murdered.

The police reaction to this report was extraordinary. A conference was convened to plan the strategy of future investigations. It was chaired personally by Paul Everingham, the Chief Minister of the Northern Territory. There was an impressive array of police, including an Assistant Commissioner, a superintendent and a number of other senior officers. Although statements had been taken from many of the witnesses prior to the inquest, it was decided that they should be re-interviewed. Teams of police were formed, one for each state in Australia. They would swoop on the witnesses simultaneously to cut off any chance of them contacting one another to compare notes.

There seemed to be a degree of paranoia about all this. The people to be interviewed were not suspected conspirators. They were decent members of the community who had had no prior contact with the Chamberlains or with each other. Unless some of them had happened to introduce themselves at the first inquest, it is doubtful that any of them would have known the identity of the others.

Arrangements were made to tape record every conversation concerning the case. Police even went to the lengths of recording conversations with each other. This was later to prove an embarrassment when the tapes came into the possession of counsel assisting the Commission of Inquiry. The hunt for a motive was to be resumed in earnest, with extensive inquiries being made concerning the Chamberlains' medical history. Ultimately, doctors and nurses were to be interviewed in three Australian states and across the Tasman in New Zealand.

Arrangements were made for a team of police to execute a search warrant at the Chamberlains' home in Cooranbong and to seize an extensive list of items for testing. A large team of police were sent to Ayers Rock with instructions to dig up extensive areas of ground near the site of the Chamberlains' tent. This was to cause some amusement to the rangers who eventually expressed the hope that they would put the Rock back when they finished looking under it. Ultimately, a Hercules transport plane was to be used to fly the Chamberlains' car to Darwin. In both its planning and execution the police investigation was to assume the dimensions of a military campaign.

Yet, as Mr Justice Morling was to point out, even if Lindy Chamberlain had been guilty of killing her child there was no evidence to suggest that the killing was premeditated or that there was any motive for it. It could only have been the act of a woman suffering from postnatal depression or the type of killing which a criminologist might have described as falling within the baby battering syndrome. In most Australian jurisdictions, such killings would only be punishable as manslaughter or infanticide and the mother could expect to be treated relatively leniently. Accordingly, whilst the taking of human life is always a serious matter, if one were to rank the various types of murder in order of seriousness, this one would seem to fall towards the lower end of the range. It clearly did not give rise to the same desperate need for urgency, for example, as an investigation into a series of seemingly random murders by a psychopathic thrill killer. A senior police officer was to brush this observation aside. There was nothing special about the police approach to this case, he claimed. All cases are equally important.

There was, however, no doubt that a number of police were left smarting by Barritt's comments. He had trenchantly castigated members of the Northern Territory police for their lack of objectivity. The criticism was not well-received. As Detective Inspector Charlwood was later to concede, some police officers had responded by announcing 'we'll show him!'

The police conversations faithfully recorded by the officer in charge of electronic eavesdropping were also to prove revealing. One police investigator was to refer to Lindy as having 'killer eyes'. The other police officer involved in the conversation obviously found something deeply sinister about Aidan. 'He's got really weird eyes,' he said. At the time Aidan was six years old.

Other calls were to reveal intense disappointment when some aspects of the case against the Chamberlains proved to be less damning than had been hoped. 'Yeah, the boss's ass really hit the ground when he heard about that,' one sergeant commented ruefully. Another police officer was to confide that 'the boss' had been so bitterly disappointed that he had not had the courage to pass on other progress reports lest his hopes be dashed again.

On 19 September 1981, a team of police led by Detective Sergeant Charlwood arrived at the Chamberlains' home with a warrant authorising them to seize some sixty items. It was a Saturday, the Seventh Day Adventists' sabbath. Michael Chamberlain was still an ordained pastor and had some commitments. It had now been thirteen months since Azaria disappeared and he felt that they could have waited another day.

'We have further scientific evidence now,' Charlwood explained 'and I've got a warrant to search the house.'

'What sort of evidence?' Lindy asked.

'I should execute the warrant first, before I tell you that,' Charlwood replied.

Despite his initial annoyance, Michael did his best to co-operate with them. He stood in the kitchen picking out from the multitude of items brought to him things which he remembered taking to Ayers Rock in August, 1980. They seemed to be particularly concerned with knives and scissors.

During the course of the search a police officer found the family Bible. A police running sheet was later to record that one passage had been underlined in red. It concerned the story of a woman who had killed her child by driving a tent peg through his head. In fact, the story had nothing to do with a mother killing her child. The officer had been looking at a passage in Judges 4 which recounts the story of an Israelite woman, Jael, who killed Sisera, the commander of the Canaanite army which had invaded Israel and oppressed its people. The story was not underlined, but some of the print from the picture on the facing page had left an impression on the text. The inscriptions on the flyleaf indicated that the Bible had been in the possession of the Chamberlain family since 1884.

When Michael went out to the garage to get the tent for Charlwood, he was unable to find the pegs. 'They were given back to you,' Charlwood reminded him. Michael explained that they had moved house since then and that he didn't know where they were.

'If they turn up, I will let you know,' he added. Charlwood was not satisfied and kept searching for them. Michael permitted them to take what they wanted and they left with nearly four hundred items. Their search had uncovered two camera bags, but it was Michael that told them that neither of them had been taken to Ayers Rock. He found the right bag and gave it to them.

Whilst the search was still in progress, a press helicopter arrived. It circled low over the house whilst some nameless member of a news team trained a camera on the people below.

The police also wanted to look at the car, but it had been involved in an accident and was at Morrisset being repaired. Michael agreed to take them to it. They found it partially disassembled and Michael signed a note voluntarily authorising the police to remove it for examination. When the Commission of Inquiry concluded in Darwin five-and-a-half years later, it had still not been returned.

Later, Charlwood drove Lindy into the police station for a formal interview. On the way he confided that the clothes had been examined by Professor Cameron. 'He confirms there was no dingo involved in the disappearance of your daughter,' he said.

'I didn't know there were any dingo experts in London,' Lindy replied sarcastically.

'He doesn't profess to be a dingo expert,' Charlwood said. 'The baby was decapitated.' Later he referred to Cameron's comments concerning 'a hand print from someone whose hand was wet with blood: a print consistent with a female hand.'

As they neared the police station, there was a short exchange. 'Did you kill your child?' Charlwood asked.

'You've asked me that before,' Lindy replied.

'I've never asked you that before. I've asked you if you knew what happened to her.'

Lindy was getting angry. Besides, she had been advised by her solicitor that she should not take part in any interview unless he was present. She was uncertain whether she could answer some questions without waiving her right to decline to answer others.

'What are the implications if I tell you?' she asked and then added with a touch of sharpness, 'You've broken your word before.'

'What do you mean?' Charlwood asked.

'Last time we spoke like this, it was about hypnotism. Then you got to the inquest and threw it up at me. What guarantees have I got that you won't throw this up at me in court?' This was a reference to an earlier conversation which Lindy had regarded as being 'off the record'. Charlwood had asked her to submit to hypnosis, but Lindy had declined on religious grounds.

'It depends on your answer,' Charlwood responded candidly.

'You don't think if I did, I could have carried out this charade all this time?'

'You are selling yourself short.'

'Oh, come on!' Lindy snorted. 'You are crediting me with the brains to commit the perfect murder and get away with it.'

'I mean it,' Charlwood said. 'You are an intelligent woman. Don't sell yourself short.'

'Ask my friends. They'll tell you I can't tell lies.'

'You haven't answered my question.'

'No, I haven't, have I?'

There was a pause as Charlwood brought the car to a halt in the police driveway and Lindy got out.

'No, of course I never killed my child!' Lindy said with feeling.

On 20 November 1981, there was an application to the Supreme Court of the Northern Territory for an order quashing the findings of the first inquest so that the matter could be reopened. The

Chamberlains were given no notice of the application and the proceedings were heard in camera. The Crown adopted this tactic because it wanted to be sure that the Chamberlains would not gain some hint of the scientific reports which were to form the basis of the case against them.

Barritt was informed of the application the afternoon before. He arranged for a barrister to represent him but, when he arrived, he was informed that he would only be admitted to the proceedings if he gave an undertaking not to tell his client the nature of the evidence. It seems that not even a magistrate, and a former policeman at that, was to be trusted with information which might have been of some limited assistance to the Chamberlains. The barrister took the view that this reduced his role to an exercise in futility and he withdrew in frustration.

11

The second inquest

THE RULES OF JUSTICE provide certain basic safeguards for an accused person. No person is liable to be punished for a serious crime unless he has been convicted by a jury of his peers.

Furthermore, the Crown carries the onus of proving his guilt beyond any reasonable doubt. An accused has no obligation to prove his innocence or to offer any explanation. He may decline to answer questions put to him by the investigating police and, in due course, sit silently in the dock while the Crown case unfolds and then, through his counsel, simply make a submission that the Crown has failed to discharge its onus of proof. If he is right in that contention then he must be acquitted.

Over the years there have been some legislative incursions into these safeguards. Difficulties of proving cases against drug peddlers, for example, have led to statutory presumptions that a person who possesses more than a prescribed quantity of a prohibited drug has it in his possession for the purpose of supply to others. In the main, however, these safeguards have been respected and with good reason. They arose not as a result of the whim of some trendy political party, but from the collective wisdom of generations of judges who, in centuries gone by, sought to forge a fair system of justice free of such barbarisms as trial by ordeal and trial by combat. In common with Americans, Canadians, New Zealanders and citizens of other countries who have inherited English legal traditions, Australians generally pay homage to the great axiom of British justice: 'It is better for ten guilty men to go free than for one innocent one to be unjustly punished.'

In the normal course of events, a person charged with a major criminal offence such as murder will find himself involved in a preliminary inquiry before a magistrate. Inquiries of this kind are normally referred to as 'committal proceedings'. Their purpose is to determine whether there is sufficient evidence to warrant putting the accused on trial for the offence charged. They are normally confined to an evaluation of the Crown case, though the accused may present evidence if he wishes to do so. The term 'the accused' is an apt one. Unless and until his guilt has been proven beyond reasonable doubt, he remains simply a member of the community against whom certain, still unsubstantiated, allegations have been made. But he has been accused of a serious offence and is accordingly entitled to the safeguards offered by the law. Consequently, he is entitled to remain silent while the Crown endeavours to prove a case against him.

By late 1981 the Northern Territory police had gathered an impressive body of scientific evidence which seemed to raise a strong case against Lindy Chamberlain. In the normal course of events, this would have resulted in her being arrested and charged. Yet, from the police point of view, such a course had one serious disadvantage. It permitted the Chamberlains to simply remain silent. If they could be inveigled into the witness box before they found out about the scientific evidence, a skilled cross-examiner might extract some admission from them before they were in a position to appreciate its significance. Equally, he might provoke emphatic denials or other statements which the scientific evidence could later expose as untrue. The problem was: how to spring the trap?

The answer to this dilemma was to be found in the normal coronial procedure. An inquest is simply an inquiry into a person's death. There is no accused, merely a number of witnesses. Of course, the evidence may disclose that a person has been guilty of a crime and, in that event, the magistrate or coroner as he is known is empowered to commit him for trial. A witness is not left entirely bereft of protection. He may object to answering questions on the ground that to do so might tend to incriminate him, but that protection is not extended automatically. A witness must actually commence his evidence and say in response to a particular question, 'I object to answering that question on the ground that it may tend to incriminate me' or words to a similar effect.

If the Chamberlains wanted to say that to a suspicious Australian public, then let them! But not even the most rabid punter would have put any money on it. They would feel constrained to give evidence and one of the major safeguards available to accused people would have been successfully circumvented.

Stuart Tipple began to get some inkling of what was in store when he sought copies of the various scientific reports. His request was flatly refused. He was surprised by the refusal because counsel assisting coroners at inquests normally adopt a very open and co-operative attitude. The matter was raised with the coroner in early December when the case was listed for the purpose of announcing the hearing date. Chief Magistrate Gerry Galvin said that he had no power to intervene.

The second inquest commenced on 14 December 1981. The Chamberlains were again represented by Phil Rice QC, but another barrister, Andrew Kirkham, had been added to the team. Even before the case began, they raised the matter with Des Sturgess, a Queensland barrister who had been briefed by the Crown to assist the coroner.

'It's out of my hands,' Sturgess told them. 'I've got my instructions and I can't help you.'

The hearing began formally with an opening address by Sturgess in which he outlined the evidence given at the earlier inquest and proceeded to tender, one by one, the various items which had been exhibits. Two video tapes were screened and the tape recording of Lindy's interview with Inspector Gilroy was played to the court.

On the second day Sally Lowe was called. She was asked to identify a statement she had made to the police on 19 September 1981, and a copy was passed to Phil Rice. He seized the opportunity to object to the cloak of secrecy.

'Mr Sturgess, for reasons best known to the authorities who instruct him, is proposing simply to call witnesses without giving a summary, even to Your Worship at this stage, of the nature, extent, or their purpose in being called.'

'Mr Sturgess?' asked Galvin, the question implicit in the tone of voice.

'I will bear that in mind and see what I can do,' Sturgess responded cryptically, but he acceded to a request that Sally Lowe's evidence be interrupted for an hour or two so that the fresh statement might be digested.

'I now call Michael Leigh Chamberlain,' Sturgess announced. This time it was Andrew Kirkham who took the objection. He referred to a witness' privilege against self-incrimination and foreshadowed relying upon some unreported decisions of the Victorian Supreme Court which were then en route from Melbourne. He then went on to the real thrust of the objection.

'Inasmuch as they have the choice, it can only be a real choice if it is known what evidence is going to be called. We don't know the nature or extent of the fresh evidence to be put before you, and neither of the parties we represent is in a position to effectively exercise their rights without knowing the nature of the evidence to be called. The fairer course would be to call the evidence, then call the Chamberlains and allow them to make an election, or to make submissions as to their rights, on the basis of what has gone on before.'

Sturgess remained unmoved. 'I am subject to Your Worship's direction but, apart from that, I control who shall be called, and when they shall be called, and the order in which the evidence is presented, not the witnesses themselves.'

Galvin adjourned the proceedings pending further argument in the light of the authorities from the Victorian Supreme Court. The Chamberlains and their legal advisers met in the conference room to consider their position. Peter Dean reported that a radio station had already announced that Michael Chamberlain had refused to give evidence to avoid incriminating himself.

'We want to give evidence,' Lindy said decisively. 'We don't want to look as if we have got something to hide.'

The situation was too important to be resolved so peremptorily and Rice insisted on taking them through their rights. But the decision had already been made.

Before Michael's evidence began, Rice rose to object again, his voice tinged by anger and frustration. 'Your Worship, we repeat our submission regarding Mr Chamberlain being called at this stage. We have no control over his being called now. We would have thought it far fairer to have called him after other evidence which the authorities have, which they claim changes the aspect of things. I merely mention this, because we cannot in any way control the time when Mr Chamberlain, or Mrs Chamberlain, can give evidence. And to that extent I rise in protest, knowing that I am impotent to do anything about it.'

Sturgess commenced to cross-examine Michael, leaving Rice and Kirkham to try to deduce the nature of the evidence to come from the form of the questions. The cross-examination was wide ranging. It dealt with the bloodstained sleeping-bag taken to the drycleaners, the possibility of more bloodstaining on a towel, the number of people who might have bled in the car at various times and the camera bag which had been taken to Ayers Rock. Later when Sturgess was cross-examining Michael about his conversation with Trevor Scadden from the *Adelaide Advertiser*, Rice again objected. There was a heated exchange.

'But is my friend alleging the commission of some sort of offence by Mr Chamberlain?' Rice demanded. 'You see, we know nothing! He has gone into the witness box at this early stage without any notice to us at all. Now, we have been very patient. But I do object. If my friend is going to suggest that he has committed some offence, why has he not been charged? And the normal processes of justice allowed to proceed, instead of putting him in the witness box and cross-examining him — under the guise of an inquest — with a view to building up a case when presumably this other evidence, this other undisclosed evidence, does not seem to have the fibre?'

The cross-examination continued, with Rice fighting a rear-guard action and interjecting from time to time to remind the court that this was not a trial and that Sturgess should not assume the role of prosecuting counsel.

When Michael's evidence concluded, Rice sought a short adjournment. He was still waiting for the Victorian authorities. Unhappily, they had not arrived by the time court resumed and he was left to argue the matter without them. Galvin again brushed his objection aside. 'If I can just indicate that I see no reason to change the ruling or the nature of the questions. I do not feel I am doing anything wrong.'

The next witness was Alice Lynne Chamberlain. Sturgess covered much of the same ground he had covered with Michael. When he came to the bunny rug, he put it in Lindy's hands and asked her to identify it. His questions were soon interrupted. Lindy broke down, her shoulders shaking with sobs. Sturgess requested a short adjournment.

Sturgess reminded her of Charlwood's question: 'Mrs Chamberlain, did you kill your child?' Why, he demanded, had she replied, 'Well, what are the implications if I tell you?' Lindy was no longer tearful. Now her blood was up.

'Because I had told him that our legal advice was not to give an interview,' she retorted. 'And although I have learned very fast how far to trust the police, I was still expecting them to honour their word. And I was not sure what he considered an interview and what he didn't. And as I had no legal advice there, I was asking him the question. Unfortunately, I was given the wrong advice.'

She conceded that Charlwood had asked her if she was prepared to give him her hand prints and suggested that the giving of them could be a means of not only tying her to the prints on the clothes, but of excluding her. 'Did you say this, or something to this effect?' Sturgess asked. ' "Yes, I realise that. I am prepared to let you have my hand prints, but I would like to talk to my solicitor first"? '

'That's correct.'

'And he said, "Yes, that's all right." Is that correct?'

'That's right,' Lindy said emphatically, 'and he promised to contact us the following day. We haven't heard from him since.'

Sturgess was clearly taken aback. 'Steady on,' he said.

There was a pause before the next question: 'Mrs Chamberlain, would you be prepared to give to the police your palm prints?'

Rice interjected, vigorously protesting at the unfairness of putting her on the spot in that manner without giving her the opportunity of taking his advice.

There was a short adjournment while they discussed the matter. It was Kirkham who explained that it was a no-win situation. If her hand print proved to be too big, they could say it was only part of the hand. If too small, they could say the clothing was bunched.

She went back into the witness box and gave her answer. 'I told Sergeant Charlwood, and I say the same thing again, I would have been quite happy to provide my palm prints to them provided my lawyers agree. They do not agree that I give my palm prints at this stage. They know I am quite happy to give my palm prints.'

Sturgess' last unfinished question was a masterpiece of disbelief. 'You are not prepared to give to the authorities your palm prints so they can be compared with. . .' He sat down.

The court adjourned to the police compound to examine the Chamberlains' car. Constable Metcalfe pointed out areas where blood had been found. He drew particular attention to the inside hinge of the front seat on the passenger's side. Then he held up a small steel plate about five inches square. He had cut this out from an area under the dashboard adjacent to the passenger's side wall of the vehicle. There was an unmistakable spray pattern on it. He climbed into the front of the car and lay on the floor looking up at the area from which the plate had been cut. He pointed upward like a character in a pantomine. The implication was chilling.

It was Joy Kuhl, a forensic biologist employed by the New South Wales Health Commission, who had tested the stains found in the car. She was to give evidence of an impressive barrage of tests.

She had begun with a 'screening' test for blood using a chemical named orthotolidine. The test was a relatively straightforward one. One applied the chemical to a small white pad and rubbed it on the suspected area of carpet. One paused to see if anything happened before adding peroxide. A bright blue reaction then indicated the presence of blood. She explained that there were other substances which could give a 'false positive', but that they gave a 'first stage' reaction easily recognisable by the formation of the blue staining before any peroxide had been added. She had obtained positive reactions to this test from the camera bag, the console in the car, the door handles, the seats and the carpet.

The second series of tests were of an immunological nature. In the main, she had used a test known as 'crossover electrophoresis'. This involved the use of an 'antiserum' which, in theory, would react only with foetal haemoglobin. One took a glass plate covered with a thin layer of agar gel and punched two rows of small holes or 'wells' in the gel. The antiserum was added to one row of the wells. A series of blood samples were added to the other row. One of those samples would be the one to be tested. The others were 'controls'. An electric current was then applied to the completed apparatus, impelling the antibodies in the serum towards the opposite row of wells and, by a process of osmosis, dragging antigen from those wells in the opposite direction. If the sample contained foetal haemoglobin, then the antigen and antibody would form a precipitin band.

The procedure was complicated by the fact that adult blood contains small quantities of foetal haemoglobin and the blood of an infant contains substantial quantities of adult haemoglobin. Accordingly, it was not so much a question of whether foetal haemoglobin was present, but whether it constituted more than, say, one per cent of the total haemoglobin in the sample. To overcome this difficulty, the samples were diluted to the point where the small amount of foetal haemoglobin contained in adult blood would no longer be sufficiently strong to react with the antiserum.

The controls consisted of a sample known to contain a large proportion of foetal haemoglobin, a sample of adult blood and samples of the blood of various animals. If the test worked properly, one would obtain a positive reaction to the known foetal haemoglobin sample and negative reactions to the other controls. By the use of this test Mrs Kuhl was able to 'demonstrate' the presence of foetal haemoglobin on the hinge of the passenger's seat, underneath the seat and on a number of items taken from the car. Two droplets had been removed from the spray pattern on the underdash plate and, although the surface of those drops had reacted negatively to the orthotolidine test, when she dug into the material removed she was able to demonstrate that it, too, contained foetal haemoglobin.

She concluded that the concentration of foetal haemoglobin necessary to produce these results could only have come from a child under three months of age.

She had also carried out tests to determine the grouping of the phosphoglucomutase, or PGM, of the blood tested. It was the same as the grouping of this particular protein in the blood of the Chamberlain family.

She had also endeavoured to establish the quantity of blood necessary to produce the pattern of staining evident in the region of the hinge on the passenger's seat. To reproduce that pattern she needed five millilitres of blood and noted that it would only run in the right direction if someone was sitting in the seat.

A South Australian policeman, Sergeant Cocks, demonstrated his ability to cut a baby's jumpsuit with a pair of curved scissors to produce damage similar to that found in Azaria's jumpsuit. When he did so he discovered that small tufts of material fell out. He had discovered similar tufts in the material vacuumed from the Chamberlains' car and three tufts in material vacuumed from the camera bag. The implication was plain enough, but it confronted one difficulty. As Cocks conceded in cross-examination, at least part of the damaged areas on Azaria's jumpsuit were heavily stained with blood, but he had been unable to detect blood on any of the tufts recovered from the car or the camera bag.

Professor Cameron came to the witness box and expressed his conclusion that death had been caused by a cutting instrument, possibly encircling the neck. He was well prepared, with slides of Ruddock's photographs of the staining said to be hand prints. He produced a transparency showing the outline of a young woman's hand and suggested that the magistrate try it himself. The magistrate had difficulty in seeing it. He was not to know it at the time, but that difficulty would later be shared by several forensic scientists and a number of eminent judges.

'Like beauty, it has to be in the eye of the beholder!' Rice said contemptuously.

The scientific evidence continued to mount. An odontologist named Sims had been brought out from London to give evidence that he too had examined the baby's clothes, but had found none of the characteristics he would have expected had the garment been damaged by the teeth of a dog. He was scarcely a dingo expert. He had had no experience with live dingoes and his observations of their dentition were limited to an examination of a single skull.

Professor Malcolm Chaikin was a textile expert who occupied a chair at the University of New South Wales. He gave evidence that the teeth of dogs and other canids could tear fabric, but could not cut it like scissors. He had examined the damaged areas of the

Azaria Chamberlain jumpsuit both with the naked eye and with a scanning electron microscope. He had observed that the severed fibres ended in an approximate plane which indicated that they had been cut rather than torn. More importantly, he had detected the presence of tufts, which, he explained, could not be produced by a tearing action. His conclusion was plain. The damage had been caused by scissors or some other cutting instrument and not by teeth.

Detective Sergeant Charlwood was called to give evidence of his interviews with the Chamberlains and of other inquiries, including the search of the house. He was to admit, in cross-examination, that he had attempted to record conversations with them and that he had never warned them of his intention to do so.

The proceedings were adjourned over Christmas.

On 1 February 1982, Joy Kuhl was recalled. Since giving evidence in December she had spent four days making a minute examination of the camera bag. She had confirmed the presence of blood in various positions and had 'identified' the presence of 'foctal blood' on the zipper clasp and part of the buckle.

Even before the addresses began the result seemed a foregone conclusion. It remained only for Sturgess to articulate the Crown allegations. The Crown case was to be that Lindy Chamberlain had taken her daughter to the car and cut her throat. The body was secreted in the camera bag or otherwise concealed near the car until later in the evening when the opportunity presented itself for her to bury it. At some stage she must have told her husband what she had done and he must have co-operated with her in concealing the crime. Later the body had been exhumed and the clothing removed from it before it was re-interred. The jumpsuit had been cut by scissors in a manner calculated to simulate dingo damage. One or both of the Chamberlains had then jogged out to the little gully near Maggie Springs and left it there as if discarded by a dingo.

It came as no surprise when they were committed for trial, Lindy on a charge of murder and Michael on a charge of accessory after the fact. The stage had been set for the most widely publicised and controversial trial in Australia's history.

PART III

THE TRIAL

12

The defenders gather

THE SCIENTIFIC EVIDENCE presented at the second inquest had left Stuart Tipple, the Chamberlains' solicitor, in something of a quandary. There were now two distinct bodies of evidence.

First was the 'eye witness' evidence, consisting of the Lowes, the Wests, the Whittakers, the rangers, the trackers and even the police who initially attended the scene, which pointed strongly to the Chamberlains' innocence. It seemed that virtually everyone who was there on the night in question was convinced that a dingo had taken the child.

On the other hand, the scientific evidence suggested that the baby's throat had been cut in the car and that blood had dripped onto Lindy's tracksuit pants and running shoes. It also suggested that the jumpsuit had been buried with the body inside it and had subsequently been disinterred before being cut in a manner apparently calculated to simulate dingo damage and deposited with the other clothing in a manner which was inconsistent with what the experts would have expected from a dingo. Each body of evidence was internally consistent and compelling. Yet they seemed totally irreconcilable.

At the time of the first inquest it had been possible to reconcile the eyewitness and scientific evidence by concluding that a dingo had taken the child, but that there had been subsequent human intervention. That conclusion provided an adequate explanation for the disposition of the clothing and the cuts to the jumpsuit. However, it offered no explanation at all for the subsequent discoveries of foetal blood in the car, blood spots on the tracksuit pants and shoes or Cameron's conclusion that the baby's throat had been cut. It seemed conceivable that the tracksuit pants may have got blood on them whilst they were lying folded on the floor of the tent, but it was difficult to imagine that any dingo could have let himself into the car and sat on the front seat while he cut the baby's throat with a sharp instrument.

Whichever way you looked at it, there was something about this case that just did not add up. During the course of the first inquest, the Alice Springs *Star* had reported a rumour that the baby had been taken not by a dingo, but by a Kadaitcha man. Such legendary Aboriginal executioners are said to strike suddenly and then vanish, sometimes leaving the tracks of a wild animal behind in an attempt to deceive the relatives of the victim. There was, of course, no evidence to support such rumours and Stuart regarded them as pretty far-fetched.

But there had to be some explanation.

When one reduced the dilemma to its lowest common denominator, one seemed to be left with a conflict between the observations of reliable witnesses and conclusions drawn from scientific testing and theory. In those circumstances it is logical to enquire whether something might not have gone wrong with the tests or whether other experts might express contrary opinions. Tipple began the long odyssey to track down experts who might advise him.

It was to prove an arduous and frustrating task. Many simply did not want to become involved. Scientists do not all share the politicians' longing to bask in the public spotlight. Others disclaimed the necessary expertise. One or two textile experts refused to become involved when they heard that Professor Chaikin had already expressed an opinion.

Mrs Kuhl's testing programme presented a particular problem. In most instances she had used up all of the bloodstain and the tests could not be repeated by an independent expert. Furthermore, there was an element of interpretation involved in assessing the results. With an orthotolidine test it is important to note the shade of blue or turquoise staining on the pad and to gauge the speed of the reaction. With immunological testing, such as the crossover electrophoresis testing, one needs to have some regard for the position and shape of any bands evident on the plate if one is to distinguish true bands from mere 'artefacts'. Unhappily, the tests had not been photographed. Furthermore, although it was possible to stain and preserve the plates, that had not been done.

The destruction of the plates and the failure to make any photographic record of them was apparently in accordance with the practice of the forensic science laboratory, a practice which was to be trenchantly criticised by George Masterman QC, the New South Wales Ombudsman. Whether sanctioned by time-hallowed practice or not, it placed the defence in a very unfair position. The Chamberlains had parted with their car voluntarily. The police had arranged for various tests to be carried out on portions of it. They had not only failed to tell the Chamberlains of those tests so that they might have independent observers present, but had gone to extraordinary lengths to prevent them from finding out about them. Then, when it was too late to do anything about it, the Chamberlains were presented with a fait accompli. The test plates had been destroyed, there were no photographs and the material had been used up. It effectively prevented any independent expert from expressing a contrary view about the results of the tests and from repeating them.

In January 1982 after the second inquest had been adjourned, Stuart Tipple wrote to Joy Kuhl seeking information concerning the antiserum used in her immunological tests. There was no reply. She returned to the witness box when the inquest resumed at the end of January and was asked if she would provide the material requested. She agreed. Stuart wrote again on 3 March and again on 30 April. He also pursued his request by telephone. The information was finally supplied by a letter dated 25 May 1982.

Professor Barry Boettcher became involved in the matter almost by accident. He was head of the Department of Biological Services at the University of Newcastle. In 1979 a friend of the Chamberlains who had been studying for an honours degree in science had worked in Boettcher's laboratory. This contact led to a request that Boettcher read the relevant material from the second inquest. He waded through the transcript and then made a meticulous examination of Joy Kuhl's work notes. He made a number of disturbing observations.

Joy Kuhl had given evidence as follows:

> While a baby — or a foetus — is in utero, it does not have any adult haemoglobin. Up till the time of birth, the foetal haemoglobin increases in concentration. After birth, it gradually decreases in concentration and the presence of adult haemoglobin begins to be seen. This occurs up to about six months of age. After approximately six months of age, detectable amounts of foetal haemoglobin are not present in a normal infant.

This was not correct, Boettcher realised. Adult haemoglobin, or Haemoglobin A, becomes detectable at about the eighth month of gestation and increases in concentration until the infant is about six months of age when the normal adult concentration of about ninety-eight per cent is attained. A newborn baby could be expected to have approximately eighty per cent Haemoglobin F and twenty per cent Haemoglobin A.

At the time of her death, Azaria's blood would have been expected to have contained about thirty per cent Haemoglobin F and seventy per cent Haemoglobin A. Doctor Andrew Scott was later to give evidence that he had tested the blood found on Azaria Chamberlain's jumpsuit by means of a haptoglobin plate. Barker was to tell the jury that he longed for those innocent days when he thought that a haptoglobin was something that grew in the bottom of his garden and by the time the trial drew to a close there were few who would not have shared that sentiment.

Yet no haptoglobin has ever gladdened the heart of a horticulturalist. It is a protein found in blood. Andrew Scott wanted to find out which of the various groups of haptoglobin were to be found in Azaria's blood. A haptoglobin plate is actually a sandwich of polyacrylamide gel between two plates of glass. It acts as a molecular sieve, the larger molecules being trapped higher up the plate and the smaller drawn by gravity down until they reach the point where they, too, are unable to further penetrate the sieve.

One can see on such a plate not only the position of the haptoglobin, shown as a diffuse band, but the position of haemoglobin. Haemoglobin molecules are smaller than haptaglobin molecules and so one looks for them further down the plate but, though both are smaller than haptoglobin molecules,

Haemoglobin A and Haemoglobin F molecules are not the same size. Consequently, when there are sufficient concentrations of both present in the blood being tested, one will see two haemoglobin bands. By comparing the relative intensity of the two haemoglobin bands Scott was able to make an estimate of the relative concentrations. He found that Azaria's blood contained approximately seventy-five per cent Haemoglobin A and twenty-five per cent Haemoglobin F. Both he and Boettcher agreed that this was within the range of what was to be expected for a child of that age.

When Boettcher turned to Joy Kuhl's work notes he found, to his surprise, that a number of the results obtained from the crossover electrophoresis tests had been recorded in a manner which suggested that the Haemoglobin F antiserum had reacted more strongly with the bloodstains taken from the Chamberlains' car and other items than it had with the control sample of cord blood. Since cord blood contained approximately seventy per cent foetal haemoglobin, nearly three times the concentration of Azaria Chamberlain's blood, that seemed an incongruous result.

She had given this evidence:

> I was getting very strong reactions against the foetal haemoglobin and much weaker ones against the adult haemoglobin, which is very consistent with gradual changing of the blood from the foetal to the adult concentration.

This suggested to Boettcher that she had also regarded the relative strength of the reactions as significant but had not been struck by their apparent incongruity because she had expected Azaria's blood to contain more foetal than adult haemoglobin.

As a number of scientific witnesses were later to point out, the crossover electrophoresis test is really designed as a qualitative test rather than a quantitative one. In other words, it is designed to determine whether or not a particular substance is present, rather than to estimate its quantity. Indeed, that was part of the problem in this case. Since there are small traces of foetal haemoglobin in adult blood, the question was not whether there was foetal haemoglobin present in the samples, but how much.

The Crown was to suggest that the qualitative nature of the tests invalidated Boettcher's comparison of the relative strengths. Boettcher agreed that the tests were primarily qualitative, but pointed out that the strength of the precipitin band formed between the well containing the antiserum and the well containing the sample to be tested was dependent upon the relative concentrations of antigen from the sample and antibodies from the serum available to form the band. Consequently, if one had a reasonably constant supply of fresh antiserum, one would expect to see a stronger band when the sample contained higher concentrations of foetal haemoglobin and, consequently, more antigen capable of reacting with the foetal haemoglobin antibodies.

Joy Kuhl was to protest that this might not be so. One frequently encountered a 'prozone' effect. The supply of available antigen so outnumbered the available antibodies that it swamped them and one obtained a very faint reaction or no reaction at all. Boettcher was familiar with that phenomenon, but pointed out that at the extreme dilutions which Mrs Kuhl had used, the supply of Haemoglobin F antigen should not have been sufficient to swamp anything. He was later to establish a graph showing the relative concentrations at which a prozone effect might be expected to occur. It confirmed his view that it offered no explanation for the incongruity of results recorded in the work notes.

Nor was this a 'one off' abberration. Of the seventeen series of tests carried out, the work notes showed nine in which the antiserum reacted more strongly with the sample from the item tested than with the foetal haemoglobin control. The other eight comparisons involved reactions which were recorded in a manner which suggested at least an approximate equivalence. In no case was there any test which was recorded as demonstrating a stronger reaction with the item tested than with the foetal haemoglobin control. This seemed to rule out chance experimental error.

Furthermore, Mrs Kuhl had also carried out a haptoglobin test on blood taken from the hinge of the passenger's seat of the Chamberlain's car. The results were recorded in her work books as 'Foetal Hb only', a result which caused Boettcher to raise his eyebrows almost to the point where his hairline had once been.

Such a result could only have been obtained from an unborn foetus. Joy Kuhl was later to assert that despite that notation there were, in fact, bands of both adult and foetal haemoglobin present. She was also to say that this test, too, was of an exclusively qualitative nature and that one could not validly compare the intensity of the bands.

This was a view resolutely rejected not only by Boettcher but by Dr Scott and Kuhl's boss, Dr Simon Baxter. Indeed, it seemed to defy simple commonsense. The bands in a haptoglobin test are not formed by reactions with anything. They are formed from masses of molecules of a particular type which congregate together at the point where they can no longer fall through the molecular sieve. The more molecules that are present, the more there is to see. An experienced biologist can therefore judge the relative proportions of molecules by comparing the breadth and intensity of the bands.

Dr Baxter was shown this haptoglobin plate by Mrs Kuhl. He was to report that 'at least fifty per cent' of the total haemoglobin present was foetal haemoglobin. He was also to agree that, whilst there is some scope for error in visual comparisons of that nature, it seemed highly unlikely that skilled and competent forensic biologists such as he and Dr Scott would be so far out in their estimates that one could estimate the proportion of foetal haemoglobin as being 'at least fifty per cent', whilst the other would estimate that there was at least three times as much adult haemoglobin.

To Boettcher the implication was plain: either the bloodstains which Mrs Kuhl had tested had not come from Azaria Chamberlain or there was something radically wrong with her testing procedure.

Boettcher's suspicion was further aroused when he found 'double banding' between the wells. The antiserum is supposed to be specific to foetal haemoglobin, that is, it should react with nothing else. The presence of two bands suggested that there were two separate immunological reactions and the antiserum was producing a reaction with two different kinds of antigen.

At first blush, that may not have seemed too serious. If the antiserum was reacting with something else in the blood as well as foetal haemoglobin, then so what? As long as one established that foetal haemoglobin was present, then what did it matter that there might be something else in the blood which was producing a second band? Yet this was dangerously simplistic. If the serum would react to one thing other than foetal haemoglobin then it was obviously defective. How did one know that it did not have two additional specificities or even half-a-dozen? Perhaps neither of the reactions were caused by foetal haemoglobin antigen.

The crossover electrophoresis test relied largely upon the principles which formed the basis for the immunodiffusion test invented by Professor Ouchterlony in 1948. That test also involved the formation of bands between wells containing antiserum, and others containing the sample to be tested. Unlike crossover electrophoresis, however, there was no electric current to drive them together. The antigen and antibodies were allowed to 'diffuse out' in their own time. Crossover electrophoresis had the advantage of speed and, to some extent, sensitivity, but the Ouchterlony test was more accurate.

A classic formulation of this test was to place the antiserum in a well in the centre of the plate and to place six other wells in a circle around it. Professor Ouchterlony himself referred to this as the 'six-shooter' formation. The biologist would then place the sample to be tested in one of the wells, the foetal haemoglobin control in an adjoining well and other known blood samples in the remaining ones. If one obtained a reaction between the serum and the sample to be tested, then one could see a band similar to what one would obtain on the crossover electrophoresis test.

However, there would also be a band between the antiserum and the foetal haemoglobin control. If this band merged into the band produced by a reaction with the sample, then one could be confident that it was caused by the same kind of reaction. One knew that the foetal haemoglobin control did not exclude the possibility of a second band being caused by a defective antiserum reacting with something else in the foetal haemoglobin control, but if there was only one band there, one could be certain that it was a true reaction with the foetal haemoglobin antigen. If it merged with the adjoining band, one then knew that that also was a true reaction. For this reason the merged bands were referred to as 'a line of identity'.

From time to time, one would see a plate in which there were two adjoining bands, but they did not merge. In some cases they simply did not meet, whilst in others they crossed over. Occasionally, one also saw lines of 'partial identity' where they was a degree of merger, but one band protruded from the other in a 'spur'. In all of these cases one was obliged to conclude that the presence of foetal haemoglobin in the sample had not been demonstrated. The antiserum was not reacting with the foetal haemoglobin molecule, but with something else. The crossover electrophoresis test provided no similar safeguard.

Joy Kuhl had carried out only one 'Ouchterlony test' as they had come to be known, but she reported that it gave rise to 'indications' of foetal haemoglobin. As Professor Ouchterlony was later to point out, she had used inadequate controls and five of the controls which she had used had all failed. A number of eminent scientists were to say that this test should not have been reported at all and Joy Kuhl was inclined to agree. She had reported it, she claimed, upon the advice of Dr Baxter, a claim which Baxter was to reject.

She was, however, to prepare another Ouchterlony plate for demonstration purposes. This plate also showed the presence of a band which did not merge in with an adjacent one and form a line of identity. This confirmed Boettcher's suspicion that the antiserum was not monospecific. Kuhl was to explain this other band as an artefact and support her conclusion by pointing out that it was not located in the centre between the two wells. All true immunological bands were to be found in that position, she claimed.

This was news to Boettcher, who pointed out that a band is formed at the 'zone of equivalence', that is, the point at which there is an equal concentration of antigen and antibodies. The position at which that point of equivalence is reached is dependent entirely upon the relative strengths of the samples. It need not be between the wells at all.

Ultimately, this question was to be resolved by Professor Ouchterlony himself who was brought to Australia to give evidence before the Commission of Inquiry in 1986. Boettcher was quite right, he confirmed, and Mrs Kuhl's assertion indicated a lack of understanding of his technique.

Boettcher was also concerned that the denaturation of the blood molecules caused by heat and the effluxion of time may have produced immunochemical complications which the routine procedures of a forensic science laboratory were ill equipped to detect. In this case, the blood samples had been taken from the interior of a motor vehicle which had been driven around for some thirteen-and-a-half months after Azaria disappeared. For some of that time it had been exposed to extremes of climatic temperatures not only at Ayers Rock, but at Mount Isa where the Chamberlains lived. If, in fact, the blood had come from some other person such as the bleeding hitchhiker, Keyth Lenehan, whom the Chamberlains had picked up from the scene of his accident and driven frantically to hospital, it may have been in the car for two-and-a-half years or even longer.

Boettcher obtained a supply of foetal haemoglobin antiserum from the same manufacturer and conducted some tests of his own. In some of the tests he used his own blood and noted, with some amusement, that he succeeded in scientifically demonstrating that his blood came from an infant under three months of age. The validity of these tests was to be questioned because they did not fit in with what was expected. Boettcher agreed. He would not have expected to see such results either. But he, too, was coming to feel that something very unusual had occurred in this case.

The relevance of the tests was also to be questioned because, in the main, Boettcher had obtained these reactions using dilutions greater than one in two thousand whilst Mrs Kuhl had been working at dilutions which she judged to be about one in a thousand. However, Mrs Kuhl had judged the dilutions by assessing the colour of the diluted sample. While some forensic biologists were to agree that one acquired a degree of accuracy in such assessments through years of practice, there were very great difficulties in assessing dilutions of old and denatured blood.

In the first place, blood became darker with the passing of time and, in a car, could be expected to be affected by contaminants. This made any comparison with the colour normally expected at given dilutions highly questionable and made it likely that a biologist would end up with a sample more highly diluted than she expected. Furthermore, the process of denaturation caused a dramatic deterioration in the level of activity of the blood molecules, but did not produce a corresponding change in the colouration. Consequently, the 'effective' dilution may have been many times as great as the colour might have indicated.

All in all, the tests left Boettcher totally unconvinced.

Meanwhile, scientists were expressing scepticism of other aspects of the Crown case.

Professor Vernon Plueckhahn was a Victorian pathologist who had enjoyed a long and distinguished career, with frequent forays into the forensic area. He examined the jumpsuit with meticulous care, but was unable to discern any bloodstained hand prints whether from a 'small adult', a 'female' or anything else. He also disagreed with Cameron's conclusion that the bleeding had been caused by an incised wound to the throat inflicted by a sharp cutting instrument. He could not exclude the possibility that it may have been caused in that fashion, but it was only one of a number of equally viable hypotheses. He pointed out that blood, like other liquids, diffuses through a fabric. If one spills water or milk onto a towel, the resultant wet patch gradually grows as the towel soaks it up.

Consequently, whilst the jumpsuit was heavily stained with blood all around the collar and shoulders, this did not prove that there had been a 'circumferential' wound. If a dingo had seized the baby's head in its jaws one would expect to find wounds on both sides. The blood from these wounds may have run down to the collar and spread out through the fabric to produce the staining now evident. Plueckhahn also had in mind the grisly hypothesis that the dingo may have eaten the head first, an hypothesis later supported by Derek Roff and others.

Professor Keith Bradley was to agree that the pattern of bleeding on the jumpsuit was consistent with puncture wounds to the neck rather than a cut throat.

Another Melbourne pathologist, Dr Rose, provided useful information concerning the pliability of a baby's skull. At nine-and-a-half weeks, much of the bone is still cartilagenous and the skull can be easily compressed.

Les Harris, the president of the Dingo Foundation, was also anxious to help. In the unique situation existing at Ayers Rock he considered it quite likely that a dingo had taken the baby. He had written a lengthy report to the first coroner, Dennis Barritt. He concluded:

> Comparisons between dingoes and domestic dogs are not particularly valid, tempting as they might be. The dingo is a natural canid (in fact a wolf, not a dog) which has to practise its hunting skills on a daily basis and at a very high level of efficiency in order to survive. In terms of strength, speed, agility and reasoning power, they compare more readily with the natural felines, i.e. tigers, leopards, et al. It is easier to underestimate the capabilities of dingoes than to overestimate them.
>
> The Ayers Rock dingoes are atypical in one respect of natural behaviour. They have had very close contact with tourists for a long time and have been fed directly and indirectly by tourists. They have maintained all of their hunting skills, plus extended their abilities to acquire food from tourists and their campsites, and you are no doubt aware that they often raid tents in their search for food. Humans, their accoutrements, their tents and caravans pose no threat, and pillaging is not uncommon. This has resulted in a very dangerous situation wherein they are not tame and they are not wild.
>
> In considering the questions:
>
> 1. Could a dingo have taken the baby?
> 2. Could a dingo or dingoes have removed its clothing?
> 3. Could a dingo or dingoes have totally consumed the baby?
>
> my answers, based on many years of observation of dingoes in their natural habitat and in captivity, would be:
>
> 1. Yes, with ease.
> 2. Probably yes.
> 3. Yes, without any doubt.

So far as the cutting ability of dingoes was concerned, Harris was to relate a particular problem he had encountered in transporting dingoes by car. On occasions they would simply bite through a seat belt leaving him to stare ruefully at the two pieces. This was accomplished with nonchalant ease and the belt was sometimes severed so cleanly that it looked as though it had been cut by scissors.

Stuart was still keen to find a textile expert willing to comment on Professor Chaikin's evidence, but he had found no takers. He discussed the matter with Chaikin himself who remained firm in his view and suggested to Stuart that the better defence might be one of subsequent human intervention, as Barritt had found in the first inquest.

On the other hand Dr Hector Orams, an odontologist from Melbourne, had found himself incapable of distinguishing between the damage to Azaria Chamberlain's clothing and damage which had been caused by dingoes. This was a difficult area, one which involved an overlap between two normally unrelated disciplines and it seemed that no-one in either field had published any report of studies concerning the affect of animal teeth upon fabrics. Orams felt that the textile men might not be aware of the efficiency of the carnassial teeth which came together in a scissor-like action. He pointed out that, despite decades of research, the masticatory processes of humans was still not fully understood and that there had been little research at all in relation to the masticatory processes of dingoes and other canids.

Stuart Tipple was later to be criticised by some Chamberlain supporters. He was too young and inexperienced, some said. Others, with the benefit of hindsight, managed to come up with all sorts of suggestions about things which he should have done. But he had done full well for his clients. He had put them in a position where, in normal circumstances, they would have had a good fighting chance.

13

The prelude

MANY AUSTRALIANS WHO HAVE NO FAITH IN GOD and little in human nature display, paradoxically, an unshakeable trust in British justice. They may regard the income tax legislation as a gun to be pointed at their heads by the chief highwayman in Canberra and may shake their heads sadly at some of the more recent statutory innovations which indicate the extent to which 'the place has been taken over by trendies', but 'real' law is different. We have the best system of justice in the world — everyone knows that. The man in the street may not be able to articulate the system's virtues with the rhetoric of a politician or the understanding of a student of jurisprudence, but there is a deep conviction that when he gets to court 'a bloke gets a fair go'.

There is, in a sense, a religious quality about this faith ,though it is shared by many who would deny any belief in the supernatural. To the religious it is a logical extension of faith: God is a God of justice. To the irreligious it seems to fill part of the void. There is a deep psychological need to believe in something and what better than justice?

The religious connotations are nowhere more evident than in the criminal courts which sit in judgment upon those brought before them and punish the guilty according to the measure of their wickedness. Perhaps this is the reason why so many criminals make a full confession, even though they have been cautioned by the police that they need not answer any questions and, in many cases, even when the case against them would otherwise have been flimsy. Sometimes there are obvious reasons for such a step, but in many cases one is left to speculate that it has been borne of the subconscious conviction that confession and forgiveness are inextricably intertwined.

Yet faith in justice is tempered by a cynicism towards lawyers. There is a feeling that the guilty frequently escape justice because some 'smart lawyer' is able to find a 'loophole', some barren technicality dreamed up by the unscrupulous to protect the guilty from the clear purpose of the law. Others imagine juries being 'hoodwinked' by the distortion of evidence, the use of subtle but misleading sophistries and beguiling oratory. This concept is neither new nor uniquely Australian. In 1875, London theatregoers flocked to the presentation of Gilbert and Sullivan's new musical 'Trial by Jury' to hear the fledgling barrister sing, 'I'll never throw dust in a juryman's eyes or hoodwink a judge who is not over wise'.

Faith and cynicism maintain an uneasy balance, but one thing is sure: human machinations may acquit the guilty, but never convict the innocent. Justice, whether he be God or ideal, would never permit it. So it was that as the Chamberlain trial approached, faith and cynicism jostled for supremacy: faith claiming those who believed in the Chamberlains' innocence and cynicism afflicting those who were convinced of their guilt.

The Chamberlains were hurt, battered and bewildered. The loss of a child is itself a crushing blow. No-one who has not experienced such a loss can really understand the devastating flood of emotions it unleashes. There is a sense of tragedy about it that one does not experience upon the death of an older person, no matter how close. There is a feeling that the child has been cheated, that her potential for a full and productive life has been cruelly snatched away. Yet there is, at the very least, a finality about it. One may feel the pain for a long time but the tragedy itself is over. There will be no new wounds. One may pick up the pieces and start again in the knowledge that no matter how deep the anguish, it will abate in time.

The Chamberlains had been denied even this limited consolation. The wounds had constantly been re-opened by the jeers of a hostile community and the procedural demands of justice. After their dramatic exoneration at the end of the first inquest, there had been some respite as if some authoritarian figure had sharply rebuked an angry mob and told them to be quiet. An undercurrent of suspicion remained, but the roar of the crowd had been reduced to the odd spiteful mutter.

Now with their committal for trial they were to feel that the mob had again been turned loose. Their supporters remained loyal, but they were publicly execrated by a press which recognised that the more vicious the content the more newsworthy the article. To go out was to run an unrelenting gauntlet. They found themselves more and more like embatttled defenders in the path of an invading army of breathtaking power and malevolence. Yet there was a strength about them, too. A writer in the Homeric tradition might have described them as 'bloody but unbowed'. Satan may have unleashed against them all the powers of hell but they would prevail against him. The promise of God was clear: 'Commit your way to the Lord; trust in him, and he will act. He will bring forth your vindication as the light, and your right as the noonday.' In the meantime, like Joshua they must be 'strong and very courageous'.

The more voluble of their adversaries may have sounded like emissaries from hell, but there was a strong groundswell of ordinary Australians whose suspicions day-by-day deepened into a conviction of their guilt. Many factors contributed to this groundswell. There was still a confidence that most people are not charged with serious offences unless they are guilty. The magistrate had obviously found the evidence against them damning. Why else would he have committed them for trial? The Chamberlains appeared so strange. Lindy had appeared on television and described the child's clothing with an apparent lack of emotion. How could a normal warm-hearted mother do that? Their story didn't ring true. Nothing like this had ever happened before. Sure, there were rumours about Aboriginal babies being left out for the dingoes, but who had ever heard of one marching into a camping area and taking a white child out of a tent?

And what about this weird religion? Who knew what they were into? Somebody suggested they were linked with the mass suicides at Jones Town a few years earlier. Maybe there was something to that rumour about Azaria's name after all. There were further reports that a file held by the Queensland Department of Maternal and Child Welfare recorded earlier incidents of 'baby battering'.

The rumours flew thick and fast, some plausible, many simply preposterous. Many were fair-minded enough to treat them as mere unsubstantiated gossip, but the assault was too sustained and, deep down, many concluded that there was so much smoke there must be fire.

There is little doubt that the police contributed to this spate of rumours. A detective told a Sydney journalist with the *Sun* that the car accident in 1981 was a cunning ploy to get rid of the last piece of damning evidence. Had it been covered by insurers it would have been written off and taken to a wrecker's yard. Stories of the 'white' coffin and the biblical story 'outlined in red' could only have come from police. Other journalists were told that the police considered Lindy was mentally unstable. Police in Alice Springs reportedly told a newspaper 'source' that they had the murder weapon.

It was in this context that the Australian cynicism became evident. One repeatedly heard comments like 'I think the bitch is guilty, but she'll probably get off.' There was a feeling that a Northern Territory jury would be too unsophisticated to grasp the damning nature of the scientific evidence and to resist the wiles of 'smart lawyers'. Besides, everyone knew that Australian juries were reluctant to convict women, especially young mothers. This feeling of pessimism was deepened when it was announced that Lindy was again pregnant. Some even went so far as to suggest that it was a 'forensic pregnancy' designed to create sympathy and to put the jury into an emotional bind about the prospect of separating mother and newborn child. Wiser heads pointed out that it was likely to have the opposite effect. If the jurors thought she had murdered one baby, they might fear for the life of the next. Such muted quibbles were generally drowned in the flood of rumour, suspicion and innuendo.

Darwin is part of the 'Top End' of Australia. It lies nearer the equator than either Hawaii or Fiji and the temperatures are consistently hot all year round, with only the humidity acknowledging changes in the seasons from 'wet' to 'dry' or vice versa. It provides shade and sustenance for some 66,000 people.

In some respects it is even more isolated than Alice Springs. The nearest major city is Adelaide some 3212 kilometres away. Like

Alice Springs, there is a frontier feel about the place, but it is a different kind of frontier. Alice Springs is an outback town, an oasis of civilisation in a sea of red desert. Darwin is a tropical city perched on the edge of the Arafura Sea and hemmed in by luxuriant greenery. Many factors contribute to that frontier atmosphere. The heat, the vegetation, the Asian presence, the four-wheel drives and 'road trains' and the perennially advertised safaris to view crocodiles, buffalo and exotic birds all play their part.

'The Mall' is the heart of the city. It is a broad, paved area bounded by shops geared to milk the perennial tourists. Leather hats, buffalo horns, big hunting knives and Aboriginal art are all displayed. There are coconut palms and purple bougainvillea. On Saturday morning it becomes a market place with fruit stalls, souvenir stands and locals selling flute stones. Aborigines play the didgeridoo and beat out a rhythm with painted sticks. Sometimes the women dance. At night the band at the Victoria Hotel beats out a different kind of rhythm. Listening is compulsory if you live within a kilometre or so.

If you can stand the heat, it is an enchanting place to visit. One can walk from the Mall to the pearl shop around the corner and then stroll through the park under the canopy of leaves from huge trees with massive trunks and tortured root systems. At the edge of the park there are the remnants of an old hall. One can stare down at stone walls two feet thick which, in parts, now rise no higher than a man's waist. They stand as mute yet striking testimony to the ferocity of Cyclone Tracy which virtually demolished Darwin in 1974.

There is an intense parochialism about Darwin. The locals are friendly and hospitable and the tourist dollar is important to the local economy, yet anything perceived as 'interference' by Commonwealth ministers or other 'outsiders' is bitterly resented. Only the locals understand the Territory. They have no need of 'bloody southerners' coming in to tell them how to conduct their affairs.

There was to be a roaring trade in T-shirts. Someone had realised that to come right out and print 'Lindy is guilty' might constitute a contempt of the Supreme Court, but the same message could be conveyed in other ways. A batch of shirts was run off with bold lettering proclaiming, 'The Dingo is Innocent'. They were to be worn by demonstrators on the footpath outside the Supreme Court building whilst the trial was in progress. Whether by accident or design, they were frequently in evidence when the jury filed in shortly before 10.00 a.m. or wended their weary way home at the close of the day's proceedings. Other T-shirts appeared. The designs were different, but each was derisive of Lindy's claim that a dingo had taken her baby. One depicted Lindy inside a dingo suit. The caption read, 'Darwin's Answer'. Like the dingo jokes, all conveyed the subtle message that no-one but a fool could accept that a dingo had taken the child.

Professor Boettcher flew into Darwin the day before the trial started. He was to stay with an old friend. Over dinner his friend commented, 'You know she's going to be convicted, don't you?'

'Don't you think that is a bit premature? The trial hasn't started yet,' Boettcher pointed out.

His friend shook his head. 'Darwin made up its mind months ago.'

14

Battle is joined

THE TRIAL COMMENCED on 13 September 1982. It was to last nearly eight weeks.

There had been changes of counsel on both sides. The Chamberlains were now represented by John Phillips, a Melbourne Queen's Counsel, destined to become the author of a book entitled *Advocacy with Honour*, the Victorian Director of Public Prosecutions and, ultimately, a Supreme Court judge. He was a specialist in criminal law and was well-regarded by his colleagues. He was thorough and capable, an effective cross-examiner and was reputed to have an almost encyclopaedic knowledge of criminal law and procedure. If he had a flaw, it lay in his gentlemanliness and the fact that he did not hail from the Territory. Andrew Kirkham was to be his junior.

The case for the prosecution would be presented by Ian Barker. Barker was the local boy made good. He had been the Solicitor-General of the Northern Territory and, when he left to practise as a Queen's Counsel in Sydney, his former partner, Brian Martin, had taken over as Solicitor-General in his stead. He was later to defend the only justice of the High Court of Australia ever to stand trial in a criminal court. Like Phillips, he was an effective cross-examiner and had a good knowledge of the law. He was renowned for his dry sense of humour. Perhaps the most telling quality was his intuitive grasp of practical psychology.

Barker was also a member of the Northern Territory Conservation Commission, the body which was responsible for parks and wildlife in the Territory and which among other things employed the rangers. The Chamberlains were to accuse this body of culpability in relation to the death of their child. The attacks on other children had been well-known and the rangers had warned of further attacks on children and babies. Yet the Chamberlains were allowed to enter the camping area with the obvious intention of erecting a tent and staying for some time without being warned of the danger to their nine-and-a-half-week old baby. The Commission was at least vicariously responsible for this default. Yet here was one of its members turning up to prosecute. An accused had become the accuser.

Barker was assisted by Des Sturgess and a Darwin barrister, Tom Pauling.

Mr Justice Muirhead had the Chamberlains arraigned and the barristers settled down to the task of empanelling a jury. A jury panel is supposed to be representative of the community. Doctors, lawyers and some other professional groups are exempted, whilst convicted felons are excluded but, in theory at least, one is left with a wide range of people who will bring a diversity of experience and common sense to their task. The procedure for the selection of individual jurors is at best a haphazard one. Names of jurors are drawn from a box. Challenges may then be made by either the defence counsel or the Crown prosecutor, but they must be made before the juror takes his seat in the jury box.

Counsel are given no background information and have no right to ask potential jurors questions to determine whether or not they harbour any bias concerning the case. A rough-and-ready assessment of character must be made, augmented, perhaps, by any pet theories which the particular barrister may espouse. At one stage, for example, it was fashionable to challenge all the women. This was not mere chauvinism. At that stage the law provided that a woman's name should be added to a jury roll only at her request. Barristers were inclined to ask themselves why anyone would volunteer to be on a jury roll when they did not have to be. One of the answers which sprang to mind was a desire to put right the evils of the world, a desire which might not be reflected in an excess of sympathy for people accused of serious crimes. They were challenged not because they were women, but because they were volunteers.

In this instance the task was particularly difficult. The

Chamberlains had their supporters but, in general, the climate of public opinion was against them. A few seconds appraisal seemed pathetically inadequate to enable one to be confident that he had rooted out any jurors likely to be guided by prejudice and presupposition rather than a fair appraisal of the evidence. A newspaper cartoon published some months before the trial began had depicted an old hobo sitting in the shade of a cactus in the middle of the desert. He looked up quizzically at the two policemen bending over him and asked, 'Lindy who?'

'Only eleven to go,' one policeman said to the other with evident satisfaction. That seemed to say it all. The whole of Australia seemed to have formed some pre-judgment about this case.

The judge was as concerned as Phillips about the effect of rumour and publicity. He explained the rule that juries must act only on the evidence and appealed for fairness:

> . . . If you were on trial for a serious offence how would you feel if you found that jurors had been influenced by matters not mentioned in the court, by matters heard outside the court, under circumstances where neither you nor your counsel could explain it or challenge it? That, ladies and gentlemen, is why it is so vital that you keep your eyes entirely on the evidence. Your job in this case is to administer justice according to law, not according to rumour, not according to preconceived notions. You will hear much of this, ladies and gentlemen, for the simple reason that possibly the publicity concerning this matter has been without precedent in our lifetime.

Yet even in the courtroom itself were ever-present reminders that this was no ordinary trial. The judge pointed out two video cameras silently watching all that occurred:

> I do not want you to feel that as you sit here you are more or less being directly telecast to Australia or that there is any direct broadcast of these proceedings. That is not so. They were put in for the convenience of the press to avoid overcrowding, to enable the press to observe these proceedings in another place close by if they wished to do so. So, do not get the idea that you are erupting to stardom or something because you are not.

The formalities complete, Barker rose to address the jury of nine men and three women. It was a masterful opening:

> A baby was killed at Ayers Rock on 17th of August 1980 during the evening between eight and nine o'clock. It was a Sunday. The child was just under ten weeks old, having been born on the eleventh of June. She was called Azaria Chamberlain, and was the daughter of the accused Michael Leigh Chamberlain and Alice Lynne Chamberlain. The body of the child was never found but, having heard the evidence concerning the baby's disappearance, you will have no difficulty determining that she is dead, and that she died on the night she disappeared. As to the manner and the cause of death, one cannot be precise because the body was never found. However, what will be proved, largely upon scientific evidence of the baby's clothes, is that the child lost a great deal of blood, in all probability from injury to the major vessels of her neck. She died very quickly because somebody had cut her throat.
>
> The Crown does not venture to suggest any reason or motive for the killing. It is not part of our case that Mrs Chamberlain had previously shown any ill will towards the child. Nor do we assert that the child was other than a normal healthy baby. The Crown does not, therefore, attempt to prove motive, nor does it invite speculation as to motive. We simply say to you that the evidence to be put before you will prove beyond reasonable doubt that, for whatever reason, the baby was murdered by her mother.

With a handful of deft sentences he had encapsulated the essence of the Crown case, acknowledged but brushed aside the obvious difficulties in his path, and created not only interest but a sense of expectancy.

He took two further sentences to dispose of the alternative, the economy of language subtly conveying the message that the Chamberlains' protestations could be brusquely dismissed:

> Shortly after the event, the mother asserted, and thereafter continued to assert, that the dead child had been taken from the tent by a dingo. The Crown says that the dingo story was a fanciful lie, calculated to conceal the truth, which is that the child Azaria died by her mother's hand.

The case against Michael was etched in with equal brevity:

> The Crown case against Michael Leigh Chamberlain is that he actively and knowingly assisted his wife to dispose of the child's body, to mislead the police about the circumstances of the child's disappearance, to attempt to have the police and the Coroner believe that the baby had been killed by a dingo, and in other ways in attempting to conceal the fact that murder had been committed. At the close of all the evidence I will invite you to find, beyond reasonable doubt, that Michael Leigh Chamberlain is guilty of the crime of being an accessory after the fact to the murder, by his wife, of his child Azaria.

Barker then began an exposition of the evidence to be called, tracing the background of the holiday, the arrival at the camping area and the events leading up to Azaria's disappearance. He made the point that 'the only witness to the killing was the accused, Alice Lynne Chamberlain' and that there was 'no evidence beyond her statement' to establish Aidan's whereabouts during 'those few terrible minutes'.

He then dealt with the seizure of the car in September 1981, already a year earlier, and its subsequent examination. That examination, he said, revealed that attempts had been made to clean up the blood in the car, but that even the residue was 'far greater in amount than all the bloodstaining found in the tent'. Furthermore, he contended, the blood in the car was 'free blood from the victim' whilst the bloodstains in the tent had been transferred from 'bloodstained hands or clothing of the child's mother'.

At this stage the other scientific opinions remained trumps in his hand to be played later in the game, but the time had come to disclose the joker. Mrs Kuhl, he told them, had found that the blood in the car was the blood of a baby under six months of age. The blood had been in the car for not less than twelve months, nor more than two years.

> The discovery of foetal blood in the car is a critical part of the Crown case. It would be preposterous to suggest that the dingo took the child from the tent and into the car, and we will submit that

> the discovery of Azaria's blood in the car destroys the dingo attack explanation given by Mrs Chamberlain, whatever else there may be to support such explanation, and the Crown says there is almost nothing.
>
> So, ladies and gentlemen, this is a case of simple alternatives. Either a dingo killed Azaria, or it was homicide, because the child could hardly have inflicted injuries upon herself. If she was killed in the car, one can at once forget the dingo.

When the court adjourned at 4.27 p.m., Barker had still not finished. Overnight the defence team reviewed the transcript of his address. It was obvious that the case he intended to present was quite different from the one put forward by Sturgess at the second inquest. There the allegation had involved an apparently premeditated murder, committed perhaps as some kind of sacrificial rite during the course of the afternoon, probably in some concealed area adjacent to Ayers Rock. Now it was apparently an unpremeditated killing for an unknown motive, committed in the car at about 8.00 p.m.

Perhaps it was the body in the camera bag, perhaps only the clothes. In either event, one wondered where the camera gear had been put. The body was buried, disinterred and reburied. The car was cleaned up. The clothes were cut and placed near the Rock. Yet when? It was all so vague. It was like shadow-boxing. There was little of substance that you could pin down and try to refute.

The second day's hearing was delayed while Phillips again raised the problem of people wearing T-shirts proclaiming 'The Dingo is Innocent' and, worse, of the press photographing and filming them. The judge himself pointed out the seriousness of this conduct:

> . . . I would regard the publication of photographs of that type of inflammatory material as likely to intefere with the calm deliberations and objectivity of a juror. . .

Later, he publicly castigated 'the fools' responsible and told the jury that he had requested the sheriff and the police to 'take such action as may be appropriate'.

Barker's address wound up shortly before the morning tea adjournment:

> Ladies and gentlemen, where does this all lead? A ten-week-old baby girl is last seen alive when she is taken in the direction of her parents' tent and car by her mother. A week later, her bloodstained clothing is discovered some four kilometres away. It had been buried, with her body in it, dug up, and cut by human hands, using scissors. In the car is found the blood of a baby under the age of six months, and the clearest evidence that an attempt has been to clean the blood up.
>
> Apart from the container of the chamois, foetal blood is found in a number of places in the car, on a towel, on a pair of scissors, on the black camera bag and in the camera bag the tufts of thread, each of which were cut and must have come from the jumpsuit or a similar garment.
>
> Now the Crown says, and we say it again, that this is a case of simple alternatives. Either a dingo or dog killed that child or the child was murdered. It is very difficult indeed to see room for any intermediate state of affairs. We will be putting to you that there is no reasonable explanation for the presence of the foetal blood and the tufts of fabric unless deposited on the night the child was killed. What was found in the car is connected with and very much part of the story of the child's disappearance. No dingo could have taken the child into the car and killed her there; only a human being could have done it. The baby could hardly have inflicted injury upon herself. The Crown says it must have been a case of homicide and the account of the child's disappearance given by Mrs Chamberlain must therefore be false.

After the morning tea break the judge again referred to people wearing clothing containing messages or other material relating to the trial and threatened to charge them or anyone photographing them with contempt of court.

Barker's junior, Tom Pauling, rose to call the first witness. Earlier in the year he had been briefed by Peter Dean to advise the Chamberlains, but he was now appearing for the Crown.

'If Your Honour pleases, I call Sally Coral Lowe.'

From a prosecutor's point of view, it was good strategy to call Sally Lowe first. If her evidence was accepted, then the Crown case was destroyed. She had heard the baby cry when, on the Crown case, it had to be dead. There was no way around the impasse. She was an apparently truthful woman who had enjoyed no prior contact with the Chamberlains and she had no reason to lie. It also seemed unlikely that she could have been mistaken. She was a sensible and articulate young mother, well attuned to the cries of young babies. In the stillness of a desert evening a baby's cry would carry and Sally had been only twenty metres from the open flaps of the tent. There were no other babies in the camping area that night and earlier suggestions of confusion due to the cry of an owl or some other ephemeral nocturnal creature seemed somewhat fanciful.

Had she been called at the end of the scientific evidence, she might well have carried the day. Territorians pride themselves on their practicality and their 'down-to-earth' attitude to people. The commonsense approach of this young mother might have seemed far more reliable than the convoluted and hotly disputed esoteric propositions advanced by the scientists.

Some of the other witnesses like the Wests who had heard the menacing growl shortly before the alarm was raised and the Whittakers who provided such a graphic description of Lindy's emotional state were equally threatening. When their evidence was considered in conjunction with that of others such as Derek Roff and Murray Haby, there seemed a strong likelihood that the jury would believe this group of practical people describing what they had seen and heard. The scientific evidence would be in danger of being discarded as too theoretical. Some of it might even be resented. One could well imagine that the jury might not warm to the proposition of an English odontologist being brought to the Territory in an attempt to give evidence of the ability of dingoes, especially when his evidence appeared to contradict the views of the rangers.

Timing, it seemed, provided the key. The opening address could imply that these people would be called, but their evidence would be overborne by the really important evidence to come. Mrs Lowe's evidence was foreshadowed, but dismissed as 'impossible'. The dingo tracks were mentioned, but dismissed as 'a red herring'. In the face of the expectations so engendered, a jury might accept this evidence only provisionally. What weight jurors did give to it would be eroded as the weeks passed and the struggle to understand the complexity of the scientific evidence mounted. By the time nearly two months had passed, there might be an air of it having been overtaken by events, of being merely views people held before the scientists discovered what really happened.

Having the most junior of the prosecution barristers lead Mrs Lowe through her evidence also seemed to subtly devalue its importance.

Her evidence, when it came, was short and to the point. It was a baby's cry, not some creature of the night. It was 'quite a serious cry but, not being my child, I didn't sort of say anything. Aidan said, "I think that is bubby crying," or something similar. Mike said to Lindy, "Yes, that was the baby; you had better go and check." Lindy went immediately to check.'

In cross-examination, Phillips read the relevant portion of Barker's opening to Mrs Lowe and explained: 'the Crown is saying that it is impossible you heard the baby when Mrs Chamberlain returned to the barbecue.'

'I disagree with that,' Mrs Lowe commented.

'Not only do you disagree with it, but you are absolutely certain that is the time you heard the baby? Are you not?'

'Yes, all the Chamberlains—Aidan and Mrs Chamberlain and Mr Chamberlain — were present. My husband, myself and child. And we heard the cry.'

'The cry came from the direction of the tent?'

'It definitely came from the tent.'

'Beyond any doubt?'

'I'm positive.'

'You know well, from your own child, the sound of a baby crying?'

'Well, I come from a big family and [I am] used to babies. I can tell the difference between a baby and an older child.'

'Apart from your own baby and rearing it through the same stages as Azaria Chamberlain, what other babies of that age had you had direct contact with, prior to 17 August 1980?'

'I come from a family of nine, and they always seem to be having children. [I am] just familiar with babies and children.'

'You are quite satisfied that the sound you heard was a baby crying out?'

'Yes, positive.'

The cross-examination continued. Lindy had 'a new mum glow about her. She was a little tired, but she still managed to be quite cheerful and happy.' Mrs Lowe saw no blood on her.

Until she and her husband moved to the motel at about ten o'clock, the Chamberlains were never out of her sight. They were 'quite visible, because you could see them crying.' She never saw them attempting to clean the car or taking any object out into the scrub.

The cry was critical and Phillips was determined that the jury were going to get the message.

'Finally, as to the duration of the baby's cry,' he asked, '. . . the cry, as you listened to it, appeared to be cut off, did it not?'

'That's right,' Mrs Lowe said. 'Going from experience with other babies, yes.'

'It seemed to you to stop suddenly?' Phillips persisted.

'Yes.'

'And that was something you noted?'

'Right,' Sally concluded emphatically.

Greg Lowe was to say that he had not heard the baby cry. He had been 'heavily involved in conversation'. He had heard Michael Chamberlain make some comment about it and saw Lindy go to check. He confirmed Lindy's account of raising the alarm.

In cross-examination, Kirkham referred him to Barker's allegation that Michael's behaviour had 'lacked urgency'. Greg confirmed what he had told the police.

'Mike and I must have searched for about half-an-hour, and this was going at full pelt through the scrub. We kept covering different areas, and then coming to our tent to see if there was any news.'

Kirkham put the allegation bluntly. 'Did he in any way, to your observation, lack endeavour in seeking his child?'

'No,' Lowe replied. 'I must point out, though, that Mike did go back to console Lindy on several occasions.'

'It is further suggested by the prosecution that there were opportunities for the Chamberlains, or one of them, to clean blood from the front of the car during the search. Did you see either of the Chamberlains engaged in any such operation?'

'No, I didn't,' Lowe replied. 'There were quite a lot of people around at that time at the tent site and I am sure if anything like that had happened it would have been noted.'

Judy West spoke of hearing Lindy's cry which 'seemed to come fairly quickly after the growl of the dog'. The Chamberlains, she said, left the area of the car twice for approximately ten minutes on each occasion. On the first occasion he had put his arms around Lindy and simply led her away. On neither occasion were they carrying the body of a child or a digging implement.

Amy Whittaker revealed that on the first of the two occasions when the Chamberlains had walked out into the scrub they had done so at her suggestion. She vividly recalled Lindy's agitation: 'They're not looking in the right place.' On another occasion she had said, 'the baby is just out there, it must be out there, under the bushes somewhere, and they are not searching, and they should be looking in that area.' Amy had taken Michael aside and said, 'Look, take Lindy out there and let her see for herself that the baby is not there.'

She described Michael as 'a man rigidly controlling some emotion that he thought may have been in danger of overcoming him'. Lindy 'was certainly numb. And she certainly appeared to be rigid, motionless, and oblivious, to some extent, of her surroundings. Those signs would be consistent with a person in shock.'

She referred to the intermittent arrival of people and vehicles during the evening. 'Every time they came, there was always the hope that maybe this time there would be some–something certain.'

Kirkham asked Amy Whittaker: 'Mr Chamberlain, on a number of occasions, approached vehicles coming up, to ask for news: is that so?'

'Yes. I saw Michael several times go towards a car. As it came down the road and stopped, he would go off to the car.'

Constable Frank Morris was led methodically through his part in the investigation. He confirmed that Lindy 'appeared to be weeping, upset'. He also related the apparent inconsistency.

'Mrs Chamberlain said that, originally, she was at the barbecue site, and she'd seen a dingo near the tent. It had what appeared to be something in its mouth.' When he raised the matter with her some time later, 'she said that the dingo had nothing in its mouth... I said back to her, "but you made the statement earlier that the dingo had something in its mouth", believing that the woman could have been upset because of the situation and could easily have made a mistake. She stated she did not recall making that statement earlier.'

Morris conceded, however, that he could not recall the exact conversations: 'Not word perfect, no.' He also confirmed that he had made no record of them until 26 August 1980. That was nine days after the conversations and two days after the discovery of the clothes which were to spark the suspicions of his superiors.

Murray Haby, an amateur naturalist, described the tracks he had found. 'There were a lot of tracks down lower, but this track stood out because it was a little bigger than the others, and quite easy to follow, and came along to an area where obviously it had put something down, this dog or this dingo, and had left an imprint in the sand, which, to me, looked like a knitted jumper, or a woven fabric. And then it obviously picked it up, because it dragged a bit of sand away from the front and kept moving. And I followed it around past Anzac Memorial, to where a car park comes off that road to the south of the sand dune, and lost it in the carpark.'

He said that the imprint was about seven inches by about five or six and roughly oval in shape. 'And there was a drop of something there. Something moist. Like saliva had spilt there beside it.'

The Chief Ranger, Derek Roff, gave evidence of the tracks which he had followed and of the drag marks with the depressions displaying a cloth imprint. Alan Barber, the manager of the Uluru Motel, gave evidence that Michael had told his mother that 'our daughter Azaria was killed by a dingo last night and we don't ever expect to find the body.' Inspector Gilroy was called to recount his part in the investigation. The dispute between Goodwin and Morris concerning the manner in which the clothes were found was canvassed. Lenehan, the bleeding hitch-hiker whom the Chamberlains had rescued from the side of the road, recounted the manner in which the good Samaritans had loaded him not on their donkey, but into the back of their hatchback with his head protuding forward toward the aperture between the front seats.

Whilst the evidence rolled continually onward, the

Chamberlains' solicitor, Stuart Tipple, continued to work behind the scenes in an attempt to marshall the strongest defence case available. He had been gathering an impressive body of evidence concerning the behaviour of dingoes and got wind of the fact that a little girl had been dragged from a car at Ayers Rock only a few weeks before Azaria Chamberlain disappeared. Roff's deputy, Ian Cawood, had confirmed the truth of the story, but had been unable to provide any record of the family's name or address. It was not until well after the trial that the Cranwells were to come forward and relate the full story of what had happened to their little daughter Amanda. Phillips applied for leave to advertise in the newspapers, but Mr Justice Muirhead dismissed the application, commenting: 'There is an abundance of evidence as to dingoes, their capacity to get very friendly, and to get very vicious, to go into rooms, and to go into tents and upset rubbish bins and behave like pests. It seems that the jury will have to approach this case knowing that.'

So far as the ability of a dingo to carry off a baby was concerned he said: 'It is not like saying the child was carried away by a wallaby, it could not happen, or it does not happen. The evidence is entirely the reverse in this case.'

The case moved on, with Barker foreshadowing the tender of the transcript of the evidence given by the Chamberlains at the second inquest. When people have made as many public statements as the Chamberlains, it is virtually inevitable that they will phrase things differently, omit details included in an earlier account or otherwise create apparent inconsistencies. Whilst there were no damning admissions in that evidence or in any of their other statements, the defence was anxious to limit the scope for what Lindy Chamberlain herself would later describe as 'nitpicking'.

Phillips asked that this transcript be excluded in the exercise of the judge's discretion to reject evidence which might prove unfair to the accused. He pointed out the obvious unfairness of interrogating the Chamberlains publicly whilst the case against them was kept secret. Mr Justice Muirhead asked: 'Could not your clients have said, "Well, under those circumstances we are not going to wander in a maze, and we decline to give any further evidence on the ground that it might tend to incriminate us"? There was that opportunity.'

Phillips responded by pointing to the potentially irreparable prejudice likely to be caused by the storm of publicity if that course had been adopted. Barker argued that, whatever the merits of the procedure adopted by Sturgess, the law permitted it and that if the Chamberlains had declined to exercise their right to object at the appropriate time, they could not now be heard to say that their evidence should be excluded.

Mr Justice Muirhead ruled that the evidence should not be admitted. He agreed that Sturgess had acted 'according to law', but added: 'At this time, the accused were the focus of national interest and national curiosity. Counsel involved in the inquest must well have known the extent of that interest. In looking to the future, the possibility of prejudice to their clients by a refusal to answer further questions about a largely unknown subject matter was a very real, albeit almost a novel, consideration. What were the prospects of their clients receiving a fair trial, by an unprejudiced jury in the Northern Territory, according to law?'

He was speaking, of course, of the specific issue under consideration, but the last rhetorical question was to provide a hollow mocking echo that would reverberate for the next five years and beyond.

15

An avalanche of opinion

A BOXING COMMENTATOR describing the trial would have said that the Chamberlains were well ahead on points. One of the old time 'masters of the metaphor' might have ground out the phrase, 'Barker's like the guy with the wheelbarrow: he's got the job in front of him.' Many thought the job an impossible one. Yet Barker had foreshadowed a flurry of knockout punches from the scientists. Besides, there is an old boxing adage that 'it's only the referee's opinion that counts'.

Sergeant Cocks gave evidence of his experiments on jumpsuits. He carried out an impromptu demonstration for the jury, using a pair of curved scissors similar to the pair found in the Chamberlains' car. He was able to produce damage of the same general shape as that evident in the jumpsuit worn by Azaria Chamberlain at the time of her disappearance. The jumpsuit which he had cut was tendered and passed around the jury box.

He explained that he had tried to reproduce the damage using a scalpel and a razor blade, but that neither produced the same result. Scissors, it seemed, provided the answer. They also produced tufts of cotton and nylon similar to those found in the Chamberlains' car and in the camera bag.

It has been said that a good jury advocate should 'go for the jugular' and Phillips wasted little time on preliminaries. He reminded Cocks of his assertion that the fibres of fabric in the collar and sleeve of the baby's jumpsuit 'were all consistent with having been cut' and contrasted that with his evidence before the first inquest that 'the majority were cut'.

Some of the fibres had withdrawn back into the weave, Cocks

explained. 'The fibres that I could examine were distinctly cut.'

The point was not without significance. The force necessary to produce tearing may cause a stretching of the fibre and a corresponding retraction into the weave when severance occurs.

'Are you saying now you could not examine all the fibres in the collar? Yes or no?' Phillips persisted.

'That is correct,' Cocks conceded.

'Do you not think you should have made that clear to the jury?'

'Possibly yes, on reflection,' he conceded.

'With people on trial for murder,' Phillips emphasised.

Phillips reminded him of his evidence at the first inquest that none of the tufts from the camera bag 'gave the reaction for blood'.

'Did you test them for blood?'

'No, I am not an expert in testing for blood.'

'How were you able to give that evidence?'

'Under a microscope you can see the appearance of blood and I did not see any trace of blood. Therefore I gave the reply, which is an accurate reply, "I could not see any blood on any of the loops and fibres, or threads or tufts, that I had removed from the car vacuumings or the bag."'

'That is not what you swore at the inquest at all, Mr Cocks,' Phillips thundered. 'What you swore at the inquest was "nothing that gave the reaction to blood. They didn't give a reaction, that is the point". That is what you swore.'

'Then what I said at the inquest, if that is how it's been recorded, is inaccurate,' Cocks conceded.

'It is not the first time you have given inaccurate evidence in your career, is it, Mr Cocks?' Phillips demanded.

'I don't consider that I have ever given what I'd call inaccurate . . .,' Cocks retorted defiantly.

Phillips reminded him of the trial of a man named Van Beelen when he gave evidence concerning the thickness of hairs said to identify Van Beelen as the assailant.

'And you gave three times the correct thickness, in your sworn evidence, didn't you?'

'I gave evidence three times of an incorrect measurement.'

'You didn't give evidence three times,' Phillips contradicted. 'I suggest you gave evidence of three times the correct measurement. Triple what it should have been.' The sergeant capitulated, but Phillips wasn't done yet. 'In that case did you produce. . . slides and photographs?'

'Yes.'

'Your evidence was wrong, was it not?'

'There was evidence that some of the photographs had been mixed up, and were in the wrong place. Yes.'

'Was your evidence wrong?'

'Yes.'

Later he turned to the fragments of vegetation which had been embedded in the fibre of the baby's jumpsuit. 'You talked about "a lot of other material; green broadleafed material."' Three small vials were produced, but each was nearly empty. It scarcely looked like the legacy of deliberate and forceful rubbing in vegetation to simulate the effects of having been dragged through the scrub for several kilometres.

Professor Malcolm Chaikin came to the witness box and reiterated his view that the jumpsuit worn by Azaria Chamberlain at the time of her disappearance had been cut by a sharp instrument rather than being torn by dingo teeth. He gave three reasons for this opinion. In the first place, when the damage to the collar was viewed through the scanning electron microscope the fibres were found to be 'pretty much in a plane'. This was not consistent with a tear. In the second place, he found one fibre which had been severed cleanly. He identified this as a 'classic scissor cut'. Thirdly, and most importantly, there were tufts associated with the severances. If a tooth or some other relatively blunt object catches in a loop of fabric, the tension may cause the fabric to tear. Once torn, the tension is released and there is no further tension available to cause a further severance of the same loop of fabric. Since tufts can only be formed by two severances of the one loop, they cannot be produced by tearing.

One had to be careful with tufts. Some were produced in the manufacturing process. But in this case there were some directly adjacent to the severance.

There were more in the car and the camera bag. Professor Chaikin examined carefully and found that of the twenty-five vacuumed from the car, five appeared to be consistent with the tufts taken from Azaria Chamberlain's jumpsuit. A further three taken from the camera bag were also consistent.

He also found a number of hairs in the camera bag, six of which appeared to be from an infant.

Evidence that the jumpsuit had been cut rather than torn was a vital part of the Crown case. It pointed clearly to human involvement. That, of itself, did not prove that the child had been murdered, as Barritt had pointed out at the first inquest. But if the cutting could be linked to the Chamberlains, it would support a strong inference of guilt. It meant that they had somehow recovered the baby's clothes and damaged them in an apparent attempt to simulate an attack by a dingo. How could they have found them when they took little part in the searches and three hundred others assisted by Aboriginal trackers failed? Why didn't they tell the rangers of their discovery? Why had they lied about it ever since? And why would they want to fabricate evidence of a dingo attack unless they were trying to cover up a murder?

Yet in reality, any links provided by the presence of tufts and hairs in the Chamberlains' car and camera bag were tenuous. The Chamberlains were to give evidence that the bag had been given to them by someone else and that they had used it not merely as a camera bag but for carrying clothing during trips. Chaikin's own evidence established that the majority of the tufts in the car had come from other sources. Why couldn't the minority of tufts consistent with those found in the jumpsuit have been produced in a similar fashion?

Chaikin's evidence did not go so far as to establish that they had come from the same jumpsuit and the knitwear manufacturer Bonds probably produce such garments by the million. Similar considerations applied to the evidence concerning the hairs. At least half apparently came from adults and the others varied from 'a light straw yellow' to 'mid to dark brown'. Chaikin concluded that 'I would not be able to say that all this hair came from the same head.' Some of it might have been Azaria's but, even if it were, there seemed no reason to suppose that it might not have got there innocently, perhaps from a cardigan or bonnet worn on some earlier picnic.

This time Phillips chose not to attack. He hoped to win more by exploring the professor's opinions in the light of other evidence and by an implicit appeal to fairness.

He suggested the use of the bag for family excursions and asked, 'In those circumstances, do you find it at all surprising that you found baby hair in the bag?'

'Well, I'd rather not comment on that. All I know is that there was baby hair in the bag. I wouldn't know how it got there.'

'Could you indicate just how many hairs a baby might lose in a day?'

'On the average baby there are fifty or sixty thousand. Babies start shedding at different times, so one cannot come to any definite conclusion. But when they start falling out, they fall out in large numbers. It can be measured in hundreds of fibres a day.'

'Even at one hundred a day, according to my indifferent mathematics, this baby would have had the potential to lose seven thousand in its short life? In nine-and-a-half weeks?'

'On the average, it could be calculated that way.'

Phillips then turned to the question of the damage to the nappy and asked, 'You are certainly not prepared to exclude that damage as being possibly caused by a dingo's tooth or claws, are you?'

'I could not. No,' the professor responded.

A good cross-examiner will not only seek to undermine the force of any evidence which may prove inimical to his client's interests, but will be alert for the possibility of evidence which may bolster his own case or undermine that given by other adverse witnesses. Professor Cameron was still to come and Phillips saw in Chaikin an opportunity to create doubts about the validity of his opinions even before Cameron entered the witness box.

'We are told that Professor Cameron, from England, will be giving evidence, and he will offer the view that if a dingo were to have taken hold of this child by the neck with the jumpsuit collar up, so that the fabric of the collar is between the child's flesh and the dingo's tooth, that would involve the infliction of damage onto the collar. Do you follow that proposition, professor?'

'I follow it,' the professor agreed.

'Your experiments would run very strongly against that proposition, wouldn't they?'

'My experiments would tend to indicate that the proposition

would not necessarily follow,' the professor replied cautiously.

'In fact, your experiments show that not only could a tooth press against a child's flesh, but penetrate it for some distance, and still not cause damage to the jumpsuit or the singlet.'

'Obviously when it was being held there would be an indentation, but subsequently that fabric would recover.'

'Exactly,' Phillips said with evident satisfaction.

Phillips pressed on. The professor had 'scanned the cut' through the electron microscope and looked at any positions where it looked as if a reasonable picture could be taken of 'either a bunch of fibres coming together or of an individual fibre that looked like it had a sharp end'. Despite that, the professor had been able to find only one fibre which had the 'classic appearance of being cut'. Furthermore, whilst the professor had carried out experiments with dingo teeth on fabric, he had ventured his opinion that a dingo tooth had not produced that damage 'without ever seeing a live dingo bite anything' and 'without ever having examined the clothing of a person who was bitten by a dingo'.

The scientific evidence was interrupted whilst the prosecution interposed Rohan Tew. Tew had once been involved in an altercation with a plate glass window and had apparently severed a nerve in his arm. He worked for a man named Floyd Hart installing car radios and cassette players and, from time to time, bumped or cut himself. If the injury occurred to part of his arm, the nerve ends would fail to signal that information to the brain and Tew would find out about it only when he saw the blood. Two-and-a-half months after Azaria's disappearance, he was working on the Chamberlains' car when he noticed blood near the console. He checked his arm, but found no sign that he had been bleeding.

The jury heard nothing of Senior Constable Graham's minute search six weeks earlier and had no idea that a doctored version of Tew's statement had been produced which omitted, among other things, any reference to his employer and his role in the installation. In due course, however, Floyd Hart became concerned that Metcalfe's promise to give the defence team a copy of his statement may not have been honoured and contacted Phillips directly. He was to say that he had carried out most of the work personally and had seen no blood.

Senior Constable Metcalfe gave evidence of his discovery of the spray pattern under the dashboard. He produced the steel plate which had been cut from the car. It was marked as Exhibit 90 and passed from juror to juror so that each might examine the 'classic arterial blood spray'. Phillips drew from him the details of an incident which was to remain unexplained not only during the trial, but throughout all of the subsequent investigations.

Four months before the trial, a plastic syringe had been found in the Chamberlains' car. It was empty and bore no needle. Disturbances to cobwebs hanging from the roof of the police compound and dust marks on the floor suggested that someone had climbed over the wire fence and crawled under the car. The gearbox had been removed, leaving an aperture wide enough to admit a person's arm.

It seemed unlikely that this could be the source of any infantile blood in the car because the use of the syringe for that purpose would inevitably have left some residue. Of course, it could have been cleaned, but it defied credulity to imagine someone using the syringe to fabricate evidence, taking it away to clean it and then returning to replace it in the car where it was likely to be found. Various hypotheses sprang to mind, but it seemed the only firm conclusion one could draw was that the police custody of the vehicle had not been as secure as one would have liked.

It was left to Sturgess to lead Joy Kuhl through her evidence as he had done at the second inquest. Metcalfe set up the screen and operated a projector on a table near the witness box, whilst she explained to the jury the rudiments of blood identification and the nature of the tests she had used. She exuded polite competence.

Both Professor Boettcher and Dr Simon Baxter, Kuhl's immediate superior, sat in court to hear her evidence. Each would later be asked to comment upon her observations.

The tests were reliable, she maintained, and foetal haemoglobin had been demonstrated. Since the second inquest she had carried out a regimen of tests to verify the specificity of the antiserum and in more than two hundred and thirty tests had obtained no positive reaction with adult blood.

In cross-examination, Phillips made the point that all of the plates had been destroyed. 'Did you take any photographs of them?

Or did you direct that any photographs be taken of this evidence before it was destroyed?' he asked.

'No. We have no facilities for that,' she replied. But as Phillips pointed out, there had been the facilities to take photographs for demonstration purposes. She replied: 'To produce my visual aids, yes.'

Phillips turned to her understanding of the changing balance of foetal and adult haemoglobin in the blood of a developing infant. To Boettcher's mind this was the key. If she had realised the proportions that should have been present in Azaria's blood, she would have been struck by the obvious incongruity of the results she was obtaining.

'Now, at the inquest did you swear this? "Human foetal haemoglobin is different from adult haemoglobin. While a baby, or a foetus is in utero it does not have any adult haemoglobin." '

'Yes, I did.'

'That was demonstrably false.'

'I used that statement for the purposes of making things clear and simple. It was not a false statement.'

'I say false in the sense of incorrrect.'

'It was incorrect, scientifically,' she conceded. 'It was used as an indication of the relative amounts.'

'You are perfectly entitled to give an explanation which you have, but the fact is, scientifically, that statement is utterly incorrect, is it not?'

'Scientifically, it is not correct,' she conceded. 'Yes.'

Phillips also challenged her about her assertion that the bloodstains could not be more than two years old. Lenehan had bled in the car when the Chamberlains picked him up on 17 June 1979. This was just outside the two year period prior to her tests in September 1981.

'Are you suggesting that we should, as it were, shut the door as at September 1979?'

'That would have been consistent with my opinion, yes.'

'These stains could not date from August 1979? Do you swear that?'

'It is an opinion based purely on experience, Mr Phillips. I can't swear that.'

'Do you swear they cannot date from July 1979?'

'Once again the same applies, no, I can't swear that.'

'Do you swear that they cannot date from June 1979?'

'No,' she conceded. That was enough for Phillips' purposes.

Phillips cross-examined at length, taking her through the procedure followed in the various tests, Boettcher's criticisms and any obvious scope for error. There were few concessions.

Eventually, he resorted to the overhead projector. Boettcher had picked up what appeared to be double bands even on the demonstration slides. Phillips pointed them out . 'There are two bands, Mrs Kuhl?' he inquired.

'Well, there is a band and a smudge,' she replied. He inserted another slide.

'Will you concede at least that there is a band, and a faint impression of a second band?' This time the response was more emphatic.

'No.' He tried a third slide.

'That is a band, is it not?'

'It is not a band. . . it is an artefact in the staining procedure.' Phillips gave it away. The jury had seen the projection of the slides and Professor Boettcher would explain their significance in due course.

Dr Simon Baxter was the senior forensic biologist attached to the New South Wales Health Commission. In 1974, while still in England, he and another scientist, Dr B. Rees, had published a paper entitled *Immunological Identification of Foetal Haemoglobin in Bloodstains in Infanticide and Associated Crimes*. He had retained an interest in such cases and, when he allocated to Joy Kuhl the task of testing samples taken from the Chamberlains' car, he had asked her to show him all of the plates displaying a positive result. There was some disagreement over this, Kuhl giving evidence that he had seen every plate whether positive or negative and Baxter remaining adamant that he had been shown only the ones displaying positive results.

He agreed that the orthotolidine test could react not only with blood, but with other substances such as bleach, horseradish and some heavy metals. He said that such 'false positives' were 'first stage' reactions, that is reactions which produced colouration before the addition of peroxide, and then usually a different shade to the vivid peacock blue characteristic of blood. When asked whether an experienced biologist could confuse such a reaction with the result likely to be obtained from a genuine bloodstain, he replied confidently, 'Not while I am around.'

He had agreed with Mrs Kuhl's interpretation of the test plates which he had seen, but conceded that even he had no experience in testing denatured bloodstains for the presence of foetal haemoglobin.

He had tested the blood of Keyth Lenehan, the bleeding hitch-hiker, for the presence of foetal haemoglobin and had obtained a negative result. He had also carried out a PGM test and discovered that it fell into a different group from that shared by the Chamberlain family.

Like Joy Kuhl, he was to dismiss most of Boettcher's criticisms. The crossover electrophoresis tests were qualitative and not quantitative. If there was a band there, it would indicate the presence of foetal haemoglobin, but one could not validly compare the strength of that band with the strength of another band in order to compare the relative concentrations. He did, however, disagree with Mrs Kuhl in relation to the haemoglobin bands evident in the haptoglobin test.

London forensic biologist, Mr Bryan Culliford, was called to provide some theoretical support for Kuhl and Baxter. He seemed to have been imported mainly because he had first adopted the crossover electrophoresis technique in the forensic science laboratory. He had not seen the plates before they were destroyed but, assuming the accuracy of what he had been told, he was prepared to agree with Mrs Kuhl's conclusions. In cross-examination, he conceded that he would only be prepared to support those conclusions if the antiserum was in fact specific to foetal haemoglobin. If the antiserum had been thoroughly tested and found to be specific, then he would regard a second band as 'insignificant'. Boettcher would not have disagreed, but it was a bit like a zoologist confidently asserting that if you had thoroughly established the species of a large cat and proven it to be a lion and not a tiger, the presence of stripes was insignificant.

Dr Tony Jones had been the first pathologist to examine Azaria

Chamberlain's clothing. Unlike Cameron, he did not regard the bloodstains on the jumpsuit as proving an incised wound to the throat. He felt unable to exclude the possibility of some crushing injury to the baby's head, although he thought an injury to the neck was more likely.

He confirmed that, although the orthotolidine test on the under-dash spray pattern had proved negative, he had later cut off five of the droplets and forwarded them to Mrs Kuhl. She had earlier given evidence that it was only when she dug into two of these droplets and tested the material extracted that she was able to demonstrate the presence of foetal haemoglobin. That testing was within the province of the biologist. Jones added his own contribution as a pathologist. The spray droplets indicated pressure from a small orifice such as a small artery.

In cross-examination, Kirkham asked Jones to examine another steel plate with a spray pattern. He asked, 'Does that spray pattern appear to you similar to the spray pattern you have described?'

'It is a fine spray of similar character,' Jones agreed. He was obviously curious, but Kirkham did not take the matter any further. It was later to be revealed that the plate had been cut from a Torana of the same model. No-one could say what had caused the pattern, but it seemed unlikely that the Reverend W.A. Roberts had cut the throat of another baby under his dashboard.

Bernard Sims, the London odontologist, gave evidence that the damage to the jumpsuit was not consistent with a dog attack. The typical hole and tear marks he would have expected were not present: the damage to the arm seemed too regular and the damage to the collar seemed too linear.

He dismissed the possibility that a dingo might have carried the child away by the neck 'without leaving any damage to the clothing'. A suggestion that it may have carried the child off by fastening its teeth into the child's face was dismissed just as readily.

'It wouldn't be able to. The facial tissues would be ripped away.' The possibility of the dingo seizing the child by the skull was dealt with by the simple expedient of producing a dingo skull and a doll dressed up as a baby. The head of the doll was described as being the size of a three-month-old baby and he was able to demonstrate the sheer impossibility of it fitting within the dingo jaws.

Kirkham took this up in cross-examination. Sims remained adamant. 'Using lay terms, if a dingo seized the head of a child with a forty centimetre circumference, the jaws would be dislocated?' Kirkham asked.

'Yes,' Sims replied confidently. Kirkham asked him to examine a photograph. It showed a live dingo with the head of a doll similar to the one Sims had used for his demonstration in its mouth.

'Do you concede, having seen that photograph, that a dog could perfectly easily encompass the head of a child of Azaria Chamberlain's size, in its jaws?' Kirkham demanded.

'If that...' Sims began, as he starred incredulously at the photograph. He started again. 'If that doll's head has not been forced into the the dog's jaws, I would accept that.'

When the Crown finally called Professor Cameron, it was as though the preliminary acts had finished. Now it was time for the star. Barker ran through his impressive list of qualifications and experience which included a paper on the Turin Shroud. He asked him how many autopsies he had carried out and was rewarded with the answer, 'In excess of fifty thousand'.

Whilst not prepared to completely exclude the possibility of an attack by a dingo, the professor saw none of the evidence he would have expected had that occurred.

'It would be very difficult for me to imagine a dog grasping the head from above. That would be the only way in which I think a dog could possibly grasp a child without damaging the collar. But, in so doing, I would've expected extensive bleeding, but not around the collar of the jumpsuit.'

'Why?'

'Because when you get a head injury [rather than a soaked bloodstained collar] you get rivulets of blood draining down and missing the collar. It goes down the front and down the back, depending on which way the head is bending. Certainly you'll get bleeding around the back of the collar, depending on how the child lay afterwards, where [the] pooling of the blood.'

He indicated the blood pattern on the jumpsuit and continued, 'I would've anticipated that it can only be described by a cut-throat type of injury.'

He was shown Exhibit 90, the plate cut from under the dashboard of the Chamberlains' car, and confirmed that the pattern appeared to be that of an arterial blood spray spurting upwards under the dashboard from a point near the firewall.

Phillips commenced his cross-examination with the words: 'Professor Cameron, I would like to ask you some questions about a famous English case, called the Confait case, in which you were involved. Because I want to suggest to you it illustrates some of the difficulties in giving forensic opinions in court.' This was a clever approach. Cameron's earlier errors would not be glossed over, but they would become an example and an object lesson in how forensic science could misfire.

The Confait case had received considerable publicity in England. Three young boys, each intellectually retarded, had been charged with murder and arson. They had been interrogated by the police and persuaded to sign confessions but had later repudiated them. One of them had come up with an iron clad alibi. He had been at a Salvation Army club until about 11.30 p.m. The time of death was therefore crucial. Other medical evidence suggested that Confait had died somewhere between 8.00 and 10.00 p.m., but Professor Cameron had testified that 'rigor was commencing' at the time he examined the body in the mortuary and that death may have been as late as midnight. One of the boys was convicted of murder, another of manslaughter and the third of arson.

After two inquiries and three years in prison the boys were declared innocent and awarded compensation. Another eminent pathologist had put the time of death at around 8.00 p.m. and Cameron himself had conceded that 'I would have thought the time of death less likely to be near the midnight mark'. It seems he had been misled because he had not known that the police surgeon had found rigor mortis complete at the scene of the fire or that a fireman had found the body stiff to touch. Furthermore, he had failed to take a rectal temperature of the body. These matters were put to Cameron over Barker's repeated objections.

'Consequently,' Phillips concluded, 'when you gave evidence at the trial, you were not armed with the correct knowledge of all of the attendant circumstances?'

'I would agree entirely,' Cameron conceded.

'Now, I want to suggest to you, Professor Cameron, that you have done the same thing in this case.'

He pointed out that the professor's opinion that a dingo had nothing to do with the disappearance of the child had been based in part upon his view that a dingo could not have removed the child from the jumpsuit with only two studs undone. There had been some conflict between the evidence of Morris and Goodwin, but it related to whether the jumpsuit was merely open to the crutch or open down one leg as well. The professor conceded that his belief that only two studs were undone had been an important factor in causing him to conclude that a dingo had not been involved and that his 'understanding was wrong'.

He had also said in his report: 'Suffice to say I have never known a member of the canine family leaving clothes in a neat bundle.' Again, the evidence of both Morris and Goodwin was inconsistent with that statement.

Phillips then turned to another part of his report. 'On reading all the evidence, it would suggest the last time the child was seen, by an independent observer, was 1530 hours on the day of the alleged disappearance of the child. Although there is evidence given that the child moved or was seen to be held by the mother, nobody actually saw the child apart from an alleged kicking motion seen at the barbecue site.' Phillips drew his attention to the deposition of Judy West who had seen the child as the sun was setting. The professor conceded that the sun would not have been setting at half past three and that his conclusion was 'a false assumption if one negates, as I have apparently negated, Mrs West's evidence'.

'Have you made any other false assumptions, before you gave evidence, Professor Cameron?' Phillips asked.

'Again, not to my knowledge,' Cameron replied. Phillips reminded him of his evidence at the second inquest. 'I rely entirely on Dr Scott's negative evidence, in that there was no saliva present.' Phillips drew Cameron's attention to Scott's deposition in which Scott had qualified his statement that he had not established the presence of saliva in the particular portions tested — 'Of course, there is no guarantee that there is no saliva elsewhere.'

Phillips took him to a further passage in his report: 'Suffice to say I have never known a member of the canine family pulling off the nappy intact.' This seemed a strange statement given Goodwin's description of the tear marks and the pieces of lining strewn over the clothing, yet the professor said that he had made that statement on the basis of the appearance of the nappy when he examined it.

He then returned to the Confait case which had revealed one further bizarre twist. Confait had died of strangulation and an English barrister studying photographs of the wounds saw what appeared to be writing in blood on his neck. Professor Cameron had preserved the neck and kept it in his laboratory. Further photographs were taken and enlarged three hundred times. The barrister was convinced that the pattern spelled out the word 'WANK'.

The professor did not agree but, when pressed by Phillips, agreed that there had been a general appearance of the letters 'WA'.

Phillips now rammed home the relevance. 'Would you not agree that blood from an injury, purely by accident, can take up apparent shapes of objects?'

'They must have a contact point. By or against an object.'

'It can occur purely by accident, an apparent pattern of an object?'

'A pattern of an object can occur, certainly, yes.'

'By accident?'

'By whatever means, accident or not.'

The point was plain. If patterns can form by accident on a neck, why not on a jumpsuit?

The Crown case was over and the defence felt they had weathered the storm and maintained their points lead.

16

The defence

AT THE CLOSE OF THE CROWN CASE, a barrister is entitled to make an application to the presiding judge for an order directing the jury to formally acquit the accused on the grounds that he has 'no case to answer'. To succeed in such an application, however, he must satisfy the judge that the Crown has failed to establish a prima facie case. If there is some evidence of each element of the offence charged, then a prima facie case has been established and the application will fail.

A judge generally has no power to bring the proceedings to a halt merely because he regards the evidence against an accused as grossly unsatisfactory. This is a strange gap or lacuna in our law and one which legislators have been curiously reluctant to cure.

At the close of the committal proceedings, at least in New South Wales, a less senior judicial officer may dismiss the information on the ground that 'a reasonable jury properly instructed would be unlikely to convict'. If the magistrate does commit the accused for trial, the Crown law authorities may intervene and dispose of the matter by filing a 'nolle prosequi', a document which does not involve any formal dismissal of the proceedings but, for all practical purposes, means that the matter will not go any further. Such a step is usually taken on the advice of prosecutors who have not had the advantage of seeing the witnesses and who are, in any event, ranked considerably below the judges in seniority and status. If there is an appeal against the verdict, the appellate court may actually overrule the jury's verdict on the ground that it was 'unsafe and unsatisfactory' in those, admittedly, very rare cases where it is found appropriate to do so.

Yet a trial judge who is on the spot, able to observe the demeanour of the witnesses and to soak up all the nuances of the drama being enacted before him, is denied all of those rights. If the accused is charged with murdering the Chief Justice of the court in which the matter is being tried and the trial judge can see the Chief Justice sitting in the back row waiting to give evidence that the allegation is at least exaggerated, he may nonetheless be obliged to carry out his part in the charade until the trial has drawn to a close in the normal manner. If there is no evidence of the murder, he may direct the jury to find the accused 'not guilty' at the close of the Crown case. But if there is some evidence, even if it comes from a witness whom the judge regards as mentally unbalanced or an obvious liar, then the case must proceed.

This was the difficulty which confronted the Chamberlains at the close of the Crown case. The case against them was entirely circumstantial. Much of the scientific evidence upon which it was based had been seriously undermined and it flew directly in the face of a strong body of credible evidence pointing to the Chamberlains' innocence. Had the law been otherwise, the case might have ended there. As it was, Mr Justice Muirhead was unable to direct an acquittal. The Crown case may not have been a strong one, but it was sufficient to raise a prima facie case and he felt that his hands were tied.

It was 13 October 1982 when Phillips opened the defence:

> Mr Foreman, ladies and gentlemen of the jury, I want to begin by mentioning some legal matters of fundamental importance to this trial. Very shortly you are going to see and hear witnesses for the defence, and it is of critical importance that, when you are listening to and looking at witnesses for the defence, you never once allow yourself to slip into an attitude of mind where you say, in effect, to the witness for the defence: 'Come on, you convince me that the Chamberlains are innocent'. You see, as His Honour will tell you later on, persons accused of crimes like these under our law never ever have to prove their innocence.

He went on to announce that both Chamberlains and 'a considerable number of other witnesses' would give evidence and then outlined the matters in dispute: firstly, the presence of foetal blood in the car and camera bag; secondly, Cameron's conclusions that the child's throat had been cut by a sharp instrument and that there were handprints on the jumpsuit; thirdly, the suggestion that there was no canine involvement in the baby's disappearance; and finally, the suggestion that the clothing had been damaged by a sharp instrument. He also foreshadowed calling evidence of dingoes attacking people, mostly children, at Ayers Rock. He concluded: 'You do not want me to spend a couple of hours telling you what the evidence is going to be, do you? You would like to hear the evidence, so let's go ahead and do that now. I call Mrs Chamberlain.'

The baby was due in four weeks and Lindy was big with child as she made her way to the witness box. The journalists who had covered the earlier inquests were struck by the sharp contrast between the woman now holding out her hand to take the Bible and the slender attractive woman who had defied Des Sturgess. Her swollen face bore the marks of burdens infinitely more heavy than the one she so obviously carried in front of her.

Phillips elicited her name, address and the family history and then deftly led her through a series of anecdotes which might account for blood in the car: both the boys had experienced nose bleeds, Reagan had cut his lip, Azaria had vomited and Lenehan had bled so profusely that two T-shirts soaked with blood had been left behind on the roadway. He asked her to explain the purposes to which the camera bag had been put, obtained a concession that moist towelettes had been kept in the glove box and then turned directly to the events at Ayers Rock. She agreed generally with McCombe's description of the incident with the dingo standing on the rock and explained that her question had been a facetious remark. She also said that she had first put the tracksuit pants on somewhere between three-quarters of an hour and an hour after the baby had disappeared. At the time of the disappearance they were with the parkas in the front left-hand side of the tent.

Phillips then asked that she be shown the clothing which Azaria had worn on the night in question. It was too much. Whatever composure she may have had was now beyond her grasp. Mr Justice Muirhead intervened to ensure that she was feeling all right. She said that she was, but the judge was still concerned.

'All right. You let me know, if you are not.'

Phillips tried another tack. 'Without opening any of those articles, do you confirm that they were the clothing your child was wearing, apart from a matter I will ask you about in a minute?'

'Yes,' Lindy replied in a small voice.

Phillips asked that the clothing be returned and the judge, obviously still concerned, again intervened. 'Right. Put the clothing back!' he snapped.

'Please state what other article Azaria was wearing,' Phillips asked.

'She had a white knitted "Marquis" matinee jacket with a pale lemon edging.' This time it was not only Lindy that broke down. At least three jurors were visibly distressed. The judge interrupted Phillips: 'Some of the jury are upset now.'

'I am sorry, Your Honour,' Phillips apologised, 'it was my fault. I should have thought. . .'

'It is all right,' the judge responded. 'Mr Foreman, how are you getting along?' The foreman's face was a sufficient answer.

'Right,' said His Honour, 'we will take a break for a quarter of an hour.'

Lindy was more composed after the adjournment and Phillips was able to complete the evidence-in-chief without further interruption. He finished on a high note, having her place her hand upon Exhibit 124, the photograph taken by Ruddock of the ultraviolet fluorescence which Cameron had thought betrayed the impression of a hand print on the jumpsuit.

'You can see the finger extending beyond the mark,' Phillips pointed out.

'Because the hand is flat,' Barker protested. The judge allowed the evidence and Phillips led from Lindy an estimate that her finger extended beyond the black mark by 'about half an inch'. But the real coup de grace was still to come.

'How many black smudges or splotches do you say you see in that light?'

Lindy counted them audibly. 'One, two, three, four.'

'Right, now just hold your finger up,' Phillips directed. 'How many spaces have you got there?' The question did not need to be answered. The jury could see for themselves that Lindy's finger contained the usual complement of two joints and three phalanges. If a hand had caused the 'impression' in the photograph, it belonged to some as yet unrecognised species of creature which had a further joint and bone in each finger.

Barker's cross-examination commenced shortly after lunch and continued until late the next afternoon.

He went straight to the question of blood on the lower portion of the tracksuit pants. 'Do you accept there was blood on the pants?'

'No.'

'You do not?'

'No.'

'Do you deny there was blood on the pants?'

'I have never seen any blood on the pants at all.'

He reminded her of Mrs Hansell's evidence. 'She said that — do you remember that she indicated with her hand the sort of splashing motion?'

'Yes.'

'She said they ranged in size from about her fingernail, "sort of tapering off with little drips, sort of and went down to very small points, very small blobs, just splattery." She said, "I would have to say between one to three dozen all told and they were tapering off and running down towards the bottom." Do you remembering her saying that?'

'Yes.'

'Do you accept that as what she saw?'

'Yes.'

'Do you deny that it was blood?'

'I have never seen any blood on myself. There could have been blood on them because they were in the front of the tent.'

'Is that the way you would account for it if there — if it were blood?'

'Well, that is the only explanation I have.'

'When do you say the blood got on the pants, if it was blood?'

'Well, I would think it would be at the same time as it got on the parkas, because they were all together.'

'Where do you think it came from?'

'My personal opinion is that it came from Azaria.'

'How?'

'The attitude of the dingo coming out of the — head-shaking indicate to me the — that there were — blood from Azaria going on that [sic] garments and the description that is given is very similar to my impression of the marks on the parka and the sleeping bag.'

He turned to the question of blood on the shoes.

'My own opinion is that there was blood on my shoes. It hasn't been confirmed by any tests,' Lindy told him. He asked how it got on them and she replied, 'I think it would be from crawling over things that were in the doorway, and things in the tent.'

This led him to the blood in the tent. The scientists had found little and the dingo 'theory' seemed to call for a lot.

'And you say that the dog shook its head at the entrance?'

'That's right.'

'And that, therefore, blood must have been dropped at the entrance to the tent?'

'Yes.'

'Splashed around, is that what you're saying?'

'Yes.'

Lindy was cross-examined about her observations of the dingo leaving the tent. She said that it went south for a couple of feet but that she hadn't watched where it went.

'Did you see again at all?'

'I saw a dingo which I have been led to believe was a different dingo.'

'Did you see the dingo standing by the side of the car on the southern side?'

'I saw a dingo standing by the car on the southern side. The — the trackers told me that it was a different animal. It was the one I chased though.'

'There were two dingoes, were there?'

'According to the trackers there was two.'

Unhappily, neither the trackers nor Dr Newsome who had made a similar suggestion at the first inquest were called. Derek Roff held a similar opinion, but whilst he was called to give evidence he was not asked any questions about the likelihood of a second dingo.

The next morning, Barker turned to the bloodstains in the car. He reminded Lindy of Mrs Kuhl's evidence of obtaining positive orthotolidine reactions for blood from the carpet from the driver's side and from the driver's seat.

'If it were the case, do you know why there would be blood on the off-side carpet?'

'No. It could've come from a number of places, I suppose. I don't know.'

'What places would you suggest?'

'Children crawling around the car, or people moving. Or from people Michael had fixed up, with injuries. I don't know.'

She was reminded of the positive reactions to the crossbar under the passenger's seat, a ten cent coin found under the underfelt, and the seat bracket and hinge.

'What do you say about that?'

'I don't know that I've got any opinion on it, particularly.' There was an interjection by the judge who explained that she was not being asked whether she accepted the validity of the findings, but merely 'if there were positive reactions, what have you got to say about it?'

Barker persisted. 'Can you account for the presence of blood on that side of the car?'

'I know Mr Lenehan's blood is on that side of the car. And a number of other incidents that I have related here in court, but other than that, I don't know anything about it.'

'The blood around the console? Can you account for that, if indeed it were blood?'

'It could've got there — when Reagan hit the dashboard. I don't know.'

He continued to go through the various items from which Mrs Kuhl had obtained positive reactions: the window handle, the chamois, the under-dash spray, the towel, the scissors, the 'large areas in both the front two compartments' and the camera bag. Lenehan, she thought, may have accounted for some of them and nasal secretions on used handkerchiefs occurred to her as a possible explanation for the reactions in the camera bag, but she was completely at a loss in respect of the under-dash spray.

She was asked whether the dingo had been carrying 'a bleeding baby'.

'That's my opinion,' she said in a broken voice.

'Pardon?'

'That is my opinion,' she repeated.

'Well, is there any doubt about it?'

'Not in my mind.'

'Is it merely "your opinion" or is it something you know as fact?'

'It is something my heart tells me is a fact. Other people don't think so.'

He came back to it again later.

'Mrs Chamberlain, you say this child was in the mouth of a dingo which was vigorously shaking its head at the entrance to the tent. That is what you firmly believe; is that right?'

'That's right.'

'The dog having taken Azaria from the bassinette?'

The reply was inaudible and the judge again intervened. 'Take it steady, Mrs Chamberlain.'

'You saw blood on the parka?' Barker persisted.

'Yes.' This time the reply was clear but the judge was still concerned.

'Would you like a spell, Mrs Chamberlain?'

'No. I'd rather get it over with, Your Honour.'

'I do not want you to have to answer questions when you are feeling distressed. Would you like me to give you a ten minute break?'

'No, I'd prefer to go on. This has been going on for two years. I want to get it over with.'

Barker took up where he had left off.

'You say the blood on the parka must have come from the baby?'

'Yes.'

'When it was in the dog's mouth?'

'Somewhere around about that time.'

'What other time could it have come from the baby?'

The reply was tinged with more than mere asperity.

'Look, Mr Barker, I wasn't there. I can only go on the evidence of my own eyes. We're talking about my baby daughter, not some object,' she snapped.

'Right,' the judge said decisively, 'I'll just give you a break, Mrs Chamberlain, for ten minutes.'

Barker turned to Morris' evidence concerning the contradiction in the two accounts Lindy had given him. Phillips let it run on for some time, but then interrupted: 'I object to selected passages being put. My recollection is, when he was cross-examined, the constable clearly said that he may be mistaken.'

'He said that it was not verbatim,' Mr Justice Muirhead agreed. 'He made no notes.'

'More than that, with respect, Your Honour,' Phillips persisted. 'He said he may be mistaken about that.'

'I was not trying to argue with you, Mr Phillips,' the judge replied. 'I was kind of basically agreeing.'

Barker began to wade through the interview with Gilroy but this time it was Lindy who protested.

'Mr Barker, that interview was a short interview, to give them some facts to work on. He told me they were coming to take a statement with all details in it. I don't pretend that everything in that is exactly one after the other as it happened. I was totally confused, and still in shock, when that was taken.'

'Is it the case that what you say here cannot be relied upon?' Barker retorted.

'I am saying that it may not specifically be lined up, one thing after the other. It may be jumbled. I am not saying it's incorrect. I am saying it may be in the wrong order.'

The cross-examination continued with Lindy at times displaying distress and at other times flashes of barely controlled anger.

Barker finished by putting to her the Crown case. She took the baby into the car, sat in the front passenger's seat and cut its throat. Blood spattered on the front of her pants and sprayed upwards under the dashboard. She had left the body in the car 'either wrapped or in the camera bag'. She had then returned to the tent, washed her hands, removed the tracksuit pants and gone back to the barbecue. When Michael asked her to check the baby, she invented the story of the dingo removing the child from the tent. She told Michael what had happened and they both stayed near the car 'because the child was in it'. 'At some stage' one of them buried the baby in the soft sand. They later disinterred the child and removed the clothes. They cut the jumpsuit to simulate dingo damage and put the clothes where they were subsequently found 'with the object of letting it be thought that the baby had been killed and eaten by a dingo.' It was all denied.

During the course of his cross-examination, Barker had made the point that her recollection of some details was extraordinarily clear. Later he was to use the term 'fantastic'. Yet in other respects her memory had been vague. The criticism was of dubious validity. One's memory tends to comprise a series of mental pictures rather than a continuous verbal narrative. One may retain a vivid recollection of some frames in the roll of film but recall others poorly, if at all. If the events have been particularly traumatic or confused, one may also confuse the order of the frames. Yet Barker's questions had conveyed the same implicit criticism again and again.

In re-examination, Phillips asked: 'Now, I will ask you to do your best with this. Would you try? You have been asked a lot about whether you remember things — different things during the hours following your child's disappearance have been put to you — you said you have not remembered a number. Just try and explain, please, in your own words how you felt that night while the searching was going on, in terms of observations you made?'

'I felt totally numb and some things came to me very clearly, and others just a complete blank — like a series of disjointed pictures put together.'

Lindy's evidence was over and Phillips called Professor Boettcher. Phillips took some time establishing his impressive credentials. Before coming to the crux of the matter, Phillips said: 'In your opinion . . . should it be concluded, on the results of any of the tests performed by Mrs Kuhl, that foetal haemoglobin was present in any of the samples tested by her?'

'No, it is my opinion that such a conclusion should not be reached from the results presented by Mrs Kuhl.'

The conclusion was simple, but the reasons for it seemed appallingly complex to the untutored. Phillips led him through a detailed exposition, systematically building up a prodigious case for those who could follow it. The press clearly didn't. The nation's newspapers reported his conclusion and his claim that the serum used by Mrs Kuhl was 'defective', but no synopsis of the professor's detailed analysis.

The main thrust of Barker's attack seemed to rely in confronting Boettcher with Baxter's experience and competence and the undoubted eminence of Culliford. Whilst that was occurring, the judge intervened to ensure that the professor's position was clear.

'You say you did find fault with her methodology, do you not?'

'I am critical of the conclusions [that have been] derived from those results, Your Honour.'

'You are critical of her interpretation of what she saw?'

'Yes.'

'And her scientific examination? Am I right in saying you believe she was misled by believing that the antisera was specific, where you say it was non-specific?'

The professor agreed.

Barker resumed the attack. 'You don't know whether it was specific or non-specific, do you? Apart from what she can tell you, and what Dr Baxter can tell you?'

'Unless one of the two batches I used was the same batch that Mrs Kuhl used,' Boettcher replied.

This was the Achilles heel of a significant part of the professor's argument. Stuart Tipple had still not been able to ascertain the batch number of the antiserum which Mrs Kuhl used in her tests. Consequently, although it was clear that Boettcher had obtained anti foetal haemoglobin serum from the same manufacturer, he could not exclude the possibility that Mrs Kuhl had used another batch which did not display the same deficiencies as the one used in his tests.

Barker also made the point that Boettcher was not a forensic scientist. Consequently, it was suggested, he did not have the same day-by-day experience as Mrs Kuhl and the other forensic biologists upon whom the Crown relied.

Findlay Cornell, a biochemist, gave evidence that blood contains in excess of one hundred different proteins. Protein can be detected by means of isoelectric focussing. Yet when he tested samples taken from the carpet in the Chamberlains' car, he detected no protein 'whatsoever'. Had blood soaked into the carpet, he said, 'I would've expected to see protein; specifically haemoglobin.'

He was also asked about the tests which showed that the PGM group of the blood in the car was different from that of Lenehan. He was not impressed. 'I think, given the age of the blood in the car, and the fact that the other was taken fresh from the person you spoke about, I'd be very wary about interpreting those results, and would not have much confidence in those results, no.'

When Les Harris was sworn he proved a mine of information. He recounted an incident of a dingo shearing through a steel cable with its carnassial teeth and another incident in which he had seen a dingo kill and carry away a twenty pound swamp wallaby.

It seemed that half of Australia had asked how a dingo could possibly have removed the body from the jumpsuit, but the jury was to hear that dingoes could prove remarkably dexterous. A further anecdote concerned five pounds of scotch fillet steak which Harris had intended to have at a barbecue until a dingo with a larcenous bent decided otherwise.

'The thing that surprised me a good deal,' he explained, 'was that the fillet — it was cut fillet — and the fillet had been placed into the plastic bag and I presume the bag would have been rolled a couple of times, and then the whole thing was put in standard butchers' paper, folded and rolled, and it was held there by one piece of sticky tape. The only mark on that piece of paper was at the corner where the tape was, and there was [sic] marks there which suggested he just slipped through with his teeth, probably the incisors, the ones across the front. The whole lot had been unrolled, the plastic bag had been unrolled and the only mark on the plastic bag was in one corner. There was [sic] two indentations which suggested that he put claws on it as he pulled the meat out of the bag and consumed it on the spot.'

The manner of taking stationary or slow-moving prey was simple. 'It will seize the entire head in its jaws, and in one motion it simply closes its jaws, and it will crush that skull. Usually they will accompany this with a sharp shake, which is calculated to break the neck of the animal at the same time.'

Kirkham asked, 'With your knowledge of dingo behaviour and capacity, are you able to offer an opinion as to whether a dingo would be capable of grasping and carrying the child?'

'Yes, it would,' Harris replied. 'There is enough showing that the dingo would make the assessment that it was a mammal and therefore viable prey. I would envisage that a dingo would, immediately after the instant of identification, make seizure, which would be of the entire head, and it would close its jaws sufficiently to render that mammal immobile. As a continuous operation, it would then continue by immediately making off with the acquired prey. It would have made the seizure by head, and it would be unlikely that it would change its grip in any way. That would have been adequate to immobilise the prey.'

Kirkham asked if there would be much blood, but Barker objected on the ground that that was a question for a pathologist. Kirkham came at it another way, asking Harris if he observed much blood from a kill in the field.

'No, there's been very little, and it's characteristic of a kill in the field that little bleeding takes place.'

In cross-examination, Barker built upon Harris' description of the dingo's strength. He was laying the groundwork for a later submission that a dingo could easily have held the baby well clear of the ground. Consequently, it need not have had its head down as Lindy had described and need not have allowed either the body or clothing hanging from it to drag on the ground. It was an interesting twist. Much of the initial suspicion of the Chamberlains' account had stemmed from the deeply ingrained belief that a dingo would not have been capable of carrying a nine-and-a-half pound child. Now the Crown was to suggest that they should not be believed because a dingo would have carried it with such superlative ease.

Professor Richard Nairn had enjoyed a distinguished career spanning some forty years. At the time of the trial he was Professor of Pathology and Immunology at Monash University in Victoria. Like Boettcher, he was emphatic that Mrs Kuhl's tests did not establish the presence of foetal haemoglobin. Unlike Boettcher, however, he had actually worked in laboratories where antisera were produced, including the laboratory in Germany operated by Behringwerke, the manufacturers of the antiserum Mrs Kuhl had actually used in the tests. He knew what could go wrong and, having read Mrs Kuhl's evidence and work notes, was convinced that the antiserum was not monospecific.

He was also critical of Mrs Kuhl's methodology. He spent some time outlining the regimen of testing and experimentation which, he suggested, should have been pursued before any tests had been carried out on samples from the Chamberlains' car. Others, including Professor Ouchterlony, were later to agree. The situation was too unusual and had too much potential for error to be dealt with by blind reliance upon a standard 'recipe'.

Barker tried the same tack as he had with Boettcher, seeking to draw a rigid delineation between the practical, hardworking forensic biologists and the armchair theorists who worked in an ivory tower atmosphere at universities. Yet even on that score he found the headway difficult.

'May we take it, Professor, that you are not a forensic pathologist?'

'In one sense I'm not,' Nairn agreed. 'In another sense, I am responsible for the forensic pathology teaching in my medical school, and have been for the last twenty years.'

Barker made the point that forensic biologists were largely occupied with the identification of blood from trace samples and old stains.

'Most of their work, of course, is on fresh stains,' Nairn rejoined.

'All your work is on fresh stains, isn't it?'

'By no means. All my work is on all sorts of tissue. Some of it is very old. I've actually made a study of the ageing of animal tissues . . .'

Barker cut him off. 'I was talking about blood.'

'Including blood, as an example of an antigen,' Nairn continued.

Barker decided to switch to specifics and referred Nairn to the Victorian Forensic Science Laboratory. Nairn agreed that that laboratory concerned itself with cases where blood had to be examined for forensic purposes.

'By forensic purposes, do we mean for the gathering of evidence for presentation to a court?' Nairn agreed.

'That is the speciality of the forensic biologist, is it?'

'Yes. As a matter of fact, the forensic pathologist to that group attended a course that I gave sixteen years ago,' the professor volunteered, 'to learn how to do it.'

Barker turned to probe the extent of his experience.

'How much of your time is devoted to the identification of blood?'

'As I said, very little. Rather more, in the last few weeks, since I wanted to make myself competent in being able to give opinions in this court.'

'When did you commence to make yourself competent?'

'I began to make myself competent twenty-five years ago.'

'When did you commence to make yourself competent to give evidence in this court?'

'When I was first asked to give an opinion about certain aspects of this case. In mid-July. I have repeated all of these things in my own laboratory.'

'And before that, was very little of your time devoted to the identification of blood?'

'I don't accept that blood is any different from any other tissue. A great deal of my time has been devoted to the identification of human and animal tissues. Some of it forensically, in the identification of remains. I am considered to be, possibly, the final consultant in this in many cases.'

'May we confine our discussion to blood,' Barker demanded.

The judge intervened.

'I think what he was trying to point out is, you can't really confine your discussion on immunology only to blood, when you are looking at questions of experience and endeavour.'

'He seems to have managed it so far, Your Honour,' Barker retorted, the frustration evident in his voice.

He tried another tack.

'If you tested your anti-foetal haemoglobin antiserum against over two hundred samples of adult blood, and if it did not react to one of them, that would be a good practical method of determining that it is not specific to any component of adult blood, wouldn't it?'

'Not necessarily,' the professor replied. 'It would depend entirely upon what test you were using, what concentration of adult blood you were using.'

'But two hundred tests,' Barker protested, 'by a competent biologist, in which no positive reaction was obtained?'

'I have already referred to the inferiority of quantity over quality. Two hundred bad tests are poorer than one good test.'

'I know your opinion of forensic biology as a science, Professor,' Barker said acerbically.

Nairn ignored the comment and continued with an explanation.

'Antisera can alter on storage. They are kept frozen and then they are taken out again for another time. This is why all testing has to be done at the time when you make the test. It can't be based upon what happened last week. Even yesterday.'

'Professor, if they are done properly, by someone who knows what they are doing, that would be rather an adequate series of tests? Wouldn't it?' Barker persisted.

'For the purpose? Were they done on the same day?' Nairn demanded. 'Or is this a series of tests done in the course of a month?' He paused, waiting for a reply, but Barker sat down.

Professor Pleuckhahn was Director of Pathology at the Geelong Hospital and senior examiner in forensic medicine at Melbourne University. He seemed almost derisive of several of Professor Cameron's opinions.

Phillips took him to Cameron's opinion that the pattern of bleeding could only be reproduced by a cut wound across the neck.

'From my experience and my study of this clothing, I would say that Professor Cameron's statement was completely unfounded,' Pleuckhahn responded. He explained that he had seen people brought into hospitals with severe head injuries which had produced patterns of bleeding on their clothing similar to that evident on Azaria Chamberlain's jumpsuit.

Cameron's proposition that 'the child would have had to have been alive for the bleeding to have occurred' was refuted dramatically. He produced a photograph showing extensive bleeding from a corpse in a mortuary at a time when the man had been dead for two days.

He also disagreed that there would be extensive bleeding: '. . . depending on the vessels punctured at the time; if it's a vein punctured as such, a tooth could well form a plug. It depends on how tight he gripped.'

'Does extensive bleeding necessarily follow from severe crushing injuries to the skull of an infant?'

'I've seen extensive crushing injuries of a child's skull, also adult for that matter, without any real, obvious external injuries.'

His response to questions about the hand print was equally emphatic: '. . . to me I can find no evidence whatsoever that would convey to me, even on this highly contrasted ultraviolet fluorescent photograph . . . the imprint of a hand. I've attempted to, but I can't.'

Barker sought leave to defer his cross-examination until the next day.

'We can go onto someone else,' Phillips said, and called Michael Chamberlain.

To the unsympathetic he would not have seemed a good witness. He had been through too much. For two years he had suffered the barbs of suspicion, hostility and, in many instances, outright hatred. He had come to feel as much a pariah as the biblical lepers who were obliged to cry out 'Unclean! Unclean!' lest anyone should approach too near and be infected. He had become acutely conscious of his powerlessness as, day by day, he watched the devastating effect upon his wife and children. It is a heartbreaking experience to hold a small boy racked by uncontrollable sobbing and know the emptiness of your soft assurances. You tell him that it will be all right, that things will look better in the morning, but you know that tomorrow is likely to bring more jeers, more taunts from children who don't understand their own cruelty. How do you explain the venom of prejudice to a six-year-old? How do you explain it to yourself?

He no longer railed against the injustice of it all. Surely God still reigned. If he chose to permit this valley of weeping, then Michael must endure it. As St Paul had asked nineteen centuries earlier, 'For who can resist his will? But who are you, a man, to answer back to God? Will what is moulded say to its moulder, "Why have you made me thus?"'

He was forbidden even the bitter smouldering anger that might have sustained another man. Had not Jesus, himself, commanded his followers to 'love your enemies and pray for those who persecute you'? This was not mere hyperbole. Jesus had said, 'for if you forgive men their trespasses, your heavenly father also will forgive you; but if you do not forgive men their trespasses, neither will your father forgive your trespasses.' Michael had confided to a journalist: 'I must not commit the sin of bitterness if I am ever to see my daughter again.'

There was no sense of fight about Michael as he entered the witness box. He was hesitant, but the dominant impression was one of resignation. He seemed like a man who had been hurt to the point where he had lost the ability to resist.

Phillips led him through his evidence. There had been no confession by his wife that she had murdered the child, no cover up, no burial, no cutting of clothing and no middle-of-the-night jaunts to plant them.

In cross-examination he conceded that his wife was the last person to see the child alive.

'And do you tell us that you are unable to say just what she told you about the child's disappearance?' Barker asked.

'In no detail can I tell you,' Michael admitted, and added, 'We prayed.'

It seemed that something of this resignation may have been evident even on the night in question. Barker reminded him of Constable Morris' evidence that on one occasion Michael had said: 'It was the will of God. There was nothing that you or I or anybody else could do about it.'

'I don't recall saying that,' Michael replied.

'You deny you said it?' Barker demanded.

'I am not going to deny it.'

'It's something you believe?'

'I believe in God's will.'

'Did you believe it as the will of God when you told Morris?'

The judge intervened, 'Just assuming you did say that?'

'Well, God's will is overall — even though we can determine.'

Michael had a tendency to adopt a very literal approach in his response to questions and this tendency had been exacerbated by his lawyers' instructions to stick to what he had seen and heard and not to give answers based upon what other people had told him. He adhered to this injunction faithfully in answering a number of crucial questions.

'Did your wife cut the sleeve?'

'I don't think so.'

'Did she cut the collar?'

'I don't think so.'

'Did you bury the jumpsuit with the child in it?'

'No.'

'Did your wife?'

'I don't think she did.'

'Did you rub [the jumpsuit] in vegetation?'

'No.'

'Did your wife?'

'Not that I know of.'

Later, Barker asked whether on the night of 17 August he had gone to the place where the clothes were later found.

'No,' Michael said.

'Did your wife?'

'I don't have any knowledge of her doing that.'

The answers were technically correct — in fact, models of precision. But the denials were so half-hearted that Stuart Tipple groaned silently. The man's wife was being accused of murder; the jury would have expected a husband convinced of his wife's innocence to have been emphatic, even outraged.

Yet whatever the impression he had created, he had shown none of the deviousness that one would have expected from a man who had been a party to such an elaborate charade as the Crown suggested.

Professor Pleuckhahn was cross-examined and another mother gave evidence of another dingo attack upon her child before Phillips announced, 'Your Honour, that is the case for the accused.' The evidence in the trial was now complete.

17

It's only words

IT IS NO EASY TASK to prepare an address in a case of this complexity. There had been seventy-three witnesses, one hundred and forty-five exhibits and the transcript now ran to more than two thousand eight hundred pages. The scientific evidence presented particular difficulties. Conclusions can be stated simply, but if one is to seek to undermine them one must meander through a verbal jungle of polysyllabic words, esoteric concepts and practical difficulties. One must canvass not only the relative eminence of the scientists concerned, but the relevance of their experience to the particular concepts at issue. Somehow or other it must all be reduced to a coherent and understandable form. If twelve members of the community chosen at random had to be called upon to resolve scientific controversies among some of the most highly qualified and experienced experts in the world, then they needed all the assistance they could get.

In criminal trials, at least in the Northern Territory and several other Australian jurisdictions, the defence counsel has to address first. This means that he must try to anticipate what the Crown Prosecutor will say in his address and to answer the prosecution's arguments even before they are advanced. One may invest a great deal of time and effort seeking to negate a particular argument only to have the Crown Prosecutor disavow it and take a different approach altogether. Alternatively, one may find that the Crown Prosecutor had never thought of an argument until defence counsel 'suggested' it. Yet it is worse still to find that one has failed to anticipate an important point in the prosecution's argument and is condemned to sit in frustration whilst it is urged upon the jury and to curse the fact that the law offers no right of reply.

Such a situation is likely to engender a passion for thoroughness, but it is a passion which must be resisted, at least to some extent. Few juries take any notes of the addresses and a defence counsel must bear in mind the likelihood that much of what he has said will be lost in the wake of the prosecutor's address. Furthermore, after the prosecutor has addressed, the judge must deliver his 'summing up' of the case. If the weekend supervenes before the jury retire, one may find that the best part of a week elapses between the close of the defence address and the time the jury actually sit down to try to resolve the issues before them. Consequently, an experienced counsel may feel it is safer to stick to the main points and to try to 'ram them home'. He will try to portray his case vividly and resort, perhaps, to analogy or humour: anything that is likely to ensure that the point remains in the minds of the jurors.

A counsel must also keep in mind that he is unlikely to hold the attention of any group of people, no matter how well motivated, for more than a certain period of time. University studies have established that the attention span of the average student is only about fifty minutes. It is frequently impossible to adequately deal with the issues in a complex criminal trial within such a period. But, despite what juries may think, barristers are usually conscious of the need to be brief. These competing considerations obviously require considerable compromise. One will weed out side issues and matters to the periphery. The difficulty is that what may seem a side issue to one person may seem crucial to another. Ultimately, the barrister must rely upon his judgment.

Phillips began with an appeal to the 'fundamentals'. He reminded them that they were obliged to act on the evidence alone and that the prosecution was obliged to prove its case beyond reasonable doubt. He suggested that they should reject any proposition Barker might make which strayed outside the ambit of his opening address on the case 'we were called upon to meet'. Then he delivered his opening salvo:

> Ladies and gentlemen, women do not usually murder their babies, because to do so would be contrary to nature. One of the most

> fundamental facts in nature is the love of a mother for her child. The love of a mother for her baby. A mother will make all manner of sacrifices for her baby. A mother will die for her baby. We all know that. It happens again and again. But we know, too, from the evidence in this trial that sometimes mothers may harm or even kill their babies. But we know from the evidence in this trial that that's not really contrary to nature at all when it happens, because we know that the natural love of those mothers for their babies has been distorted and warped and removed by the effect of severe depressive illness. So that the killings by mothers of babies in that connection can be said to be motiveless killings; killings without reason.
>
> Just listen to what Dr Milne — Mrs Chamberlain's doctor — had to say about it.
>
> Question: 'On the occasions you saw Mrs Chamberlain. . . ' — and I interpolate: we know there were many, daily in hospital and routine check-ups thereafter — 'on the occasions you saw Mrs Chamberlain, did she show any symptoms, even of a mild form of post-natal depression?'
>
> Answer: 'No.'
>
> The result of that, is this, isn't it? That the defence which doesn't have to prove anything has proved beyond any doubt that Mrs Chamberlain does not come within the category of mothers who might commit a motiveless killing, because we know that's confined to mothers who suffer from this severe form of post-natal depression — and she didn't even have a scrap of symptoms, even of a milder form. So the question of a motiveless killing caused by illness in this case is gone forever, in our submission. Now, what are the alternatives? There is only one alternative and that is a killing with motive; a killing with reason. . .

He broke off to deal with Barker's proposition that the Crown did not have to prove motive. As a matter of law that proposition was perfectly true but, for practical purposes, it had 'nothing to do with the circumstances of this case'. He then returned to the attack:

> You know, the learned prosecutor put many allegations to Mrs Chamberlain when she was in the witness box, didn't he? Many, many. But there was one allegation, the most important allegation

> in this trial, that was never put, and it's the allegation which would have started with the words: 'Mrs Chamberlain, I put it to you that the reason that you cut your child's throat was . . . ' That's the most important allegation. It was never put. It was never put, because Mr Barker, one of the best men in the business, just cannot think of any reason why she would do it. The prosecution have had two years and three months to think of a reason, any reason, good, bad or indifferent, and they can't. They can't supply you with a reason why she should do it. And we have excluded a motiveless murder, haven't we, on Dr Milne's evidence? In this area of the case, the supply of a reason why this mother would kill her baby, the prosecution are bereft. They are stone, motherless broke. They are bankrupt. There's no other way to look at it.
>
> But we're not bankrupt in this area of the case. The defence isn't bankrupt in this area of the case because we have been able to obtain from witness after witness after witness, ninety per cent of them independent of the Chamberlains, proof after proof after proof of this mother's love and affection for her baby. That's what we've been able to obtain, and we are not bankrupt in this area, ladies and gentlemen. If anything, we are suffering from an abundance of riches.

He went through the evidence, referring them to witness after witness who had spoken of Lindy as a warm and affectionate mother who had loved her baby:

> Now, where have we got — ten people there from north, south, east and west of our country — Tasmania, Western Australia, Queensland — every one of them telling you the same thing. And we've traced it, haven't we ladies and gentleman, from the time of the pregnancy through to the birth, through the nine-and-a-half weeks and up to within minutes of that child's disappearance. And all these people tell you the same thing. This mother was not the sort of mother that Dr Milne explained might commit a motiveless killing, a mother who has rejected the child. These people all tell you the same thing. This lady was a caring mother a mother who loved the child, a mother who wanted it, who welcomed it and who looked after it.

He then turned to the evidence of Sally Lowe. He reminded them of her confidence that it was a baby cry and not some creature of the night. He dealt with the matter at some length, taking pains to cut off any possible avenue of attack that Barker might elect to pursue in his address:

> I submit to you that that woman's evidence ought to be accepted, applying any criteria you like to it — accuracy, firmness, independence, knowledge of what she is talking about — and I submit to you that that evidence stands as an absolute barrier, on its own, to a conviction for murder in this case.

His address was logical and forceful. He ran through the evidence of those who had been present at the camp site and barbecue area, then turned to the evidence of the tracks and drag marks which had been seen on Sunrise Hill, the sand dune to the east of the tent. He reminded them of the unusual spate of attacks and other uncharacteristic behaviour by dingoes at Ayers Rock in mid-1980. All of this evidence, he suggested, pointed strongly to the Chamberlains' innocence. He reminded them that the Chamberlains had little, if any, chance to bury the child and clean up the car as the Crown suggested. He dealt with the Crown's criticisms of the Chamberlains' response to the tragedy and then commenced the long task of wading through the scientific evidence. He was later to confide to a journalist, 'we've answered the Crown, scientist for scientist. I had never seen a defence case better put together.'

He concluded with an appeal to fairness:

> Now you don't want a lecture from me about beyond reasonable doubt, do you? We've all got that perfectly clear. We all understand the fundamental importance of it. You can't go wrong, in our respectful submission, if you keep that centrally in your thoughts while you're considering the case. By all means, give Mr Barker the same fair hearing you've given me. But remember, he has got to prove his case beyond reasonable doubt. The defence does not have to prove anything. I cannot stress that rule of law too much. A distinguished judge once described it as the golden thread that runs through the fabric of our criminal law. That's how important it is. If you stick to that, you won't go wrong.

In the weeks to come John Phillips, like Stuart Tipple, was to receive his share of criticism. Most of it was ill-informed. The rest relied heavily upon the wisdom of hindsight. The Chamberlains themselves took no part in this. They remained grateful to Phillips for all that he had done. Yet the thing that is most hurtful is not the criticism of others, but the self-doubt that frequently follows the loss of a case which the barrister regarded as a just cause. One tends to agonise along these lines: 'surely if I'd just done this or that it might have made all the difference.' The devil of it is that one may be right. Not even the most eminent of Queen's Counsel will brag of conducting cases perfectly. There is always something that might have been done better.

Furthermore, many of the questions which a barrister is called upon to resolve simply have no right answer. Either alternative involves an element of risk. If the decision he makes proves successful, he is applauded: if it backfires, he may be denigrated as an irresponsible fool. Yet the criticism may be no more valid than abusing a two-up player for calling 'heads' instead of 'tails'. Experienced barristers understand these things, but they offer little consolation to a man who fears that an innocent woman may have been sentenced to life imprisonment because he failed her. John Phillips was to take the loss of this case very hard.

In reality, his approach to the case had been well-nigh impeccable and his final address had drawn the threads of the evidence together and welded them into a series of seemingly unanswerable arguments. By the time he sat down, there was a general feeling that the case was as good as over. It didn't matter what Barker said. He would never be able to sway the jury in the face of the defence case, the force of which John Phillips had so ably demonstrated.

A student of literature might have recalled the contrasting speeches which Shakespeare attributed to Brutus and Mark Antony. Brutus, too, presented an argument of impeccable logic. The crowd was with him to such an extent that Mark Antony could get a hearing only by assuring them that he did not intend to blame him for killing Caesar. 'I come to bury Caesar and not to praise him' was the opening line. Yet as the speech progressed, he built up sympathy for the slain emperor until the groundswell of outrage had totally erased the logical arguments of Brutus. It was a scene which reflected a deep understanding of human nature.

Mere reason is not always an adequate answer.

One of the Australian legal magazines was later to publish an article on Ian Barker. The cover of that edition bore his photograph with the caption: 'The man who won the Chamberlain case'. It was certainly not printed at Ian Barker's instigation and he probably found the caption as offensive as the various professional bodies who wrote to complain. But there was an element of truth about it. His final address was brilliantly persuasive.

He began in a way which might have seemed strange to the uninitiated:

> It's just as well, isn't it, that we wear wigs and gowns in courts. I don't know why law reform societies and commissions seem to want to do away with them. It permits people like me to take one faltering step towards people like Mr Phillips in elegance if not in eloquence; and a gown, of course, enables me to cover up my old shirts. That's what distinguishes the Melbourne Bar from the Sydney Bar.

Yet there were a number of subtle hints conveyed in those innocuous sentences. The force of Phillips' address lay in his eloquence not in the justice of his cause. Phillips was a 'silvertail' from down south brought up to play the role of the 'smart lawyer'. By contrast, Barker was a humble practical man: one of them. He was to reinforce these concepts again and again:

> You've heard a very skilful address by counsel for the accused in which references to evidence has been selective, perhaps necessarily so but nonetheless selective. I'll try to fill in the deficiencies.

He did not make the statement that there were deficiencies. The implicit assumption seemed to be that that was self-evident. His task was merely to spell out what they were. He gave a number of examples before returning to the theme of Phillips' address:

> These are matters to which I will have to take you but, without being critical of my learned friend, you have heard what I suggest is a rather one-sided view of the evidence. Again, you've heard Mr Phillips as he had to try to have the best of all possible worlds with the evidence of Mr Harris.

> In other words, what he's really suggesting is that you should pay attention to the examination-in-chief, but disregard the cross-examination, which was where we had the image of the dog with its head erect and the child in its mouth coming from the tent, the head well above the shoulders: a fact which, if it be the case, rather devastates the story told to you by the accused, Mrs Chamberlain, that the dog emerged from the tent but she was unable to see the baby because the head was below the shoulders and in darkness.

Again, the underlying message is clear. Phillips' address was a skilful piece of oratory, but it depended upon a selective and one-sided approach to the evidence which would simply not stand up to an honest appraisal.

He then turned to Phillips' criticism that much of the Crown case had been purely speculative:

> Now, speaking generally, as I must at this stage of the address, Mr Phillips said to you a couple of times, and rather unkindly I thought, that some of the allegations of the Crown are mere theories advanced by me and no-one else. Well, it was a little unkind and really he does know better because I am not here to propound theories and I haven't done so. All I've done is to suggest to you that as intelligent jurors you can draw inferences from proven fact. Because that's what you're here for. This is probably a classic textbook case of circumstantial evidence. We don't have eyewitnesses in the sense that anyone saw the child killed, so the whole case must be, in substance, a drawing of inferences from established facts. If those inferences point to the guilt of the accused, and if there was no room for alternative reasonable inferences, well then, your duty is to convict. . .
>
> With great respect to Mr Phillips, his approach to all this rather suggests that nobody could ever be convicted of anything unless he did it in the presence of an eyewitness. Or that nobody could ever be convicted of anything if some eyewitness were to put forward a contrary proposition . . . Out the window would thereby go a huge body of scientific learning from fingerprints to blood grouping because, as I understand the argument, such evidence goes only to support theories, whereas if you want good evidence you need eyewitnesses. . .
>
> Please, let's be sensible.

Of course, Phillips had never suggested that all circumstantial or expert evidence should be ignored. But the message had been subtly conveyed that what he had said was not merely untenable, but silly. By equating the Crown case with a 'classic textbook case', the message was being conveyed that other juries had convicted in similar cases and the appeal to be sensible really suggested that the absurdity of Phillips' position was manifest: the real question was whether they would act capriciously or responsibly.

The possibility of a dingo having taken the child was ridiculed:

> What is this dingo supposed to have done? It managed, if her story is true, to kill the child in the bassinette, drag her from the basket, divest her of two blankets and a rug and shake her body vigorously at the entrance to the tent, and carry her off into the night in such a way that it left virtually no clues in the tent in the way of blood or hairs or anything else. . .
>
> At the shortest it walked some four or five kilometres, if the story is true, to the base of Ayers Rock and, if during part of that distance it walked through the bush, it managed to do so without tearing or pulling the fabric of the jumpsuit, collecting almost nothing in the nature of seeds or sticks or other vegetation along the way. So, all in all, ladies and gentleman, it was not only a dexterous dingo, it was a very tidy dingo. . .
>
> It managed to cut the collar and the sleeve with a pair of scissors. An unlikely circumstance, you may think, even if we're dealing with the most intelligent and perceptive of animals. . .
>
> But supposing the dingo were on trial here. How could you possibly convict it on this evidence? Where is the evidence? Where is there one substantial clue, apart from the account given by the child's mother, pointing to the killing of this child by dingo? There isn't one. The case against the dingo would be laughed out of court because it's a transparent lie.

He turned to the various accounts of dingoes biting children and otherwise harassing tourists:

> But don't be confused by all this. The way the defence is presented, we are here dealing with a man-eating dingo who raided the tent like a tiger in an Indian village. Indeed, it's even suggested by Mrs Chamberlain that the animal planned the attack.
>
> Now I don't contend, ladies and gentlemen, that dingoes are

> gentle creatures, nor do I contend that they are never dangerous, but what we do know as Australians, and you don't need experts to tell you, is that they are not notorious man-eaters. In the same way that you know as Australians, particularly as Northern Territorians, you don't need experts to tell you that crocodiles are notorious man-eaters. Now, no doubt the ordinary crocodile would go out of his way to eat this baby. The experience of Australians suggests that the dingo does not bear such a reputation, and in saying this I am conscious of Mr Roff's evidence about the peculiar conduct of dingoes at Ayers Rock, and that is something which you will take into account, but if this case was set at Cahill's Crossing on the East Alligator and not at Ayers Rock, and if this were a crocodile case and not a dingo case, well, you might have much less difficulty with it and questions of inherent improbability might not arise. But you are entitled to take account of your general knowledge and commonsense in a case like this, and if your general knowledge tells you that dingoes are not known as a species for killing and eating human beings, then you can take all that into account, in deciding the likelihood of the truth of the dingo theory.

All this was brilliantly done from a tactical point of view. The ridicule implied that the suggestion that a dingo might have taken the child was an affront to common sense. Indeed, Barker later said so specifically. Humour can be a devastating weapon in the hands of a skilled advocate. If the jury laugh about a particular proposition, they are unlikely to accept it. The reason for this is not entirely clear. Perhaps it is because jurors tend to be insecure about their role. It is not easy to announce that you believe an assertion which has proved a source of amusement to eleven of your fellows. Perhaps it is merely that the humour drives home any apparent unlikelihood in a vivid manner that is likely to be remembered when the jury come to consider the issue. Whatever the reason, it seems to work and Barker was using it in a particularly effective way.

In March 1987, a man was taken by a crocodile near Cahill's Crossing on the East Alligator River. One of the journalists covering the Chamberlain Commission of Inquiry made a brief excursion to the morgue to see if he could learn any details. He ran into Senior Constable Metcalfe who had assisted Joy Kuhl in examining the Chamberlains' car. Metcalfe reminded him of this passage of Barker's address.

'That Barker, he's always right. He predicted that this would happen and now it has.'

The jury was not to know that Barker would be credited with the gift of prescience, but the appeal to the jury's experience as Australians, 'particularly as Northern Territorians', was an effective tactic. Barker was well-known as a local identity. He had been the Northern Territory's first Solicitor-General before moving to Sydney to establish a successful private practice as a Queen's Counsel. He was in an ideal position to appeal to fellow Territorians by contrasting a familiar and very real peril with a situation that seemed infinitely less threatening. It was also an appeal which subtly conveyed the message: 'never mind what these smart southern lawyers say; only we Territorians understand these things. We don't need outside experts to come in and tell us what is likely to happen in our own backyard.'

The evidence of the tracks and the depressions in the sand on Sunrise Hill were dismissed with equal scorn:

> Let me talk about the tracks in the sand. When I opened this case, I said they were a red herring and I still say they are a red herring. If there were as many eccentric snow-dropping dingoes as the evidence suggests, ladies and gentlemen, it would be surprising if that ridge were not covered in dingo tracks and strange dingo tracks, as these busy marauding creatures ran about, resting from time to time with their suitcases and portmanteaus, washing and assorted articles of underwear, stolen from tourists. Well, that's the evidence. One wonders where all this material finishes up, but the point I make is that the evidence of tracks is totally at variance with that of Mr Harris. That is that a dingo can carry — according to him — a twenty-five-pound wallaby three-quarters of a mile without putting it down. Why, you may wonder, would it drag a nine-pound baby?

He was scathing in his treatment of the scientific evidence:

> I am sorry, ladies and gentlemen. I can do no more than give you the world's leading forensic biologist. I am not asking you to

genuflect at the shrine of Mr Culliford, as Mr Phillips suggested. The rather disdainful, with respect to him, Professor Nairn can deprecate all he likes the backward methods employed by scientists who daily work in an environment quite alien to Professor Nairn's elegant ivory tower. The fact is you've heard from a man who commands international respect in the field of forensic biology, who you will remember was neither assertive nor dogmatic nor disdainful of the opinions of others. . .

Mrs Kuhl says it is foetal blood, and I suggest to you that she ought to know, and Dr Baxter ought to know what it is he is dealing with, because you know really, if the suggestions made about their work in this court have any substance, people in New South Wales are in constant danger of being wrongly convicted whenever there's some blood involved. And it's really, I suggest, rather too ridiculous to contemplate that she would come into this, in the course of her daily work, as a professional forensic biologist, and muck it all up, not knowing whether she was dealing with adult blood or the blood of a child under three months of age. What we ask you to do is to respect her opinion. She didn't come here for her greater glory; she came here because she got into the case as an employee of the New South Wales Health Commission.

Well, as with some other issues in this case, the defence side found experts to disagree and Professor Boettcher came along and criticised Mrs Kuhl and criticised the quality of the antiserum without ever asking her if he could test the actual antiserum which she used. Professor Boettcher, whose academic university life was preceded by life as a school teacher, and who has never been actively engaged in the day-to-day routine work of testing bloodstains, whose qualification to enter the arena seemed to be based in part upon a lofty concept of what he was pleased to call the 'scientific method', who teaches and engages in pleasant research and writes for learned journals about learned articles, never about forensic biology. Never about the dirty side of the profession: the sex crimes and the murders, the old bloodstains. He's never been confronted with the difficulties which the poor old practical hardworking forensic biologist is confronted with — a biologist who, we say, does an honest and competent day's work and goes to court to offer her honest opinion and finds herself confronted with the criticisms of academics who have probably never in their lives entered a forensic science laboratory. Because such things do not

> exist in the quiet halls of institutes of academic learning. And I say this with very great respect, but perhaps when Professor Boettcher has tested a few thousand trace samples of blood, and when Professor Nairn has scratched around in a car for a few days, testing it for blood, and when Professor Nairn takes time off from research and manages to test more than one blood sample a week, then each may be qualified to criticise Joy Kuhl. Until then, you might think, they should recognise that there are scientists who work at teaching and there are scientists that work at testing blood, and they should leave the field to the professionals.

As a matter of cold hard logic all this offered little answer to the defence criticisms. Nairn had worked in the laboratory that actually produced the antiserum and knew, perhaps better than anyone else, the potential for such antisera to react with other things. Both Nairn and Boettcher had relied upon an apparent incongruity evident upon Mrs Kuhl's own work notes and evidence, and both had been critical of her methodology. In fact, both Kuhl and Baxter had admitted to having very little experience in testing denatured blood samples for the presence of foetal haemoglobin in sufficient quantities to indicate that the blood came from an infant. The suggested disparity in experience was, therefore, largely irrelevant.

Furthermore, much of what Nairn and Boettcher were saying was based upon their knowledge of the composition of blood and the manner in which its molecules were likely to behave in given circumstances. The characteristics of blood do not change from one laboratory to another and an inadequate procedure does not become adequate merely because the biologist who carries it out is entitled to put the adjective 'forensic' before her title.

Yet as rhetoric it was devastating. Both Nairn and Boettcher were put into the category of people least likely to find favour in the eyes of Darwin locals. They were outside experts, armchair theorists and disdainful ones at that. In contrast, the Crown experts were painted as practical hardworking types, the sort who would roll up their sleeves and get stuck into whatever needed to be done. It was people of that sort who had rebuilt Darwin after Cyclone Tracy and who, even now, made the place work.

The reference to people in New South Wales in constant danger of being wrongly convicted was also brilliant. It drew upon the Australian faith in the system. It suggested that if Kuhl and Baxter were wrong, then perhaps all sorts of people could be wrongly convicted. Clearly, such a thing could never be tolerated by the authorities. It was simply absurd. Nairn and Boettcher *must* be wrong. In reality, of course, the circumstances of this case were quite unique. There had never been a case in New South Wales which depended upon the identification of foetal haemoglobin in aged blood samples and the opinions of Nairn and Boettcher did not impinge upon the more routine testing. Phillips was to protest about this statement and the judge was to deal with it in his summing up, but by then it had contributed to the overall effect of Barker's withering attack.

The significance of the other plate bearing a similar spray pattern to the one found under the dashboard of the Chamberlains' car was also swept aside with a string of stinging invective:

> We say at the very least it's irrelevant. At the most it's another red herring. See, what's it all about? We know it was produced from the car of a clergyman at East Maitland. We were not favoured with an explanation of how the spray got there. We were not favoured with an explanation of how long it's been there. We were not favoured with an explanation of what it is. . .
>
> It's not suggested that the spray on the real plate may be paint or vice versa, or whether they are both blood or both paint. I don't know that you are asked to find that all Toranas are sprayed under the dash with the blood of an infant as some sort of benediction or ceremonial rite when the cars are sold. . .
>
> A possibility is that it is blood and that a man on the assembly line suffers from thalassemia, or maybe he's one of the six or eight people in the world with this rare genetic disorder which overloads him with foetal haemoglobin. Look, you know, in a way I am talking nonsense. With great respect, what's the plate there for? We know that on the real plate there is blood. We know the blood is part of the pattern. It's been dug out of the pattern. It's not incidental to or somehow covering up what's there. We know there was blood on the leading edge and all we say to you is that that plate is irrelevant.

His conclusion was emphatic and definite:

> The blood in the car came from Azaria. The blood in the camera bag came from Azaria. All these things we put to you, you are entitled to find as facts. If there was no dingo, the child was murdered. The question who did it is brutally answered. You can leave out Michael Chamberlain, and you can leave out the two boys, and no-one else was there. It is not consistent with reason to suggest that it was anyone but the accused, Alice Lynne Chamberlain.
>
> You are entitled to find that she invented the dingo lie. She had blood on her pants and her shoes. She had the opportunity. She's lied about the animal, its appearance, what it did, where it went, what she did. She's lied about the blood in the car, the tracksuit pants, the dress, the giggle hats, the space blanket and the baby's blankets. We submit to you, with respect, you are entitled to find that she's lied constantly and persistently and so has her husband.Well, what does all this mean? In our submission, this case has strength, it has cohesion and it has volume, and each bit supports the others, but the whole case does not depend on every part. It's not a chain in which each link depends upon another. It's the proverbial bundle of sticks: if you put them all together they can't be broken. And if you put only part of them together, you can't break the bundle. There's only one conclusion, we say, there's only one verdict open to you, and that is that each accused should be found guilty!

Mr Justice Muirhead's summing up commenced on the morning of 28 October 1982 and concluded at 2.21 p.m. the following day. He explained the relevant law and went through the evidence in considerable detail. Towards the end of his summing up, he embarked upon a precis of the case:

> If the Crown assertions are accurate, we start off on the evidence with a slightly tired, but apparently happy mother nursing her baby to sleep. Other people, strangers, to whom she and her husband are talking, are in the vicinity, including Aidan. She leaves, apparently to put the child to bed in the bassinette which has been made up. There is some illumination from the light you have seen in the area, on the tent. She doesn't put the child to bed, as the Crown says; she enters the front of the car, which, of course, we know faces the barbecue light. She cuts Azaria's throat with

small scissors, perhaps, or with something, and causes injuries resulting in death. It would have been a pretty bloody event.

She conceals the body somewhere in the car and she returns to the tent which she disarranges the contents of, leaving traces of blood and some drops of blood on its contents. Those drops must have dropped from somewhere; on the Crown case, they must have dropped from her.

The Crown suggests, then, that she may have washed her hands in the teat bath, which she leaves in the tent, and which she later empties pretty close to Mrs Elston. Be that as it may, Aidan, who is and was always around the place, is hungry. She goes to the car and gets out beans and a tin opener. She returns to the barbecue area with Aidan and the beans.

You'll recall a witness cleaned up those beans later. The problem, ladies and gentlemen, of concealing this killing lies ahead of her. Providentially, her husband says he hears the baby crying. She doesn't, but at her husband's request she starts to walk the short distance to the tent and then, as she nears the tent, she is heard to cry out: 'My God, my God, a dog has taken my baby', or words to that effect.

If it was a plan to conceal murder, it was very quick thinking. Her husband and people come from here or there and later, to their credit, from far and wide and there, during the earlier parts of the evening, she and her husband remain, he searching from time to time until, at the suggestion of others, they go to the motel. Until they went there, ladies and gentlemen, there was a light erected by the police so close to the car, illuminating the scene: the car with the body and blood still in it.

They were in a very dangerous situation: people and police and rangers coming and going. So, some time that evening, in that situation, with caring women around her, talking to her and you may think watching her, she and her husband take the body from the car and they go and bury it in the dunes and, as I understand the Crown case, some time later they go out and locate the burial spot, dig up the body, cut off the singlet, possibly rebury the body. A horrible concept.

It is suggested by the Crown that the car is cleaned, or partially so, that the blood is mopped up, or partially so and, at some time, someone puts the bloodstained clothing — or perhaps the body or something bloody — in the camera case and, of course, we know later that night her husband invites Mrs Elston to travel in the car, and she is asked to remain in it next morning in daylight with the children.

At some stage, the Crown asserts that they place the clothing at the base of the Rock. Despite extensive searching that night and for a long time afterwards, the body is never discovered and, if she had buried it, it could not have been that very far from the tent.

Ladies and gentlemen, if you are to convict her, this is the Crown case as it has been led. This is the situation, or much of the situation of which you must be satisfied beyond reasonable doubt. But there's an important factor that I omitted in that summary. It was not only Mr Chamberlain who heard the baby's cry; it was not only Mr Lowe who said he heard someone mention a cry before she left the car. Mrs Lowe, the first witness in this case, told you on oath she heard a baby's cry which definitely came from the tent. She says she is positivie of that and she was there, and she is an apparently independent person.

You are here to determine whether you are satisfied beyond reasonable doubt that Alice Chamberlain murdered Azaria, and whether her husband is proved to the same degree of proof to have been an accessory after the fact to that murder. If upon that evidence you are so satisfied beyond reasonable doubt, your duty of course is to convict. If you are not so satisfied your duty is to acquit, simply because by law they are entitled to the benefit of any reasonable doubt that the evidence may leave in your mind.

At 8.33 p.m. the parties were given notice to reassemble in court. The jury had reached a verdict. Michael and Lindy had spent most of the trial sitting behind their counsel where they could discuss the case and give instructions. Now they were asked to take their places in the dock. They made their way into it and sat quietly, Lindy wearing a pale blue dress with white trim and Michael in grey slacks and a white shirt with a red tie. The court rose while Mr Justice Muirhead entered and took his seat. He directed the Sheriff's Officer to bring in the jury. The first chill of apprehension began to occur to journalists who had covered numerous jury trials. It is not a good sign when the jury keep their eyes averted from the accused. The Foreman stood and was asked whether the jury had reached unanimous verdicts in the cases before them.

'We have, Your Honour,' he replied.

'Do you find the accused Alice Lynne Chamberlain guilty or not guilty of the charge of murder?'

'Guilty,' came the reply. There was not a sound in the courtroom. The Foreman looked a trifle confused. 'Guilty,' he repeated a little more loudly. A similar verdict was pronounced in respect of Michael whilst two women jurors wept quietly.

In the Northern Territory life imprisonment is mandatory for murder. A judge has no discretion. Mr Justice Muirhead said simply: 'Alice Lynne Chamberlain, you have been found guilty of murder by this jury. There is only one sentence open to me under the law. You will be imprisoned for life with hard labour.'

The case was adjourned until Monday 1 November when Michael would be sentenced. He was to be sentenced to eighteen months hard labour, but ordered to be released immediately upon entering a recognisance to be of good behaviour for a period of three years.

The trial of the century was over.

PART IV

THE AFTERMATH

18

Another child is born

MICHAEL AND LINDY were assisted from the court. Michael, sobbing uncontrollably, had been released on bail. He was led away by his lawyers.

There had been no initial reaction from Lindy. She seemed stunned. She stood silent and uncomprehending whilst the sentence of life imprisonment was imposed, and then turned woodenly and let herself be led away. Then she, too, burst into tears. She was led down to the cells in the bowels of the Supreme Court building to await the arrival of the prison vehicle.

There was something vaguely symbolic about it, like the soul of the damned being taken down to the underworld. Long after she had disappeared from view, the sounds of muffled sobbing still came fitfully to those who still lingered outside the courtroom. Phillips and Kirkham went down to her, no doubt wondering what they could say that would not sound fatuous and hollow.

At about 9.20 p.m. she was driven to the Berrimah Penitentiary. The pastor's wife had commenced to serve her life sentence for the murder of her child.

The Berrimah Penitentiary is located about fifteen kilometres to the east of Darwin. It is a harsh, uncompromising place characterised by mesh fences with sections of razor wire at the top and ever-present warders with rifles looking down from the tall observation towers. It stands on a slight rise amidst the open plain. During the wet season, when the humidity sometimes exceeds ninety per cent, the heat can seem almost unbearable. Nearby there is an old abattoirs. The extent of the stench depends upon the prevailing winds and the humidity. The locals say you get used to it within a few months, but a newcomer may find something vaguely disturbing about the smell of cast-off flesh left to rot in the sun. Perhaps it strikes too close to home.

Yet the women's section, at least, is not uncompromisingly spartan. It is a modest single-storey complex, set in the midst of well maintained lawns and gardens. There are never more than a handful of inmates at any given time.

Lindy was destined to spend three years of her life there. She was to feel the effects of confinement acutely, suffering not only from the loneliness and isolation, but from the knowledge of Michael's anguish and the fact that her children were growing up without a mother. She was to lose some twenty-five kilograms in weight. There were no special vegetarian meals in gaol. The authorities saw no reason to 'mollycoddle' prisoners or pander to their fads.

From time to time one of the police involved in the investigation would bring his vehicle to a halt and come to peer at her through the wire fence. It seems that the spoils of victory were to include gloating over the vanquished.

On 3 November 1982 Betty Hocking, a member of the ACT House of Assembly, was approached by a constituent to circulate a petition and to speak at a 'Free Lindy Chamberlain' rally in Brisbane. The rally was held three days later. It attracted about 500 people, including a dozen or so hecklers. There was a smaller meeting of 'organisers' which led to the formation of a body tentatively named the Chamberlain Enquiry Committee. By the time Mrs Hocking returned to Canberra, she had petitions containing some 1600 signatures seeking Lindy's release and a review of the case.

By mid-November, support groups of various kinds were springing up throughout Australia and in New Zealand. They were, in the main, small independent groups of people grouped under such names as 'Plea for Justice', 'Free Lindy!' or 'Aid the Chamberlains'. Mrs Hocking made some attempt to co-ordinate their activities through a new body named The Canberra Plea for Justice Committee of the National Freedom Council.

During the course of the trial the *Sydney Morning Herald* had proclaimed that 'November 11 is the day for Lindy's baby'. It seems that the press had somehow discovered that Lindy's new baby was due on Armistice Day, a day which Australians also remember as the anniversary of their greatest constitutional crisis. It was upon this day in 1975 that the Governor General, Sir John Kerr, sacked the duly elected Prime Minister, Gough Whitlam, for the first and only time in Australia's history. In the end result, Kahlia Chamberlain was to prove reluctant to add to the significance of this day and exercised a lady's prerogative to be a little late. She was born on 17 November.

On the same day Betty Hocking sent a telegram:

> Michael and Lindy Chamberlain. Congratulations. The love and prayers of 30,000 signatories of petitions and protests are with you both. Isaiah 54:17.
>
> Plea for Justice Committee, Canberra.

Kahlia's birth received the kind of publicity normally reserved for the arrival of a new heir to the English throne. It made the headlines in all of the Australian papers and even the *New York Times* proclaimed: 'Australian killer gives birth'.

For Lindy, the pregnancy had been like a reminder that God had not turned his back on her. Despite all of her prayers, Azaria had been cruelly snatched away. She did not doubt that Azaria had died below the 'age of accountability' and that they would be reunited when Christ returned to raise the dead. Yet one cannot rush the onset of eternity and she had wept bitterly for the little girl whom she would never again see in this life. The events of the last two years had added to her grief and strained her faith to breaking point. The pregnancy had been confirmed during the furore which immediately followed the second inquest. She was realistic enough to realise the cynicism with which many would greet the news, but to her it signalled the first glimmerings of a revival of hope. God would not have permitted it to occur unless he had intended that the baby would be born and would receive adequate care and nurture.

When the baby proved to be another little girl, it was as though God had given Azaria back to them. So strongly did they feel this that they considered giving her the same name, though they quickly discarded the idea due to fears of further hostile publicity.

Their fears were justified when a journalist got wind of the proposal and dubbed her 'Azaria II'. Irrespective of the name, Lindy's heart went out to her. Two years and five months after Azaria had been born, another precious little girl lay cradled in Lindy' arms.

Four hours later, this baby, too, was snatched from her. This time there was no marauding dingo and the child was safe with her father. The Northern Territory government had simply decided that she could not keep the baby with her in prison. There was to be a storm of protest about the inhumanity of this decision but, in reality, the prison officials had little choice. She had been convicted by a jury of murdering one baby daughter. The prison officials could scarcely be expected to ignore that fact or to assume that she had been wrongly convicted. *If* she had killed Azaria, it was a killing without any apparent motive. How could they be certain that a new baby would be safe?

Unhappily, the remorseless logic of officialdom does nothing to assuage the distress of a mother whose baby has been taken from her. It is a hard thing for a woman to give up her baby for adoption even when she has chosen to do so because she wants him to have the family warmth and security she would be unable to provide. It is infinitely worse when she knows that she could provide all of those things, but that her child must be deprived of a mother because she has been deemed unfit to be trusted with her. Lindy clung to hopes of succeeding in an appeal, but Stuart Tipple had explained the difficulties and in the cold light of day she knew that the child might have to grow up without her.

She was warned before the birth that she would not be able to keep the child. She was later to say: 'I worked so hard against that birth because I knew the minute she was born she was no longer mine. I didn't want her to be born!' The thought of her having her baby taken from her was so strong that it inhibited her labour. When the nurses told her to push down to help the baby out, she found that she was actually trying to restrain herself, despite the added pain it caused. 'I couldn't control these instincts,' she explained.

In an ideal world it would be part of the training of forensic scientists to spend some time in a prison and observe first-hand what some people suffer. It might serve as a reminder of the very great responsibility that is theirs. Australians have been brought up to worship at the shrine of science and to regard its high priests as possessing almost papal infallibility. In many cases one gets the impression that the jury regards a scientist's theory or finding as a matter of certainty when the scientist himself would recoil from such a conclusion.

This is not merely the observation of a disaffected lawyer. During the Commission of Inquiry, one of Australia's leading forensic scientists privately expressed the same concern. Yet, alas, it is not a perfect world and scientists work in an environment far removed from the people likely to be most affected by their conclusions. Some are subtly influenced by what they have been told by the police. They are, after all, flesh-and-blood men and women like the rest of us and few of us are not influenced, at least to some degree, by our own expectations. The problem is that those expectations may provide an undergirding of confidence not justified by the results of the tests alone. Alternatively, they may erode the scientists' caution in expressing qualifications and reservations about his conclusions. One gets the impression that in the esoteric atmosphere of the laboratory it may be easy to forget that the issues are of more than academic interest to someone whose fate may be teetering in the balance.

As it happened, mother and daughter were to be reunited within a matter of days. Two days after Kahlia's birth, a Full Bench of the Federal Court of Australia decided, by a majority of two to one, to grant Lindy bail pending the hearing of her appeal. There were stringent conditions including the requirement that she live at Avondale College at Cooranbong and that she report to the police weekly though, as it turned out, the police chose to call on her rather than run the risk of having to control ugly scenes at the police station. On 21 November 1982 Michael, Lindy and Kahlia flew home to Avondale.

They were together again as a family, but Lindy was still a convicted murderess and a sentence of life imprisonment still hung over her head.

19

The appeal to the Federal Court

AN APPEAL FROM A JURY'S VERDICT is a far more limited proceeding than is commonly imagined. In some jurisdictions an appeal involves a rehearing of the case. A transcript of the earlier proceedings is usually tendered to avoid the necessity to hear all of the evidence again, but counsel for the appellant may insist that witnesses be recalled for further cross-examination so that the judge may make his own assessment of the credibility of the people concerned.

Consequently, when a magistrate in Sydney convicts a person of a minor theft, the judge hearing the subsequent appeal may quash the conviction on the ground that, although the magistrate accepted the evidence of one of the prosecution witnesses, he is not satisfied beyond reasonable doubt of its truth. Because he is considering the matter afresh, the judge will usually regard any errors the magistrate may have made as being quite irrelevant. Accordingly, one may hear an irascible judge interrupt a young counsel's eloquent exposition of the deficiencies in the judgment appealed from with the question: 'What on earth makes you think I have any interest in the magistrate's opinion?'

Appeals of this nature offer a considerable safety net for disaffected litigants. If the defendant's case was not adequately presented during the course of the first hearing he may make up for those deficiencies when the appeal is heard. It offers a second chance unfettered by anything done or left undone in the initial hearing.

An appeal against a jury's verdict is quite different. There is a presumption that the verdict appealed from is correct. An appellant will succeed *only if* he can establish that the trial may have miscarried for some reason. He may establish, for example, that the judge misdirected the jury as to the law which it was to apply, that he admitted evidence inimical to the appellant's case when the law required that it be excluded or, conversely, that he excluded favourable evidence which should have been admitted. Even then, the appellate court may dismiss the appeal if it is satisfied that no substantial miscarriage of justice was likely to occur as a result of the error.

Appeals from superior courts do not proceed by way of a rehearing but by argument based upon the transcript of the evidence already given. Because the witnesses are not recalled, appellate judges take the view that they are not in a position to make any findings about the credibility or otherwise of the people concerned. If the appeal is from the decision of a judge hearing a civil case, they will have access to his reasons, including any findings about the credibility of particular witnesses.

Countless appellate judgments repeat the same refrain: 'His Honour was in a position to see and hear the manner in which the witnesses gave their evidence. His view of their credibility was based not only upon what they said but upon their demeanour in the witness box. We are denied the same opportunity and cannot, therefore, say that His Honour was wrong.' There may be slight variations in the wording, but the principle remains the same. It is invoked like some kind of magic incantation to strike down any suggestion that a judge might have been wrong in his assessment of a particular witness' veracity or reliability.

A barrister may advise his clients that he thought the witness was an obvious liar whose evidence was completely refuted by three or four others, but he will be obliged to explain that an appeal could not succeed on that ground. This has led generations of frustrated lawyers to deride appellate courts as 'Judges' Protection Societies'. In the main, this criticism has been quite unfair. The appellate courts are not concerned to protect judges against criticisms but to uphold the principle that a superior court's findings of fact should remain unchallenged. It would be immensely expensive and time-consuming to permit a rehearing of every major case in which one or other of the litigants was dissatisfied with the result and hoped to obtain a better view of his witnesses from an appellate court.

In recent years, however, there has emerged a qualification to the general rule. In 1979 the High Court of Australia ruled that, whilst a judge's findings concerning the credibility of witnesses were to remain sacrosanct, any inferences which he had drawn from the more direct evidence were open to challenge. This principle has become known colloquially as 'the rule in Warren v Coombe'.

Unlike judges, juries do not give any reasons. In some cases, one may deduce from the simple word 'guilty' that they must have accepted the evidence of a particular witness because there was no other conceivable basis for such a decision. In more complicated cases it may be quite impossible to know what evidence the jurors accepted and what they rejected. In a malicious wounding case, for example, they may have believed the complainant, may have thought the comments which the accused had made to the investigating police displayed a 'consciousness of guilt' or they may have been persuaded by scientific evidence of bloodstains and the like. They may, of course, have been persuaded by a combination of factors. One simply does not know.

This causes considerable difficulty in the determination of any subsequent appeal. It is not merely a matter of an appellate court announcing: 'We cannot say that the jury was wrong to believe Mr X.' The appellate court does not know whether the jury believed Mr X or not. This dilemma has led appellate courts to fall back upon the principle that juries, like customers, are always right. If there were a number of alternative bases upon which the jury might have reached its decision and any one of them would have been legally defensible, then the court will assume that was the basis for the decision. Furthermore, in determining whether there was some defensible basis for the decision, the court will assume that the jury decided that each piece of evidence which may have supported such a contention was credible and that each piece of evidence tendered to undermine it was not. Of course, this may not be the case, but the appellant has the task of impugning the correctness of the verdict. If he cannot establish its basis, then he can only accomplish this task by establishing that it was 'not open' to the jury to come to that decision no matter which of the witnesses they believed.

When the case against the accused depends upon circumstantial evidence, the Crown must satisfy the jury beyond reasonable doubt that it has excluded any reasonable hypothesis consistent with innocence. The Crown usually seeks to discharge this onus by producing a diverse array of evidence concerning the surrounding circumstances. Some of this evidence may be accepted by the jury, some may be rejected and some may be regarded as doubtful. The jury will then seek to draw inferences from the facts which it regards as having been established by the evidence it has heard.

Whilst the rule in Warren v Coombe might provide a legal basis for an appellate court to review the inferences, it does not know what inferences were drawn or what evidence they were based on. Consequently, if counsel for the appellant is to show that the verdict was wrong, he must do it the hard way by assuming that all the evidence which favoured the Crown was accepted, all the evidence that favoured the defence was rejected and persuading an appellate court that, even on that basis, no inferences could validly be drawn which would be sufficient to exclude one or more hypotheses consistent with innocence.

It was for this reason that Stuart Tipple had been cautious not to build up Lindy's hopes when he saw her in the Berrimah Penitentiary the day after the verdict. She had been so hopeful, so convinced that the verdict could not be permitted to stand. Justice could not be so blind, at least not in Australia in the 1980s. He had been unwilling to completely quench her hopes. God knows the woman needed something to cling to. Besides, as he told her, it was a very technical area. In a lengthy summing up, a judge could easily make an inadvertent slip which might provide a viable ground of appeal. There had been one or two things which had caused Stuart some concern but, overall, the summing up had been quite fair. If anything, it seemed to lean in the Chamberlains' favour. The trouble with being treated so fairly was that it left one with little to complain about on appeal.

The Federal Court would not entertain an argument that the jury might have been influenced by publicity and rumour and one could not appeal on the ground of the prosecutor's brilliance.

There were other possible grounds but no adequate evaluation of Lindy's prospects of success could be made until the defence lawyers had had the opportunity to go through the transcript exhaustively and consider the various possibilities in the light of judgments handed down in earlier appeals.

The Chamberlains had five months at Avondale with their new little daughter. Lindy was breastfeeding the baby and they made few trips out into the glare of public scrutiny. But in the years to come, Lindy was to look back on this time with her family as an oasis of tenderness in a nightmare of desolation that seemed to have no end. Michael and Lindy would stroll through the college grounds watching the boys run ahead of them on the green fields. At least here they were free from harassment. The boom gates at the entrance to the college were manned and journalists were resolutely excluded.

The appeal commenced on 7 February 1983 before Sir Nigel Bowen, the Chief Justice of the Federal Court of Australia, and Justices Forster and Jenkinson. Phillips and Kirkham had withdrawn in favour of an appellate specialist from the Sydney bar and the Chamberlains were now represented by Michael McHugh QC and his junior, Glen Miller. There were twenty-three grounds of appeal and the legal argument did not finish until 3 March 1983.

McHugh sought leave to tender a number of affidavits containing fresh evidence as to some of the issues at the trial.

Whilst Derek Roff had given evidence at the trial, he had not been asked about his observations when he went to the position near the rock where the clothing had been located. His affidavit stated:

> On 24 August 1980 I observed the clothing lying on some low green vegetation which was flattened and depressed in an area approximately four feet by two feet and this was consistent in my experience to an area where a dog or dingo had laid.

Professor Carrell had also sworn an affidavit. In their subsequent joint judgment, Sir Nigel Bowen and Mr Justice Forster outlined its contents:

> Professor Carrell is Professor of Clinical Biochemistry, Christchurch Clinical School, University of Otago, New Zealand.

> He has high qualifications concerning haemoglobin stability and abnormalities of haemoglobin and plasma proteins. His evidence would challenge certain evidence given for the Crown by Mrs Kuhl, in particular her evidence regarding the comparative stability of foetal and adult haemoglobin, and her evidence regarding the margin of error in diluting denatured blood samples. In general he would be critical of her testing and her conclusions.

A further affidavit had been sworn by Professor Boettcher outlining the results of further tests conducted since the trial.

The court refused leave to tender these affidavits. None of them, it held, constituted fresh evidence 'in the accepted sense'. This referred to the accepted rule that evidence will only be regarded as 'fresh' if it was not available at the time of the trial and could not have been obtained by the exercise of reasonable diligence, though it has been said that 'great latitude' should be allowed the appellants in considering this requirement. The majority judgment added:

> It is true that the Federal Court may consider further evidence although it does not qualify as 'fresh' evidence. It will consider the further evidence together with all the evidence at the trial to see whether innocence or a reasonable doubt is established. In doing this it will pay regard to the facts as the jury having regard to its verdict may reasonably have found them to be.

They concluded, however, that the further evidence 'lacked cogency in the relevant sense'.

Another argument related to the obvious difficulty of having a jury of bank clerks, storekeepers, secretaries and those from other walks of life representative of the community at large endeavouring to resolve scientific disputes when some of the world's leading experts were aligned on each side. The majority judgment suggested that no matter how esoteric and convoluted the arguments might be, it was within the province of the jury to resolve the issue:

> Had we seen and heard all the evidence on this topic being given we might have concluded otherwise, but situated as we are, we have no doubt that the jury was entitled to prefer the evidence of one group of experts to that of the other group. A number of close

> examinations of the evidence on this topic and a consideration of the arguments and criticism of counsel for the appellants does not lead us to the conclusion that the evidence of the appellants' experts is so strong that we could say the jury was wrong to accept the evidence of the Crown experts.

More specifically, the majority rejected criticism of the scientific evidence concerning the spray pattern on the under-dash plate:

> . . . If Mrs Kuhl's test results were accurate and her opinion correct, unexplained foetal haemoglobin was found under the dash. The Crown argues that it may properly be inferred that this foetal haemoglobin came from Azaria, the spray coming probably from a cut artery in her neck. The jury was entitled to accept Mrs Kuhl's evidence and to draw this inference. If they did so, we are unable to say that they were wrong.

Mr Justice Jenkinson took a different view:

> In my opinion the jury might, in reliance upon expert evidence of scientific opinion, reasonably have found, on a balance of probability, that matter from the car and articles associated with the car which Mrs Kuhl had tested contained foetal haemoglobin. But no such finding could in my opinion have been reasonably made beyond reasonable doubt. Those means of evaluating evidence which the jury enjoys by hearing and watching witnesses, and which are denied an appellate tribunal, could not in my opinion have enabled the jury reasonably to have eliminated the doubt as to whether the matter tested contained foetal haemoglobin, which a careful consideration of the transcript of evidence and the exhibits raises in the mind.

He added that Boettcher and Nairn were giving evidence 'on matters of science within disciplines of which each was a master, and at a level of difficulty and sophistication above that at which a juror or a judge might, by reasoning from general scientific knowledge, subject the opinions to wholly effective critical evaluation'.

In his view, however, the balance of the evidence was sufficient to leave a finding of guilt open to the jury:

> I think that the jury might reasonably have founded their verdicts upon the issue as to whether it was established that a dingo had not taken the child.

His judgment also provided a stark reminder of the limitations of the appellate system:

> . . . No final determination of the issue against the appellants could precede a consideration of their own sworn testimony and of the testimony of Sally Coral Lowe. No determination of the issue against the appellants is reasonable unless Mrs Lowe's evidence of hearing Azaria cry out immediately before the discovery of the child's disappearance can be rejected. I do not think that Mrs Lowe's evidence could reasonably have been found to be deliberately untruthful, but a conclusion that she was mistaken could in my opinion have been reasonably reached. Not having seen or heard those three witnesses, I cannot say that the jury's judgment of the appellants' veracity or of Mrs Lowe's reliability as to the noise she swore she heard was unreasonable. A final determination of the issue against the appellants could not have preceded a careful consideration of the psychological improbability of the appellants' conduct which verdicts of guilty necessarily impute to them. But again I cannot characterise the jury's evaluation of those circumstances as unreasonable when the jury had the appellants, whom I have not seen, under observation in the court for weeks and in the witness box for days.

Mr Justice Jenkinson would have regarded the evidence of Professor Carrell and the further evidence of Professor Boettcher as 'fresh' evidence. However, he expressed the view that the evidence given at the trial that the car contained foetal haemoglobin should not have satisfied the jury beyond reasonable doubt and it was not necessary to admit further evidence about that issue. Consequently, he concluded that the fresh evidence was not 'cogent in the relevant sense' and would not have affected the result.

The Chamberlains' counsel also argued that the jury's verdict was 'unsafe and unsatisfactory', but the court held that it had no power to entertain such a ground of appeal in view of the earlier decision in Duff v The Queen (1979) 28 ALR 663, a case in which the accused had been charged with kidnapping the Indian Military Attache.

Judgment was delivered in open court on 30 April 1983. The court unanimously dismissed the appeal. The nature of the appeal seemed to elude most of the journalists and from time to time the press reported that three appellate judges had also found the Chamberlains guilty. In fact, of course, they had done no such thing. They had merely held that the appellants had been unable to demonstrate that the jury must have made an error.

The Chamberlains were keen to fight on, but it seemed that so many of the factors which may have influenced the jury could not now be challenged. Like generations of appellants before them, the Chamberlains were finding that an appeal is frequently little more than an exercise in trying to shut the barn door after the horse has bolted or, as Ian Barker quaintly put it, 'Trying to kick goals by moonlight'.

20

The appeal to the High Court

WITH THE FEDERAL COURT'S DECISION to dismiss the appeal, Lindy's bail expired. She was taken back into custody and returned to Berrimah Penitentiary. Kahlia was five months old. She was to be without her mother for three years.

On 16 August 1983, a Sydney newspaper, the *Daily Telegraph*, reported that 'one of Australia's most distinguished judges has expressed doubts about the verdicts of "guilty" in the Azaria Chamberlain trial.' Sir Reginald Sholl had said that he did not discount the claim that a dingo had taken Azaria Chamberlain and that he believed there was a 'genuine probability' of her parents' innocence. He said that the case had left him with more doubt in his mind than any other trial he could remember. He believed that the trial judge, Mr Justice Muirhead, 'had summed up the case in favour of the Chamberlains but the jury had gone against him.'

On 31 August 1983, the Tasmanian *Examiner* printed a letter penned by a person who adopted the pseudonym of 'True Justice'. The letter asserted that 'a significant percentage of Australians are not satisfied that fair and impartial legal process led to her conviction and hold grave doubts as to her guilt and consider she may been the victim of a miscarriage of justice. A public inquiry must be commissioned immediately to investigate this situation.'

A week later, the paper carried a further letter. 'How could I fail to respond to the rational letter penned by "True Justice" (Aug. 31) which so accurately sums up the plight of the Chamberlain family? Without wishing to disclose any evidence in public, I fully endorse the comments made.' The letter was signed by Greg Lowe.

On 23 September 1983, the *Darwin Weekend Star* carried a front page story on Lindy Chamberlain. It quoted a prison source which described Lindy as 'the model prisoner'. 'When the command is snapped: "Chamberlain, clean the toilets" she does so without fuss. The female warder says Lindy is quiet and humble, but always courteous. She regards herself as just another prisoner. . . There are no frills or fancy requests. If anything, she keeps requesting to help other prisoners, despite how minute their problems might be. There are several people on the staff in this institution who firmly believe Lindy did not kill her baby, Azaria.'

On 20 November 1983, the *Sun Herald* carried a headline, '80,000 sign plea for Lindy'. The article also reported Betty Hocking's concern for the trauma being suffered by the Chamberlain children. 'Aidan is a very disturbed little boy and the younger one wakes up in the middle of the night looking for his mother. He sleepwalks and goes around looking behind furniture for Lindy. Kahlia has been well looked after by a lovely lady who weaned her own child so she could breastfeed her she was in such a state when she was taken from her mother.'

On 24 November 1983, Les Smith, a Seventh Day Adventist scientist, reported that the spray on the plate under the dashboard of the Chamberlain car was sound-deadening material; in fact, Dulux Dufin 1081. He had examined about forty Holden Toranas and found four others with a similar spray pattern on the same steel plate. The cutting of babies' throats had not reached epidemic proportions and it seemed reasonable to suspect that there was some other explanation. Smith found that if he took a photograph of the brackets and extended the line of individual spray marks back towards their origin, they converged at a point approximately 200 millimetres in front of the bracket. Further observations showed that the spray always hit the bracket at an angle of about twenty-two degrees from the side of the car. From these observations it was possible to pinpoint the source of the spray. It was found to be a plenum drain hole from the wheel arch of the car. Sound-deadening material is sprayed into the wheel arches to deaden the sound of stones being thrown up by the tyres and it seemed that during the manufacturing process, overspray would sometimes come through the drainhole and leave a pattern on the plate under the dashboard.

To confirm this theory, Smith removed some of the material from the spray pattern on a plate and compared it with material removed from the wheel well of the same car using infrared spectroscopy. He reported that 'this technique, which is somewhat akin to chemical fingerprinting, showed that the two materials were the same'. He also examined the spray pattern from the Chamberlain vehicle under a microscope and, later, took photographs which he had enlarged. He found that 'yellow flecks of paint overspray could be seen uniformly distributed over the bracket and the spray material. Consequently, the spray material must have been deposited on the bracket before the car was painted.' He found the same overspray on the other four brackets.

This was obviously vital evidence, but it was to prove a great source of frustration for Stuart Tipple. McHugh had advised that it could not be relied upon in the appeal before the High Court of Australia and Stuart was condemned to sit in frustration whilst the debate proceeded on a footing he knew to be factually wrong.

In days gone by, the High Court of Australia had no permanent home. As the final court of appeal and the arbiter of disputes between states or one or more states and the Commonwealth, it was considered appropriate that the High Court sit in the various capital cities around the country. Consequently, the judges who were appointed for life and regularly heard cases well into their seventies were obliged to travel around Australia like so many horses on a merry-go-round. They are now accommodated, more or less permanently, in an angular building of concrete and glass perched on the edge of Lake Burley Griffin in Canberra. The ceiling of the main courtroom soars the height of a seven-storey building. A stranger venturing into these august surroundings might be excused for thinking that the architect had been so impressed by the solemnity of the proceedings he had thought it prudent to cater for the possibility that God himself might decide to take part.

It was here that the Chamberlains' final appeal commenced on 28 November 1983. This time the legal arguments were confined to five days. They ranged over much the same ground as they had before the Federal Court, but the High Court was not bound by Duff's case and McHugh urged the judges to accept that the verdict should be set aside if it could be shown to have been unsafe or unsatisfactory.

McHugh also challenged the proposition that the scientific disputes could be resolved on the basis of the manner in which individual witnesses impressed the jury. It was not good enough, he suggested, to simply say that the jury were entitled to look at the demeanour of the witnesses and the manner in which the evidence was given and utilise commonsense and judgment. He commented: 'Your Honour, poor Professor Einstein might have had some trouble if he was trying to validate some of his theories as opposed to some slick professional witness who was used to giving evidence and was dogmatic and well-groomed and well-assured.'

It can be an interesting experience appearing before the High Court of Australia. The process may seem not too dissimilar to a private being simultaneously interrogated by five generals. Barker did not have an easy time of it. The questions were coming thick and fast. In the Chamberlain camp, hopes began to rise. There was no longer any suggestion of 'kicking goals by moonlight'. The game was still very much alive.

Ultimately, the five judges delivered four separate judgments. Sir Gerald Brennan decided the matter upon the basis that the question was one for the jury and an appellate court could not intervene:

> In my opinion, this was a case where the question of 'guilty' or 'not guilty' turned entirely upon what evidence was accepted and what was rejected. That was pre-eminently a question for the jury and the jury alone. An appellate court possesses no superior ability to decide whether facts should or should not be found when they are facts of the kind upon which the verdict in this case depended or, in the circumstances of this case, to decide whether or not an inference of guilt should be drawn. In my opinion, as there was evidence before the jury which entitled it to find Mr and Mrs Chamberlain guilty of the crimes charged against them, and as there was no error of law affecting the conduct of the trial, there was no ground for interfering with the jury's verdicts and the Federal Court was right to dismiss the appeal.

In a joint judgment the Chief Justice, Sir Harry Gibbs, and Sir Anthony Mason were to approach the matter somewhat differently though they stressed that:

> The responsibility of deciding upon the verdict, whether of conviction or acquittal, lies with the jury and we can see no justification, in the absence of express statutory provisions leading to a different result, for an appellate tribunal to usurp the function of the jury and disturb a verdict of conviction simply because it disagrees with the jury's conclusions.

Nonetheless, they held that if an appellate court thought that the conviction was unsafe or dangerous and that the jury should have entertained a reasonable doubt, it might set the verdict aside. They then embarked upon an examination of the evidence.

When it came to the evidence of Professor Boettcher and Professor Nairn, their Honours agreed with the view taken by Mr Justice Jenkinson in the Federal Court:

> We do not doubt that if the question was whether there was evidence to support a finding that the blood in the car was foetal blood, the question should be answered in the affirmative. But when the question is asked whether such a finding could safely be made, it seems to us that the answer must be in the negative. The conflicting evidence should have raised a doubt in a reasonable mind . . .

Their Honours referred to 'some obstacles to the acceptance of the Crown case': Mrs Lowe's evidence that she heard the baby cry and heard Mr Chamberlain say that he had heard it, the complete absence of motive or explanation for the crime, the position of Aidan in or near the tent, the fact that there was little opportunity available to Mrs Chamberlain to clean the blood from her hands or clothing, the difficulty of disposing of the body, the tracks suggesting that something like a knitted garment had been dragged or carried by an animal and 'the difficulty of understanding why Mr or Mrs Chamberlain, assuming their guilt, would have taken the risk of exhuming the body and leaving the clothes where they might be found.' These matters were undeniably important, but they may have been outweighed by the other evidence:

> These were all matters for the jury to consider and weigh. They were such that they must have raised doubts in the mind of a reasonable jury. However, in our opinion, the other evidence in the case was sufficient to remove the doubts.

They referred to 'the condition of the baby's clothing when it was found, the quantity and the position of the blood in the tent and car respectively, and the presence of the tufts of fabric in the car and in the camera bag.' They mentioned other aspects of the Crown case and concluded as follows:

> . . . none of these facts, regarded in isolation, would have entitled the jury to infer that Azaria had been murdered or that Mrs Chamberlain was responsible for the murder. When the evidence of all these matters is considered together, however, its probative force is greatly increased. When, in addition, one considers the evidence as to the presence of the blood on Mrs Chamberlain's tracksuit and track shoes, the presence of the tufts and the conduct of the accused, including their statements which the jury were entitled to regard as false, the evidence as a whole entitled the jury safely to reject the hypothesis that the baby was removed from the tent by a dingo, and to be satisfied that the baby's throat had been cut in the car by Mrs Chamberlain.

Mr Justice Murphy disagreed strongly with this approach.

> The error in this approach is that the jury's view of the exculpatory evidence may well have been taken in the light of their acceptance of the scientific evidence as reliable, an acceptance contributed to by the trial judge's summing up. Likewise with other adverse conclusions, and the finding of guilt itself. If, in accordance with the directions, the jury accepted the evidence that the blood was foetal, it was irresistible that they should then disbelieve Mrs Chamberlain and the other evidence pointing to her innocence. . .
>
> Once it is accepted that it was unsafe to conclude that there was foetal blood in the car, then the conviction of Mrs Chamberlain was unsafe. . .
>
> Not only for that reason, but because I am of the firm view

> that the rational hypothesis advanced by the defence was not excluded beyond reasonable doubt and that the presumption of innocence was not displaced, Mrs Chamberlain is entitled to a judgment of acquittal.

He added that if Mrs Chamberlain was acquitted the verdict against Mr Chamberlain could not stand, but that in any event 'the presumption of his innocence was not displaced. He should have been acquitted.'

Sir William Dean provided the fourth judgment. He pointed out that 'the principle that no person should be convicted of a serious crime except by a jury on the evidence has no corollary requiring that every person who is found guilty by a jury's verdict should remain so convicted. The safeguard provided by trial by jury is not dependent upon any assumption of the infallibility of the verdict of a jury. It would be foolish to deny that a jury may be prejudiced, perverse, or wrong.'

His summary of the case was revealing:

> I have found the question whether the evidence failed to establish beyond reasonable doubt that Mrs Chamberlain murdered Azaria a difficult one. As the judgments in the Federal Court demonstrate, the circumstantial evidence against her was strong. There is much about the defence story of a dingo that strikes me as far-fetched. The Crown case against Mrs Chamberlain was, however, neither comprehensive nor, in itself, impregnable. The body of the alleged victim was never found. The evidence established no motive for the alleged murder; to the contrary, it was to the effect that Mrs Chamberlain was the loving mother of a normal child. Indeed, it would seem fair to comment that the Crown case was... directed more to destroying Mrs Chamberlain's defence of the dingo than to positively establishing her guilt. Much of the material upon which the Crown relied — camera bag, scissors, bloodstains on the tracksuit pants — was directly or indirectly volunteered by the Chamberlains. The evidence led by the Crown supported much of the Chamberlains' own account of the context in which the attack on Azaria occurred: it established that Mrs Chamberlain was engaged in conversation at the barbecue area; that she was nursing Azaria 'with a new mum glow about her'; that she left the area to put a sleeping Azaria to

> bed; that, within minutes, she returned to the barbecue area showing no sign of distress; that when she left and when she returned she was accompanied by Aidan, who was, apparently, also behaving quite normally; that when she returned she had a can of food in her hand for Aidan; that Mr Chamberlain — who was not suggested to have been other than an accessory after the fact — made a comment about Azaria crying; that Aidan, in subsequent conversations that evening, indicated that he believed his mother's assertion that Azaria had been taken by a dingo. In that context the Crown case . . . strikes me as being, in its own less spectacular way, almost as unlikely as is the story of the dingo. And there remains the clear evidence that the baby was heard to cry after, according to the Crown case, she was dead.

He referred to Mr Justice Jenkinson's view that human intervention could not explain the damage to the clothes because there was no apparent motive for anyone to intervene in that fashion. He found this reasoning unconvincing: 'In this case of the bizarre, however, I am unpersuaded that it is plain beyond reasonable doubt that that damage was not caused by some such unexplained intervention.'

He concluded that 'I have finally come to a firm view that notwithstanding the jury's verdict of guilty, the evidence did not establish beyond reasonable doubt that Mrs Chamberlain killed Azaria. That being so, the verdict that she was guilty of murdering her child is unsafe and unsatisfactory and constituted a miscarriage of justice. It necessarily follows that the evidence failed to establish beyond reasonable doubt that Mr Chamberlain was guilty of the crime of which he was convicted.'

Four of the five judges had found that the jury should have entertained a reasonable doubt about whether Mrs Kuhl's tests had demonstrated the presence of foetal haemoglobin in the car. They had also clarified the law governing cases that depended upon circumstantial evidence, holding that each primary fact which forms a basis for an inference of guilt must be proven beyond reasonable doubt. Yet, in the end result, the Chamberlains had lost by the barest margin: three – two.

21

Serving time

THE LOSS OF THE HIGH COURT APPEAL was a crushing blow. The High Court of Australia is the ultimate appellate tribunal. The Chamberlains had had to obtain special leave in order to have their appeal heard. Now that it had been dismissed, they faced the harsh reality that they had reached the end of the road.

The law offered no further remedy save for a judicial inquiry of a kind which would not be bound by the limitations of appellate procedure. The difficulty lay in obtaining such an inquiry. A convicted person has no automatic right to one. He does not even have the right to apply to a court for an order appointing an inquiry. His only hope is to approach the government and seek to persuade it that there are sufficient grounds to warrant one being held. A cynic might be pardoned for protesting that this involves going cap-in-hand to the body which initiated the prosecution in the first place. He might also wonder whether a decision might not be based on purely political grounds.

In fact, there have been only a handful of such inquiries throughout the entire legal history of Australia and New Zealand. The Northern Territory did not even have any relevant statutory basis and, when an inquiry was ultimately granted in 1986, it was necessary to pass a special Act of Parliament. The history of such earlier inquiries as McDermott in New South Wales, Thomas in New Zealand and Splatt in South Australia does suggest that they are usually offered as a concession in the face of intense political pressure.

Yet as Lindy wept in the Berrimah Penitentiary and four

thousand kilometres away Michael looked despairingly at a toddler who might be in her teens before her mother was released, the groundswell of public opinion was continuing to mount. Perhaps it was a desire to atone for the trial by media which had condemned the Chamberlains even before the trial began. Perhaps it was a recognition that the prospect of an innocent young mother having been wrongly convicted for the murder of her own child was more likely to recapture the public interest now that she had been convicted and all available rights of appeal had been exhausted. Perhaps it was nothing more complicated than a growing unease about the reliability of the Crown case in the face of the brooding storm of scientific criticism. Whatever the cause, speakers addressing Chamberlain support groups throughout the country were being widely reported. Again and again, newspapers revealed that yet another expert had criticised some aspect of the evidence which had contributed to the Chamberlains' conviction.

This produced some defensive reactions. Mrs Kuhl publicly announced that she had resigned from the Forensic Science Laboratory operated by the New South Wales Health Department to join the Northern Territory Police Forensic Science Unit. She also announced that she had carried out further tests on the anti-foetal haemoglobin serum and her opinions remained unchanged.

A person claiming to have been a juror at the trial was interviewed by the press apparently with the consent of the Northern Territory Department of Law. His anonymity was preserved whilst he announced that the scientific evidence had played no great part in the conviction. It seemed the jury simply did not accept that a dingo had taken the baby. Lawyers have always treated the statements of former jurors with considerable caution. Deliberations in the jury room are confidential and the possibility of their disclosure sparking subsequent controversy and criticism may have serious implications for the conduct of future trials. Furthermore, there are twelve jurors and it is always difficult to know whether one self-appointed spokesman has managed to accurately convey any more than his own perceptions. This extraordinary step seemed to have been taken in order to allay growing fears that the jury may have been misled by a reliance upon scientific evidence now under serious challenge.

Yet if the statement were literally true, it indicated that the worst fears of the community were fully justified. All three of the judges in favour of dismissing the appeal to the High Court had regarded the scientific evidence as crucial. As Mr Justice Brennan put it, 'even if the jury were not entitled to find beyond reasonable doubt that the areas of blood in the front section of the car contained foetal haemoglobin, they were entitled to have regard to those areas of blood as showing first that there was blood in the car which could have been Azaria's blood, and secondly, that that blood was unlikely to have been deposited where it was found by any other person who had bled in the car.' They had also held that the jury was entitled to rely upon the evidence concerning: the significance of tufts; the pattern of staining to the jumpsuit; Cameron's opinion that the death had been caused by an incised wound to the throat; evidence of soil and vegetation impregnated in the clothing suggesting that it had been buried, disinterred and treated in a manner designed to simulate rough handling by a dingo; the nature of the severance to the fabric; the condition of the camera bag; and other attendant facts all established by the scientific evidence. The evidence of the lay witnesses virtually all favoured the Chamberlains. Had the High Court been as willing to sweep aside the scientific evidence, the Chamberlains might well have won five – nil.

In 1986, another juror was to make a pilgrimage to Cooranbong to apologise for the verdict and tell Lindy that she was now convinced that the decision had been wrong. It must have required immense courage to have made such a trip and to have confronted the woman who had been torn from her family by a decision which she now bitterly regretted. A television camera recorded these two women strolling together in the grounds of a private home near Avondale College, chatting about the trial and about the impact it had had on the lives of this small Australian family. They were later interviewed. Lindy made it plain that she bore no resentment towards her or the other jurors.

The parents of young Amanda Cranwell who had been dragged from the family car by a dingo two months before Azaria Chamberlain disappeared finally came forward and provided a detailed statement of the incident.

On 16 March 1984, *The Australian* published a letter from six research scientists from the Australian National University calling for a review of the scientific evidence concerning the blood. The letter indicated that the scientists had 'listened to Professor Barry Boettcher's description of the forensic evidence in the Chamberlain trial during his visit to Canberra on March 1 and urged that the immunological evidence in the case be reinvestigated by a scientifically competent tribunal.'

On 24 March 1984, the *Sydney Morning Herald* reported the response of Dr Simon Baxter, Joy Kuhl's superior at the time of the investigation:

> These attacks have been going on continuously since the trial. It has probably got worse. We have been accused either on radio or in the written word of being incompetent, of being biased or of being 'police scientists'. I object to all this because for a start my mob here work in the Health Department. We are not in the Police Department. Even if we were, it is our job and our reputation on the line and we would only present the facts as we find them. We don't change the facts to suit the police case or prosecution case, or the defence case.

Nine days later, twenty-five members of the Australian Society for Immunology and six other scientists wrote an open letter to the Chief Minister of the Northern Territory, Paul Everingham, expressing the view that the tests conducted by Mrs Kuhl did not justify the conclusions which the Crown had sought to draw from them.

Whilst this debate was raging, Michael Chamberlain resigned from the Seventh Day Adventist ministry. Lindy's next newsletter contained the comment, 'May God forgive those who have done this to me and mine.'

It is the monotony and pointlessness of prison life that is so dispiriting. There are few decisions to be made. One gets up when the bell sounds. One leaves the cell when the door is opened. One eats the breakfast that is dished out. One never has to decide when to leave, where to go or when to return. All is predetermined by a prison regimen of unrelenting monotony. In time, it seems that the ability to make decisions and to exercise initiative simply atrophies. It is partly for this reason that prisoners released on parole after serving long sentences find it so difficult to resume living independently.

Lindy was already an accomplished seamstress, but in prison she took up leatherwork, weaving and other crafts. She made clothing for the children. She could not be with them, but she could send home some token of a mother's presence.

The Aboriginal women were tragic oddities amidst the trappings of a white prison. Some were thin, almost to the point of emaciation, their gaunt faces and expressive eyes lending a lost waif-like quality to them. As if to provide a counterpoint to the thinness of the others, there was one enormously buxom woman. The other prisoners used to peg her brassieres on the line at both ends and sit basketballs in the cups. None of them found confinement easy. They had few of the skills that might have helped them while away the hours of monotony. Lindy spent some time teaching several of them to read. She found that few of them had any real understanding of their legal rights and wondered what chance they had had in the white man's courts of justice.

On 15 May 1984, the *Adelaide Advertiser* printed a letter from Betty Hocking, referring to the petition calling for Lindy's release and for a judicial review of the case: 'Seven thousand of the 131,450 signatures came from countries as far afield as Britain, Germany, the US, Malaysia, Mauritius, New Zealand and Hong Kong, and these were also initiated without any approach from us. Although the petitions were presented on May 3, another thousand signatures were on hand by May 4, and they are still coming in.'

On 18 May 1984, *The Australian* reported that Dr Gregory Woods QC, the New South Wales Deputy Senior Public Defender, had called upon the Commonwealth Attorney-General to introduce legislation for a judicial inquiry into the Azaria Chamberlain case. His statement said:

> Many people in the legal profession are deeply disturbed about what seems simply to be a wrongful conviction for murder, with a woman languishing in durance very vile indeed for a crime she did not commit.

> I believe the Attorney-General for the Commonwealth would be derelict in his duty if he were to allow arguments as to the supposed independence of the Northern Territory to impede a decision by him to bring forward legislation to establish a judicial inquiry into new aspects of the Chamberlain case. The refusal by the Territory administration to hold such a judicial inquiry should not be allowed to prevail.

On 16 August 1984, Frederick Smith, a government psychologist who interviewed Lindy at Berrimah prison, made a statement on national television:

> Psychologically, I am unable to account for any criminal behaviour on her part. On the contrary, all the indications available to me suggest that Mrs Chamberlain is clearly among those persons in society who would be least likely to engage in crime, whether in an habitual or isolated fashion.

He expressed his feelings even more clearly when he wrote to the Governor General:

> Having interacted closely with hundreds of prison inmates as a psychologist, I believe Mrs Chamberlain to be the only one whom I have known who is totally innocent.

On 18 September 1984, Hans Brunner, one of the world's leading experts on hairs, wrote to Stuart Tipple confirming that he had examined hairs that had been removed from Azaria Chamberlain's clothing and had been held in the custody of the High Court. Of the eight hairs he examined, he found that six were definitely guard hairs of a dog. He was later to explain that dog hairs differ from the hairs of a cat in diameter, 'medullary fraction' — the size of the medulla or core of the hair compared to the overall diameter — and the nature of the medulla itself. Under a high-powered microscope, the differences are unmistakable. Barker had been right in his contention that a dingo would have left hairs on the jumpsuit. It had. The Chamberlains had owned no dog for several years.

On 20 December 1984, Professor Randall R. Bresee, a textile expert attached to the Kansas State University, wrote to Stuart Tipple. He had examined Azaria Chamberlain's clothing. He quoted the evidence of Sergeant Cocks: 'When you find you can achieve a match, then that is the most likely method that was used . . . the most likely cut is the one that I demonstrated here in court.'

Bresee did not agree:

> The fallacy of this conclusion is obvious since one can produce any phenomenon many different ways. As a result, I agree that the damage of Azaria Chamberlain's jumpsuit was caused by cutting, but very strongly disagree that the most likely method used to produce the cutting of the jumpsuit has been shown to be the rather complex scissor mechanism proposed by the prosecution.
>
> Great effort was expended in reproducing damage to the Azaria Chamberlain jumpsuit using scissors and a complex combination of operations was proposed in surprising detail to reproduce the jumpsuit damage. On the other hand, no experiments were performed to investigate cutting damage to the jumpsuit by canines. This is somewhat surprising in light of the fact that canines such as coyotes are known to be capable of cutting in a way that is remarkably similar to cutting with a sharp object such as a knife.

Les Smith, having solved the mystery of the under-dash spray, had turned his attention to the fabric damage. He and Ken Chapman had carried out an extensive series of experiments by feeding cloth wrapped around meat to dingoes in pens. Smith's report contained a series of photographs meticulously arranged so that various features evident in cloth damaged by dingoes could be compared with similar features in Azaria Chamberlain's jumpsuit. Bresee found his conclusions compelling:

> The evidence presented in this report clearly demonstrates that canines are capable of producing the type of cutting damage seen in the Azaria Chamberlain jumpsuit. It is important to note that all the damage of the Chamberlain jumpsuit can be accounted for in a straightforward manner by the results of this study. Furthermore, the results of this study are consistent with what is known about canine cutting of animal skin . . . Explaining the damage by cutting with scissors, on the other hand, requires a complex set of operations and there is no evidence available to conclude that the

scissor mechanism is 'the most likely that was used' to produce the damage to the Azaria Chamberlain jumpsuit.

The pressure for a judicial inquiry continued to mount with public rallies around the country. At the same time Stuart Tipple was steadily gathering scientific evidence to support such an implication. The evidence already to hand suggested that several of the facts upon which the majority of the High Court had relied in dismissing the appeal could no longer be sustained. Surely, Tipple thought, the Northern Territory authorities would not dare to ignore the wealth of material which now demonstrated that the jury had been misled in several important respects.

On 11 June 1985, the *Sydney Morning Herald* reported that Professor Julius Stone, Australia's leading exponent of jurisprudence, had concluded that 'every element' of the Crown case 'rested on speculation'.

'A formal application for a further judicial inquiry has now been lodged by the Chamberlain Innocence Committee with the Northern Territory government,' the article reported. 'The inquiry should be granted. None of the doubts concerning the verdict against Mrs Chamberlain have been resolved in the past three years. The new evidence that has been gathered is significant and should be tested. The case, in other words, still cries out for review.'

Yet once again, the Chamberlains' hopes were dashed. In a lengthy document which quickly became known as the Martin Report, the Solicitor-General dismissed the fresh evidence and recommended that the petition be declined. The report was tabled in the Northern Territory parliament on 12 November 1985. There was no dispute as to 'what Mr Smith found' but it was dismissed as too late. The other material which had come to light since the trial was treated similarly. 'No-one has suddenly come forward to give evidence which could not have been given at the trial by that person or someone else, nor are they putting forward any recent scientific advance.' The Cabinet duly accepted his recommendations.

The Chief Minister, Ian Tuxworth, made a statement to the press. 'This campaign has as its intended effect the building up of antagonism towards the Northern Territory government, which it seeks to portray as hard, cruel and lacking in compassion. At stake is law and order and faith in the due processes of a legal system recognised as the fairest in the world.'

The report produced a storm of protest. Senator Colin Mason raised the matter formally in the Commonwealth parliament. If the Northern Territory government would not hold an inquiry, he said, it was time that the Commonwealth did. The legal and political ramifications of such a step were intimidating. The Northern Territory had recently gained virtual independence, but had not yet acquired formal statehood. The Australian Labor Party had paid a price for using the Commonwealth's treaty power to overrule the Tasmanian government and prohibit the damming of the Gordon and Franklin Rivers in an area listed by the World Heritage Commission. That decision had been a crucial election issue and the Labor Party had lost every Tasmanian seat. Territorians bitterly resented any interference from Canberra. To unilaterally appoint an inquiry into the correctness of a conviction by a Northern Territory jury after the highest court in the land had found that the trial was conducted according to law and that the verdict had been open to the jury would have caused a furore.

On 20 November 1985, the *Canberra Times* reported that the Australian Labor Party Caucus 'ruled out a conscience vote yesterday on a bill to establish a commission of inquiry to review the convictions of Mrs Lindy Chamberlain and her husband, Michael. The government will therefore vote against the bill if its proposer, Senator Mason, persists in its introduction.' The report continued:

> A conscience vote was raised in Caucus yesterday by Mr Brown who said that senators and members should be allowed a free vote on the bill. . .
>
> However, the move was opposed by the Minister for Resources and Energy, Senator Evans, who made references to the Martin Report tabled in the Northern Territory last week. . .
>
> Caucus heard that the Labor Party's position on conscience votes was fairly clear and federally this applied only to such issues as abortion.
>
> Mr Brown's motion was lost 41 votes to 22.

On 3 December 1985, Sir Reginald Sholl wrote an open letter to all members of the Commonwealth parliament. He referred to the Caucus vote and to a similar vote taken by the Liberal-National Party Coalition which 'reached a similar decision by a narrow margin'. He went on to say:

> The reasons for these decisions were apparently: (1) To intervene could be interpreted as an invasion of the 'State rights' of the Territory under its recent self-government legislation; and (2) the Chamberlains having exhausted their legal remedies up to the High Court, it would constitute a threat to the judicial system, and to public confidence in it, to allow a further inquiry. . .
>
> With great respect, both reasons make nonsense. As to (1), the Northern Territory is still a Territory of the Commonwealth, and it is acknowledged by all parties that the Commonwealth still has the right to intervene by legislation in its affairs. . .
>
> As to (2), if it is based on the naive belief that courts can never be wrong , it is time that Members of Parliament woke up to the serious defects in our legal system, which have been recently referred to by the late Professor Julius Stone, and by the present Mr Justice Kirby, among others. It should surely be obvious to any intelligent Australian that Parliament must retain the right to remedy cases of miscarriage of justice — a right recognised and enforced recently in England, New Zealand and South Australia in well-known cases where wrongful convictions for grave crimes were set aside. . .
>
> Finally, if one assumes that there is even a possibility, let alone a practical certainty (as 4,000,000 Australians according to a recent poll believe) that an innocent young mother is rotting away in a Darwin gaol for a crime she did not commit, may we ask how any decent, fair-minded Australian politicians can bring themselves with a clear conscience to say to her: 'Well, we know we have the power to intervene, and at any rate to investigate the case again, but — sorry young lady — we are afraid of offending the Northern Territory government in its new-found grandeur; we know there is quite a lot of new evidence which if accepted would be likely completely to exonerate you, but (without waiting to hear what your advisers say in answer to the Northern Territory's Solicitor-General's attack on it) we, like Pontius Pilate, wash our hands of the whole affair. . .

> So, as the present decisions stand, will the whole of the Labor members, however their consciences may trouble them, and at least a majority of Liberals and National Party members, vote to leave this woman to the sole charge of the Northern Territory government, for an unknown number of years to come?
>
> . . . If anyone could regard that attitude as anything but weak, heartless, and thoroughly un-Australian, we feel sorry for them, and hope they have a happier Christmas than Mrs Chamberlain will have.

There were hurried consultations in an endeavour to arrive at some compromise which might ensure that justice was done, but still enable the Northern Territory government to save face. They proved fruitless. The Northern Territory cabinet remained adamant that there would be no inquiry. When John Bryson's book *Evil Angels* was published at the end of 1985, his detailed analysis of the evidence led at the trial and the few subsequent disclosures made available to the general public prompted the press, in an orgasm of self-expiation, to clamour for the case to be reopened. A journalist for *The Australian* said, in his review of the book, 'I defy any right-minded person to read this book and conclude beyond reasonable doubt that Lindy Chamberlain killed her child.'

'I don't care what Mr Bryson or anybody else says,' the Northern Territory Attorney-General replied.

The Martin Report was to be challenged by others. The Leader of the Northern Territory Opposition, Bob Collins, was dismayed at the manner in which some of the scientific criticism had been brushed aside. He also noted that part of the report referring to the cross-examination of a particular witness was in the first person as if written by the cross-examiner himself. Collins consulted the transcript. The cross-examiner had been Ian Barker QC. It appeared that some of the report had either been written by him or, more likely, by someone who had drawn upon his advice. To Collins' way of thinking, Barker was perfectly entitled to provide advice to the Northern Territory government or any other client who sought it, but the government should have realised that the substantial body of scientific evidence now available demanded an objective and impartial assessment from someone other than the most senior member of the team which had presented the case.

He contacted Dr Andrew Scott, the senior forensic biologist employed by the South Australian government. The government had repeatedly relied upon the fact that Professor Boettcher and Professor Nairn had little experience in the forensic area. This, it was said, virtually invalidated any criticisms they might make of Mrs Kuhl's procedure. It was a criticism that left large sections of the scientific community bewildered. The identification of blood depends upon the same principles whether the results are to be used in a hospital or a courtroom. Experience was important, but neither Crown nor defence scientists had ever had any experience testing old and denatured bloodstains for foetal haemoglobin in sufficient quantities to indicate that it had come from an infant.

Andrew Scott had been a witness for the Crown at the trial and it was to his laboratory that the Northern Territory police normally sent biological material for examination. The New South Wales Forensic Science Laboratory had been approached with a view to examining the Chamberlains' car only because Cooranbong was near Sydney. Scott was obviously concerned at the manner in which the criticisms made by Boettcher and Nairn had been brushed aside. Like Joy Kuhl, he was a forensic biologist, in fact the senior forensic biologist in South Australia. He had a doctorate and more than ten years' experience. His report revealed that he shared the concern of the two professors.

On 5 December 1985, another prisoner, Helena Mantz, wrote a letter concerning her contact with Lindy Chamberlain in prison. Miss Mantz described herself as 'a street kid, stealing in my younger days to stay alive'. She had been raised in a series of institutions, homes and gaol. When she had been sent to the Berrimah Penitentiary, she had decided to 'bash up' Mrs Chamberlain because she believed she had killed her baby. Despite her initial hostility, she said that she had 'grown to love and respect this woman, who has been sentenced to life imprisonment unjustly by the NT government.' She referred to Lindy's 'unique personality' and said that 'her stronger character attracts all the female prisoners who have failed in society and have weaker character themselves.' Miss Mantz said that her intended victim had become 'a guiding influence and my adviser to help me step into maturity.'

She also described the limited visits to the prison allowed to Michael Chamberlain and the children. 'The children stay close to their mother and hardly ever move away from her.' As the time begins to run out, 'they are irritable and crabby with one another, all wanting the most of their mother's attention . . . fighting over who sits on her lap or next to her. . . She should not be here in this place away from the children who love and need her and who she loves too.'

The letter had been seized by the gaol censors and returned to Miss Mantz by the Assistant Secretary of the Department of Correctional Services. By the time it was smuggled out of prison, it bore a postscript. 'The Minister and Secretary to the Minister both refused me permission to send it out. I don't think they want people to know the truth and want all to stay ignorant on this matter.'

The Northern Territory's response was predictable. The Acting Minister of Correctional Services said that the conduct of the prisoner would be investigated and any disciplinary action resulting from broken rules would be at the discretion of the Secretary of Correctional Services.

An application had been made for Lindy's release on licence. It, too, was refused. Lindy spent her third Christmas in prison.

22

Release

IN THE MIDST OF THIS GROWING POLITICAL STORM, fate was to play another card.

An English tourist, David James Brett, had come to Ayers Rock. He was a young man, still in his twenties, who had previously spent four years in Australia before returning to his home in Kent. He had become fascinated by the occult and had dabbled in mystic rituals. He mixed with others who shared his fascination and together they explored the so-called 'black arts', seeking not merely good fortune but fulfilment and a sense of purpose. They sought guidance in these matters from the spirit world but, when it came, his friends were more convinced than he was. It was his destiny, they said, to find purpose in his own suicide. That was enough for Brett. He packed up and went home to England.

He had returned to Australia in mid-1985. But the command from 'the other side' continued to haunt him. He had a premonition of his impending death and spoke of it as an event that would have significant consequences.

It is hot at Ayers Rock in January. The sun blazes down onto the rock like a blowtorch trained on an anvil by some celestial blacksmith. It would have been foolhardy to have attempted the climb during the full heat of the day and Brett decided to leave it until late in the afternoon.

Uluru can be scaled at only one point, a sloping spur of rock on the eastern end of the rock known to white men simply as 'The Climb'. To the Pitjantjatjara this place is *Itjraitjrai*. It was here in the Dreamtime that a ***kuniya***, or python woman, came to bury her eggs. The task complete, she travelled south to ***Alyurungu*** where she and her people made camp. They were there attacked by *Liru*, or poisonous snake warriors. *Alyurungu* lies on the south-western face of the rock about halfway between *Itjraitjrai* and *Mitakampantja*, the place where the arrow-shaped patch of lichen still reminds the Pitjantjatjara of the fate of the two lizard men who perished in the fire set by the enraged bellbird brothers. At *Alyurungu* may be seen the marks of this battle between the *Kuniya* and *Liru*. Pockmarks in the rock are said to be the scars left by the warriors' spears and the bodies of two slain *Liru* remain as the blackened marks left by the spasmodic flow of water that courses down a vertical cliff face.

David Brett probably knew little of the spirit creatures whose domain he was entering as he commenced his climb though, with his interest in mysticism, it is doubtful that he was completely indifferent to the spiritual significance of this place. It was nearly sundown and he had taken some additional clothing in case it became cold. Several people saw him climb. He followed the chain strung from a series of short pipes embedded in the surface of the rock as a guide to tourists. Above that, one reaches a point which seems to be the apex when one is standing on the ground looking up hopefully. But at that point there is still as far to go again. Brett was a fit man, but he rested a while there before swinging his knapsack over his shoulder and resuming the climb. Some tourists on the way down saw him as he made his way higher.

Ayers Rock does not rise to a sharp peak. The top is a vast undulating plateau of stone. Climbers follow white marks painted on the stone over protuberances, down into fissures, and then up the other side until they reach a point near the centre marked by a cairn to indicate that the summit has been attained. At the shoulder of the rock the route swings from the south-east to the north-east, the path having obviously been chosen with care to keep tourists away from the precipitous sides which plunge two or three hundred metres to the ground below.

Precisely what happened may never be known. Perhaps the heat proved too much. The Rock operates like a gigantic thermal bank and the western side, in particular, remains hot long after the sun has ceased to burn the necks of the climbers. Life in Kent would have offered little preparation for such an extreme climatic condition. Perhaps he simply became distracted by the grandeur of the place and lost his way. Those of a more mystical bent, be they Pitjantjatjara or whites of the kind who had foretold Brett's early death, would no doubt have assumed a more arcane explanation. Whatever the cause, he was seen moving uncertainly near the shoulder of the cliff by a well-educated young Pitjantjatjara couple, with the delightfully anglicised names of Tanya and Ewen Edwards. They immediately went for the rangers but, when they returned, they could see no trace of him. They assumed that he had made his way back down.

The body was found on 2 February 1986, seven days after he was last seen on the shoulder of the rock. He had fallen into an area between the side of the rock and the small hill of dirt and rock beside it. This area was immediately adjacent to the little gully where Azaria Chamberlain's jumpsuit, singlet and nappy had been found. The two massive patches of lichen merge into an arrow only when they are viewed from the south looking obliquely along the south-western face of the rock. From that vantage point, the gully and the area beside it are almost aligned. Though it had taken a week to find, the body, like the clothing which had been found five-and-a-half years earlier, had been pinpointed by this huge 'arrow' that was already ancient when Captain James Cook first set foot in Botany Bay.

The body was badly decomposed and several parts including the right arm were missing, apparently chewed off by dingoes or goannas. Sergeant Van Heythuysen roped off the area and called for assistance to search for the missing parts of Mr Brett's body. He hoped to at least find some of the larger bones. One of the volunteers was John Beasy, who had been the mechanic at Ayers Rock at the time Azaria Chamberlain disappeared. It was at a point which Van Heythuysen was later to estimate as being seventy to a hundred metres from the body where he found the matinee jacket. It was dirty and half-buried in an area of red sand within a rough semicircle of vegetation. The area in which it was located was later excavated and a small white button was found. It was one-hundred-and-fifty-three metres from the position in which the other clothing had been found in 1980.

At the trial the Crown had invited the jury to be sceptical about the existence of this matinee jacket, but Lindy had given the police a good description right down to the fact that it was a 'Marquis' size 000 with a lemon-scalloped edging. On 5 February 1986, she was driven from the Berrimah Penitentiary to Police Headquarters in Darwin. She broke down when she was shown the jacket, but she had no hesitation in identifying it as Azaria's. The lady who had given her the jumpsuit had knitted a bonnet and booties to match and those garments were still in Lindy's possession. Furthermore, a comparison of the jacket with the jumpsuit showed a correspondence of bloodstains on the two garments. The Crown did not dispute that it was the right jacket.

Following the discovery of the jacket, the Northern Territory Police Commissioner, Peter McAuley, recommended the establishment of a judicial inquiry. It seems that this recommendation did not meet with immediate acclaim and, according to a Darwin newspaper, until 9.00 a.m. on Friday 7 February, 'government officials were confident that no inquiry would be ordered and that Mrs Chamberlain would remain in gaol'. Shortly thereafter the Chief Minister, Ian Tuxworth, who had been visiting a school, apparently received a phone call and made an immediate return to his office. He met with the Commissioner of Police and then attended a special meeting of Cabinet at about 10.00 a.m. The Attorney-General, Marshall Perron, later held a press conference, to announce:

> I am here to advise that the Territory government has decided to institute an inquiry into the Chamberlain case.
>
> The decision follows advice received from the Solicitor-General and Police Commissioner on what they regard as significant new evidence.
>
> They have advised me that the discovery of a baby's matinee jacket near the base of Ayers Rock and its subsequent identification by Mrs Chamberlain may have a bearing on the case.
>
> The government proposes to take whatever steps are necessary, including the possible introduction of legislation at the forthcoming sittings of the Legislative Assembly, to set up the inquiry.
>
> At this stage terms of reference have not been drawn up nor has the composition of the inquiry body been decided.

> I can also advise that a short time ago His Honour, the Administrator, accepted the advice of the Executive Council that the balance of Mrs Chamberlain's life sentence be remitted and that she be released from Darwin prison.
>
> I expect that will take place this afternoon.
>
> The decision to so recommend to His Honour was made in the light of Mrs Chamberlain's need for unrestricted access to legal advisers to prepare for the inquiry.
>
> Although Mrs Chamberlain's remission is subject to the usual condition of good behaviour, it is not my intention that she be taken back into custody — regardless of the outcome of the inquiry.

The next day the *Adelaide Advertiser* carried the headline 'Leaked Letter Prompted Jail Release'. It seems that the *Northern Territory News* had obtained copies of the reports by Dr Andrew Scott and Professor Orjan Ouchterlony and had decided to contact Behringwerke in West Germany. They were informed that Dr Baudner and Dr Storiko had written to the Department of Law on 20 January 1986 expressing concern at what they perceived as a misunderstanding of their position. It seemed astonishing that this document had not been disclosed.

The *Northern Territory News* is normally supportive of the government, but this was a story which demanded to be printed. They set it up as the lead story.

Bob Collins had provided the reports not only to the *Northern Territory News*, but to a number of other journalists on the basis that these reports would remain confidential, pending a press conference at 2.00 p.m. The Attorney-General's press secretary was apparently warned of what was to occur. The story was subsequently printed, but not that day. About fifteen minutes before the presses were due to start rolling, the acting editor received a telephone call from the Chief Minister.

'I know what's on the presses, but I've got a better story for you,' he announced. 'We're letting her out.'

The press conference at which the historic announcement was made followed at 2.00 p.m., the time which Bob Collins had nominated for his conference to publicly reveal the reports. His conference proceeded, but to an empty room.

By the time the story was run the next day its impact had been sapped by the drama of Lindy's sudden release. If the earlier recommendations had contained 'a number of inaccuracies and errors', as Dr Andrew Scott had suggested, who cared? She was out now. The real interest lay in her impending reunion with her family and in the inquiry to come.

The Chief Minister, Ian Tuxworth, later explained Lindy's sudden release in the following way:

> When the garment was found in the area where the English tourist fell to his death we considered this to be new evidence. It was obvious that an inquiry must be held and it would be proper to release Mrs Chamberlain on bail or parole or whatever until the outcome of the inquiry was known.
>
> We would not want her to languish in prison while an inquiry was in progress. I think any government would have done this. Because she has served more than three years' imprisonment already we had to also look at possibilities of the future. The inquiry outcome might not be known for anything up to a year. So, we decided that she had served enough imprisonment regardless of the possibiltiy of being confirmed as guilty. For this reason it [was] decided to remit the balance of her life sentence.

He protested at the scepticism of the press.

'It is very simple. It has been explained several times to the press when they ask, but no-one seems to be able to grasp the plain facts.'

Despite this reassurance, a number of questions remain unanswered. What happened between 9.00 a.m. and 12.00 noon which led the Cabinet to make this decision, notwithstanding the confidence of senior government officials that she would remain in gaol? If the decision was nothing more than a responsible cabinet acting upon the advice of the Police Commissioner, then why was it taken in such obvious haste?

Furthermore, why was the recommendation obtained from the Police Commissioner at all when the Solicitor-General, Brian Martin, had provided a lengthy analysis of the fresh evidence only shortly before? Why was it accepted when McAuley himself conceded that he was 'not aware of any facts connected to this piece of evidence which affects the veracity of the prosecution's original case'? Was it really just coincidence that this decision was taken only fifteen minutes before the presses started to roll on a story that would have accused the Northern Territory government of withholding vital evidence?

The editorial in the *Sunday Territorian* two days later described the decision as a 'sudden and unexpected government cave-in'. It also mentioned that a letter advising Bob Collins of the decision contained 'several typographical errors' and was 'obviously drafted in a hurry'. Why? Was the decision dictated by the demands of justice or political expediency? Would Lindy Chamberlain still remain a prisoner had it not been for the impending storm of criticism?

PART V

THE COMMISSION OF INQUIRY

23

'The fight has only just begun'

SHORTLY AFTER 2.00 P.M. on 7 February 1986, Lindy Chamberlain was informed that she was to be released. By then the *Northern Territory News* had known of her impending release for two hours, a fact which may have said something about the Cabinet's sense of priorities.

But none of that would have mattered to Lindy even had she known. What mattered was her release. She would be reunited with her family. Once more, Aidan, now twelve, Reagan, now nearly ten, and Kahlia, a bubbly and adventurous three-year-old, would have a mother. She and Michael could pick up the pieces of their marriage and start again.

Yet, perhaps even more important was the assurance that God had not forgotten her. The last five years had involved an enormous struggle – what the old pilgrims would have called a 'travail of spirit'. No person made of flesh and blood could fail to have cried out in anguish, 'My God, why did you let this happen to me?' As Jenny Ransom and others knew, Lindy Chamberlain was a woman of great faith. She had endured not only the loss of her daughter, but a chronicle of suspicion, hate, imprisonment and a succession of bitter disappointments that would have broken any normal person. She had frequently been thrust into pits of despair, but she had climbed shakily to her feet again and again.

Sometimes when a person has lost everything — home, family, friends, reputation, aspirations for the future and even physical freedom — he finds within himself some inner resource, some wellspring of meaning which provides a reason for living and for maintaining the struggle. This inner resource was to be found in

Lindy's conviction that God loved her. In time, she believed, the truth would come out. No matter what else they did to her, they could not take away her faith. She had come to that strange mixture of resignation and defiance in which Job had cried, 'Though he slay me yet will I trust in him!' Now that faith had been vindicated.

It was nearly midnight on Sunday 9 February when Lindy Chamberlain arrived back at Cooranbong. It was an emotional homecoming. The drive into Avondale College is fully one-and-a-half kilometres long and the fence and trees had been draped with a profusion of yellow ribbons. It seems that the Adventist community had taken the old song to heart for, as the 'Azaria Newsletter' was to explain, it had been 'three long years'.

On the first Sabbath of Lindy's freedom, the Chamberlains went to the Avondale Church to worship God and to give thanks. More than a thousand people had gathered to worship with them and to welcome Lindy back. Amidst exuberant applause, Lindy and Michael came to the rostrum whilst Lindy spoke. 'Words are totally inadequate to express our gratitude for your love, care and prayers. It reaches out like a blanket to surround us. It is totally tangible.' She struggled for a moment to retain her composure before continuing. 'You may think it is all over but, believe me, the fight has only just begun. It is not just for our freedom; it is for you as well. We do not ever wish to see what has happened repeated in Australia again. God bless you all.'

The Adventists are not known for demonstrative displays in church. As St Paul commanded, everything must be done 'in decency and order'. Yet as they left the rostrum, there was a standing ovation. St Paul might have raised one eyebrow, but then he, too, had spent a long time in prison.

Lindy's release prompted further political controversy which went far beyond the borders of the Northern Territory.

The New South Wales Premier, Neville Wran, expressed personal delight over the decision to release her from prison. It was reported that he had supported the call for a Federal inquiry when it had been raised by Senator Colin Mason. He said that he supported any inquiry that could get to the truth and commented on the extent of Mrs Chamberlain's suffering.

The Premier of Queensland, Sir Joh Bjelke Petersen, commented that he was sure the Northern Territory government 'did the right thing' when they released Lindy Chamberlain. He told the Brisbane *Sunday Mail* that he had always believed that a dingo might have taken Azaria. 'To me it was quite simple and easy to believe . . . the dog theory, and perhaps somebody was involved later on. Having been out there, I've told many people I've seen dingoes there. They are out there scavenging food all the time because they get it off the tourists. It was always easy for me to believe it could happen.'

On 11 February 1986, Mr Peter Duncan MHR rose to his feet in the Commonwealth House of Representatives to refer to an editorial in the *Sydney Morning Herald* and to ask: 'In light of the widespread and justified concern over the Northern Territory government's capacity to conduct an impartial inquiry, will the Attorney-General offer to make available a Federal judge to conduct the inquiry?'

Lionel Bowen, the Deputy Prime Minister and Attorney-General replied:

> I did see the editorial in the *Sydney Morning Herald*. I must say that it was more than fair comment as to the now very widespread concern across Australia as to what might have happened in the administration of justice in the Northern Territory, particularly in respect of this trial. It is well known that a family tragedy has occurred.
>
> . . . As I understand the present position and, rather surprisingly, the Attorney-General in the Northern Territory has announced, as a result of the finding of what is deemed to be a further piece of evidence, that the accused mother has been released and irrespective of the outcome of the inquiry which he proposes to institute, no further action will be taken in respect of her alleged involvement in that tragedy.
>
> I think that is worth commenting now — the *Sydney Morning Herald* adverted to it — that there appears to be very strong evidence that the forensic tests that were carried out were not in accordance with established procedures and that was known to the prosecution. There is other evidence from forensic experts in Australia that the evidence given was not in accordance with what

> one would call scientific capacity or understanding of what should have happened in terms of undertaking those tests. That was not adverted to.
>
> Further, when the inquiry was instituted, particularly involving the appropriate agents that were to be used in pursuing those tests — they came from Germany — the responsible scientist there was not consulted as to whether the tests carried out would be accepted as being proper evidence to justify what was led by the prosecution in endeavouring to obtain a prosecution.
>
> Finally, there seems to be the further evidence that, when there was a reassessment of that inquiry by the Solicitor-General in the Northern Territory, it was not a fair assessment because those matters were not brought into consideration. . .
>
> The allegation is that there has been an attempt to cover up the actions of the administrators of justice in the Northern Territory actions in endeavouring to obtain a conviction rather than looking at the fairness of the evidence that should have been presented to the jury. It is a matter of record that there is some comment from one member of the jury that the jury now feels that it might have had at least an opportunity to acquit the accused rather than otherwise. These are not new accusations; they are known to the government of the Northern Territory. . .
>
> One of the matters of concern is why that has not been acted on before in view of the fact that it was known that there was evidence that obviously had not been led. It will obviously come out in the course of an inquiry. . .
>
> The obligation now is to guarantee that the inquiry be far-reaching, wide-ranging and impartial. The only way to achieve that would be by having an independent inquiry with somebody appointed from outside the Northern Territory with the capacity to examine all the evidence that is now available.

These remarks were the more striking because Bowen had been adamant that the Commonwealth should not take the initiative to institute an inquiry. Since the enactment of the Northern Territory (Self Government) Act in 1978, such matters were the responsibility of the Northern Territory government alone.

His remarks provoked an angry response.

Marshall Perron, the Northern Territory Attorney-General, immediately issued a press release challenging Mr Bowen to repeat his remarks outside parliament. He claimed that the Commonwealth Attorney-General had attacked 'the integrity of eight judges, three Northern Territory Attorneys-General, the Territorial police force, the Territory Department of Law and crown witnesses in the Chamberlain case'.

Former Northern Territory Chief Minister, Paul Everingham, also challenged him to repeat his comments outside the parliament and to relate them to his role as Northern Territory Attorney-General during the Chamberlain trial. Like Marshall Perron, it seemed that he had in mind a potential defamation action. It would have been a fascinating exercise: a former Northern Territory Attorney-General suing the present Commonwealth Attorney-General for criticising the manner in which he had discharged his role and administered justice. The statements 'seem to adopt all manner of wild allegations against the fairness of the administration of justice in the Northern Territory', he complained. 'Let me say unequivocally that the Chamberlains were not in any way discriminated against by Northern Territory law authorities.'

Intriguingly enough, his statement included the comment that 'it is difficult to see the jacket being of any help to Mrs Chamberlain'. Yet that statement merely served to highlight the apparent incongruity of his successor's decision. If the discovery of the jacket appeared to be so inconsequential, then why have an inquiry and why release her 'to prepare for the inquiry'?

Everingham himself added, 'But justice must not only be done, it must be seen to be done.' It was, of course, an unarguable truism but it seemed to offer little explanation for the decision. After all, why should the need for justice to be seen to be done demand a lengthy judicial inquiry into an inconsequential piece of evidence?

On 19 March 1986, six weeks after Mr Perron had so scathingly denounced Mr Bowen's comments, the Northern Territory parliament was asked to pass a bill providing for a judge of the Federal Court of Australia to be appointed to inquire into doubts that had arisen into the convictions of Michael and Lindy Chamberlain. In introducing the bill, Mr Perron told the parliament that there was no existing legislation that would provide the basis for such a commission of inquiry and that it was necessary to pass a special statute dealing exclusively with the Chamberlain matter.

In late February, Ray Martin, a journalist for the television program *Sixty Minutes*, spent five days at Cooranbong interviewing the Chamberlains. His film crew also filmed the emotional meeting between Lindy and the juror who had come to Cooranbong to express her regret. The interviews were screened on 2 and 9 March 1986. Ray Martin pointed out that some people had formed adverse impressions of Lindy Chamberlain and asked if she could offer any explanation.

'If I cried I was said to be putting on an act, if I smiled I was heartless,' Lindy replied. 'I knew there were people ready to jump on everything I said and did. I cried in private behind closed doors. I didn't see any reason why they should see the effect on me. I wouldn't give them that pleasure. I am definitely not going to lie down and die for something I didn't do. I have to clear my name and that of my family. . . I have been called a liar. I don't like it because I know I am not.' Later she added, 'Would you lie and say you had done something that you had never done when you could tell the truth? It's made me very angry to think that I have been told over and over again that if you'd lied and said you'd done it you'd be out of gaol, but if you tell the truth you stay in gaol. You shouldn't have to lie to get justice.'

Several times during the interviews, Lindy broke down and wept. She denied having murdered her daughter Azaria and said, 'I loved that little girl.'

When asked about the attitude of the Northern Territory, she commented, 'It was quite obvious by the time we got to the second inquiry. It didn't really matter much what we said, the Northern Territory was not prepared to listen. They said to me outright: "If we don't get you this time, we'll get you next time. We'll have this inquest and another one until you get charged because we are going to get you." '

She also revealed why she had offered Michael a divorce when she first went to gaol. She had reached the nadir of despair. There was the possibility of an appeal and, from time to time, she would use it to build up some fragile edifice of hope. But her lawyers, who had been so confident about the trial, were now guarded in their prognoses. They hadn't told her that the position was hopeless, but they had displayed little optimism. There came a point at which one had to face up to the harsh realities of life. She had been sentenced to life imprisonment.

It was a sentence of indeterminate length and there had been various estimates of the time she was likely to spend behind bars. Some had suggested that it could be twenty years. It might be a long time before she would be able to be a wife to Michael. It takes time to adjust to living in a nightmare and there were many things she would have to work through. But one thing was clear: she loved Michael. There was no need for his life to be ruined, for him to be left shackled to a woman who was not free to be his wife. It was better to give him the chance to make a new life with someone else. The children, too, needed a mother. She wept as she told him, but she meant it.

Michael would not have it. They were in this together. He would not abandon her.

The Northern Territory government promptly nominated Trevor Morling as the Federal Court judge to conduct the inquiry. The Chamberlains' legal advisers had not been consulted about the choice of Mr Justice Morling, but were well content. He was renowned throughout the Australian legal community as a judge of unquestioned ability and fairness. The Chairman of the Chamberlain Innocence Committee, Sir Reginald Sholl, himself a former judge of great distinction, welcomed the appointment of Mr Justice Morling whom he described as 'an eminent, experienced and distinguished judge'.

Ultimately, Mr Justice Morling received two commissions. He was appointed by the Attorney-General of the Northern Territory pursuant to the Commission of Inquiry (Chamberlain Convictions) Act 1986 and also received from the Governor General of the Commonwealth of Australia Letters Patent pursuant to the Royal Commissions Act 1902. He formally opened the Commission of Inquiry on 8 May 1986 for the purpose of receiving applications for leave to appear and resolving various procedural aspects.

Chester Porter QC and his junior, Bill Caldwell, had been appointed to assist Mr Justice Morling. Porter was a shrewd man with an aquiline face and receding curly grey hair. He was renowned for beguiling witnesses into making damaging admissions by his friendly smile and relaxed manner. It was this habit which led a Sydney newspaper to dub him 'the smiling funnel-web'.

The Crown was to be represented by Ian Barker QC and by Michael Adams, a barrister of generous proportions. Later a third barrister, Elizabeth Fullerton, was to be added to the team.

The Chamberlains were to be represented by John Winneke QC and a barrister with the improbable name of Brind Zichy-Woinarski. Winneke was to be described by one disaffected journalist as 'the rumpled silk from Melbourne', but he was tall and imposing and was to bring to the inquiry a prodigious capacity for absorbing the intricacies of alien disciplines. A third barrister was added to the team before the inquiry commenced in earnest. It had been intended to have Michael Chamberlain separately represented so that the Chamberlains would have the opportunity for 'two bites at every cherry'. It would have been a good tactical manoeuvre but there was concern that the press might misconstrue such a step and assume that separate representation indicated a rift between the Chamberlains. There was no rift, but the Chamberlains had been constant victims of equally unfounded speculation. The plan was abandoned and the forces consolidated.

A barrister named Bennett sought leave to appear for a group of seven people who had been publicly accused of involvement in a conspiracy to cover up the taking of Azaria by a dingo named 'Ding'. That leave was later extended to Marcus Einfeld QC. It was subsequently revoked when it became apparent that none of the other parties to the proceedings were alleging any misconduct on the part of the seven people concerned.

The Pitjantjatjara trackers were separately represented by an Alice Springs lawyer, Jon Tippett, who was married to an Aborigine and had a better understanding of the difficulties his clients might encounter in giving evidence than many of his colleagues.

Chester Porter outlined the proposed procedure. He would call all of the witnesses, leaving counsel for the other parties to cross-examine as they saw fit. Lawyers around the world have often debated the merits of the two main systems of procedure.

Countries such as France and Italy adopt an inquisitorial procedure whereby a magistrate or judge makes his own inquiries to inform himself of all of the relevant facts. Australia and other countries which have inherited the English system follow an adversarial procedure. Lawyers for each side present the evidence which favours their case, leaving the judge or magistrate to assess the evidence which they choose to present and to make a decision. The Commission of Inquiry would be a synthesis of the two.

Porter proposed that the matinee jacket be examined by the Victorian Forensic Science Laboratory. As he pointed out, its personnel had not previously been involved in any matter concerning the Chamberlain case and, if outside experts were required, they could be selected by the officers of that laboratory. The Crown suggested that the testing should be carried out by scientists selected by the Crown, but conceded that defence experts might be present during the course of any testing. Winneke submitted that Porter's proposal was to be preferred. 'Rightly or wrongly, Your Honour, perceptions have arisen about the independence of various persons, including those whom Mr Barker now asserts are best qualified to carry out these tests.'

The judge adopted Porter's suggestion and adjourned the proceedings until 5 June. The long-awaited inquiry had begun. It was to last until March the next year and to cost in excess of $6,000,000. Some of its revelations were to prove profoundly disturbing.

24

The inquiry opens

THE INQUIRY COMMENCED IN EARNEST on 5 June 1986. It began with an opening address by Chester Porter, an address that was to last all day and well into the next. He referred to the convictions of Alice Lynne Chamberlain and Michael Leigh Chamberlain and to the nature of the charges against them.

'Those convictions drew considerable comment, not merely because the nature of the case was sensational, but because the sudden translation of a mother who had lost her child to a dingo into a murderess without a motive obviously raised considerable concern amongst interested people studying the case.'

Porter mentioned that the evidence appeared to fall into three categories: firstly, the primary evidence, that is the evidence of people who were there at the camping area on the night in question; secondly, the accounts of the Chamberlains; and thirdly, the scientific evidence.

Porter announced:

> I am here to assist Your Honour in inquiring into both aspects of the case, guilt or innocence. We have investigated so far as we could, and we have gone through the very thorough police work done in making obvious and necessary inquiries in Mount Isa with regard to the birth of the child and those who knew them and so forth. No possible motive has turned up for Mrs Chamberlain to kill her baby. . .
>
> The position therefore as at the time she went to Ayers Rock was that she was an apparently loving mother, happy with her child, and no motive to kill it. . .
>
> Both of the Chamberlains were persons of excellent

> character. Michael Chamberlain, I think as everyone knows, was then a pastor of the Seventh Day Adventist Church. I think this should be said, although it must be obvious to most people that there is absolutely nothing in the doctrine of the Seventh Day Adventist Church which would in any way suggest the killing of young children. The doctrines of that church are very similar to the evangelical doctrines of many Protestant churches, and they involve a belief in life-after-death. The doctrines involve various matters that might give comfort to people who lose a relative, and that may become relevant.

He referred to the unusual boldness of the dingoes at Ayers Rock and to the spate of attacks on children. He foreshadowed calling a number of experts to give evidence about dingo behaviour and commented that there was '. . . no real conflict, I think, that a dingo in the circumstances at Ayers Rock could, quite possibly, have taken a baby. There is a great deal of controversy as to how it might have gone about it. I have been quite amazed by the conflict of evidence between dingo experts as to just how pure-bred dingoes are supposed to behave.

'. . .The experts all qualify their views by saying, of course, that a hybrid, that is a dingo with a little of the domestic dog in it, might behave quite differently again. Let us make this perfectly clear, that no-one really knows whether the dingoes who were undoubtedly present around the time that Azaria Chamberlain disappeared were hybrids or pure-bred dingoes. It's just simply not known.'

Porter referred to a number of people who had seen Mrs Chamberlain with the baby and concluded that 'the evidence of the witnesses who saw Mrs Chamberlain that day with her baby certainly is inconsistent with any intention then in her mind of killing the child. Rather they give the impression of an affectionate mother.'

He continued to go through the evidence, pointing out the various issues that would have to be resolved. The judge interrupted his account to inquire whether there was any evidence that Mrs Chamberlain was left alone with her 'two surviving children' to the knowledge of Mr Chamberlain after the baby had been taken. Porter undertook to deal with the matter in the evidence and the judge commented that 'it might be thought unlikely that Mr Chamberlain would leave his wife alone with the surviving children if he had been told that she had murdered the youngest'.

Later Mr Justice Morling interrupted Porter again to inquire whether there was any evidence as to whether she had received medical or psychiatric care upon her return to Mount Isa. The implication was obvious. It was difficult enough to imagine a man assimilating the information that his wife had just murdered his child and deciding to help her cover up the killing, all without 'giving the game away'. It was even more difficult to imagine him trusting her alone with the other children and doing so without any attempt to ensure that she received adequate psychiatric treatment.

Porter outlined the nature of the scientific disputes and then referred to the Crown's allegation that there were inconsistencies in her various statements which indicated that she had lied. He pointed out that there were 'two extreme positions and there is no intermediate ground. Either this lady when she gave all these statements was a murderess, or she was a mother who had suffered frightfully and was being accused of murder.' He went on:

> If one assumes the latter, to test it — if she was in fact innocent and she was accused of murder — one might expect that some of what she might say would be distorted: memory would be distorted in the emotional turmoil caused by the whole concern. In fact, if perchance under those circumstances she conscientiously lied, it would not be indicative of guilt. If someone is accused of robbing a bank and that someone was unfortunate enough to be walking down the street at that time, the fact that he says he was somewhere else does not necessarily mean he was guilty. He may be scared to admit to the incriminating matters.

John Winneke QC also made a short address:

> We venture to suggest to Your Honour that their trial was unique in this regard in the history of Australian criminal law in that it fuelled rumour, speculation and innuendo. Very little of that was favourable to the Chamberlains. Rumour, as Your Honour will be told, had them as religious fanatics, sorcerers, callous and cunning

liars, and notwithstanding the well-motivated intentions of the first coroner in seeking to quell those rumours by announcing his findings on national television, Your Honour will be invited to conclude that the probabilities are that it had the opposite effect. It was within the currency of public knowledge before this trial that Azaria, the name Azaria, was a synonym for 'sacrifice in the wilderness', that Azaria was a brain-damaged child, that Azaria had indeed been killed well before 8.00 on the night of 17 August, that the Chamberlains were weird religious fanatics with predilections towards sorcery, that they kept a family Bible in their home opened at a page heavily underlined in red where a biblical character had driven a stake through his child's head, and many more rumours had circulated about the Chamberlains at the time when they came to trial in Darwin.

Your Honour, our law prides itself on being able to bring people to trial in circumstances of fairness and before a jury free from preconceptions, but we will be submitting that the equipment the law has to ensure a fair trial did not operate in the case of the Chamberlains and that it was impossible, no matter how much care had been taken, to be satisfied that this trial took place in a climate free from preconception.

As if to confirm the validity of this comment, a member of the public approached Porter with a 'Darwin's answer' T-shirt she had bought in the Darwin Mall that morning. Their sale was not likely to influence Mr Justice Morling, but there was some concern that public opinion might be further inflamed. The judge described them as being 'in the worst possible taste' and publicly asked those responsible to stop selling them. His comments were ignored and the sales continued.

A fresh spate of rumours broke out concerning the death of David Brett. It was suggested that he had the word 'Azaria' tattooed on his buttocks, that he had fled to Ayers Rock to escape from a group of Seventh Day Adventists and even that he had told his mother that they wanted him to be a sacrifice in the wilderness so that through his death Lindy might be released. It was all nonsense and Porter did not ventilate these rumours in open court.

Porter then began the slow process of calling the witnesses to the so-called primary facts. He ran through the Aboriginal trackers, the rangers, the police and the other people who had been in the camping area on the night in question.

Greg Lowe now revealed that he had seen Lindy Chamberlain come back out of the tent and put her arm around Aidan's shoulder. He had watched her go to the car and open the boot. She had carried no baby.

He had said nothing about this for almost three years and was rigorously cross-examined by Ian Barker. He said, however, that he was certain of his recollection. It had not been until after the first inquest that he had realised the significance of his evidence. Until then, he had understood the Crown case to allege that the baby had been killed several hours earlier. When he did realise its significance more than a year after the event, he kept quiet about it because he was afraid that he would be accused of lying. In fact, he went to the lengths of obtaining legal advice from the Legal Aid office in Tasmania. He was concerned that the Crown might persuade the jury that he had made it all up and that it might weaken the force of the balance of his evidence. Worse, he feared that suspicion might also taint his wife's evidence. Sally's evidence of hearing the baby cry was absolutely crucial. It meant that Lindy Chamberlain could not be guilty. He had fully expected that evidence to be accepted and Lindy to be acquitted. All in all, he had concluded that it was not worth jeopardising her credibility.

The Commission sat in Darwin throughout most of June and August, hearing the evidence of more than seventy witnesses. It was striking that those who had been present on the night in question had entertained no doubt about the authenticity of the Chamberlains' explanation. The rangers had been convinced. It was the sort of attack they had feared might happen and the tracks seemed quite conclusive. Despite his evidence of some inconsistency in the two accounts she had given him, Frank Morris gave evidence that he had accepted Lindy's explanation at face value. Inspector Gilroy had also accepted the truth of the Chamberlains' explanation.

The only discordant note had been struck by the impression De Luca, Gilroy and, later, Buzzard had formed of Michael's lack of emotion. Whilst Gilroy had thought it odd, he apparently attached little significance to it. He later advised police headquarters in

Alice Springs that there appeared to be little doubt that the baby had been taken by a dingo. In fact, it was a strange criticism to make. The Crown had never accused Michael of having any involvement in the actual murder of his child. Indeed, it was part of the Crown case that he remained unsuspecting until, at some stage during the evening, Lindy told him that the baby had not been taken by a dingo but that she had murdered it. It is difficult to see how a perceived lack of emotion could have supported such an allegation. Michael was obviously distraught when the baby disappeared. One could scarcely imagine him regaining his composure had his wife smiled reassuringly and said, 'Don't worry, dear. A dingo didn't take the baby. I just cut her throat and stuffed the corpse in the camera bag.'

In any event, there was an abundance of evidence from people such as the Lowes, the Wests, the Whittakers, Bobbie Downs, who was now Mrs Elston, and John McCombe who had noted the Chamberlains' distress during the course of the evening. The gist of their evidence was that Michael was clearly upset but 'trying to put on a brave face'. McCombe said that Michael was obviously doing his best in 'a vain attempt to conceal his grief', but that later in the evening he 'broke down and sobbed'.

No less than six people gave evidence that there was no sign of blood on Mrs Chamberlain's hands or clothing.

The Ptijantjatjara people have no need to leave notes when they call and find a friend not home. The footprints in the sand will tell the friend not only who has called, but the approximate time of his visit, which members of his family accompanied him and even the identity of any neighbouring dogs which may have decided to come along for the trip. Some of their better trackers are among the finest in the world.

Yet there are difficulties in interviewing them which may not be apparent to a stranger. It is not merely a matter of language, though few of them speak English fluently and some of them have no understanding of it at all. The problem is one of *concept*. The Ptijantjatjara do not speak, for example, of alternatives. It is confusing to ask a question such as: 'Did you go to the store or stay home?' A Ptijantjatjara may understand the words, but they will convey to him two separate and unrelated questions. He is likely to answer 'yes', or simply shake his head. If he shakes his head the questioner is likely to assume that he did neither of those things and ask further questions to try to find out what he did do but, in fact, he may be simply signalling his confusion.

In common with other Northern Territory tribal Aborigines, the Ptijantjatjara are also an extremely courteous people. If a question is asked with sufficient intensity, they will feel an obligation to provide the answer the questioner seems to want. A series of forceful and leading questions may produce smiling assent, but the witness may have done no more than to placate a 'white fella' who seemed to be getting upset. For this reason, the Supreme Court of the Northern Territory has laid down a series of guidelines for police to follow when interrogating Aboriginal people. They include such innovations as the need to have a trusted friend present. Failure to comply with the 'Anunga rules' as they have become known will usually mean that the court rejects any evidence of the conversation.

It was, perhaps, these kinds of linguistic and conceptual difficulties which had led to reports of Nipper Winmatti having made statements at variance with the evidence he was later to give. For example, in his book *Azaria, The Trial of the Century,* Steve Brien stated that 'Nipper Winmatti told me that he doubted the whole dingo story. . .'

In June 1986, Nipper gave evidence that 'the dingo came from the north and he went around the tent to the front entrance, and from there he backtracked around the tent'. When asked by Mr Adams, for the Crown, 'How far from that canvas floor outside the tent did you see the tracks that were in front of it?' he replied, 'Tracks walk in' and added, 'I seen the tracks with my own eyes. They had gone in and come out.' Asked by Porter, 'Are you able to say what it was that the dingo was carrying?' he replied, 'It was the baby the dingo was carrying and as he was trying to climb up the rise of the sandhill it was really hard for him to climb up.' At the top of the hill he had seen marks where the dingo had put the baby down. 'The marks look like there was hip bones like gone deeper into the ground and the heel of the foot.'

The Commission had gone to great pains to ensure that the Aboriginal witnesses were able to give evidence in their own words free from any pressure to meet the expectations of others. Aboriginal interpreters were available to assist them and Jon Tippett was on hand to object to any questions which may have proved confusing and to confer with his clients and offer any necessary clarification.

Nipper had been called as a witness at the first inquest, though not at the trial, and had then given evidence of his conviction that a dingo had taken the baby. He had maintained that position in discussions with Derek Roff, Arthur Hawken and other locals whom he trusted.

His evidence concerning the tracks received substantial corroboration from Nui Minyintiri and Barbara Tjikadu as well as the white men Derek Roff, Murray Haby, Michael Gilroy and John Lincoln.

There was also significant evidence given concerning the timing of the Chamberlains' emotional reactions. The Lowes were adamant that when Mrs Chamberlain returned from the tent with Aidan, both were composed and apparently relaxed. Lindy even had the presence of mind to pick up the conversation with Sally where she had left off. When the alarm was given, Lindy was obviously devastated and Aidan became a distraught little boy who was obviously convinced that the dingo 'had bubby in its tummy'.

Those who arrived at the tent found the blankets disarrayed and spilling from the baby's bassinette towards the entrance and the centre pole of the tent askew. Some also saw blood on various items.

Barker's suggestion that the 'dingo story' had 'almost nothing to support it' was beginning to sound hollow.

25

It's in the blood

BLOOD HAS LONG CAPTURED the imagination of man. From William Shakespeare's *Macbeth* to Rafael Sabatini's *Captain Blood* novels, our literature has abounded with stories of blood. It has been the hallmark of the sinister, the macabre and the violent. Countless swashbuckling tales of romance and adventure would have been poor insipid things had 'Neptune's great ocean' washed it from their pages.

The first scientific witness was Tony Raymond, a senior and experienced forensic biologist attached to the Victorian Forensic Science Laboratories. He had been responsible for much of the independent testing carried out on behalf of the Commission. He presented a paper entitled 'What is blood?' and explained it with the aid of an overhead projector. It was a scholarly exposition lamentably lacking in anything remotely swashbuckling. Within each drop of blood lay, it seemed, a world of unbelievable complexity. Had its intricacies been known to Shakespeare, we might have been treated to the spectacle of Lady Macbeth becoming demented at the thought of phosphoglucomutase and a hundred other polysyllabic proteins clinging tenaciously to her fingers. Yet it was from these myriads of tiny molecules that the Crown was able to construct a case every bit as damning to Lindy Chamberlain as the blood of the slain Duncan.

Four of the five judges of the High Court of Australia had held that it would not have been open to the jury to have been satisfied beyond reasonable doubt that Mrs Kuhl's tests had demonstrated that the car contained blood from an infant. Consequently, evidence to that effect should not have been used as the basis for any inference of guilt. As Mr Justice Murphy pointed out, one simply did not know what effect this evidence might have had upon members of the jury, but three judges had held that it was at least open to the jury to convict the Chamberlains on the balance of the evidence. That evidence included, of course, the presence of substantial amounts of blood in the car which the jury might infer had been the blood of Azaria Chamberlain even if they doubted the validity of the conclusions drawn from Mrs Kuhl's tests. The High Court pointed out that the presence of blood in the car had been largely unchallenged at the trial. The dispute had raged over whether it had come from an infant or an adult.

Now both the Crown and the defence had an opportunity to fight these issues again. The Crown, for its part, intended to call more witnesses and to rely upon further tests. Whilst it may not have been open for the jury to be satisfied beyond reasonable doubt that the presence of infant blood in the car had been demonstrated by the scientific testing, the Crown would contend that the further evidence called before the Commission did justify that conclusion. On the other hand, the defence wished to contend that there was probably no blood in the car at all. If there were, it was limited to a small amount on the hinge of the front passenger's seat which might have come from the bleeding hitchhiker or some other innocent source.

The evidence of blood in the car was crucial. The Crown contended that the child had been murdered whilst Lindy sat in the front passenger's seat and held the baby out in front of her under the dashboard. As the child's throat was cut, an artery spurted blood at a trajectory of approximately forty-five degrees, producing the spray pattern found on the plate. More blood dripped downwards, producing the marks found on her tracksuit pants by Mrs Hansell. Other blood dripped into the carpet. This was demonstrated by the positive orthotolidine reactions. True enough, one could not see blood in the carpet, but there was practically nothing else that would produce a second stage reaction of vivid peacock blue characteristic of blood. The implication was obvious: the blood had been cleaned up, but the Chamberlains had been unable to completely eradicate it. Telltale trace elements remained. Blood had run down the side of the seat and hinge in a manner that could occur only when the seat was occupied, and there was more blood on the crossbar and under the carpet and underfelt beneath the seat. There was blood on a towel which suggested, perhaps, that it had been caused when a knife had been wiped clean. There was also blood on a pair of scissors which may have been the murder weapon or may have been used to cut the jumpsuit later in the evening. As if all that were not enough, Mrs Kuhl's tests established that the material comprising two of the droplets cut from the spray pattern, the stains on and under the seat, the marks on the towel and stains on the camera bag were all blood from an infant under three months old. There were 'strong indications' that the blood on the scissors was also infant blood.

Clearly, if all these allegations could be confirmed there could be little doubt that the child had been murdered.

By the time the Commission of Inquiry got under way, the first chink had appeared in the Crown's impressive armada of evidence. The research by Smith had established that the under-dash spray was not comprised of blood, whether infant or otherwise, but of sound-deadening material. There were more revelations to come.

Sergeant Huggins of the Victorian Police Force had examined the stains on the crossbar under the seat and under the carpet. They could not have got there from blood flowing down the side of the seat, as the Crown had suggested.

A number of forensic biologists gave evidence about the use of orthotolidine. There was general agreement that it was merely a screening test. A positive result indicated that the substance might well be blood and that it was worth carrying out further tests to determine whether it was. However, as the Queensland forensic biologist, Freney, pointed out, it was 'quite wrong' to treat a positive reaction as even prima facie evidence of the presence of blood.

At Andrew Scott's direction, Craig Fowler carried out a series of tests to determine whether copper dust would produce a similar reaction. He found the reaction so similar that even an experienced forensic biologist might be deceived. The Chamberlains, of course, had lived in Mount Isa, one of the greatest copper-producing areas in the world.

This was of immediate interest to Professor Boettcher, but it is one thing to obtain a positive result from ore taken from a mine and another to establish that dust tramped into a car by the feet of its occupants might produce a similar reaction. The Professor travelled to Mount Isa and collected samples of dust from thirty-two different areas. The results varied from place to place. Some were 'extremely strong', others involved 'only specks of blue colour on what otherwise was a negative background', and others were 'perfectly negative'. However, some of the results were particularly significant. Sandy material collected from the roadway on the street where the Chamberlains had lived produced 'some specks' of the immediate peacock blue reaction characteristic of blood. Dust taken from the floor on the passenger's side of a Daihatsu motor vehicle also provided a strong positive reaction, as did dust in a groove of the dashboard light switch. These results were obtained even though the Daihatsu had been thoroughly washed prior to the tests. Boettcher concluded that 'since the Chamberlains lived at Mount Isa when Azaria disappeared, it would be expected that a number of their items would have collected Mount Isa dust capable of producing the peacock blue colour expected in a positive orthotolidine test with blood. Mrs Kuhl's description of the reaction given by tests on the outside of the camera bag — 'in the seam grooves there were discrete specks that were strongly positive for the orthotolidine test' — was, Boettcher said, 'a good description of the sorts of results that I obtained in literally dozens of tests at Mount Isa.' As Chester Porter dryly pointed out, it was difficult to imagine that the whole district was awash with blood.

The suggestion that there were blood spots on the tracksuit pants was to prove equally dubious. Mrs Hansell had said that she thought the spots were blood. They looked like blood and they were removed by a blood solvent she referred to as the 'green label'. Yet the stains had never been tested scientifically. Dr Scott was to suggest that a drycleaning operator might easily have been confused by drops of fruit juice or other liquids. It seemed that even an experienced forensic biologist would have difficulty in identifying blood from a visual inspection, especially if it were on a dark background such as the navy-blue portion of the tracksuit pants. Scott explained that 'really on a dark material all you are going to see is a dark stain and whether it's blood or tomato sauce or fruit juice that's all you're going to see, a dark stain.'

During the earlier sittings in Darwin, it had emerged that Noel Dawson, a witness who had seen Lindy and Azaria at Ayers Rock, was the laboratory manager of a company that produced drycleaning solvents similar to the one used by Mrs Hansell. He had been involved with such products for more than twenty years and it was his lot to advise drycleaners as to any difficulties they encountered in removing stains. The manner in which Mrs Hansell had attempted to clean the garment was described to him and he agreed that such a process might also remove 'fruit juice, raspberry cordial or something of that nature'. He was asked: 'But would it be fair to say that there are many kinds of stains that could be removed by the application of that chemical in that manner?'

'There'd be quite a few stains, yes,' he replied.

Scott agreed. One could not use the efficacy of the drycleaning solvent as a valid means of deducing the presence of blood.

Mrs Hansell had found that one application of the solvent was normally sufficient to remove bloodstains but recalled that the stains on the tracksuit pants were not so amenable. It was necessary to repeat the treatment. They had been taken to the drycleaners immediately after the Chamberlains returned to Mount Isa and the stains would have been quite fresh. Their uncharacteristic resistance to the drycleaning solvent suggested that the stains may not have been blood.

Mrs Kuhl maintained that the immunological tests did establish the presence of infant blood. Dr Baxter said that he had agreed with her conclusions. Bryan Culliford was too ill to come to Australia again, but the Crown relied upon the evidence he had given at the trial and on a report in which he said that, although he no longer had any notes of them, he 'would have' carried out certain tests. Nonetheless, the validity of Mrs Kuhl's conclusions was questioned on a number of grounds.

In the first place, a number of witnesses gave evidence that the crossover electrophoresis, or counter-current electrophoresis test, was an inadequate procedure to adopt. Professor Ouchterlony explained that 'the usual thing is to run the counter-current electrophoresis as a presumptive test and then, when you've got something which seems to be positive, then [sic] verify by additional tests so that you have a proper identification of what you register in the preliminary tests and that, as far as I understand, has not been done. . .' He explained that the technique had been invented for the purpose of providing a means of 'rapid clinical diagnosis', but that it was necessary to verify the results by other techniques.

Professor Leach, Professor Nairn and Professor Boettcher all agreed. Professor Nairn added that it was a complete waste of time to carry out 'crossover tests' unless one went on to other tests to provide a positive identification. He said that he was 'strongly of the view' that Mrs Kuhl's tests did not establish the presence of foetal haemoglobin in the car. Professor Boettcher commented that no reaction between the antiserum and an old and denatured stain could be relied upon. Even Dr Baudner, the Research Director of Behringwerke, the manufacturers of the antiserum, agreed that it was 'not good enough' to use crossover electrophoresis. It was necessary to verify the reactions by use of the Ouchterlony or some other technique.

In the second place, if one were to make the best of an inadequate technique, one would need to carry out a series of tests to determine the manner in which the particular antiserum would react when used to test a range of blood samples by means of the testing procedure as set up in that particular laboratory. Professors Ouchterlony, Leach, Boettcher and Nairn and Dr Lincoln, a forensic biologist from London, all stressed the need for such a regimen of testing.

Nairn pointed out that unless this was done, the biologist was in no position to make any adequate interpretation of a line found on the 'crossover plate'. Dr Lincoln agreed. He said it would be 'exceedingly unwise' to try to interpret results without carrying out such tests. The Crown sought to rely upon the evidence of Mr Martin, but even he agreed that it was 'undesirable' not to 'pretest' the antiserum. Dr Baudner emphasised that the antiserum was merely a research product. It was up to the user to determine that it was reliable in her hands.

In the third place, a number of witnesses gave evidence that the antiserum was not monospecific. It would react with something other than foetal haemoglobin. The evidence was not all one way. Dr Lincoln, Dr Scott and Culliford's successor, Peter Martin, had all used the antiserum in crossover electrophoresis testing at dilutions of approximately 1:1,000 without obtaining cross reactions with adult blood. However, techniques and apparatus differ from laboratory to laboratory and it is necessary to establish that an antiserum is specific in the hands of the person using it. Furthermore, Mrs Kuhl's demonstration plates provided undeniable evidence of the type of reaction which the antiserum could produce. Professor Nairn said that the 'double banding' evident on the plate suggested that the antiserum was not monospecific. He said that when you see such double banding, you 'first think of bispecificity' and then you 'find out what it is'. Professor Boettcher agreed.

Dr Baudner was not prepared to concede that the antiserum was not monospecific, but he agreed that one would need to find the cause of the double banding before one could rely upon it.

Dr Baxter and Mr Martin both suggested that the double banding might be explained by two identical proteins which had 'differing electrophoretic mobilities'. In other words, there might be two groups of foetal haemoglobin molecules, each of which would react with the antiserum, but because they migrated across the plate at different speeds, they would encounter the antiserum at different points and produce two distinct bands. Professor Ouchterlony dismissed the suggestion. The first reaction would create an immunoprecipiten barrier. The antigen from the sample being tested would not be able to pass it in order to create a second reaction with a further set of antibodies. That could only happen if the antigen passing through were of a kind which would not react with the first set of antibodies, but would react with the second and that could not occur if they were immunologically identical as Baxter and Martin suggested. The only explanation, Ouchterlony said, was that there were two 'immune complexes'; in other words, there was a bispecific antiserum reacting with two different kinds of blood molecules. The serum, he concluded, had a second specificity 'and that cannot be argued with'.

Boettcher's queries regarding the specificity of the antiserum had obviously caused some consternation, at least on the part of Behringwerke's Sydney agents. Seven days after the trial ended, they sent a telex to their principal conveying the request of the Department of Forensic Medicine for supplies of the batch Boettcher had used. The telex concluded: 'We would appreciate if you do not make any mention of our association with the Department of Forensic Medicine with any communication you may have with Professor Boettcher.'

In the fourth place, it emerged that, so far as any of the experts knew, no-one had ever attempted to test denatured blood for the presence of foetal haemoglobin in sufficient quantities to indicate that the blood had come from an infant. Though she may not have known it at the time, the situation facing Mrs Kuhl had been unique in the history of forensic science. As Mr Freney put it, 'it was tiger country'. Whilst Dr Baudner was dubious about suggestions that the serum had more than one specificity, he agreed that one simply could not rely upon a reaction between the antiserum and a denatured blood sample.

It fell to Professor Nairn and Professor Leach to explain the nature of the problem. The antiserum is made by taking blood containing foetal haemoglobin and injecting it into a rabbit. The rabbit's immune system then sets to work busily manufacturing antibodies to the foetal haemoglobin molecules. The difficulty arises from the fact that even cord blood, that is blood from the umbilical cord of a newborn baby, contains about thirty per cent adult haemoglobin. The manufacturer has to remove this before the blood is injected into the rabbit. He does this by subjecting the blood to a centrifuge and by exposing it to adult haemoglobin antibodies which 'absorb out' the adult haemoglobin.

This can never be done with complete accuracy. Some adult haemoglobin may remain and may, in due course, produce some antibodies. Equally, the rabbit may have other antibodies already in his blood stream. Furthermore, the process adopted to remove the adult haemoglobin results in the denaturation of some of the molecules. The denaturation causes the molecule to change shape and to expose different 'antigenic determinants', the parts of the molecule which determine the antibodies with which it will react.

The blood sample, including the denatured molecules, is

injected into the rabbit which manufactures not only antibodies to foetal haemoglobin, but antibodies to the denatured molecules. Those antibodies may later react with a denatured blood sample whether it contains foetal haemoglobin or not. The biologist is likely to be completely deceived by this kind of reaction because the antiserum will not react with her controls of adult blood or samples of animal blood. In theory, that will prove that the serum is monospecific, but in fact it has not reacted with the controls because they were fresh samples containing no denatured molecules. In reality, the test may have proven nothing more than that the sample was old and denatured.

Denaturation occurs naturally with effluxion of time, but it is accelerated by heat. General Motors Holden confirmed that the interior of a car can reach eighty degrees Celsius. Dr Baudner had advised Boettcher that if foetal haemoglobin was heated to that temperature for half-an-hour, there would be no reaction with the antiserum. The Chamberlains' car had been exposed to extreme heat at Ayers Rock and Mount Isa. It was examined by Mrs Kuhl more than thirteen months after Azaria disappeared and more than two years after the dash to hospital with the bleeding hitchhiker.

The Crown suggested that the results of these tests had been confirmed by the presence of a foetal haemoglobin band on the haptoglobin plate. However, it again encountered difficulties. Dr Baxter conceded that one has to be 'very cautious' before concluding that foetal haemoglobin was present as a consequence of reading a haptoglobin plate. 'You can't distinguish it with one hundred per cent certainty,' he said, and explained that it was 'only a confirmatory test'.

Both Mr Raymond and Dr Scott expressed the view that one would not normally expect to find double haemoglobin bands present on a plate of that nature when the sample was thirteen months old. Dr Baxter had carried out certain tests during 1986 which demonstrated that, under extreme circumstances, the denaturation caused the haemoglobin bands to disappear after fifteen days.

Both Professor Boettcher and Mr Raymond reported encountering double bands from adult blood and Professor

Boettcher actually produced a sample plate demonstrating this phenomenon.

Mrs Kuhl conceded that she had used no 'foetal control' on the haptoglobin plate and Dr Scott expressed the view that such a control was necessary before one could be confident that the band that one could see was, in fact, foetal haemoglobin.

The bands also seemed to be the wrong colour. They were reddish-brown and Dr Baxter himself conceded that it would be surprising to find reddish-brown haemoglobin bands from blood of that age.

Dr Baxter's view that the band in the 'foetal position' amounted to 'at a conservative estimate at least fifty per cent of the total haemoglobin' was quite inconsistent with the estimate of twenty-five per cent foetal haemoglobin which Dr Scott made upon his examination of blood taken from Azaria's jumpsuit. This seemed to suggest that, if what was being tested was in fact blood, it was not the blood of Azaria Chamberlain, but of an even younger baby which had bled in the car quite recently.

All in all, it seemed that even if one assumed that all the tests had been carried out and recorded competently, the results still fell far short of proving that there had ever been any infant blood in the car. Even Dr Baxter, who had been shown at least all of the positive results, said that he could not say either 'yes' or 'no' and that 'at this stage' his position was 'ambivalent'.

The real question seemed to be whether the Commission could be satisfied that there had been any blood in the car at all. Raymond had carried out an extensive programme of tests but had detected blood only in a nasal secretion on the back of a seat. As he readily conceded, it was difficult to imagine that Mrs Kuhl could have 'got it so wrong'. Not only Raymond, however, but Scott, Baxter, Boettcher and Nairn all expressed the view that if there had been significant quantities of blood present in 1981 they would have expected the tests in 1986 to have detected it. Raymond and Baxter were at pains to point out that some of it may have been removed by the testing in 1981 and that it was conceivable that further denaturation had accounted for the lack of any reaction in 1986. Nonetheless, it was 'surprising' that no blood at all was found, particularly on the hinge.

Dr Cornell's evidence also became important in this light. He said that the PGM grouping test may have been inaccurate due to the denaturation of the material being tested. Freney agreed. A partly denatured stain could give misleading results. Others expressed surprise that Mrs Kuhl had obtained any PGM results at all. Dr Baxter had seen 'typable' PGM stains eighteen to twenty-four months old, but agreed that it was quite exceptional. Mr Raymond and Professor Renate Meier had found eight months about the limit. Mr Martin said that 'we are surprised when we get activity at eight months'! Dr Scott said that the chances of being able to group PGM in a denatured stain thirteen months old were really quite small. Boettcher agreed that it was unexpected and said that it would seem that it must be more fresh than that. Dr Baxter conceded what was by then apparent: a PGM result can always be a question of some controversy between biologists. Dr Cornell also gave evidence of his tests for protein in the carpets of the car during 1982. Even at that stage he had been unable to find any trace of the hundred or more proteins found in blood. It seemed difficult to explain the result of that test by further denaturation since Mrs Kuhl's tests.

Furthermore, in the light of subsequent evidence, it was less difficult to accept that the results of Mrs Kuhl's tests may have been wrong. As Mr Fowler and Professor Boettcher demonstrated, the results of the orthotolidine tests were quite unreliable. The material may have been copper dust. There is another screening test known as the Kastle Meyer technique. It is somewhat less sensitive than the orthotolidine technique though it has been used to detect bloodstains up to twenty years old. It also produces fewer 'false positives' than orthotolidine. Mrs Kuhl had used both techniques and Dr Lincoln found it 'very significant' that she had obtained positive results to orthotolidine but negative to the Kastle Meyer technique.

Equally, it seemed that the crossover electrophoresis tests carried out on the droplets cut from the under-dash spray pattern were equally unreliable. The Crown did attempt to suggest that, although the spray pattern was actually sound-deadening material and not foetal blood as the jury had been invited to infer, it was conceivable that some foetal blood had splashed onto the two drops tested by Mrs Kuhl. Mr Raymond had established that there was no blood of any kind remaining on the plate and Mr Justice Morling was quick to point out that it would have required an enormous coincidence for particles of foetal blood to strike the plate in such a manner that the blood was confined to the surface of two droplets and then for Dr Jones, who was merely seeking a representative sample of the spray pattern, to remove those two droplets and send them to Mrs Kuhl.

The contention also overlooked the fact that when Mrs Kuhl tested the spray pattern with orthotolidine, the result was negative. It was possible that the surface of those blood spots, but apparently no other blood in the car, became so denatured that it would not react or that some other substance landed on top of them and screened them from the orthotolidine. But, in either case, the chances seemed infinitesimal. What seemed infinitely more likely was that something had gone so radically wrong with these tests that a mixture of paint and bitumen had been demonstrated to be foetal blood.

Even Mr Martin, upon whom the Crown heavily relied, conceded that if there had been blood on the towel he would still expect to get some reaction from it and that the fact that the tests had proved negative suggested that it was not blood. He concluded that if there was blood in the car at all when Mrs Kuhl tested it, the quantities must have been 'very small'. Boettcher and Nairn agreed, but Nairn made it clear that he was not confident that Mrs Kuhl's tests had established that there had ever been any blood in the car.

Ironically enough, it was left to one of the scientists who had been called at the Crown's request to administer the coup de grace to this aspect of the case. Professor Ferris was an eminent forensic pathologist and President of the International Society of Forensic Scientists. He had been brought from his home in Canada to give evidence concerning the inferences which might be drawn from the pattern of bloodstaining on Azaria Chamberlain's jumpsuit. He brought to the inquiry not only extensive experience in investigating deaths due to accident or crimes of violence, but experience gleaned from examining bodies and clothing taken from bodies of people who had been mauled or partly eaten by grizzly bears and timber wolves. He explained that if the child had been killed in the car in the manner the Crown suggested, there would have been 'visible and readily detectable amounts of blood present in the car almost in spite of whatever means was used to conceal it'.

Yet, the evidence was plain. None had been seen by the Demaines, Bobbie Downs or anyone else on the night in question. None had been detected by Senior Constable Graham when he conducted a minute search of the car some six weeks later. Dr Cornell had been unable to find any protein when he tested the carpets in 1982 and Raymond had not been able to detect any residual traces of blood in the car, though no less than seven scientists had expressed the view that they would have expected some positive reactions had there been any substantial quantities in the car when Mrs Kuhl examined it in 1981. All this seemed to point to the one conclusion. There had been no blood in the car other than, perhaps, minute quantities of the kind which Mr Martin said one might expect to find in any family car.

The 'evidence' of the blood, upon which the Crown case had so heavily relied, did not exist.

26

Where and when

IN THEORY, AT LEAST, THE CROWN'S INABILITY to establish that the child had been killed in the car did not mean that Lindy could not have killed the child. Ian Barker, as quick on his feet as a Thai kick boxer, was later to point out that she may have murdered the child anywhere in the vicinity of the camping area. Winneke protested that the Crown should not be permitted to 'make a new case' at this late stage of the proceedings, but Mr Justice Morling ruled that it was open to the Crown to make such a submission. Yet there was an air of 'clutching at straws' about it. Compelling arguments about the classic arterial blood spray and a car virtually awash with the blood of an infant had given way to speculation about what might have been.

Such a scenario offered the Crown none of the strong evidentiary support with which the 'murder in the car' theory had been rammed home. The correlation of an arterial blood spray under the dashboard, blood spots on the tracksuit pants and traces of blood in the carpets had been the most damning part of the Crown case. In addition, the car had belonged to the Chamberlains and had been parked immediately beside their tent. Lindy had admitted going to it. It also offered both a measure of visual concealment and a means of containing any cry which the baby may have made or the sound of any emotional outburst by the mother.

No alternative site could offer the Crown a case of such strength. The obvious need for concealment suggested that any site would have had to have been some distance from the tent. Yet the accoutrements of murder and concealment of the crime were all to be found in the car. It seemed difficult to imagine one small woman setting out on an expedition into the desert with the baby in one arm and an assortment of knives, a towel, container of water, shovel and, perhaps, camera bag in the other. Murder elsewhere, it seemed, required at least a second trip even if one put aside the macabre suggestion of two or more burials.

It was also obvious that any other site involved considerable risk of discovery. Perhaps the most likely possibility was the ablution block, but Lindy would have had to have skirted the barbecue area which lay between the tent and the block and to have been willing to take the child into a well-lit area. The baby disappeared at about 8.00 p.m., a time at which mothers might be expected to take young children to the toilet or showers before bed. Had she left the corpse inside, it might have been discovered. On the other hand, had she attempted to remove it she might have run into someone at the entrance who could scarcely have failed to notice the extensive bloodstaining.

The child could have been killed in the scrub on the slopes of Sunrise Hill, but in that event it seemed unlikely that Lindy would have directed the searchers to that area when she pointed out the path taken by the dingo.

If the child's throat had been cut anywhere near the camping area, it seemed inconceivable that three hundred searchers, assisted by black trackers and at least some dogs, would not have picked up the shallow grave. Roff had thought that the dingo might bury the child's body and had directed the searchers to look for the telltale signs of recently disturbed sand, which at that time of the night would have been of a different shade from the surrounding surface. Yet, if the child's throat had been cut some distance away, it was difficult to imagine how Lindy could have accomplished the murder and all that the Crown suggested within the limited time available, even if she had enjoyed the good fortune to escape detection by fellow campers and to have had Aidan remain quiet and unsuspecting in the tent.

It was also difficult to imagine that Lindy would have nonchalantly strolled back to the tent without at least wiping the blood from her hands and clothing. To have failed to do so would have been to court discovery by any wandering camper. Yet, there were significant bloodstains in the tent which the Crown could explain only by suggesting that they were caused by blood smears from the murderer returning to the tent to change.

In fact, the blood in the tent was not confined to the odd smear. Blood was proven to be on Michael's sleeping bag, two purple blankets, Reagan's parka and a floral mattress. In addition, Mrs Prell, who was employed at the motel, saw blood on Lindy's sleeping bag and the Chamberlains showed Constable Morris bloodstains they had found on Aidan's parka. Unfortunately, no attempt was made to photograph or accurately describe these bloodstains until some weeks later. By then the articles had been extensively handled. Most of the material, other than the purple blankets, does not absorb blood which can abrade from the surface. However, even if one ignored the amount of blood presumably lost due to handling and transport, there was obviously a significant amount of blood left on items in the tent.

Both Dr Jones and Dr Scott, each of whom had been Crown witnesses at the trial, expressed the view that Lindy's hands or clothing would have had to have been literally dripping with blood to account for all of the stains found in the tent. The spots on the tracksuit pants would have been completely inadequate even if they had been blood and no other portion of Lindy's clothing was ever suspected of having been bloodstained. It seemed fanciful to suggest that she would have walked some distance back to the tent with such copious quantities of blood still dripping from her hands. If she didn't, then how did she clean them? No bloodstained rags were found when Constable Noble loaded the contents of the tent into the police vehicle and the only water in the tent was seen to be clear. And how did she manage to remove the tracksuit pants, as the Crown contended, without getting blood on the waistband?

The evidence also suggested that at least some of the blood in the tent was caused by a direct flow or dripping rather than by smearing. Both Constable Morris and Mrs Lowe noticed drops of blood. Mrs Lowe also noticed a pool, whilst Mrs West referred to a spray of blood. Dr Jones said that he could not imagine the blood on the mattress having simply flowed from someone's hands. Dr Scott seemed to agree, but added that it was difficult to conceive of what fabric could hold so much blood that it could transfer to the floral mattress sufficient to account for the stain. He added that the sharp edge of the stain was also suggestive of direct flow blood. Some of the blood on the sleeping bag he examined was characteristic of a spray or splash of blood. Overall, this seemed to suggest that the baby had actually been bleeding in the tent.

The relative positions of these stains were also significant. One of the purple blankets upon which blood was found was described by Mrs Lowe as being 'out of the cot towards where Reagan was sleeping'. Mrs Lowe described a pool of fresh blood about one-third of the way into the tent. She described it as being 'a squashed oval shape' and said that there were a few drops of blood towards the opening of the tent. The Crown suggested that Mrs Lowe was mistaken about this pool of blood because it was not discovered in the course of subsequent scientific examinations, but Dr Scott did discover a significant bloodstain on the floral mattress which would have been in the position Mrs Lowe described.

Furthermore, the mark was roughly the shape which she described, though it was somewhat smaller. It may be that Mrs Lowe was mistaken as to the size or that further blood had abraided from the surface before Dr Scott examined it. In either event, the shape and direction of the drops were perhaps more significant than the size of the pool. It was impossible to reconstruct the precise position of the stains in the tent with absolute precision. But the Chamberlains were methodical campers who knew that the only way to manage with three children in a small tent was to have a specific place for each item. When the various items were repositioned to accord not only with the Chamberlains' recollection, but the memories of others who had entered the tent on the night in question, the stains were positioned in areas which may have been consistent with a trail of blood, and certainly indicated a number of areas of blood, between the bassinette and the opening to the tent.

Bloodstains in that region could have been the legacy of a dingo removing its prey, but seemed quite inconsistent with the odd smear which one might expect from a distraught mother returning to the tent to clean up and conceal the murder of her child.

The Crown had suggested that if a dingo had taken the child, there would have been more blood in the tent. Some support for this view was obtained from Professor Ferris, who said that it was improbable that a dingo could take a child from a tent without the child shedding a great deal of blood, even if the child had been dead for two minutes. He conceded, of course, that he had had no experience with dingoes. Dr Jones expressed the view that there was a 'scenario' whereby the baby could have been removed from the tent without a great deal of blood being spilled.

Both Professor Pleuckhahn and Professor Bradley agreed. If the dingo grasped the child by the back of the skull and maintained the pressure, the bite would occlude the wound and inhibit the flow of blood. Considerable support for this theory was obtained from observations of the dingo experts. Dr Corbett said that if the dingo had killed Azaria for food, there would not be much blood. Indeed, there might be none at all. Newsome, Thompson and Brechwoldt all confirmed that very little blood may be shed when a dingo kills prey. Brechwoldt gave evidence of two incidents in which post mortems had been carried out on animals to determine the cause of death, because there had been no visible signs of injury at all and those investigating suspected that the animals may have died of fright. In fact, they had been killed by biting, but virtually no blood had escaped from the wounds.

The Crown also sought to exclude this possibility by leading evidence, based on skull measurements, that a dingo's jaws could achieve a maximum gape of approximately forty-three degrees. Beyond that, it was said, the dingo's jaws would become disarticulated. This, the Crown contended, established that no dingo could open its jaws wide enough that the gap between the points of the canine teeth would exceed eight to nine centimetres. Since the skull of a baby nine-and-a-half weeks old would be approximately ten centimetres across, it was argued that a dingo could not have taken the skull in its jaws.

This argument was to provide a classic example of the manner in which courts could be misled by a purely theoretical approach to possibilities outside the common experience. Dr Morrison, a dingo expert from South Australia, heard this evidence with considerable interest. He then produced a video tape of a simple experiment he had conducted. He had taken a frozen chicken from his freezer and measured it with a pair of calipers. It was 13.5 centimetres across. He left it substantially frozen so that it could not be compressed and placed it on the floor. He then let a medium-size dingo into the room. Both the video tape and some still photographs of the experiment revealed that the dingo had not received the benefit of the Crown's esoteric arguments concerning its angle of gape. It simply seized the chicken, its jaws encompassing the 13.5 centimetre width, and marched triumphantly out the door with its prize.

There was, of course, still one major objection to the conclusion that a dingo had taken the baby. Professor Cameron's evidence had suggested that the cause of death was an incised wound to the throat with a sharp cutting instrument and that he had seen the impressions of a small adult hand in the bloodstains on the jumpsuit. Before the Commission of Inquiry, however, he conceded that the determination of the nature of wounds which produced particular blood flow patterns is not a precise science, but a matter of general impression.

Drs Jones, Scott and Bradley and Professor Pleuckhahn all gave evidence that they had been unable to see any impression of a human hand in the stains on the jumpsuit. Furthermore, Mr Raymond confirmed that the pattern of staining was consistent with the proposition that the jumpsuit and matinee jacket were both on and done up to the neck when the blood flowed. Dr Scott agreed that the bleeding pattern on the jumpsuit was consistent with the blood flowing whilst it had been covered by an outer garment.

Whilst Professor Cameron was being cross-examined, the jumpsuit and matinee jacket were fitted to a lifesized doll. The Professor agreed that, with the matinee jacket in place, it would have been extremely difficult to place a hand on the shoulder in the position necessary to cause one of the impressions he had described. He pointed out that there was ready access to the position where the other impression was located. There had, however, been further testing carried out on that staining. Eighty per cent of it was not blood at all, but ferric oxide. It seemed that the child had not only bled sound-deadening material, but red sand.

Dr Jones did not agree that the bleeding must have been caused by an incised wound to the throat. He felt that substantial skull lacerations could have caused the bleeding. Dr Scott stated that, in his experience, cut throats produced a different pattern of bleeding, at least in adults. He suggested that if the throat had been cut, he would have expected to find blood falling down onto the front of the garment.

Professor Pleuckhahn had carried out some experiments which showed that blood applied to both sides of the head of a doll would trickle down to the neck of the jumpsuit and spread out through the fabric to form a circumferential stain. He concluded that the blood on Azaria Chamberlain's jumpsuit could have come from a head injury rather than a circumferential injury to the throat. In fact, he thought that that was more probable. The blood pattern was not 'regular around the neck', as one would have expected from a circumferential injury.

Professor Ferris was dubious about the effect of those experiments because Professor Pleuckhahn had used blood with some anticoagulant added. If he used pure blood, the clotting might have inhibited the seepage through the fabric. He concluded that the injury had been 'circumferential' in the sense that there had been injuries to several parts of the throat, but agreed that the wounds could have been caused by an animal bite. On the whole, however, he felt that that was unlikely because he would have expected small particles of fat and tissue to have been found in the bloodstains. An instrument, such as a knife, cuts more cleanly and is less likely to produce such particles.

Professor Pleuckhahn and Professor Cameron both expressed the view that the absence of these particles did not prove that a dingo had not been involved. In the end result, the disagreement proved to be of academic interest only. The clothes had been out in the open for a week before they were found and Dr Scott, who carried out the examination, had not been looking for such particles. He told the Commission that he could not say that the examination would have picked them up unless they had been as large as two millimetres.

Both Professor Nairn and Professor Ferris referred to the spurting that accompanies the cutting of a throat in the manner suggested by the Crown. The jumpsuit did not appear to contain evidence of the vast quantities of blood which they expected would be lost in such an exercise. Professor Ferris spoke of the 'zig zag' pattern of spurting caused by the severance of a major artery. Both also confirmed that it would be extremely difficult to restrain spurting of that nature with a towel and to prevent blood from spraying not only over the jumpsuit, but over the clothes of the murderer. For this reason, Professor Ferris concluded that the stains on the jumpsuit had probably been caused by post-mortem bleeding. None of the other pathologists disagreed with him.

Cameron had inferred the cause of death from the pattern of bleeding. If Ferris was correct and the bleeding had occurred after the child was already dead, then the Crown was left without any evidence of the cause of death.

Later, when Lindy came to give evidence, Ian Barker omitted to put to her the Crown's case as to the cause of death or the scene of the murder. He obviously felt unable to do so, given the state of the evidence. The oversight did not go unnoticed. Mr Justice Morling asked him to consider the matter and, in due course, to give him the scenario the Crown considered most likely. Barker was later to suggest that the child may still have died from a cut throat and that there may have been ante-mortem bleeding before the post-mortem bleeding.

It was true, of course, that one could not rule out the possibility of some ante-mortem bleeding, but there was no evidence whatever to suggest that it had in fact occurred. Furthermore, there was no sign of the 'zig zag' pattern typical of arterial bleeding or the fine spray typical of venous bleeding from a live body evident upon the jumpsuit. Consequently, if there had been any ante-mortem bleeding, it did not come from a lethal wound to the throat.

The possibility of such bleeding being masked by means of a towel seemed unlikely. Professor Ferris said that one would need 'a great deal of good luck'. It seemed equally unlikely that it could have been masked by subsequent post-mortem bleeding. The ante-mortem blood would have spurted beyond any area which post-mortem blood could have been expected to reach.

Alternatively, the Crown suggested that 'if the child was already dead it is difficult to see an explanation for the wound not consistent with the proposition that the child was murdered'. There were obvious difficulties with this proposition. If there is no evidence as to how a person died, then how can one possibly conclude that he was murdered? One was entitled to ask: when, where, why and how? The Crown appeared to have no answers to any of those questions.

When Professor Ferris' reservations concerning Scott's failure to find particles of tissue, fat and the like were swept aside, it became apparent that the pattern of bleeding on the jumpsuit was unlikely to have been caused by wounds inflicted by a human assailant. A murderer would have had to have killed the child in some indefinable way without cutting its throat, stabbing it through the body or causing other injuries of a kind which would produce spurting. It would then have been necessary to wait for some time before returning and cutting the throat in a cirumferential manner.

Whilst mutilation murders do occur, it would be unusual for a murderer to wait some time after the killing before embarking upon further injuries to the body. Furthermore, Professor Nairn had given evidence that if the throat had been cut or the child had been decapitated, the heart would have gone on beating for some ten minutes and there would have been terrible convulsions. It seemed unlikely that Lindy could have been away from the barbecue area for any more than eight to ten minutes. There would not have been time for her to have killed the child, waited until that process had exhausted itself and then cut the child's throat to produce the post-mortem bleeding evident on the jumpsuit.

That would not, of course, have been the end of the exercise. She would still have had to dispose of the body, return to the tent, clean herself up, ensure that the blankets were left in disarray and the pole was knocked askew and then obtain baked beans from the car for Aidan.

What seemed far more likely was that a dingo had in fact taken this child. It had stopped at the back of the tent where it caught the baby's scent, travelled around the side of the tent to the front where it had entered, and seized the baby as it lay in the bassinette. It had taken it by the exposed portion, namely the skull. It was classic dingo behaviour to maintain its grip and that had produced at least a partial occlusion of the wounds. Sufficient blood had been lost to provide something of a trail to the entrance, but there had not been the massive bleeding which was to come.

The dingo had then taken the child in an easterly direction up Sunrise Hill. Part of the matinee jacket had trailed on the ground producing the drag mark seen by Derek Roff. At the top of the rise when it had covered sufficient distance to feel safe from pursuit, it had rested for a moment and the weight of the baby had produced the depressions in the sand with a cloth imprint in them.

Later, the animal had sat down to consume his prey. Roff had given evidence that dingoes frequently eat the head of their prey first. Whilst it is grisly to contemplate, there seems little doubt that this would have produced bleeding of the kind which could account for the pattern of bloodstaining on the jumpsuit and matinee jacket.

27

The dingo experts

A NUMBER OF PEOPLE EXPERT in the behaviour and abilities of dingoes were called to give evidence and asked a set series of questions. Porter obviously wanted to be in a position to compare their answers.

'In or about August 1980, was it within the bounds of reasonable possibility that a dingo might attack a human baby?' he asked.

Mr Cawood: 'Yes.'

Mr Roff: 'Yes.'

Mr Harris: 'Yes. Given the increased need for food, possible reduction of food, I would say that it is . . . an outright acquisition of prey.'

Dr Corbett: 'Yes, I think it's possible, but unlikely.'

Dr Newsome: 'Yes.'

'Was it within the bounds of reasonable possibility that a dingo might carry the baby away for consumption as food?'

Mr Cawood: 'Yes.'

Mr Roff: 'Yes.'

Mr Harris: 'Well, at the risk of sounding silly, it would not have taken the baby for any other reason whatsoever but food. Given what I said a few minutes ago about the camping area being regarded as a common foraging ground, I would not expect a dingo to stay in that area once it had acquired food or prey which was beyond its capacity to eat on the spot. It would have removed it to a place where it was unlikely to be challenged for possession.'

Dr Corbett: 'I think it is possible; again, unlikely.'

Dr Newsome: 'Yes.'

'Would the dingo have the ability to carry the weight of a nine-and-a-half pound baby?'

Mr Cawood: 'Yes.'

Mr Roff: 'Yes.'

Mr Harris: 'Yes, quite easily.'

Dr Corbett: 'A dingo can move a nine-and-a-half pound baby from A to B, yes.'

Dr Newsome: 'That would depend on the distance.'

'Assuming a den is four to six kilometres away, would it be able to carry the baby that far?'

Mr Cawood: '[It] could take the baby to the den near where the clothes were found.'

Mr Roff: 'Right to the den. The den where the clothes were found was within a reasonable range for a dingo seeking to feed its puppies.'

Mr Harris: 'I can't refer to empirical evidence; I can only draw on my general observations of dingoes over more than a decade in the field and in captivity, and my opinion that a distance of four to five kilometres and the weight of about ten pounds would present absolutely no problem to a dingo.'

Dr Corbett: 'It would get the baby that far, yes.'

Dr Newsome: 'Judging from what I know of dingoes it would be a possibility. I'd imagine that it wouldn't be able to carry that kind of weight clear of the ground the entire way, for a number of reasons; not just the weight, but trying to have an even distribution of that weight and there may require some adjustment.'

'Is August a month when dingoes usually have puppies at Ayers Rock?'

Mr Cawood: 'Yes.'

Mr Roff: 'The puppy season is in August.'

Mr Harris: 'The cubs are born in July, August — there is a slight variation around Australia — and we have found from observing captive litters that as soon as the teeth of cubs erupt they are prepared to tackle solid food . . . about eighteen days.'

Dr Corbett: 'Yes, it would be puppies; it is not the normal month.'

Dr Newsome: 'Yes.'

These answers were confirmed by Constable Morris, who reported that a lactating bitch had been shot near the site where the clothes had been found.

'Does the male dingo, in a dingo pair, normally help feed the puppies?'

Mr Roff: 'Yes.'

Mr Harris: 'Our observations of captive stocks are yes. Our observations in the field are not unequivocal in this matter. We have seen males carrying freshly killed prey and going back to where we know there is a female and a litter. But we have not in this field directly seen males arriving at a den and presenting food.'

Dr Corbett: 'It doesn't normally help feed them. Not directly. I have not seen the male bring back food for the pups directly.'

Dr Newsome: 'I have not seen that, but I have not seen as much of feeding or dens as Dr Corbett.'

'Does the dingo normally or occasionally bury its prey?'

Mr Cawood: 'Yes, for various reasons [at Ayers Rock], but it is not its normal habit.'

Mr Roff: 'Yes, dingoes in the vicinity of Ayers Rock do.'

Mr Harris: 'This seems to vary. We have been unable to attribute controlling factors to the burying of prey. We have seen prey buried in our captive stock and in the field. So the answer to the question is yes, the dingo does bury prey from time to time, but we don't understand the controlling factors yet.'

Dr Corbett: 'I have not seen dingoes burying prey.'

Due to an oversight, Dr Newsome was not asked this question.

'Does the dingo have a habit, like the fox, of eating its prey head first?'

Mr Cawood: 'I don't know.'

Mr Roff: 'Yes, it's true of most carnivores.'

Mr Harris: 'Again this depends on the size of the animal. With the larger animals they tend to eat the contents of the abdominal cavity first and then move on to the solid meat, but with smaller animals they usually tend to eat the prey head first.'

Dr Corbett: 'It eats some prey head first, but it is not typical of dingoes to decapitate the head for a start and eat from the head.'

Dr Newsome: 'I've been surprised at that suggestion. I can't recall.'

The Crown relied heavily upon the evidence of Drs Corbett and Newsome, each of whom expressed the view that the 'overall scenario' was unlikely. In one sense, this was hardly a controversial suggestion. Whatever the explanation for the disappearance of Azaria Chamberlain, the incident had been unique in Australia's history. It was obvious that something quite extraordinary had happened. Furthermore, both Corbett and Newsome had drawn primarily upon their experience with dingoes in the wild. The point which both Roff and Cawood had made as early as August 1980 was that opinions of the kind which Corbett and Newsome had expressed were undoubtedly correct if related to dingoes in the wild, but that a unique situation had existed at Ayers Rock with 'semi-wild, semi-tame' dingoes behaving in an uncharacteristic manner. Dr Corbett himself readily conceded that Derek Roff would be well-informed about contacts between dingoes and humans at Ayers Rock at the relevant time, whilst he did not 'really know that much about it'. He also agreed that he had never heard of any other area where so many people had been attacked by dingoes in such a short period of time.

The distinction was important, for many of the things which Lindy had said occurred had been dismissed by a sceptical public on the basis that 'dingoes don't do such things'. It had been said, for example, that dingoes would normally be extremely reluctant to enter a tent or any other confined area. Yet the evidence of Roff, Richard Dare, Rohan Dalgleish and Peter Elston established that dingoes frequently entered tents at the camping areas near Ayers Rock. A Mrs Foster reported that one had burgled the annexe to her caravan whilst Mr Dare referred not only to the one which was accustomed to strolling nonchalantly down the aisle of his bus accepting titbits from his passengers, but to dingoes which had entered motels. Roff was emphatic that a dingo would not hesitate to enter a tent for food. Richard Dare said that 'you couldn't leave anything unattended around the camping area'. A dingo would be 'in and off with it like a shot'.

The Crown had also relied upon Dr Corbett to lend some support to a theory that the dingo would have dropped the baby if it had been disturbed as Mrs Chamberlain claimed. Again, this was probably typical of dingoes in the wild, but it left the locals sceptical. Both Roff and Cawood gave evidence that it was not true of dingoes at Ayers Rock. It was certainly not the experience of

Erica Letsch, who created quite a disturbance when the dingo took the pillow from under her head and then returned for her sleeping bag. But it was left to a tourist, Mr Love, to demonstrate just how ready the local dingoes were to ignore the expectations of experts. He and his family had decided to have a picnic. It was to be a magnificent repast with a five kilogram leg of pork assuming pride of place on the table. He stepped back to record this joyous occasion on celluloid, but looked through the viewfinder in time to see a dingo, who obviously shared his love of fine food, climbing onto the table. He let out an outraged shout, but the dingo took off with his leg of pork held securely in its jaws. He gave chase, uttering the appropriate white man's imprecations, but the dingo was too fast and he gave up after running for several hundred metres. Intriguingly enough, that incident also occurred shortly after sunset and the animal actually took his prize from an esky with the lid on.

The Crown also suggested that Lindy could not have seen the dingo shaking its head because it is not characteristic of dingo behaviour to shake prey in order to kill it. It seemed little more than an exercise in clutching at straws because Dr Corbett, at least, had seen dingoes kill large rats by shaking them in order to break their necks. It seemed that some prey might be killed in that fashion whilst others would not, and, of course, no-one had ever seen how a dingo might treat a human baby. Furthermore, no expert had any experience as to how a dingo might be expected to manipulate any kind of prey after it had already collided with a tent pole and was trying to get out between swinging flaps. It was all speculative and probably irrelevant. Lindy had never claimed that she had seen the baby in the dingo's jaws and, if Roff and Newsome were right in their theory that there had been two dingoes and that the 'warning growl' heard by Bill West had been uttered by the one with the baby, it was probably that Lindy had seen the wrong dog.

Despite the evidence that it was the puppy season and that a lactating bitch had been shot nearby, the Crown sought to suggest that there had been no puppies at the den near the position in which the clothes had been found. Dr Corbett gave evidence that a dingo den could normally be identified by the amount of rabbit skins littered within thirty to forty metres. Dung is also evident especially when the pups are a little older. He said that he simply could not imagine a dingo den which was not surrounded by food remains.

Yet in 1979, the year before Azaria disappeared, Dr Morrison had made a television documentary. He had filmed one particular den in which he could both see and hear the puppies. The video tape was screened in court. It showed Dr Morrison approaching the den and pointing out various features but, as he later said in his evidence, there were no noticeable skins outside the den. The surrounding area was 'relatively clean' except for the puppies' tracks immediately in front.

One thing which did emerge with clarity was that dingoes were unpredictable. Mr Harris said that he would be very suspicious of anyone who claimed to be definitive about their behavioural patterns. Dr Corbett emphasised that each dingo is an individual and that one could not make predictions with any certainty based upon general observations. One could suggest normal behavioural patterns, but there would always be exceptions. Dr Murray agreed. One had to be 'very careful' before making dogmatic statements about what the animals might do.

These notes of caution were important. The Crown's contentions really boiled down to an argument that, if an expert would not have expected a dingo to behave in a particular manner, then one could be satisfied beyond any reasonable doubt that it did not do so. One could then assume that any evidence that the dingo did was unreliable and, if it came from the Chamberlains, was deliberate perjury displaying a 'consciousness of guilt'.

There were obvious leaps of logic in any such approach, but when the propositions were related to the unique character of the events surrounding the disappearance of Azaria Chamberlain, the leaps became pole vaults. The opinions were at best educated guesses, based upon dubious extrapolations from the familiar to the unfamiliar. Only the rangers were able to give evidence of the peculiar behaviour of dingoes at Ayers Rock in 1980. The other experts were reduced to drawing upon their experience of dingoes in the wild and endeavouring to make some kind of adjustment to what might be expected in the circumstances described by others.

Even that tenuous exercise was only the first step in the process of reasoning. They then had to consider how those particular dingoes might go about taking a baby for food. There had been instances of Aboriginal babies having been taken. Mr Perron gave evidence of one such incident, Les Harris had been told of another and Nipper Winmatti's evidence at the first inquest suggested that there may have been more. But none of them had been the subject of any detailed investigation and no-one really knew how even a wild dingo would have seized or carried a baby.

The Inquiry then had to go to the next step and try to come up with a set of expectations about the manner in which the clothing worn by the baby might have been damaged in such an attack. Later evidence was to reveal that Professor Gustafson of Sweden may have been the only scientist in the world who had carried out an extensive study of the manner in which fabric was likely to be damaged by animal teeth and even he had studied neither dingoes nor attacks upon human prey.

The dingo experts clearly did their best to be helpful, but there were obvious difficulties in trying to relate experiences of wild dingoes attacking small fleet-footed mammals in the open to an attack by a semi-tame dingo upon a fully dressed child sleeping in a bassinette at the back corner of a tent.

Tony Raymond said that the Healesville experiments had shown that dingoes could pick up the dolls by the clothing without causing visible damage. As Professor Fernhead explained, the jumpsuit material is elastic. It could be held without the teeth actually penetrating the weave. In the light of the expert evidence, there appeared to be little doubt that a dingo could have taken the baby and carried it to the area in which the clothes were subsequently found without causing significant rips or tears.

The experts also had little doubt that a dingo could have removed the baby's body from its clothing. The real issue seemed to be whether the damage found in Azaria's jumpsuit was consistent with the damage which a dingo might have been expected to cause in the removal of the body.

The evidence established that dingoes were surprisingly dexterous creatures. Richard Dare gave evidence of a dingo which had 'gently unwrapped' a cake which had been sealed in aluminium foil. There were 'a few minor tears', but the dingo had been able to gently unfold the foil without any major rips. Derek Roff had seen a dingo open a bar of chocolate 'which to me was extremely amazing, the way he did it without ripping and tearing'. He confirmed that 'in stress situations' they tend to 'rip and grab and swallow extremely fast', but in situations where they did not know that they were being observed, 'it is a very fastidious process, almost, of investigation, of opening . . . I know that they can be extremely efficient'. Les Harris, no doubt with thoughts of a vegetarian barbecue still on his mind, agreed that dingoes could be 'thoughtful and methodical at anything they do' and that they could 'unwrap things with care and consideration'.

When asked how a dingo would be likely to treat a prey wrapped in cloth, Derek Roff replied, 'Well, the dingo would obviously extract the prey from the cloth. It depends on circumstances at the time, I would suggest, as to how that would be done.'

Dr Corbett agreed that a dingo could easily open the press studs of a jumpsuit with its nose or teeth. The fact that most of the studs were undone was consistent with a dingo having nuzzled into the jumpsuit in an attempt to remove the body. The animal would have been sufficiently intelligent to be able to extract the limbs of the baby from the extremities of the garment. Overall, he concluded that a dingo could have removed the body from the clothing altogether, although he felt that it was unlikely that a dingo would not have caused some damage to the jumpsuit.

Sims, the London odontologist, would have expected more 'florid' damage than was evident in the jumpsuit. However, neither he nor Corbett had been shown the results of an experiment conducted at the Adelaide Zoo in which the decapitated body of a goat kid dressed in a jumpsuit had been placed in a dingo pen. A dingo had removed the kid and the jumpsuit was later found to have only two studs undone. Sims agreed that this experiment demonstrated that the Australian dingo had considerable manipulative skills in getting food out of clothing. He commented that it would require more skill to get the clothing off Azaria than to remove the clothing from the goat in the experiment, but conceded that he had been surprised that a dingo could have removed the goat kid and caused so little damage. Dr Newsome had also been surprised.

Further experiments had been carried out at Healesville in Victoria using dolls and pieces of meat in jumpsuits. Tony Raymond found that the dingoes 'would go for the head first'. He said that he had been told by 'the expert' that dingoes would start at the head area and work down and 'that's what happened'.

To his immense interest, he also found that the dingoes would attempt to remove the jumpsuits from the dolls by pulling on the extremities. The jumpsuits came away leaving the booties inside the feet. Azaria's booties had also been found in the feet of her jumpsuit and Raymond had been unable to imagine how a dingo could have removed the body and left them behind. These experiments provided the answer.

The Crown dismissed the experiments as 'failures'. It suggested that the damage to Azaria's jumpsuit 'looks wrong' and referred to a number of witnesses who had expressed the opinion that the damage was not what they would have expected. It was able to extract some support for that proposition from an impressive number of witnesses. However, Professor Cameron and Professor Ferris were pathologists who hailed from England and Canada respectively, both countries which are noted for the paucity of dingoes. Dr Scott was an Australian, but he was a biologist who had formed his opinion on the basis of a comparison between Azaria's jumpsuit and a single experiment about which he, himself, suggested there was a need for caution.

Corbett and Cawood both knew a lot about dingoes, but neither of them had made any study of the manner in which they were likely to damage clothing. Furthermore, neither had seen the results of the experiments. This was important, given that both Newsome and Sims had expressed surprise at the small amount of damage which had been caused. Of the witnesses who supported this proposition, only Sims was an odontologist and he had literally never seen a dingo at the time he wrote his first report. Whilst it was plain that a number of people would have expected more damage, the early experiments demonstrated that the expectations of experts were not always fulfilled.

Sims was not the only odontologist to give evidence. Professor Gustafson had been referred to as 'the father of forensic odontology'. He had written the first book on the topic in 1966 and was still generally acknowledged as the world's leading expert in the field. His extensive research concerning the effect of animal dentition on fabrics was without parallel in the world. He was now eighty years of age, a white-haired old man with twinkling eyes and an almost encyclopaedic knowledge of his subject. His wife had also been a university professor and, like her eminent husband, was sharp and perceptive. They were a delightful couple. During the course of a conference, she explained that her husband had invented a technique involving the use of ultraviolet light for use in the identification of various kinds of damage to fabric. He had done so whilst at the Folies Bérgére watching a scantily clad young lady dancing. He found the effect on her costume fascinating as she wafted in and out of a beam of blue light. His wife waved her finger reprovingly and said with a wry smile, 'Only my husband could come up with an invention that required him to keep going back to the Folies Bērgēre for research purposes.'

Professor Fernhead had been Professor of Dentistry at the universities of London and Hong Kong and now held the Chair at a Japanese university which had offered him not only more money, but far better facilities than his countrymen were able to provide. Sims had been one of his proteges.

Dr Orams gave further evidence before the Commission of Inquiry. His qualifications and experience stamped him as Australia's foremost forensic odontologist and his opinion obviously commanded respect.

It would have been difficult to imagine a more distinguished group of odontologists giving evidence in the one case, yet they were unanimous that the damage evident in Azaria's jumpsuit was quite consistent with causation by the teeth of a dingo.

They were to receive a striking degree of support from an extensive series of experiments conducted by Les Smith and Ken Chapman. Derek Roff's observations also sounded a note of caution. Dingoes seemed to adopt a fastidious method of dealing with prey only when they were not being watched. Expectations based upon observations were likely to prove misleading unless, of course, they had been carried out from a concealed position using, perhaps, a telephoto lens. Dr Corbett had produced a film of a number of dingoes feeding on a carcass but this, again, seemed to provide little guidance. In the circumstances shown in the film some competition for the food was inevitable. It would have been intriguing to find out how many of the experts who expected more damage to the jumpsuit would have given the dingo any chance of extracting a bar of chocolate without tearing the wrapper.

Azaria's clothing had not been found neatly folded as some reports had suggested. Neither Morris nor Goodwin — who found them — suggested anything remotely approaching such a situation. But the clothes had been grouped together within a relatively small area. Dr Corbett said that he could not imagine the clothing being left in the vicinity of a den without being disturbed and scattered. Others were to agree, but Derek Roff was not so sure. 'I find myself having difficulty giving an answer to that,' he said. 'I mean to say, every animal is possibly going to be different, and I would expect, yes, sure it could be scattered, and sure, it could be exactly like this.' Later he explained that 'every dingo is a character in his own right. He's got his own expertise.'

If Corbett was right, it would have suggested the possibility of human involvement. On the other hand, if Roff was correct and there were puppies in the den nearby, it was quite likely that a dingo had brought the baby to that very point and had left the clothes in the manner they were found. Ian Cawood raised a third possibility:

> There's another point that I did think of: that after the clothing was found — it was found in a bundle — that a dingo will take up a bloodstained object and move it, take it back to a lair or take it somewhere but normally chew it. And this was a thought that crossed my mind at the time, that the clothing could have been in fact somewhere in a disarranged fashion and another dog or dingo could have picked it up and by doing so would have rebundled it into a compact sort of an area and take it back and just drop the clothing somewhere after it was first put somewhere else — or first, if the child had been taken from it, but again I would imagine the clothing would have to be torn by the first dingo or the second if that was the case.

Speculation about some form of subsequent intervention, whether by a human being or another dingo, received some support from the extensive pattern of searching carried out by Charlwood's 'task force'. The evidence suggested that those searches continued until the Thursday after Azaria disappeared. The little gully where the jumpsuit was found was apparently not searched, but the police were confident that they would have found the matinee jacket if it had been in the place where it was found in February 1986. The Chamberlains went home on Tuesday. If the jacket was placed there by human hands, the hands were not those of the Chamberlains.

28

Ripping yarns

THE EXTENSIVE SERIES OF EXPERIMENTS by Smith and Chapman had established that the teeth of dingoes could cut fabric. They could also produce tufts indistinguishable from those in Azaria's jumpsuit. Professor Chaikin was surprised. He had described the tufts as the strongest evidence that the jumpsuit had been cut, a fact which excluded causation by a dingo. He then suggested that dingoes' teeth could not produce 'snippets' which he later explained were very short tufts of nylon. Again, however, he was surprised. The experiments showed that dingoes produced not only tufts but snippets. These conclusions were confirmed by Tony Raymond of the Victorian Forensic Science Laboratories and, ultimately, were conceded by Professor Chaikin. The main thrust of his evidence at the trial, that the jumpsuit had been cut and not torn, had abruptly become irrelevant.

It seemed surprising that this was not known at the time of the trial. Professor Gustafson's book *Forensic Odontology* had referred to the shearing action of the carnassial teeth when it was published in 1966. However, it was obvious that Stuart Tipple had experienced great difficulty in finding other textile experts willing to become involved in the matter. Professor Chaikin, giving evidence that Tipple had been to see him shortly before the trial, said: 'He started off by saying that there was no recourse to any other textile expert in Australia and therefore it was important for the defence to receive the benefit of my knowledge on the textile and fibre aspects of the case.' Furthermore, Professor Gustafson was an odontologist rather than a textile expert. It was understandable that a textile expert may not have been familiar with his work. Whatever the explanation, it was now clear that one could not exclude the possibility that the jumpsuit had been damaged by a dingo merely because it had been cut rather than torn.

Before the Commission of Inquiry, Professor Chaikin took a different tack. Whilst cuts might be caused by either a sharp implement or by the teeth of a dingo, it was possible to distinguish between the types of cuts. Cuts caused by a sharp instrument, he said, may exhibit 'planar array'. This was defined as an alignment of the severed ends of the fibres within a number of consecutive yarns. The phrase seemed to have been invented for the purpose of the inquiry, but Professor Chaikin had referred to the concept of the fibres being in alignment during his evidence at the trial. He suggested that the limit of deviation in the planarity would be about 'one-tenth or one-twentieth of a millimetre between the fibres, or two or three diameters' difference . . . or just a coarse human hair difference' and later added, 'well, you can have an approximation. In fact they line up as seen yesterday, one or two hairs' difference.'

In November 1986, Professor Chaikin asked his colleague, Dr Griffith, to examine the jumpsuit. Dr Griffith formed the opinion that the cut in the collar had been formed by a single stroke of a knife. He carried out demonstrations by holding the collar of a jumpsuit in a folded formation against the neck of a doll and slashing a knife across the throat.

Ultimately, a number of jumpsuits damaged in that fashion were tendered. They displayed cuts which resembled, in varying degrees, the damage to Azaria's jumpsuit.

Dr Griffith defined the concept of 'planar array' somewhat differently from Professor Chaikin. He insisted that it must extend over a line of at least five millimetres, but suggested that the degree of deviation could be as much as a whole yarn, which was about seven times the thickness of an individual fibre.

Dr Robinson was a microscopist. He had operated the scanning electron microscope when Professor Chaikin first made his observations of the jumpsuit. He also regarded 'planar array' as being characteristic of damage by sharp scissors, but defined the concept as an alignment within a tolerance of a distance equal to one fibre diameter.

Dr Griffiths had acknowledged that two competent and intellectually honest scientists could come to different conclusions about the presence of planar array in a particular cut. This was evident not only in the disagreement among the Crown witnesses concerning the degree of deviation permissible, but as to whether there had to be a continuous sequence involving every fibre in a number of consecutive yarns or whether the phenomenon could be intermittent. Dr Robinson favoured the view that there must be a continuous sequence, whilst Dr Griffiths held that the planarity might be intermittent.

The experiments conducted by Smith and Chapman had produced many samples of cloth cut by the teeth of dingoes. Some of these cuts were quite straight and, even when examined under an optical microscope, appeared to exhibit the phenomenon which the 'Chaikin team' had referred to as 'planar array'. The Crown countered by leading evidence from Chaikin, Griffiths and Robinson to the effect that one could only determine the presence of planar array by examination under a scanning electron microscope which offered a considerably higher level of magnification and a greater depth of field. Smith and Chapman acknowledged that they were not textile experts, though it seemed that no textile expert or odontologist, save for Professor Gustafson, had carried out an extensive programme of experimentation as they had.

Towards the end of 1986 Dr Bill Pelton, a Canadian textile expert now working in Australia, was asked to review their findings and to offer his own opinion of the degree of similarity between the dingo-damaged samples and the cut evident in Azaria's jumpsuit. He supported the conclusions of Smith and Chapman. The damage was remarkably similar. He also dismissed the suggestion that one could only make a valid assessment with the aid of a scanning electron microscope. The degree of magnification was too great. One could only see one or two yarns at a time. The fact that the cloth had to be wrapped around the stub meant that one could not 'sight along' a flat line of severance. The angle at which the severed ends of the yarns were viewed could also be misleading and that risk was increased by the much-vaunted depth of field which sometimes gave the impression that two fibres were side by side, when in fact one was considerably lower than the other. With the optical microscope one could manipulate the sample at will and sight along the edges of the cut yarns. With the scanning electron microscope one had to work from a series of two-dimensional images. Photographs — or 'micrographs' as they were known — were taken of these images and the individual micrographs were then pieced together in an attempt to obtain a continuous image. The resultant 'montage' might consist of a crooked line of micrographs joined together in a pattern which reflected the line of cut yarns. Dr Pelton was supported in his view that the optical microscope offered an equally valid means of determining the planarity of the fibres by Professor Bresee and Professor Fernhead.

Ultimately, Mr Justice Morling asked Porter to endeavour to find an independent microscopist who could throw some light on this controversy. Porter duly obtained the assistance of Dr Hoschke of the Commonwealth Scientific and Industrial Research Organisation (CSIRO). Dr Hoschke gave evidence that the experts in his laboratory used scanning electron microscopes for the purpose of studying the severed ends of individual fibres. A fibre was so fine that the added magnification offered by such an instrument was indispensable. When it came to determining the planarity of a line of severance, however, they normally went back to an optical microscope.

Dr Hoschke also suggested that the term 'planar array' had been misused. The concept involved an alignment of fibres within very fine tolerances. In order to achieve such planarity, CSIRO scientists actually went to the lengths of sharpening scissors under a scanning electron microscope to ensure that they were as sharp as human ingenuity could make them. Such a degree of planarity was not evident in the damage to Azaria's jumpsuit. Indeed, one could not produce it in terry towelling material. It could be accomplished only in a fabric which had a tight weave. The degree of deviation suggested by Dr Griffiths and others fell well outside the normal concept of planar array. It, no doubt, delineated a degree of planarity, but it was a novel concept to suggest that some semi-planar configuration could be used to distinguish between damage caused by teeth and that caused by a sharp instrument. He went on to say that even the presence of planar array as it is usually understood may have offered a means of distinguishing cuts from tears, but that he had never heard any expert suggest that it offered a means of distinguishing cuts caused in one manner from cuts caused in another.

Dr Robinson had produced montages for the purpose of illustrating the difference between a true planar array caused by a scalpel and a mere straight cut caused by dingo teeth. These montages were later shown to Dr Hoschke. He was not impressed. The scalpel cut shown in the montage produced as an example of planar array was, he said, less planar than the damage caused by dingo teeth shown in the montage produced to demonstrate the difference.

Dr Pelton agreed that the montage of damage caused by cutting with a scalpel did not display planar array. Tony Raymond said that if the term was used to denote the damage in the 'V' cut evident in Azaria's jumpsuit when Dr Robinson pointed it out to him under the scanning electron microscope in November 1986, then he had seen planar array in material damaged by dingoes. Professor Bresee agreed.

The Crown argued that the observations of Professor Chaikin and Dr Robinson in 1981 established that the jumpsuit had been damaged by a cutting instrument even if that conclusion could not be formed on the basis of an examination in 1986. However, Dr Robinson had taken few notes and no photographs of what he had seen in 1981. Neither he nor Professor Chaikin had realised that dingo teeth could cut and, consequently, each had understood that their task was merely to distinguish cutting from tearing. Futhermore, if Dr Hoschke was correct, their observations were of little value because a study of the planarity of the fibres was not a recognised means of distinguishing one type of cut from another, no matter how contemporaneous or accurate the observations may be.

Furthermore, Dr Brown, the dentist who had given evidence at the first inquest, had taken photographs of the damage at a relatively early stage. When those photographs were compared with the current state of the damage, they revealed little change due to the passage of time. That impression was confirmed by the condition of the scissor cuts which Dr Scott had made when he removed a sample of the material for testing. Those cuts had retained their planarity since late 1980. Tony Raymond gave evidence that the appearance of the 'V' cut in Dr Brown's photographs was not inconsistent with damage by a dingo.

Whilst Dr Robinson was not mentioned at the trial, he had done much of the work upon which Professor Chaikin relied for his conclusions and conceded that much of Chaikin's report had reflected his views. At that stage only one dingo experiment had been conducted. When it became apparent that dingoes could not only produce tufts but snippets, Professor Chaikin did conduct some further experiments using scissors, steel bars and a 'Stoll' tester but not dingo or dog teeth. By the time he was called to give evidence before the Commission of Inquiry, Dr Robinson had seen a few more samples of dingo-damaged fabric but his observations had, in the main, been confined to relatively straight sections of the cuts, an approach which Dr Hoschke described as being 'less than scientifically rigorous'. Dr Robinson rejected this criticism and pointed out that one only needed to examine a single pair of scissors to understand how they worked. However, the evidence of the odontologists established that, unlike scissors, there were enormous variations in the cutting capacity of dingo teeth. Dr Orams pointed out that dingoes living in a sandy environment, such as the region surrounding Ayers Rock, might be expected to have sharper teeth than their brethren living in more fertile regions.

The Crown suggested that the absence of detritus, biological fluid such as blood and/or saliva capable of binding the fibre ends together, offered a significant indication that the 'V' cut in the collar of Azaria's jumpsuit had not been caused by a dingo. There were two difficulties with this argument. Firstly, there was evidence that the fibre ends in the 'V' cut had remained relatively straight *because* they had been bound together by detritus. As Dr Pelton pointed out, the combination of compression and detritus was significant. It was what one would have expected from the shearing action of the carnassial teeth. Secondly, there were samples of dingo-damaged fabric in which the severances were apparently free from detritus. Consequently, even if Dr Robinson had been correct in his assertion that there was none present in the 'V' cut, it would not have justified the conclusion for which the Crown contended. In fact, Dr Hoschke found that the montage of dingo-damaged fabric which Dr Robinson had prepared displayed no sign of detritus.

Another distinguishing feature was said to be a 'classic scissor cut'. When fabric is cut by scissors, the thickness of the yarns produces distortion of the individual fibres which, in the main, will be broken rather than cut cleanly, although to the naked eye the overall appearance of the yarn would suggest a cut rather than a tear. Every now and again, however, a microscopist will pick up a fibre end which has been cut cleanly and shows signs of compression from both sides. These are the characteristics of a classic scissor cut. It differs markedly from a classic 'razor cut' which is characterised by a flat uncompressed end marked by striations in the direction of the cut. A classic scissor cut had been found in the sleeve of Azaria's jumpsuit. Dr Robinson gave evidence that he had never seen a classic scissor cut in dingo-damaged fabric and the high probability was that one could never be found. Dr Pelton and Dr Hoschke both stated that at least one was evident in Dr Robinson's own montage of dingo-damaged fabric.

The 'V' cut was of particular interest to Dr Sanson, a zoologist who had made an extensive study of the manner in which kangaroos and other macropods chew plant fibres. The other damage, he conceded, could well have been caused by a dingo, but he found it difficult to conceive of any mechanism by which the teeth of a canine could have caused the 'V' cut. Mr Justice Morling was to find him an 'impressive witness', but even he was not prepared to assert that causation by a dingo was impossible.

Dr Griffiths' theory of the 'V' cut being caused by a single knife stroke injected a note of drama into the textile evidence. Professor Cameron had said that the baby's throat had been cut. Now it seemed that the same slash of the knife, or perhaps another in a series of slashes, may have caused the damage to the collar of Azaria's jumpsuit. The 'V' cut was no longer a subsequent attempt to simulate a dingo attack, but the legacy of a murder.

The collar, the Crown suggested, had by coincidence been

folded in a particular manner. Griffiths' experiment demonstrated that the cuts in the collar could be aligned in a manner which would explain how they could have been cut by a single knife stroke if the collar was folded in that manner. Unhappily, he too had carried out no research into the nature of the fabric damage likely to be caused by dingoes. However, he maintained that his hypothesis would account for the damage.

'. . . [S]ince you see no other way in which it could be reproduced, therefore it must have been reproduced in that way?' the Crown asked.

'Yes,' Griffiths replied, 'I say that.'

As Mr Justice Morling pointed out, this left even the Crown experts divided. Professor Chaikin and Barry Cocks had both suggested that the damage had been caused by scissors. On the other hand, Sims had conceded that the 'V' cut in the collar was the sort of damage which might have been expected from carnassial teeth and that it would be difficult to replicate it with scissors. Now Griffiths had suggested that it was not caused by scissors but by a knife. Counsel for the Chamberlains were to accuse the Crown of endeavouring to resolve conflicts of this kind by a selective use of the evidence:

> Professor Chaikin and that doyen of South Australian forensic science, Mr Cocks, are applauded when they give evidence of scissor cuts, but ignored when Dr Griffiths' brand-new Wiltshire Staysharp knife hypothesis is propounded. Dr Sanson, on the other hand, is applauded for his comments about the 'V' cut in the collar, but ignored when he concedes that the remainder of the damage to the jumpsuit may be consistent with damage by a dingo.

A similar selectivity also seemed evident in the Crown's approach to the evidence concerning the manner in which the 'V' cut may have been caused. It was suggested that the opinions of Smith and Chapman were of little value because they failed to resolve the 'geometric problem'. They had demonstrated that dingoes could produce damage which corresponded to each feature in the 'V' cut, but had not demonstrated that they could produce the overall pattern. As Barker pointed out, to prove that a dingo could produce ten straight lines did not prove that it could produce a perfect star-shaped formation.

When it came to Griffiths' experiments, however, the Crown sought to rely upon the fact that he had produced the 'ingredients' and to suggest that the rest was within the range of 'experimental possibilities'. Not only Sims but Professor Fernhead, Professor Gustafson and Dr Orams all agreed that a dingo could have caused the damage. Chapman suggested one possible mechanism which, however, Dr Sanson found unacceptable. Professor Gustafson suggested a number of possible mechanisms, but added '. . . It's a guess. As every opinion concerning this are guesses. No-one has seen a dingo cutting it on the baby.'

There were further hurdles in the path of the knife theory. Dr Griffiths had said that it would explain not only the 'V' cut in the collar, but also the damage to the sleeve. Yet the sleeve damage contained a classic scissor cut which could only be produced by opposing forces coming together in the manner one would expect of scissors or teeth, but not a knife on a soft background. Dr Hoschke also confirmed that his experiments had indicated that a planar array could not be obtained by means of a sharp knife used on fabric stretched over even a moderately soft surface, such as a newspaper on a table. It seemed likely that the soft surface of the baby's neck would also have made it more difficult to retain the configurations of the folds. Dr Griffiths, himself, conceded that it was easier using dolls of hard plastic. Furthermore, when Dr Pelton examined the samples which Dr Griffiths had produced by means of his experiments, he found that they did not reproduce all of the features of the damage to the collar of Azaria's jumpsuit and, in fact, contained a number of 'points of dissimilarity'.

However, Dr Pelton's evidence did not merely cast doubt on some of the Crown's conclusions. He had carried out an extensive study of the samples of cloth damaged by dingoes in the experiments conducted by Smith and Chapman. He found twenty-eight points of similarity between dingo-damaged fabric and the damage in Azaria's jumpsuit. Of those twenty-eight points, he found that twelve would have been difficult to reproduce with scissors even if one had known what kind of damage to cause. Four points of similarity would have been very difficult, if not impossible, to reproduce with scissors. He noted that even Sergeant Cocks, who was armed with sharp curved scissors, a seemingly limitless supply of jumpsuits and ample time in which to practise, was unable to reproduce these features despite having the original jumpsuit in front of him to use as a pattern. Dr Pelton pointed out that one would need more than a pair of scissors because the damage was a mixture of cutting and tearing and the yarns had been pulled in a manner which would have required the use of tweezers if it had been caused by a human being. Furthermore, the evidence suggested that no textile expert or odontologist in the world would have been able to anticipate the nature and range of the damage likely to have been caused by a dingo.

The Crown seemed to be reduced to suggesting that this weary and distraught couple sat up in their motel room in the early hours of the morning, 'took a stab at it' and, by the merest coincidence, produced nothing inconsistent with damage by a dingo but twenty-eight points of similarity. Not surprisingly, Dr Pelton concluded that the damage was 'highly unlikely' to have been caused by human intervention and 'highly likely' to have been caused by a dingo or dog.

29

Were the Chamberlains believable?

BEFORE THE COMMISSION OF INQUIRY the Crown again attacked the Chamberlains' veracity. Both Lindy and Michael were cross-examined at length. Suggestions of lying sparked a sharp retort from Lindy. 'I do not like you, Mr Barker. I never have and I never will.' Later she was to accuse him of a 'nitpicking' approach to the evidence.

The Crown suggested that Lindy could not be telling the truth about seeing the dingo emerge from the tent. If the dingo 'emerged from the tent in full view of her gaze' then, as the Crown asked the jury, 'How could she possibly have been unable to see, in the mouth of that animal, her child, Azaria?' Yet she had constantly maintained that, although she saw the dingo shaking its head, she had been unable to see anything in its mouth. The Crown suggested that it was impossible to reconcile her ability to describe the head and ears of the dingo in minute detail with her claim that she had been unable to see anything in the animal's mouth. Lindy countered by suggesting that the baby may have been obscured by the log which formed the rail of a low fence delineating the boundary of the area set aside for camping or, alternatively, by one of the low shrubs which grew between the barbecue area and the tent.

At the trial, the Crown had been able to rely upon the evidence of Les Harris to the effect that a dingo is likely to carry prey with its head erect. Consequently, it was argued , if the dingo had taken the child it would have emerged from the tent with its head held high and the baby would have been readily visible to Lindy. Evidence given before the Commission of Inquiry, however, suggested that, whilst that opinion might be right, one could not count on it. No-one had ever seen a dingo try to manoeuvre through the flaps of a tent with a baby in its jaws and no one really knew how it might go about such a task, even if there had not been two dingoes as Roff and Newsome surmised. It was all speculative.

The Crown also suggested that she could not be telling the truth when she claimed that she believed that the dingo had the baby yet 'dived straight for the tent'. In fact, Lindy gave evidence that as she approached the tent she saw that the bassinette was empty. She cried out, but still 'dived' into the tent to check. It was a perfectly normal, human reaction. Some things are too horrific to be easily assimilated. One does not want to believe the evidence of one's own eyes. Even when the harsh reality of the situation is inescapable one hopes against hope that one might be wrong. As Lindy explained at the trial, 'To know something is true and to accept it are two different things.'

When further pressed about this aspect of her evidence, Lindy explained, '[M]y mind refused to accept that it had her in its mouth — although sort of — it must be it.' When interviewed by Detective Sergeant Charlwood on 30 September 1980, she told him that she had felt in the carry cot to make sure the baby was not there 'even though I could see she wasn't'. Neither Morris nor Roff were willing to discount the possibility that the child may have been simply tipped out of the bassinette and concealed in the blankets strewn nearby. Each took the precaution of checking for himself.

At the trial, Barker had been able to make one devastating point. Lindy had not only claimed that there were paw marks on the space blanket, but that several members of her family had also seen them. Yet none of them had been called to give evidence in her support. How could the jury believe her if even her mother would not support her story? Before the Commission of Inquiry, the position was different. Not only her mother, but her brother and sister-in-law had all given evidence of seeing the prints. Yet another source of suspicion had been shown to be without foundation.

Equally, the Crown had been able to 'refute' the suggestion that a purple blanket had been damaged by the claws or teeth of a dingo by pointing to evidence that the damage had, in fact, been caused by insects. The implication was obvious. The insect damage had been there all along and the Chamberlains had sought to take advantage of it by passing it off as tears or rips caused by a dingo. However, the evidence of Mrs Hansell established that there had been no damage to the blankets when the Chamberlains left for Ayers Rock and Hilary Tabrett had seen cuts in them within a few days of Azaria's disappearance. Her evidence was supported by the examination of Dr Pelton, who found that insects could not have accounted for the whole of the damage. This allegation of lying had also been based upon a misconception.

The Crown also suggested that there was something sinister about the production of two Army 'giggle' hats which Mrs Chamberlain produced to the police during the course of their search in 1981. The Chamberlains had apparently taken the hats to Ayers Rock with them and Lindy handed them over when she was asked to produce anything which might have blood on it. Scientific testing ascertained that the stains on the hats were not blood, but a substance similar to gum arabic . The Crown suggested that this could not have been an honest mistake. Mrs Chamberlain must have endeavoured to deceive the police or 'taunt' them with evidence which would subsequently prove to be of no value.

It was a strange submission. Gum arabic and similar substances are found in a number of food additives and in varnishes and other household liquids. The hats had simply been thrown into a large cupboard and there was no evidence to suggest that the stains had not come into existence innocently, perhaps, through some childhood project. Not only Inspector Charlwood but even Joy Kuhl thought that the stains looked like blood and there appeared to be little reason to suppose that Mrs Chamberlain had not been similarly misled.

Ultimately, the criticism seemed to rest upon an implicit assumption that any mother would be able to adequately explain the nature and origin of stains found on any piece of cloth within her family home, a proposition which most mothers would have regarded as more than a little dubious. Furthermore, the Chamberlains had already sat through the first inquest and had heard evidence of scientific tests to determine the presence of blood. It seemed highly unlikely that they would not have realised that any attempt to pass off gum arabic or some similar substance as blood was doomed to failure.

Both of the Chamberlains had also been criticised for their limited participation in the searching. However, the evidence established that Michael had taken part in the searches initially and that he had, in fact, run feverishly into the scrub, returning only to find a torch. Within a relatively short period of time, a major search had been organised. The Chamberlains had given evidence that they had been asked to wait near the tent for any news. In any event, they had two young boys — one of whom, a four-year-old, was fast asleep. Two more searchers would have made little difference and it was scarcely unreasonable for them to conclude that they should comply with the police direction and remain with their children.

Michael Chamberlain was also criticised on a number of bases. He had clearly given varying descriptions of the baby's cry. He had referred to it variously as a 'faint cry', 'an insignificant short cry', 'an urgent cry, not loud', 'cut off', 'as if the baby was being squeezed', 'a short sharp cry', 'a cry of someone being squeezed, almost out of breath' and 'a significant cry'. It is no doubt difficult to adequately describe a cry which may have occupied no more than a second or two and the varying descriptions may have reflected nothing more sinister than different attributes of a cry related in response to different contexts.

During the course of his evidence before the first inquest, Michael made it plain that he was finding it difficult to describe the cry with precision. 'That is a very hard question to ask me,' he explained, 'but I will do my best . It seemed to me a cry of someone being squeezed almost out of breath, as if it were a cry — or it sounded to me as a pretty important cry. Mothers have instincts and, I guess, fathers have instincts too.'

Mr Justice Morling was to conclude that there were 'some slight differences in these descriptions, but they are of no great consequence.'

Michael was criticised for failing to inquire about the progress of the searchers during the day after his baby had disappeared. Mr Justice Morling was to find that there was little weight in this criticism. He was in the midst of a very small community and was entitled to assume that the police would contact him immediately they had anything to report. Furthermore, he had by then resigned himself to the fact that his child was dead, a resignation confirmed by Morris when he asked him to complete a 'Notification of Death' form for the coroner.

A further basis for criticism was Michael's apparent failure to exhibit sufficient grief on the evening of Azaria's disappearance and the following day. He explained that by reference to the comfort which he had obtained from his faith and by his desire to demonstrate the reality of that faith to others. Several witnesses had referred to him as a man who was obviously undergoing a considerable struggle to maintain self-control and, all in all, there seemed little doubt that he had been distraught at the death of his child. One solicitor in the public gallery was to confide that she had behaved in a very similar fashion when her son had been killed in a car accident. She had gone back to work the same day and had exhibited no sign of distress, though she had deeply loved her son and had been heartbroken by his death.

People react to grief in such diverse ways. To suggest that a stoical exterior was evidence of complicity in murder seemed preposterous. On any view of the evidence, Michael had lost his daughter. Why should he have been expected to have experienced less grief if she had been murdered?

Mr Justice Morling was to suggest that the most suspicious aspect of Michael's conduct was his statement to Derek Roff, about half-an-hour after Azaria's disappearance, to the effect that he did not expect Azaria to be found alive. However, as he pointed out, Michael had been told by Greg Lowe that 'there's not going to be any joy for you, mate.' The prospect of his daughter having been devoured by a dingo was obviously an horrific one. It was suggested that, in the context, Michael was seeking Roff's reassurance that the baby would have died quickly. If there was no other consolation available to him, he wished to be assured that she had not been left hideously mauled to suffer a lingering death.

Mr Justice Morling also referred to Michael's bent for 'theatrical language'. This, he said, gave some of his evidence 'a ring of unreality'.

He described Michael's description of the quantity of blood in the tent as 'patently ridiculous' and pointed out that it could not have deceived anyone who had been inside the tent to see for himself. The Crown had relied upon this description as branding Michael a liar, but Mr Justice Morling concluded that it did no more than 'reflect his proclivity for hyperbole'.

There was an obvious need to exercise caution in considering the various criticisms made by the Crown. Many of the earlier statements said to be lies had been shown to be true. The jury had, for example, been invited to doubt the existence of the matinee jacket. Furthermore, both Lindy and Michael had been through an appalling experience. Their minds must have been full of the horror of it all. Many people would have become incoherent or hysterical in such circumstances and even the most level-headed or stoical could have been forgiven for becoming confused about details.

There were also strong grounds for suggesting that the Chamberlains were people of integrity. The evidence established that they had been people of impeccable character, who had shared a strong Christian faith and an adherence to the traditional Christian principles of morality. There had been no motive for Lindy to kill the child and it seemed unlikely that a mother who still had the 'new mum glow' about her would do so. She had displayed no symptoms of post-natal depression or any other psychological disturbance that might account for such a seemingly inexplicable act.

It was difficult to imagine that Lindy had had time to accomplish everything which the Crown suggested within the limited time she was away from the barbecue area. It seemed equally unlikely that she could have done so without alerting Aidan and without displaying any sign of distress when she returned.

Michael's suggestion that he had heard the baby cry at a time when, on the Crown case, it must have been dead, was corroborated by Aidan, Mrs Lowe, and possibly another camper, Mrs Dawson, who had heard the baby cry at about that time but could not be certain it had been on the Sunday night rather than the night before. It seemed highly unlikely that Lindy had had the opportunity to tell Michael what she had done by then and he apparently had no motive to lie. It seemed fanciful to suggest that all three of them had simultaneously made the same mistake. It also seemed surprising that Mrs Chamberlain had not decided to 'hop on the bandwagon' and claim that she, too, had heard the cry if, in fact, she was a murderess seeking to provide herself with an alibi.

The distress she displayed after giving the alarm was obviously genuine and, whilst it was possible that a woman who had killed her child would be equally distressed, it seemed unlikely that she would have been able to maintain a calm demeanour prior to giving the alarm if she had already known that the baby was dead and had been forced to contend with such a strong emotional response.

The direction which she indicated had been taken by the dingo proved to correspond to the direction of the tracks found by Derek Roff, yet he had picked them out some seventeen to eighteen metres from the tent on the side away from the barbecue light and it seemed unlikely that Mrs Chamberlain would have been able to see them in the dark.

The very fact that she had not claimed to have seen the baby in the dingo's mouth also suggested candour. If she had been making up the whole story, then why should she have passed up the opportunity to say that she had seen the baby in the dingo's jaws?

The questions which Mr Justice Morling had raised during Porter's opening address were also of great significance. It seemed fanciful to suggest that Michael would have left his surviving children with Lindy in the morning if he knew that she had murdered Azaria the night before. It seemed even more implausible that he would have permitted her to continue raising them without taking steps to ensure that she received adequate psychiatric treatment.

The Chamberlains' conduct upon their return to Mount Isa could only have been described as remarkable if they had been attempting to cover up the commission of a murder. Michael had written to the Northern Territory Conservation Commission suggesting the erection of a dingo-proof fence and other steps to protect children from attacks by dingoes. The letter almost invited an inquiry into the incident. Lindy had blithely shown her tracksuit pants to Mrs Ransom and asked her to take them to the drycleaners. It seemed an extraordinary step to take if the pants had borne the telltale marks of a murder. It seemed equally unlikely that she would have volunteered the suggestion that there had been blood on her tracksuit and shoes, especially since no one else had claimed to have seen it. The fact that the correct camera bag had been produced and that the Chamberlains had displayed an extraordinary degree of cooperation in identifying the items taken to Ayers Rock would also have been amazing given that no one could have known what was there and what was not.

There were also remarkable examples of candour in Lindy's evidence. The Crown had been at a loss to explain how Lindy could have washed her hands until she answered a question about 'a water bottle'. 'When you say water bottles,' she volunteered, 'there were big two or four gallon containers and we had four of them. Three of them were right back in the boot area with the petrol — two of them in the boot and one on the roof or one on the roof and two in the boot and the juice container was down at my feet.'

Lindy was equally candid in her concession that a bloodstained towel could have been hidden in a green garbage bag. She also told the Commission that there had been an esky in the boot, although there had been no hint of that in any of the police evidence. She agreed that it would have been big enough to have hidden the body of a baby. When asked about Sergeant Cocks' experiments designed to reproduce the damage in Azaria's jumpsuit with a pair of scissors, she volunteered the fact that she was a dressmaker and that she could have done a better job of it than he had done.

In many respects, Michael seemed to display an equal degree of candour. He frequently went to considerable pains to make it plain that he was not sure about evidence that would have been in his favour.

There was also the obvious problem that, if Lindy's story of having seen the dingo was a lie formulated on the spur of the moment, she must have been an incredibly fortunate woman because the tracks indicated that a dingo had stopped at the rear of the tent adjacent to the bassinette, had then come around to the front, entered the tent, re-emerged with an object which proved to be wrapped in coarse cloth and had departed in the direction Lindy indicated had been taken by the dingo she had invented.

The coincidence seemed remarkable.

30

The arguments

BY THE TIME THE LAST WITNESS LEFT the box, it was obvious that the evidence was radically different from that led at the trial:

☐ there was no arterial spray of blood, let alone infant blood, on the plate under the dashboard;

☐ there was no blood, or at least no detectable amount of blood, in the carpets of the car;

☐ there may well have been no blood on the tracksuit pants;

☐ if there had been any blood in the car at all, it was present in small amounts consistent with bleeding by Mr Lenehan or, more probably, by some child who had bled in the car since August 1980;

☐ the blood on the jumpsuit was probably caused by post-mortem bleeding;

☐ consequently, death had probably not been caused by an incised wound to the throat;

☐ the teeth of dingoes could cut fabric and, in doing so, could produce tufts and snippets;

☐ paw prints had been seen on the space blanket;

☐ there had been a matinee jacket;

☐ if there were any marks which could be construed as impressions of hand prints, one was in such a position that it could not have been caused during the act of murder, and the other one was primarily red sand rather than blood;

☐ there were tears in the purple blanket which could not be accounted for by the action of insects;

☐ there were dog hairs on the jumpsuit which might have been consistent with the guard hairs of a dingo;

☐ the Chamberlains had not kept people away from the car but had, in fact, invited the Demaines to it shortly after Azaria disappeared;

☐ there was much stronger evidence concerning the likelihood of a dingo attacking a child at Ayers Rock in August 1980;

☐ there was much stronger evidence of the tracks of a dingo in positions which could only be described as sinister; and

☐ many of the grounds for suggesting that the Chamberlains had lied had been misconceived and, in those respects at least, the Chamberlains had been vindicated.

The addresses occupied some nine days and were supplemented by literally hundreds of pages of written submissions.

John Winneke commenced with a stinging attack on the Crown case:

> This was clearly a unique murder case. There was no body, no weapon, no motive and, far from any confession, a protestation of innocence based on facts contemporaneously stated and which, if true, themselves reveal the enormous travesty of justice which has been occasioned to the Chamberlains. This was not a case where an alleged murder victim had disappeared in circumstances of isolation where opportunities to kill and dispose of a body are obvious; rather this was a case where the alleged victim disappeared from a public camping area within metres of persons known to be there by Mrs Chamberlain and in circumstances where hundreds of people responded within minutes to her call for help.
>
> It was, accordingly, not a case where there was a shortage of reliable and independent witnesses to the events surrounding the disappearance of the victim. On the contrary, there were campers, locals, police, rangers and Aboriginal trackers. These people, we submit, have almost universally supported the Chamberlains — and with good reason.
>
> It must, indeed, be a very strange murder case giving rise to very strong doubts when the chief ranger of the National Park . . . maintains and always has maintained that not only was the mother's explanation for the disappearance of her child an inherently believable one because of the behavioural patterns that had been established by dingoes at the time, but that . . . he has absolutely no doubt that, tragic and unusual though it may have

> been, Azaria Chamberlain was, in fact, taken by a dingo. And even if Mr Roff stood alone, doubts would always accompany a murder conviction which spurned his views. But he does not stand alone. In fact, we submit it is fair to say that every person closely associated with the Chamberlains on that night and who assisted in the search for their child entertained no doubt as to the truth of the mother's explanation.

He turned to the opinion evidence which he described as 'carelessly formed and fundamentally in error':

> The Chamberlains were the victims of it and have suffered a gross miscarriage of justice on account of it. Not only have they suffered the injury occasioned by the tragic loss of their daughter in circumstances entirely beyond their control, but they have suffered the insult of the convictions, the direct consequences which followed, and the ignominy thrust upon them by a lusting and disbelieving community. . .
>
> It is a measure, we submit, of the inadequacy of this case that it can never be particularised, can never be pinned down. Its very nature enabled the Crown to skate from one hypothesis to another. It is not, we submit, a murder case. It is rather a chameleon and a nightmare for the people charged.

He demanded that the Crown face up to a number of questions:

> Firstly, why would Mrs Chamberlain have killed her daughter whom she so obviously adored? How could she have done it in the time available to her? Why would she and how could she do it in the presence and in the vicinity of her seven-year-old son and still retain his obvious love, respect and confidence? How could she retain a relaxed composure in the presence of other people? How could she have done it without showing any signs of blood on herself or her clothing? How could she tell her husband about it with so many people around and obtain his full confidence without apparent demur? How could they have concealed and disposed of the baby without anybody knowing or suspecting, and how could they have disposed of the clothing on the night of this tragedy without someone knowing about that or suspecting that it occurred? These improbabilities are the very matters which would have made cautious people suspect the validity of the expert opinion evidence which was led in defiance of it.

Winneke went back to the evidence of those who had been present on the night Azaria disappeared and stressed the significance of their evidence.

'It cannot be denied sensibly that Mrs Lowe and Mr Chamberlain and Aidan heard a cry which they believed was the cry of Azaria or that it came from the direction of the Chamberlains' tent.' The incident, he said, was important for two reasons. Firstly, 'Azaria must have been alive at the time and therefore the Crown case is quite wrong.' Secondly, it was an event 'perceived by others and not by Mrs Chamberlain.'

> If, as the Crown alleges, that was nothing more than the commencement of a gigantic fraud and cover-up, then it was indeed an extraordinary coincidence that she was given the chance to perpetrate it, not by her own initiative, but by the initiative of others. The significance of this evidence has always been apparent to the police and the Northern Territory Crown. And that is why, no doubt, they tried so very hard to break Mrs Lowe down, to use their own words, to such an extent that she and her husband went to a solicitor to see what rights she had as a witness. But having failed to break her down, it is now asserted that she is an unreliable witness. Another explanation might just be that the Northern Territory authorities, and particularly the police, are so obsessed with their belief of the Chamberlains' guilt that they have become quite unprepared to accept with an open mind any material which suggests to the contrary.

Winneke referred to the Demaines' evidence that Lindy had asked them to bring their dog to the car and that she had opened the door and rummaged around for some clothing to give it the scent:

> The significance of this evidence, we submit, is obvious. Firstly, it is conduct quite inconsistent with the proposition made by the Crown that very shortly beforehand Mrs Chamberlain had cut her daughter's throat in that very part of the car. Secondly, the evidence destroys the assertion made by the Crown at the trial that the Chamberlains were attempting to turn the car into some sort of a shrine during the night so that they could protect their secret. This was an utterly baseless allegation that was made.

He pointed out that whatever the Chamberlains said they could not win. If they said something incriminatory, it was used against them; if they said something exculpatory, they were accused of lying. 'It is, with respect, Your Honour, unusual that on the one hand people would want to use Mrs Chamberlain's frankness and openness for one purpose and then at the same time say, "She is being terribly devious in another way". The same thing has happened about her wretched tracksuit and her sandshoes. I mean, why on earth could anybody suspect that she knew that there was blood on the tracksuit when she had already cleaned the sandshoes and told the police that, in her view, there had been blood on them?'

His submissions included an invitation for Mr Justice Morling to make sixteen separate findings of fact. Winneke summarised their effect:

> In short, we submit to Your Honour that the facts tell a story of a stifled baby's cry being heard by Mrs Lowe, Mr Chamberlain and probably Aidan, coming from the Chamberlain tent. They tell a story of a mother in a composed state returning to the tent to check the reason. They tell a story of an anguished cry of that mother that a dingo had taken her baby, and of a complete change in the mother's state of composure. They tell a story of a little boy, aged about seven years, crying, "the dingo has got my bubby in its tummy", of the baby's blankets being in a state of disarray in the tent, and with blood and holes in them suggesting that a baby had been yanked out of the bassinette by force.
>
> They tell a story of experienced trackers and rangers finding tracks around the tent and in the sandhill behind the tent which convinced them that a dingo had taken the baby and that the mother's explanation was true; and they tell a story of canine paw prints being found, at the first available opportunity after the event, upon an item which was within the tent and which lay between the tent's entrance and the baby's bassinette. The facts therefore, we submit, tell a story that substantiates in the most material respects the explanation which the mother gave for the tragic loss of her child.

He then turned to the scientific evidence:

We submit to Your Honour that in the long run you should not hesitate to find that Professor Cameron's highly prejudiced opinion as to the existence on this jumpsuit of hand prints in blood is not only incorrect as a question of fact, but was uttered with carelessness and with the knowledge that it was likely to cause mischief back in Australia; and it did. This Commission should find, we submit, that Professor Cameron's opinion as to the cause of death is little more than speculation based on very tenuous support and expertise. . .

We submit that you should find that Mrs Kuhl was demonstrably wrong about the existence of foetal blood under the dashboard, and on the scissors, and on the camera bag, and on the chamois, and on the towel; and further, that the whole of her approach to her task was infected by a lack of understanding of the task which she had at hand. Accordingly, we submit that you should find that the very damaging and prejudicial allegations made against the Chamberlains on the basis of her evidence really had no evidential foundation at all. . .

In so far as Mrs Kuhl's evidence was used as a basis for suggesting that the Chamberlain car was awash with blood, and foetal blood at that, we submit that it was just plain wrong. The evidence before this Commission strongly supports the view, we contend, that whatever it was that Mrs Kuhl was dealing with in this car, it was not Azaria's blood; and, indeed, there is a very strong reason for suggesting that she was not dealing with blood at all, and that if she did find any blood in that car it was in minimal quantities and far more recent than it would have to have been if it was Azaria's blood. . .

The Commission now knows that the opinion, expressed at the trial, of the hairs found on Azaria's clothing as probably cat hairs was quite wrong; they were dog hairs. It also knows that there was no evidential basis for making the very damaging allegation that fibres found in the car and the camera bag came from the baby's jumpsuit after it had been cut, or that the hairs found in the camera bag may have come from Azaria. This Commission now knows, we submit, that the evidence given by Professor Chaikin to the effect that the jumpsuit had been cut by sharp scissors and not by a dog, and referred to by the Crown as unassailed and unassailable, is now very much assailed and, on his own concession, very much assailable. . .

> In short, we submit that this Commission has a very graphic demonstration of the shortcomings of the expert opinion evidence relied upon so heavily by the Crown to convict the Chamberlains; and the net result of the evidence before this Commission is that the Crown, we submit, can no longer prove a cause of death, a scene of death, or an interference with the clothing by the Chamberlains.

Having marked out the field of battle, Winneke then turned to specifics.

Professor Cameron, he said, 'stands absolutely alone in suggesting that these were hand prints on this garment. He agreed that he could no longer support the suggestion that they were prints in blood . . . He was constrained to agree . . . that it would have been very difficult to get a hand over the right shoulder with a matinee jacket on, but he took refuge in the proposition that the hand print on the right shoulder "was one where I did not pay as much attention to it as I did at the first inquest". Professor Cameron, we submit to Your Honour, has been completely discredited in respect of these hand prints. Not only has the factual foundation for them gone, but he has, in effect, conceded that he is using his imagination. Indeed, we submit that he gave the impression of a very subdued witness wanting to hold onto a discredited opinion come what may.'

Winneke referred to Mrs Kuhl's conclusions and suggested that 'on every other occasion upon which someone has been given the opportunity to confirm her findings, no such confirmation has been given'. He referred to Messrs Raymond, Ross, Scott, Smith and Doctors Cornell, Lincoln and Scott:

> It is indeed surprising, we would submit, that if Mrs Kuhl is correct in her findings, that not one of these reputable scientists has been able to confirm them in any way, shape or form. Perhaps that surprise dissipates somewhat when it is now known that she has made the demonstrable error in respect of the visible material still there to be seen and tested underneath the dashboard. Various explanations have been put forward during the course of this inquiry. Mrs Kuhl has said that it may well be that Dr Lincoln had a more contaminated sample from the floorwell. It was suggested by the Crown to Dr Cornell that he might have missed protein in the carpet if there were any trace amounts of it present. It has been

suggested that there may have been blood in the spray pattern, which coincidentally Mrs Kuhl might have tested, but has since disappeared. It is suggested that there may be no blood to now be found in the car either because it was all used up in her testing procedures or, alternatively, has denatured to an extent that it can no longer be detected.

One gets the impression that so many excuses or possible explanations or hypotheses have been put forward by the Crown that it has almost become an act of desperation to try and find some excuse for Mrs Kuhl, when, in truth, the real answer is that inexperience, incompetence, unreliability and prejudice have combined to produce results that were never there to be found in the first place.

The Crown case concerning the damage to the jumpsuit was attacked just as vehemently:

Professor Chaikin's evidence was based on the proposition that scissors cut and dogs tear. Professor Cameron, Mr Sims, Sergeant Cocks adopted entirely the same approach. None of them, it appears, had any idea of how a dog taking a clothed body as prey would deal with the clothing. They each assumed that it would rip and tear. None of them, of course, performed any experiments for the purposes of informing himself what range of damage a dog or dingo could or would do to this type of fabric in any type of circumstance. . .

We submit to you, sir, that the evidence given by Professor Chaikin and relied upon so heavily by the Crown at the trial and relied upon, we submit, so heavily by the appellate courts thereafter: the evidence said to be unassailed and unassailable was, in fact, evidence that was misconceived, misleading and careless.

. . .The fact is, as this Commission now knows, that dogs and dingoes can cut this fabric, and very effectively cut it, with the carnassial teeth, and in doing so will produce tufts, will cut without disturbing the base fabric by way of distortion, and will produce fibre ends coming together in a plane. It is a regrettable fact, we submit, that none of this was realised by the experts who gave evidence for the Crown at the trial and the only person who appeared to realise it was Dr Orams, who was called by the defence, but was ridiculed for not being a forensic scientist. It is, we submit, regrettable that Professor Chaikin has tended to

> demonstrate more of a desire to protect his own reputation than to exhibit a concern that he might have contributed to a miscarriage of justice.

Having completed a lengthy analysis of the scientific evidence, Winneke came to his conclusion: 'We submit to Your Honour that in the circumstances of this case, once the opinion evidence has been swept away, you are left with the full glare of what we submit is reliable and independent eyewitness testimony that leads the reasonable mind to the conclusion that the Chamberlains could have had nothing whatever to do with the disappearance of their daughter, Azaria, whom they both loved and adored very much indeed, and that having regard to the totality of the material before Your Honour, Your Honour ought to come to the conclusion that they should be entirely exonerated.'

All of this had left Barker quite unmoved, as the following address indicates:

> With respect to my learned friend, Mr Winneke, it is a waste of words to challenge the Crown to face up to what the Chamberlains' advisers see as impediments in the way of a finding adverse to their clients. They were, Your Honour, faced up to at the trial. We do know about them. So did the jury. So did the Federal Court and the High Court. No body, no motive, the cry, Aidan, the time element, the difficulty in washing the blood off her clothes, the problem of the disposal of the body, her demeanour, the disposal of the clothes, all these problems had to be confronted and set aside by the jury. They were no less real than they are now, and if they presented as immovable objects in the way of the Crown case, however irresistable, then the jury would have acquitted, but they did not. Equally, with respect, they are problems facing this Commission, but they are not to be looked at separately from the rest of the case, or each in isolation.

Barker referred Mr Justice Morling to some comments made by the Chief Justice of the High Court and Sir Anthony Mason and then turned to challenge Winneke's suggestion that the Crown case rested upon speculation:

> As we have said, there is evidence before this Commission which, it is suggested, proves murder. In a separate submission, we

> contend that there is proof before Your Honour that the child bled in the car. If that be accepted, it is likely she died in the car. Beyond that, we cannot make a submission which would enable the Commission to make a positive finding as to just how and when and where the child was killed. We cannot do so because the evidence is inadequate for the purpose and, with respect, we should not be challenged to do so.
>
> We can, consistently with the evidence, point to possible scenarios. They will remain no more than possible. Leaving aside the blood in the car, that which prevents us from making the submission that it may be accepted beyond reasonable doubt that the child was killed in a particular place at a precise time and in a precise way is that the evidence would not support such a submission.
>
> The Crown's position is that all the facts are not known and never will be known because the sole repository of all the facts is Mrs Chamberlain and she will not disclose what happened. We can, however, make submissions as to the likely cause of death. We have made other submissions as to why evidence is capable of acceptance and why it should be accepted and what conclusions should be drawn from it.
>
> In suggesting possible murder scenarios, we are not inventing hypotheses. If there is or are a possible scenario or scenarios, it follows that murder, if otherwise proved, is not to be disproved on the basis that there was no place or means or opportunity for it to have happened. There are ways it could have happened. The Crown says it did happen because that is the only rational conclusion capable of accounting for the demonstrated facts.

Barker launched a lengthy attack upon the credibility of the Chamberlains:

> Wherever you go in this case looking for things that Mrs Chamberlain said about the events, it is very hard to find a consistent pattern. It is not the case, as Mr Winneke asserted, that there is a significant consistency in it all. Sure, the basic fact is consistent, that a dingo took the baby. But when you look for the details of how and when it happened, and what she really saw, it is like trying to put your finger on quicksilver; and when you examine it all, in the end it is impossible to know whether she is really saying she saw the dingo coming out of the tent from some

> distance back and yelled out, 'The dingo's got the baby': in other words, she knew at that stage; or when she got to the door of the tent; or when she got into the tent and looked in the basket; or when she was leaving the tent. And what it is she thought she saw or thought was happening is submerged in this mass of conflicting stories which are not simply inconsistencies, but amount to irreconcilable accounts of what happened.

He also suggested that their conduct was eloquent of guilt:

> The Chamberlains, we submit, were peculiarly and, indeed, startlingly inactive on the night she disappeared and thereafter. Their inactivity is explained by their sure knowledge the child was dead and would not be found. It is for this reason that so much was subsequently said about how quickly the baby would have been dead. In this regard, it is convenient to consider the evidence of both Mr and Mrs Chamberlain. At the very least, much of what was said publicly was wild exaggeration, and it is difficult to conceive of a grieving parent in the circumstances being moved to wildly exaggerate matters surrounding the child's death unless prompted to do so by self-interest and the consciousness of guilt.

Mr Justice Morling interrupted to invite his comments concerning the significance of the Crown's inability to establish any motive for the alleged murder.

'I cannot assign a reason,' Barker conceded. 'We have never tried to assign a reason. It is one of the problems which has confronted the case right from the start... I do not attempt to deny its real importance; but if Your Honour comes to the view that the Crown contends for, with regard to the probable cause of death, with regard to the improbability of any animal having been involved in it, and paying due regard to the fact that she was the last person to see the child alive and paying due regard to what she thereafter said about it, then Your Honour may well come to the view that the question of motive is not of such importance, but it is a matter of balancing one proved fact against another.'

Barker challenged Winneke's submission that the Chamberlains' prospects of obtaining a fair trial had been prejudiced by a one-sided approach on the part of the police.

'The attack on the police in this regard, like so many other of counsel's criticisms, is carping and querulous and part of a rummage amongst the minutiae of the investigation to see what might be found which could possibly discredit the police. It serves only to confuse the issues arising from evidence obtained in the course of proper investigations.'

He then came to the main thrust of the Crown case:

'Then, Your Honour, we come to the submission which is at the heart of the case, and that is what is the evidence as to the probability or improbability of:

(i) Azaria being taken from the tent by a dingo, and

(ii) Azaria's clothes being removed from her body by a dingo?'

He referred to part of the Crown's written submissions and suggested that the 'short question' was whether the child's disappearance could be satisfactorily accounted for by a dingo seizing her in the tent, carrying her four kilometres away, removing the clothes and then eating the body:

> We say it cannot, the known circumstances being the amount and position of blood in the tent, the clothes being left some four kilometres from the tent for no explicable reason, the arrangement of the clothes at the site where they were found, the pattern of bloodstaining and the gross damage to the clothes, together with the known or at least likely behaviour of dingoes at Ayers Rock, establish that there was no canine involvement in the child's disappearance or its death.
>
> Ultimately, whether the child was taken from the tent by a dingo is not separable from the question of whether a dingo removed the child's clothes and devoured it. While it may be theoretically possible that a dingo entered the tent in search of food and carried Azaria off as live prey . . . the gross appearance of the clothing and the manner in which it was left, together with the lack of sufficient indications of canine presence at the site, establish that a dingo was not involved in the child's disappearance.

Michael Adams then took over to present a series of arguments concerning the validity of the immunological tests and other evidence said to demonstrate the presence of foetal blood in the car. He concluded with a spirited defence of Mrs Kuhl:

> . . . My submission is that she was competent. Dr Baxter, who had

> no love for her, believed that she was a competent forensic biologist. She had some years of experience; she knew what a result was. She used animal antisera. She by and large used adult testing. The techniques that she used were said by Mr Martin to be precisely the techniques he would have used. Dr Scott said it was not unreasonable for her to act in that way, although he would have liked to have seen adult controls on every plate. Dr Lincoln said as long as they are on the same plate in the series that would be acceptable. It is true that when she appeared in court her evidence was, in some respect, confused, but in relation to the fundamental matter which is: did she see what she said she saw, confirmed by Dr Baxter they are reliable results on which Your Honour can act with confidence [sic].

Barker returned to the attack like the second member of a tag wrestling team. However, the written submissions were very lengthy and he saw little point in wading through the details orally. He closed his address with a series of questions pointing to the main features of the Crown case:

> Why there was no blood in the bassinette; why there was no more blood in the tent; why there was no sign of active bleeding in the tent; why there was not massive spurting or splatters when the child was shaken, as she must have been if Mrs Chamberlain is telling the truth, at the entrance to the tent; why there was no blood immediately outside the tent; why there was no blood in the tracks which are said to be the tracks of the animal; why there was no blood in the area of the depression, so-called, where it is said that the child might have been put down.
>
> It is really, with respect, impossible to imagine that all that could have taken place with the only blood being the small quantity we have been told about in the tent which stopped at the entrance to the tent and that fact, I respectfully submit, stands squarely in the way of the proposition that all this happened as the Chamberlains would have Your Honour believe. In our submission, the story is nonsense and it is a powerful reason for Your Honour finding that on this evidence there was a murder, and if there was a murder it could only have been at the hands of the child's mother.

In reply, Winneke stressed the inherent implausibility of much of the Crown case:

The case predicates that the Chamberlains were in some way able on the night of 17 August to separate the clothes from the body of the child and thereafter dispose of that body. It predicates that they, or one or other of them, sat down in the early hours of the morning with an armoury of equipment, be it scissors, tweezers, knives, sharp-pointed instruments or any other variety of weapon, for the purposes of inflicting a variety of damage to the jumpsuit, singlet and nappy. The case postulates that quite coincidentally they were able to inflict upon the jumpsuit damage of a type which replicates dog damage in a manner which the evidence suggests that no lay person could have foreseen. It suggests that in doing this they studiously avoided the outer garment, the matinee jacket, and inflicted damage solely on the undergarment. It suggests that they managed to inflict the damage on the undergarment in a normal position where there is still to be seen a stain suggesting biological fluid of some kind; that they then removed the outer garment, leaving the top button done up, but they were able to inflict damage upon the nappy which parallels, we submit the evidence shows, in the minutest way, known dog damage.

It postulates that they then jogged three kilometres in the dark, found a dingo den that even Roff and Cawood did not know existed, that they flattened the vegetation in a manner consistent with the way it would look if a dog had lain there and managed to do it in a way so as to ensure that it was still seen a week later, and on the way in they dropped off the matinee jacket, having dragged it at ground height so as to collect the ground-hugging calotis seeds; that they then ran on with the remainder of the clothes and picked out a rare species of paretaria and rubbed the jumpsuit and the singlet in it and, in the course of doing this or at some other time, they rubbed the clothes so heavily in soil so as to thoroughly impregnate the garment and collect a teaspoon full of soil inside it, but making sure that they got that soil from different locations.

In short, we submit, the Crown case about this clothing attributes to the Chamberlains considerable skills as odontologists, textile experts, bushwalkers and botanists, and yet having so meticulously planned and executed this operation they then simply drop the clothes in a heap, leaving booties within the jumpsuit in a manner which any layman would think was quite inconsistent with the way in which a dog would leave them.

> Having completed this rather remarkable exercise, they then stood back, as if in some form of benediction, and sprinkled the torn shreds of the nappy over the remainder of the crumpled heap and, as if to put icing on the cake, threw in a few dog hairs for good measure.

All of this, Winneke submitted, would 'just not hold water'.

On 19 March 1987, proceedings were adjourned, leaving counsel on both sides to make their way home to Sydney, Melbourne and Canberra and to draft further written submissions. Chester Porter and Bill Caldwell were to be fully occupied assisting Mr Justice Morling with his report, but the others were shortly to be free to contemplate the euphoria of one-day cases.

The Chamberlains, for their part, were to return to Cooranbong to 'sweat out' whatever time it would take for Mr Justice Morling's report to be made public. The wait was to prove agonising. The evidence had seemed clear and they were confident that, this time, they would be vindicated. But their hopes had been dashed so many times in the past.

PART VI

BREAKTHROUGH

31

The Morling Report

MR JUSTICE MORLING'S REPORT WAS DELIVERED to the Governor General and the Administrator of the Northern Territory under covering letters dated 22 May 1987. It ran to 379 pages.

He outlined the nature and scope of the Commission of Inquiry and the background to the convictions. He then turned to the question of blood in the car. His analysis of this topic alone consumed 108 pages.

'At the trial, counsel for the prosecution submitted to the jury that they should conclude that Mrs Chamberlain had endeavoured to keep people away from the car after Azaria's disappearance for fear that they might notice signs of the alleged murder. It appears that the Demaines were present at the trial under subpoena, but were not called to give evidence.'

He pointed out that, 'since [Lindy Chamberlain] was away from the barbecue area for only five to ten minutes, there would have been very little time for her to have cleaned up the car thoroughly. She was under observation by others, particularly Mrs Whittacker and Mrs West, for most of the time between the raising of the alarm and her departure for the motel later in the evening. Except for the occasion described by Mr and Mrs Demaine , Mrs Chamberlain was not seen to enter the car. . . It therefore appears that she had little or no opportunity to clean up any blood in the car after the alarm was raised and before leaving for the motel.'

Bobbie Downs, who had travelled in the passenger seat of the car, 'did not see, feel or smell any blood and she did not pick up any blood on her clothing'. Neither she nor the people, including

Constable Noble, who assisted in packing the car prior to the trip to the motel, saw any blood. She had spent some time in the driver's seat of the car on the following morning but, again, had not noticed any blood. Pastor Cozens had also packed items into the car on the following day and, like Bobbie Downs, saw no sign of blood. On 1 October 1980, at Mount Isa, Senior Constable Graham had carried out a lengthy inspection of the car. 'He would have expected to have been able to identify signs of removal of blood from the vinyl or metal surfaces of the car, since there would have been variations in surface textures and colours if stains had been removed without using the same method on the whole of the surface. He did not detect any sign of blood having been removed from the car.' Despite the Crown's criticisms of the lighting, Mr Justice Morling was satisfied 'that Graham was able to carry out a proper and thorough inspection of the car for the purposes described'.

He then turned to the immunological testing, referring, at some length, to the risks inherent in testing old and denatured bloodstains for the presence of significant quantities of foetal haemoglobin and quoting Freney's delightfully picturesque description: 'It is what I call tiger country; the old stains: you have got to be very careful with them.'

Mr Justice Morling concluded that 'although Mrs Kuhl might not be expected to have been aware of all the difficulties posed by the age of any blood in the car and the temperature to which it had been exposed, they do raise doubts as to the reliability of her immuno-chemical results and, in particular, those depending upon the use of the anti-foetal haemoglobin antiserum'.

After discussing the distinction between non-specific reactions and true immuno-chemical reactions, he concluded that 'it appears, therefore, that Mrs Kuhl depended upon bases... which, in the particular circumstances of this case, may have been unreliable'.

He referred to the concern expressed by Professors Boettcher and Nairn that 'the recorded result was stronger with anti-foetal haemoglobin antiserum than with anti-haemoglobin. This was because only twenty-five per cent of the haemoglobin present would be of the foetal type if the blood were Azaria's whereas one hundred per cent of the haemoglobin present would be reacting with the anti-haemoglobin antiserum. Mrs Kuhl's response was to point out that these tests, as conducted by her, were non-qualitative in the sense that the results did not permit the concentrations of particular antigens to be measured. While this is clearly correct... in the absence of a clear explanation of why it occurred in particular instances it remains a matter of concern.'

Considerable evidence had been given concerning the need to test each bottle of antiserum for its specificity. However, Mr Justice Morling was 'unable to conclude whether the particular bottles used by Mrs Kuhl were tested in this way or not'.

Mrs Kuhl had not enjoyed the position that she might have been in 'if she had carried out detailed and systematic testing with known controls...It therefore appears that she suffered from a significant handicap in the accurate interpretation of the results which she obtained with the antiserum.'

Mrs Kuhl had conceded that, although she had told the jury that she had screened over 230 adult blood samples and that 'the anti-foetal haemoglobin has never reacted against adult blood', an examination of the laboratory records revealed that positive reactions had been obtained from six samples of blood which should have contained an adult concentration of haemoglobin.

Mr Justice Morling commented that, even if the explanation of a false reaction due to the presence of ammonia was correct, there was a problem:

> The apparent recording of the results in the result book as being genuine immuno-chemical precipitates and the lack of any precise explanation as to how they came about adds weight to the concern about reliability of interpretation to which I have already referred. If the wrong results arose from the presence of ammonia or technical problems in 1982, it is very difficult to be confident that, without a comprehensive system of pre-used testing and confirmatory testing of the results from particular samples, the plates were correctly interpreted in 1981.
>
> On the evidence, I am unable to conclude whether any of the six positive results with adult bloods was the result of a genuine immuno-chemical reaction or not. However, it seems that, for inadequte reasons, Mrs Kuhl accepted as correct results which

tended to confirm the specificity of the antiserum and rejected those results which cast doubt upon it.

Considerable reservations had been expressed concerning limitations of the crossover electrophoresis method. 'As Professor Ouchterlony pointed out, even with a proper set of controls on the same plate as the sample, with everything right in the crossover test, the operator can be misled . . . it appears that its use in this case may have prevented Mrs Kuhl from eliminating other possible causes of the reaction seen.'

Mr Justice Morling also commented that it was apparent that 'the use of proper controls and the methods adopted in testing the samples from the Chamberlains' car were essential in arriving at correct interpretations of the results. Certain important controls were lacking in Mrs Kuhl's tests.'

He discussed trial evidence suggesting that the antiserum may have reacted with substances other than foetal haemoglobin and commented: 'for these reasons I could not be satisfied beyond reasonable doubt that this antiserum, when used in the crossover electrophoretic technique or the tube precipitan technique, was specific only to foetal haemoglobin'.

All in all, it was clear that 'the task which Mrs Kuhl was called upon to perform in testing the Chamberlains' car and its contents, posed most substantial difficulties, even for the most highly skilled and experienced forensic biologist. It was much more apparent before the Commission than it was at the trial that there were many traps for the unwary in carrying out immuno-chemical tests upon samples which were old and which had been exposed to severe conditions.'

Having dealt with the risks inherent in the procedures, Mr Justice Morling then turned to consider the validity of particular results. He began with the testing of the 'under-dash spray'. Since Professor Jones' examination in 1981, a number of forensic pathologists and biologists had examined it both with the naked eye and under microscopes: '[All] now agree that it does not look like blood, in either the shape of the droplets or the pattern of the spray.'

The Crown had suggested that there may have been some blood superimposed on the bitumenous spray pattern, but Mr Justice

Morling commented: 'If it was, why it would not have been detected by the orthotolidine test is not apparent. For it to have remained undetected, it must have been covered by another substance. There is no evidence of the existence of any such substance.'

The recording of the results of the tests on the samples from the under-dash area caused him some concern. 'The result book discloses twelve occasions when the recorded results of the tests of these three samples were crossed out or changed. In contrast, it is quite unusual to find results crossed out or changed in the rest of the book.'

He referred to the evidence of Senior Constable Metcalfe that Mrs Kuhl had given him the results of tests carried out on those samples on the same day as he had delivered them. This was significant because Mrs Kuhl had given evidence that she always allowed the plates to be washed for twenty-four hours before reading them. 'Since Senior Constable Metcalfe's evidence is well supported by contemporary written records, I accept it as establishing the probability that Mrs Kuhl did read and report on the results of these tests before washing the plates. She agreed that if she had done this it would have been improper since she would have been committing herself to a result before she could have been scientifically satisfied of that result. Of course, it is now impossible to say whether this had any effect on the conclusion she reached. However, the fact that Mrs Kuhl was prepared to do this in response to requests by the police is a matter of concern.'

He referred to the testing of 'the other two samples from under the dashboard area', one of which had been negative and the other 'non-specific':

> It was unsatisfactory that neither of these tests was mentioned in the work notes which were produced at the trial and which were represented to be a complete record. It is also unsatisfactory that they were not mentioned by Mrs Kuhl when she was questioned about these samples in the witness box. . .
>
> Another unsatisfactory matter appearing in Mrs Kuhl's work notes is an entry on the reverse side of the page immediately before the entries relating to the samples from under the dashboard. The entry reads: 'No reaction with animal antisera

(pig, sheep)'. When compared with the entries in the result book, it became apparent that, in respect of the first test of one of these samples, no animal antiserum was used at all and the crossing out of others raised doubts as to whether they were used.

Mr Justice Morling concluded that 'the strong probability is that any sample lifted out of the spray pattern on the metal plate was sound-deadening compound and contained no blood at all. The sample tested as Item 33 was dug out of the spray pattern with a scalpel, but Mrs Kuhl concluded that baby's blood was present in it. The fact that she could come to such a conclusion about something which was, very probably, sound-deadener casts doubt upon the efficacy of her testing generally and upon the accuracy of her other results.'

He referred to the results from the tube precipitin tests and commented that the method was 'an old one with acknowledged drawbacks... Further, in order to detect foetal haemoglobin reliably, it is clear that the use of a known adult blood as a control and the obtaining of appropriate results would have been necessary. At the trial, Mrs Kuhl said that she used adult and foetal controls for all these tube precipitan tests. However, they are not recorded in her work notes, there is no laboratory result book record of the tests at all, and before the Commission she said that her evidence at the trial was incorrect and there were no adult controls in these tests.'

He commented that there were 'fundamental objections to the acceptance of Mrs Kuhl's findings of baby's blood in the area of the off-side rear hinge of the passenger seat and the floor beneath.'

There had been significant debate concerning the immuno-diffusion or Ouchterlony test carried out on stains found on a small pair of scissors which had been in the Chamberlains' car when the police took possession of it. Mrs Kuhl had reported that there were 'indications' of the presence of blood of foetal origin. This conclusion was criticised on a number of bases, including the fact that the necessary controls had failed. 'Raymond, Scott, Baxter and Martin were in agreement that when controls fail in a test such as this, the result should be rejected as worthless.'

Mrs Kuhl's explanation of the failure of the controls 'was rejected by other experts, including Professor Ouchterlony...

While it appears that Dr Baxter discussed the result with Mrs Kuhl in September 1981 and made some suggestion that she could report indications of foetal blood, Dr Baxter has now said that, considering all the failures in the test, it should have been forgotten. I accept this is the appropriate assessment of the results.'

He also pointed out that 'on the evidence, one could not even find that the scissors were in the car at Ayers Rock in August 1980.'

Mr Justice Morling referred to the evidence of blood on the towel:

> Professor Boettcher and Dr Baxter were in substantial agreement that the failure to obtain reactions to this [absorption/elution] test, if the test were conducted properly, would indicate that no blood was present... It can be seen that the positive results in relation to this towel are unsatisfactorily supported and are contradicted by many other results...
>
> If the towel was used to wipe a murder weapon or to clean up blood from the car, it is difficult to accept that the Chamberlains would have left the towel in the boot of the car for over thirteen months, particularly if it had been their intention to clean up the traces of blood in the car. The lack of a sensible explanation for such strange conduct would raise doubts about the evidence of baby's blood on the towel, even if the results of the test were much more acceptable than they are.

He was also sceptical of the results obtained on the chamois:

> The chamois was damp when Mrs Kuhl removed it from its container. It was common ground among the experts who gave evidence to the Commission that the conditions in which the chamois was kept, namely in humidity and heat, were most conducive to denaturation of bloodstains. Mr Martin said that, under these circumstances, he would not have tested the chamois or its container. Professor Nairn said that he would be astonished to get a result on something like these articles. Mrs Kuhl agreed that she was surprised by her result. Her surprise was not expressed at the trial.
>
> A second reason for doubting this result is the absence of a control of known adult blood, either upon the same plate or a plate run at the same time. It was common ground among the experts

> that such a control is necessary. The absence of such a control was not apparent at the trial since Mrs Kuhl's work notes included a note at the bottom of the relevant item referring to controls being good and specifying those controls as 'adult human' and 'human [cord blood]'. It is apparent from the laboratory's result book that the former was not used. The making of this incorrect entry in the notes was not satisfactorily explained.

The camera bag had been an item of particular significance. Mrs Kuhl had obtained various positive orthotolidine reactions from it and had obtained a positive reaction with anti-foetal haemoglobin antiserum using the crossover electrophoresis test on a stain taken from the zip clasp of one compartment. The Crown had 'relied upon Mrs Kuhl's evidence that she thought the camera bag had been washed' and this was a factor relied upon by the Chief Justice and Sir Anthony Mason in dismissing the Chamberlains' appeal.

It had now become clear that Dr Andrew Scott had examined it before the second inquest. 'He saw nothing that would indicate blood upon it.' He had tested some areas with orthotolidine and had sprayed it with luminol, a screening substance which 'fluoresces on contact with blood and other substances', but he found 'nothing to indicate to him the presence of blood in significant amounts. He thought there was nothing that required further testing. Nothing appeared to him to indicate that the camera bag had been washed.' Dr Lincoln had examined and tested the camera bag in May 1982, some four months before the trial. 'His screening test did not demonstrate the presence of blood.'

Given the discovery that orthotolidine would react with copper dust, Mr Justice Morling found it 'significant' that Mrs Kuhl obtained the orthotolidine reactions with 'small amounts of grit found in the bag'. He pointed out that she had not obtained positive reactions with the stitching in the seams of the bag where 'one would be most likely to find remnants of blood . . . In her evidence before the Commission, Mrs Kuhl accepted that there appeared to be inconsistency between the results she obtained and the notion that the camera bag had been washed to remove blood.'

Mr Raymond had tested the bag in 1986. He obtained 'non-specific reactions' which to him 'looked real before the plates were stained . . . He said this clearly indicated to him the possibility of a person falling into error if he tested the metal parts of the bag without undertaking full testing.'

He pointed out that 'the accuracy of Mrs Kuhl's conclusions was given considerable support at the trial by Dr Baxter and Mr Culliford. Dr Baxter said that he saw the plates and gels used by Mrs Kuhl in her experiments and agreed with her conclusions. Mr Culliford said that he had read Mrs Kuhl's laboratory work notes and her evidence and approved of her methods and conclusions.'

Mr Justice Morling observed that Mrs Kuhl had prepared six written reports and that it was the practice for 'such reports to be approved and initialled by Dr Baxter before they were typed, unless he was not present.'

> It is surprising that in a case where Dr Baxter had given special instructions, at least to the effect that he be shown positive results, three out of the five handwritten draft reports tendered to the Commission were not initialled by him. This suggests that the checking of Mrs Kuhl's work was not as extensive as it might have been. Overall, Dr Baxter's lack of recollection of the results he saw and the failure to record his checking of any results significantly diminished the weight of his support for Mrs Kuhl's conclusions.
>
> . . . So far as Mr Culliford is concerned, the approval he expressed at the trial of her methods and conclusions could not be further explored since he was too ill to give evidence to the Commission. However, Mr Martin, Mr Culliford's successor at the Metropolitan Police Forensic Laboratory in London said that, although he had not read all of Mrs Kuhl's evidence, he found her work notes extremely confusing. On the information before him, it was impossible for him to pass judgment on the reliability or accuracy of her testing procedures.

Mr Justice Morling concluded that Mrs Kuhl 'lacked the considerable experience required to enable her to plan and to carry out these complex and difficult testing procedures, at least without careful guidance from a more experienced biologist. Indeed, there appears to be doubt whether any practising forensic biologist would have been sufficiently qualified to perform these tasks without extensive consultation with leaders in immunological research.'

The results of the phosphoglucomutase or PGM tests were swept aside peremptorily. Professor Nairn had described these results as 'highly suspect' and Mr Justice Morling commented that 'I accept this is a fair assessment'. He commented that the possibility that the blood had come from Lenehan 'had not been eliminated' and that, in any event, the blood could have come from a very large number of persons, including the other members of the Chamberlain family.

> The fact that the results were obtained, having regard to the customary difficulty in obtaining any results with blood over the age of eight months, itself suggests that any blood producing such results was shed after 17 August 1980. Accordingly, I do not think that any conclusion adverse to the Chamberlains can be drawn from these results.

Mr Justice Morling then grappled with the more difficult question of whether, even if the tests were inadequate to show it had come from a baby, blood of some sort had been found in the car in significant quantities. He concluded that it had not been shown to be present in most of the places suggested including the camera bag. He commented, in passing, that even if some small amount of blood had been found on the camera bag it could be 'readily explicable by the use of the bag by someone with a minor cut to a finger. It would not justify the drawing of any inference adverse to the Chamberlains.'

After weighing the competing considerations he said, 'I would not conclude that beyond a reasonable doubt that blood was present in the car, even upon the hinge area of the passenger's seat. However, having regard to the number of positive results from the various tests obtained by Mrs Kuhl in relation to the area of the hinge of the passenger's seat and the floor beneath, I think it is more probable than not that , at the time of her testing, some blood was present in these areas.'

The evidence at the trial justified the impression that 'the car floor was awash with blood'. The evidence before the Commission was quite different:

> Other experts found it very difficult to arrive at any estimate of the volume of blood from Mrs Kuhl's work notes and evidence.

> However, having regard to the number of samples taken by her and the fact that Mr Raymond was unable to detect the presence of any further blood in 1986, there was general agreement between the various experts who gave evidence to the Commission, that if there were blood present in the car when it was first tested, there could have been only a very small amount of it.

Lenehan had given evidence that he had bled quite profusely from scalp lacerations on the right-hand side of his head. Mrs Chamberlain had used a gauze bandage and had a towel on her knees in an attempt to staunch the flow of blood. The trip to the hospital had taken approximately forty-five minutes and his head had continued to bleed. Mr Justice Morling found that it was 'likely that Mr Lenehan's head was in the appropriate position at that time when he was bleeding for his blood to have fallen in the area of the back of the passenger seat and the hinge on its off-side'.

When all things were considered, Mr Justice Morling concluded that 'if there was any blood present in the car, it was present in only small quantities in the area of the hinge and on the passenger seat and beneath. I conclude that none of Mrs Kuhl's tests established that any such blood was Azaria's. The blood shed by Mr Lenehan could have been the source of stains in the area of the hinge of the passenger seat and beneath . . . The presence of a small quantity of blood in this area would not justify the drawing of any inference adverse to the Chamberlains.'

After considering the evidence of a battery of dingo experts, forensic pathologists, odontologists and, in particular, the opinions of Professor Bradley and Dr William Rose, he concluded that 'the quantity of blood found in the tent is not inconsistent with dingo involvement'. Indeed, he found the presence of this blood highly significant:

> It was the Crown case that Azaria was killed in the car. It seems absurd to suggest that Mrs Chamberlain carried Azaria's bleeding body from the car back to the tent, where she would have been under Aidan's observation. The presence of Azaria's blood in the tent, unless it be shown to have been transferred there upon Mrs Chamberlain's personal clothing, is inconsistent with the Crown case. . .
>
> I have concluded earlier. . . that many of the stains found on

> articles in the tent were probably caused by blood dropping directly either from a wound or from a blood-soaked object . . . I am unable to conclude from the appearance of the stains which of these two sources of the bloodstains is the more likely. However, the proposition that all the bloodstains found in the tent came from the bloodstained hands or blood-soaked clothing of Mrs Chamberlain has inherent improbabilities. According to Dr Jones and Dr Scott, for this to have happened it would have been necessary that her hands or clothing be literally dripping or soaked with blood. There is no evidence supporting the existence of any clothing or article blood-soaked in this way. Had such a quantity of blood been on Mrs Chamberlain's hands, there are difficulties in explaining how it would not also have been upon her clothing in large and visible quantities, given the short time she had to clean up before her return to the tent and barbecue area. Further, it seems inherently improbable that she would have run the risk of Aidan seeing her hands dripping with blood. The allegation that she returned to the tent in blood-soaked clothing or with bloodstained hands does not sit easily with the Crown's allegation that she cleaned up the blood in the car after the murder.
>
> It has not been shown by the Crown that the blood in the tent was transferred there from the clothing or person of Mrs Chamberlain. On the contrary, the evidence points to this being an unlikely occurrence.

Mr Justice Morling approached 'with considerable caution' the competing opinions concerning the deductions which could or should be drawn from the staining on Azaria's clothing as to the likely cause of death. 'The question is one which lies on the boundary of the field of expertise of the forensic pathologist. While experience in that field may provide some assistance in the interpretation of such bloodstaining, I do not consider that, in relation to this question . . . it provides the basis for the firm conclusions.'

He pointed out that Professor Cameron had given evidence at the trial to the effect that 'the distribution of blood on the jumpsuit necessarily involved the baby being alive at the time of bleeding'. Professor Pleuckhahn had disagreed. He had expressed the view that , since considerable oozing of blood can occur after death, it could not be said whether the bleeding took place before or after death. Before the Commission of Inquiry, Professor Pleuckhahn's view was supported in that respect by Professor Nairn, Dr Jones and Mr Raymond, and Professor Cameron was 'less dogmatic in his opinion, saying that the bleeding took place at or about the time of death, and that he saw nothing to indicate arterial bleeding'.

Professor Ferris 'favoured the view that the bleeding was post-mortem. According to him the science characteristic of venous and arterial bleeding could not be seen and there were other characteristics of the bleeding which were more typical of blood dropping from an accumulated area of blood.' Mr Justice Morling pointed out Professor Ferris had given evidence at the request of the Crown. He concluded that it was impossible 'to conclude with certainty whether or not the bleeding took place before or after the time of death'. However, he noted that 'if Professor Ferris' preferred view were adopted, the most serious difficulties would arise for the Crown case. His view would make impossible of acceptance the pivotal point in the Crown case put to the jury based on Professor Cameron's evidence, namely that Azaria died when her throat was cut with a sharp instrument.'

Professor Cameron had relied upon Dr Scott's failure to detect the presence of dingo saliva as establishing that no saliva had been present. Mr Justice Morling commented that 'this was not a proper inference to draw'.

Cameron had also relied upon his experience of dog attacks on humans. Mr Justice Morling pointed to the limited nature of that experience and concluded that 'it is clear that Professor Cameron was not justified in holding the opinion that he did not require experimental evidence'.

Mr Justice Morling concluded that 'the pattern of bloodstaining does not support the contention that there was a cutting of the throat with a blade done with an intent to kill the child'.

He referred to Professor Ferris' expectations concerning small pieces of tissue or fat globules upon the clothing, but suggested that several explanations emerged from the evidence. 'Accordingly, while that failure gives no support for dingo involvement, I conclude that it is not necessarily inconsistent with such involvement.'

He also referred to the stain associated with the damaged area of the left sleeve 'apparently from a biological fluid'. At the trial, the Crown had relied upon the absence of any blood or tissue near that area and Mr Justice Morling commented that whilst its 'significance may be slight... it would seem to be more consistent with canine damage' than an attempt to simulate it.

He commented that Professor Cameron's evidence concerning the impression of hand prints had been given on the erroneous assumption that the stains had been comprised of blood when most of the material was sand. Professor Ferris had been the only other expert prepared to give 'even the faintest support' for his opinion. He had said that the stains 'might convey an impression of fingers to some observers', but that similar linear marks might have been produced in other ways:

> None of the other experts was able to detect any impression of hand or fingerprints in the staining on the jumpsuit. These experts included Drs Scott and Jones, Professors Bradley and Nairn and Mr Raymond. Professor Nairn examined the jumpsuit and the photographs taken by Mr Ruddock using special goggles so that they might be interpreted more accurately. He could not define any pattern on the clothing that indicated any particular object had ever come against it. Upon my examination of the photographs of the jumpsuit itself, I could not discern any such pattern.
>
> I therefore conclude that there were no detectable prints of hands or fingers, whether in blood or any other material, upon the clothing.

He examined the extensive controversy concerning the concept of 'planar array' and the proposition that it could only be properly determined with the use of a scanning electron microscope. In the end result, he concluded:

> I am unable to adopt the planar array test as a reliable test for distinguishing between canine teeth cuts in fibres and cuts caused by a knife or scissors. It may well be that the phenomenon of planar array can be used to assist in determining the difference between cuts and tears, but this is not the same as distinguishing between cuts made by canine teeth and cuts made by scissors or knives.

On the other hand, Mr Justice Morling remained unconvinced by the detailed comparision of fabric damage carried out by Dr Pelton and Messrs Chapman and Smith. 'I am not persuaded that a comparison of Azaria's and the other jumpsuits of itself leads to the view that Azaria's probably was damaged by a canid. But this is not to say that a canid could not have produced the damage.'

He was equally unconvinced by Dr Griffiths' hypothesis:

> Although Dr Griffiths' experiments are interesting, they do not persuade me that the damage to the jumpsuit was caused in the manner he suggested. . .
>
> Dr Griffiths claimed that the circular severance in the left sleeve of the jumpsuit was produced by the cutting of the bunched fabric, followed by the ripping or tearing out of the incompletely severed material. Sergeant Cocks demonstrated how he thought it was produced by the use of scissors. This evidence is too speculative to be of much value, particularly having regard to the contrary evidence given by other witnesses, especially Dr Pelton.

He found the evidence of the odontologists and of Dr Sanson, the zoologist, also inconclusive. Dr Sanson's evidence was 'impressive' but even he had not been prepared to say that it was completely impossible for a dingo to have inflicted the damage on Azaria's clothing. He noted that Professors Fernhead and Gustafson thought that the damage to the jumpsuit was not inconsistent with dingo damage, and commented that 'they are both highly qualified in the field of canine odontology'. Professor Gustafson disagreed with Dr Sanson that a dingo could not bite twice and maintain a straight line in the bite. He, like Dr Orams, stressed 'the manipulative and holding ability of the dingo's lips, tongue and gums, and the strength of its jaws'.

He commented that 'the appearance of the nappy is yet another puzzling feature of the evidence. On balance, it seems to support the theory of dingo involvement. However, it has to be borne in mind that dingo from the nearby den could have damaged the nappy after a human being had removed it from Azaria's body.'

Mr Justice Morling was obviously concerned about whether a dingo could have removed Azaria from her clothing 'without causing more damage to it than was observed.' He commented that he would have found this difficult to accept 'were it not for the conflict of expert opinion on this question':

> However, Mr Roff's evidence cannot be lightly dismissed. He is a practical man with much knowledge and experience of dingoes. He is a disinterested witness. As senior ranger at Uluru National Park, it was not in his interests to support an allegation that a dingo had taken a child from a camping area within the park for which he had general responsibility. It is apparent from the evidence that Constable Morris (and probably other police officers) recognised his great experience and deferred to it. Moreover, his opinion gains support from Professor Gustafson's evidence. In these circumstances, I conclude that, although a dingo would have had difficulty in removing Azaria's body from her clothing without causing more damage to it, it was possible for it to have done so.

At the trial, Professor Cameron had expressed the view that the appearance of the staining of the jumpsuit suggested that it had been buried in sand. It had, however, been extensively handled before it was seen by Mr Cameron more than a year after its discovery:

> It is therefore desirable to consider the evidence of the first scientist who examined the jumpsuit, Dr Andrew Scott... He said that he did not see any indication that the clothes had been buried. Professor Cameron agreed that the handling and vacuuming of the clothing before he saw it may have caused a significant difference in the appearance of the sand upon it. He said he would defer to Dr Scott's opinions.

Evidence concerning the composition and origin of the soils found in the jumpsuit had been given by Dr Collins and Mr Torlach. Mr Justice Morling commented:

> [It] appears that most of the soil in the jumpsuit could have come from a large number of places in the Ayers Rock region, many of those places being in the sand dune country lying generally in an easterly direction from the camp site. As Dr Collins said, his findings would not be inconsistent with the jumpsuit being dragged across the sand dunes in that area.

> The geological evidence did not further support the suggestion that the clothing had been buried, rather than dragged along the surface.
>
> Samples taken from the vicinity of the Uluru Motel clearly did not match the soil in the jumpsuit. The closest place in which a reasonably matching sample was taken was from a desert oak about one kilometre from the motel. Thus there is no support for any suggestion that Azaria's clothed body may have been buried near the Uluru Motel late on the night of 17 August 1980.

In the light of further botanical evidence from Drs Leach and Latz, 'it appears that plant materials typical of the plains country lying between the campsite and Ayers Rock were present in significant quantities upon Azaria's clothing. Further, it appears that seeds of four of the eleven species identified upon the jumpsuit could have come from the sand dune area east of the campsite.' It was to this sand dune that the tracks had led. 'The botanical evidence is not inconsistent with a dingo carrying the clothed baby from the camping area across the plains country to the Rock.'

Mr Justice Morling concluded that the seeds and other fragments found on the clothing 'may have come from the immediate vicinity in which the clothing was found':

> In my view, the evidence in relation to the plant material on the clothing does not lend substantial support for the contention that it came there by deliberate rubbing on the vegctation by human hand. The presence of the plant material on the clothing is not inconsistent with it having been picked up as a consequence of an animal agitating the clothing against vegetation.

He concluded that 'if the clothing had been merely taken from the car, buried, disinterred and later placed at the Rock by the Chamberlains, one can imagine it may have picked up some plant material but it is difficult to conceive how it could have collected the quantity and variety of plant material found upon it.' Equally, 'whilst it is not inconceivable that the plant fragments came upon the clothing by deliberate dragging by human hand through a variety of low growing vegetation, in the absence of other evidence this does not seem likely.'

Mr Justice Morling referred to the evidence of Mr Brunner and to Dr Harding's concession that hairs found on Azaria's clothing had been dog hairs. He commented that 'it now appears also that a further two hairs in the tent were dog hairs. Since no search was made for hairs in the tent and its contents until some considerable time after 17 August, it is possible that more hairs would have been found if a search had been made immediately after Azaria's disappearance.'

He referred to the evidence of Dr Corbett and Dr Newsome which reinforced 'my own impression that, if clothing were removed from a baby by a dingo, it would be likely to be more scattered about than this clothing was when found.' However, he noted that Mr Roff did not consider the appearance of the clothes to be inconsistent with dingo activity and that Mr Cawood had agreed that the flattening of the undergrowth 'was consistent with an animal having lain down'.

He rejected the Crown's submission that he should place no weight on the tracking evidence and, in particular, the Crown's contention that the tracks seen by the Winmattis on the morning after Azaria's disappearance could not have been the same as those seen by Roff and Minyintiri the night before:

> . . . Mr Roff said that they were remarkably well preserved next morning when he showed them to the Winmattis. The fact that this is quite surprising, as Roff himself said, is no reason for rejecting his evidence. I found Roff to be an impressive witness, not given to exaggeration. His veracity was not attacked and is beyond question. I refer elsewhere to his great practical experience.

He also found Nui Minyintiri to be 'an impressive witness' and commented that Mrs Winmatti, also known as Barbara Tjikadu, 'had the reputation of being an excellent tracker'. Overall, the evidence gave 'greater credence to dingo involvement in Azaria's death'.

So far as the space blanket was concerned, he found Sergeant Brown's evidence as to the loss of his notebook 'less than satisfactory' and regarded the fact that his diary made no mention of him having collected the space blanket as 'surprising', if 'indeed he did'. He commented that Superintendent Grey's evidence was 'at odds with the evidence of Inspector Gilroy, and with contemporaneous written records kept at the Alice Springs police station. Gilroy said that he spoke to Inspector McNamara at Mount Isa, not Grey.' He concluded that Lindy's mother, brother and former sister-in-law were 'all honest witnesses and that they saw marks on the space blanket that they thought may have been made by a dingo'. Morling himself was left 'in considerable doubt whether the marks which were observed were paw or claw prints left by a dingo', but had no difficulty in accepting that, if Mrs Chamberlain genuinely believed a dingo had taken Azaria, she would also have believed that the small cuts and holes had been caused by the claws of a dingo walking across the blanket. Accordingly, there was no reason to consider the matter of the space blanket as 'reflecting adversely on Mrs Chamberlain's credit'.

He also concluded that Mrs Hansell's evidence did not establish that there was blood on the tracksuit pants: 'I think it is inherently improbable that the marks on the pants were caused by blood which flowed from Azaria if and when her throat was cut by her mother.' He commented that 'it would have been astonishing for her to have been so rash as to wear them in the presence of others, including a policeman in a lighted motel room which she did later in the evening after Azaria disappeared'. It would also have been 'astonishing conduct on her part to have sent the pants to be dry-cleaned if there were incriminating bloodstains on them'. In the end result he concluded: 'On the whole of the evidence, I am of the view that the marks on the tracksuit pants were not bloodstains.'

Mr Justice Morling considered it dangerous to place any weight upon Aidan's evidence more than six years after the events he described, but concluded that weight should be given to the statement which he made on 1 October 1980:

> Several considerations lead me to this conclusion. First, when Scott interrogated Aidan on 1 October, a period of only six weeks had elapsed since Azaria's disappearance. Secondly, the expert evidence establishes that a child of Aidan's age would have had good powers of recall of events which had occurred six weeks previously. Thirdly, Aidan and his parents were given little, if

> any, warning that he was to be interrogated. Fourthly, Scott was an experienced police officer and formed the opinion that Aidan's answers were not the result of prompting by his mother. Fifthly, I find it difficult to accept that a seven-year-old child could be so well coached in his answers that an experienced police officer would be unable during the course of an interview exceeding one hour in duration to satisfy himself that the child had no independent recollection of the events of which he was speaking.
>
> Finally, I think it is probable that, if Mrs Chamberlain took Azaria to the car and returned alone, Aidan would have noticed this and would not have assented to his mother's statement that a dingo had taken the child. It is unlikely that he would have told Mrs Lowe that the 'dog's got baby in its tummy'. Thus an important part of the statement made by him on 1 October is consistent with what he said at a time when there would have been no real opportunity for his mind to have been affected by statements made to him by his parents.

The Crown had not asserted that Mrs Lowe gave deliberately untruthful evidence and Mr Justice Morling was emphatic that he 'would, in any event, reject any such suggestion'. He commented that the question remains, however, as to whether she was mistaken in her belief that she heard Azaria cry and that such a question could only be addressed in the light of the whole of the evidence. He then referred to the evidence of Mrs Dawson that on the night of either 16 or 17 August she heard a 'fairly short cry' of a baby. Other evidence established that Azaria's crying on 16 August had been more prolonged because she was hungry. Furthermore, most of the campers between the Dawsons' tent and the Chamberlains' tent left the area on the day Azaria disappeared and Mrs Dawson felt that it was more likely that she heard the cry on the night of Azaria's disappearance.

Mr Justice Morling commented:

> She did not appear to be unduly sympathetic to the Chamberlains and, indeed, some of her evidence as to her observations of the Chamberlains' conduct during the day of 17 August is mildly critical of them. Her inability to fix the night of 17 August as the time when she heard a baby's cry deprives her evidence of the weight which otherwise might have attached to it. However, her

> evidence is at least consistent with Mrs Lowe's evidence that she heard a baby cry shortly after Mrs Chamberlain returned to the barbecue and affords some marginal support for Mrs Lowe's evidence that a small baby was heard to cry shortly after Mrs Chamberlain returned to the barbecue.

In his summary of the matter, Morling referred to the two strands in the Crown case, the first consisting of evidence suggesting that Mrs Chamberlain had taken Azaria to the front passenger's seat of the car and cut her throat, the second consisting of evidence suggesting that a dingo did not take the baby:

> The effect of the new evidence on the first strand in the Crown's case is to leave it in considerable disarray. . .
>
> Taken in its entirety, the evidence falls far short of proving that there was any blood in the car for which there was not an innocent explanation. It is plain that great reliance was placed by the Crown on the findings of blood. The real dispute in this part of the case at the trial was whether the blood came from a baby. The question whether there was any blood in the car went almost by default.
>
> The doubt cast upon the findings of blood in the car is of more general importance than might first appear . . . The new evidence shows that it cannot be safely concluded that more blood was found in the car than was found in the tent. Moreover, the Crown's inability to prove that there was any of Azaria's blood in the car leaves the hypothesis that the blood found in the tent was transferred from the car without any factual foundation.
>
> In the light of the new evidence, the opinion expressed by Professor Cameron at the trial that the pattern of bloodstaining on the jumpsuit was consistent only with a cut throat cannot be safely adopted, nor can it be concluded from that pattern of bloodstaining on the clothing that Azaria's throat was cut with a blade. Further, Professor Cameron's evidence that there was an imprint of a hand in blood on the back of the jumpsuit has been weakened, if not totally destroyed, by new evidence that a great deal of what he thought was blood on the back of the jumpsuit was, in fact, red sand. . .
>
> The new evidence before the Commission discloses that Dr

> Andrew Scott, the first Crown expert to examine the jumpsuit, did not see any indication that the clothes had been buried... although Azaria's clothing may have been buried, the quantity and distribution of sand on it might well have been the result of it being dragged through sand.

It had also become clear that a reasonable match of the soil found in the jumpsuit could be found under bushes which were widespread in the sand dune country and other desert oak trees which:

> grow both in the dune country and on the plains at scattered points throughout the Ayers Rock region. Moreover, the new evidence concerning plant fragments on the clothing is consistent with the clothed body of the baby being dragged through low vegetation of kinds which grew in the dune country and on the plains between the camping area and the Rock. In the light of the new evidence, it is difficult to conceive how Azaria's clothing could have collected the quantity and variety of plant material found upon it if it had been merely taken from the car, buried, disinterred and later placed near the base of the Rock. It is more consistent with the new plant and soil evidence that Azaria's clothed body was carried and dragged by an animal from the campsite to near the base of the Rock rather than it was buried on the dune and later carried there.

Mr Justice Morling commented that new evidence was not as 'destructive' of the second strand of the Crown's case, but that 'it greatly diminishes its strength'. Evidence of the 'tracks of a dingo carrying a load which might have been Azaria's body' was stronger. He continued:

> The Crown expert has conceded that the hairs found in the tent and on the jumpsuit which were said at the trial to be probably cat hairs were either dingo or dog hairs. Dog hairs are indistinguishable from dingo hairs. The Chamberlains had not owned a dog for some years prior to August 1980...
>
> The evidence given at the trial by Mrs Chamberlain that she saw marks on the space blanket is now supported by plausible new evidence...
>
> The new evidence negates some of the most cogent evidence

> relied upon by the Crown at the trial to support its claim that the damage to the purple blanket which had covered Azaria in the bassinette was caused by moths. Mrs Chamberlain's claim that the damage to the blanket was caused by a dingo is more credible as a result of the new evidence.
>
> The quantity and distribution of blood in the tent has been shown to be at least as consistent with the dingo hypothesis as it is with murder. . .
>
> At the trial, there had been no evidence from a textile expert disputing Professor Chaikin's view that the jumpsuit was cut, probably with fairly sharp scissors, and that the severances on the clothing were not caused by a dingo . . . From the great volume of new expert evidence as to the possible causes of the damage to Azaria's clothing, it cannot be concluded beyond reasonable doubt that the damage to it was caused by scissors or a knife, or that it was not caused by the teeth of a canid. . .
>
> There is no reason to doubt that when Azaria disappeared she was wearing the matinee jacket discovered in 1986. The jacket would have covered much of the jumpsuit worn by the child. The failure to detect dingo saliva on the jumpsuit is made more explicable than it was at the trial.

He then turned to address the crucial question of whether there were doubts as to the Chamberlains' guilt:

> I have referred elsewhere to the unsatisfactory features in Mrs Chamberlain's account of having seen a dingo at the tent and I do not underestimate their importance. It can fairly be said that there are inconsistencies and improbabilities in her story and in the various versions she has given of it. However . . . there are possible explanations for many of the apparently unsatisfactory features of her evidence.
>
> On the other hand, the obstacles to the acceptance of the Crown's case are both numerous and formidable. Almost every facet of its case is beset by serious difficulties.

He referred to the absence of any motive and the undisputed evidence that she had been 'an exemplary mother' who was 'delighted at Azaria's birth'. She had not suffered from any form of mental illness, nor had she ever been violent to any of her children and she exhibited no sign of stress, irritation or abnormal behaviour before taking Azaria to the tent to put her to bed. Mr Justice Morling continued:

> If Mrs Chamberlain left the barbecue with the intention of killing Azaria, it is astonishing that she took Aidan with her. It would have been easy for her to have left him at the barbecue with his father. Having taken Aidan with her, it is even more astonishing that she should have murdered Azaria, on the Crown case, a few feet from where he was waiting for her return to the tent. It was a great coincidence that Mrs Lowe not only thought she heard Azaria cry, but also thought she heard Mr Chamberlain or Aidan say that he had heard the same cry. It is surprising that Mrs Chamberlain did not attempt to bolster her story by saying that she also heard the cry.
>
> If Mrs Chamberlain did not intend to murder Azaria when she left the barbecue, it is difficult to understand why, for no apparent reason , she should have formed the intention almost immediately after she left it. There is nothing in the evidence which could account for the formation of such a sudden intention.
>
> It seems improbable that Mrs Chamberlain, having murdered Azaria in the car or elsewhere, would have returned to the tent with so much blood on her person or clothing that some of it dripped onto the articles upon which it was found in the tent. Unless she did, there is no explanation, except the dingo story, for the blood found in the tent. Such conduct on her part seems inconsistent with her donning the tracksuit pants (as the Crown alleges) so as to avoid telltale signs of blood.
>
> It is extraordinary that the persons present at the barbecue area at the time of and immediately after Azaria's disappearance accepted Mrs Chamberlain's story and noticed nothing about her appearance or conduct suggesting that she had suddenly killed her daughter and nothing about Mr Chamberlain's conduct suggesting that he knew that she had done so. She must have been a consummate actress if, having killed her daughter, she was able to appear calm and unconcerned when she returned to the barbecue a few minutes after the murder.

He referred to the different steps which she would have to have taken if she had committed the crime in the manner the Crown alleged and commented that 'the short period during which Mrs

Chamberlain was absent from the barbecue made it only barely possible that she could have committed the crime alleged against her.' He also pointed to the evidence which suggested that it would have taken up to twenty minutes for Azaria to have died if her carotid arteries had not been severed. He pointed out that the bloodstaining on the jumpsuit indicated 'an absence of arterial bleeding'.

Morling found it very difficult to accept that Aidan did not notice that his mother took Azaria from the tent and returned without her and did not comment on that fact when his sister was found to be missing. He went on:

> It was indeed fortuitous that a dog or dingo should have been heard to growl and a dingo should have been seen not far from the tent very shortly before Azaria disappeared and that on the night of 17 August a canid's tracks should have been found hard up against the tent.
>
> It is surprising that, if Mrs Chamberlain had blood on her clothing, nobody noticed it in the hours after Azaria's disappearance. If Azaria's body was left in the car after the alleged murder, it was foolhardy for Mrs Chamberlain, in the presence of the Demaines and their dog, to open the car door and give the dog the scent of Azaria's clothing. The risks involved in the Chamberlains burying and disinterring Azaria when there were so many people who might have observed them were enormous. It is difficult to explain how the variety of plant material found on Azaria's clothing could have got there if she'd been murdered. It seems improbable that, the murder having been so cleverly accomplished and concealed, the clothing would have been so left as to invite suspicion.
>
> If Mrs Chamberlain told her husband that she had killed Azaria, it was extraordinary conduct on his part to leave his two sons, the younger of whom was aged only three years, in her sole custody on 18 August. . .
>
> Their conduct upon their return to Mount Isa is inexplicable if she had murdered Azaria. For instance, it is almost incredible that she should have told people there was blood on her shoes if she had murdered her daughter. Further, it was bravado of a high order for Mr Chamberlain to tell the police at Cooranbong that they had taken possession of the wrong camera bag if Azaria's

> body had been secreted in the one which he then produced. . .
>
> The Crown has no direct evidence of the Chamberlains' guilt to overcome the cumulative effect of all these formidable obstacles. Even so, their guilt would be established if, in spite of so many considerations pointing to their innocence, the conclusion was reached that it had been proved beyond reasonable doubt that a dingo did not take the baby. In the light of all the evidence before the Commission, I am of the opinion that such a conclusion cannot be reached.

Mr Justice Morling embarked upon a summary of the evidence which led him to that conclusion and expressed the view that 'taken in its entirety, it falls far short of proving that Azaria was not taken by a dingo. Indeed, the evidence affords considerable support for the view that a dingo may have taken her. To examine the evidence to see whether it has been proved that a dingo took Azaria would be to make the fundamental error of reversing the onus of proof and requiring Mrs Chamberlain to prove her innocence.' He went on:

> I am far from being persuaded that Mrs Chamberlain's account of having seen a dingo near the tent was false or that Mr Chamberlain falsely denied that he knew his wife had murdered his daughter. That is not to say that I accept that all their evidence is accurate. Some of it plainly is not, since parts of it are inconsistent with other parts. But if a dingo took her child, the events of the night of 17 August must have been emotionally devastating for Mrs Chamberlain. Her ability to give a reliable account of the tragedy may have been badly affected by her distress. The inconsistencies in her evidence may have been caused by her confusion of mind. Where her evidence conflicts with the Lowes' account of what she said and did in the few seconds after she commenced to run back to the tent, it may be the Lowes' recollection, not hers, that is at fault. The belief that people might unjustly accuse her of making up the dingo story might have led her, even subconsciously, to embellish her account of what happened, and this may explain some of its improbabilities. Her failure to see Azaria in the dingo's mouth is explicable if, as is quite possible, there were two dingoes, not one. These considerations afford at least as convincing an explanation

> for the apparently unsatisfactory parts of her evidence as does the Crown's claim that she was lying to conceal her part in the alleged murder. Having seen Mr and Mrs Chamberlain in the witness box, I am not convinced that either of them was lying.

He pointed out that he had not found it necessary to consider the possibility of human intervention between the time of Azaria's disappearance and the finding of her clothes. 'It is difficult but not impossible to imagine circumstances in which such intervention could have occurred. It is not inconceivable that an owner of a domestic dog intervened to cover up its involvement in the tragedy or that some tourist, acting irrationally, interfered with the clothes before they were later discovered by others.'

His ultimate conclusion was blunt and to the point. 'It follows from what I have written that there are serious doubts and questions as to the Chamberlains' guilt and as to the evidence in the trial leading to their conviction. In my opinion, if the evidence before the Commission had been given at the trial, the trial judge would have been obliged to direct the jury to acquit the Chamberlains on the ground that the evidence could not justify their conviction.'

32

Flaws in the system

NO-ONE COULD FAIRLY DESCRIBE the Chamberlains as lucky people. Countless mothers throughout countless centuries had put their babies to sleep in tents, yet Lindy had lost her baby from a tent erected in a government-run camping area in a country virtually free of natural predators. The suspicion, the rumours of her arrest, trial, conviction and imprisonment were all the result of misconceptions and errors. Lindy had been imprisoned for three-and-a-half years, but the whole family had been pariahs in their own land for seven years. It had taken a heavy toll on them all.

Yet their God of mercy had permitted fortune to smile upon them in ways that were later to prove significant. A number of people who had flocked to comfort them or to take part in the searches for their baby were to prove impressive witnesses. Had the Chamberlains been camping alone or among people who were as vague about detail and prone to confusion as the rest of us, their position, even before the Commission of Inquiry, would have been more precarious. The Chamberlains were also fortunate in having the support of the Seventh Day Adventist Church. The church provided them with a home at Cooranbong in the midst of a community of people willing to offer them not only shelter but protection and comfort. They may have felt like refugees in their own country, but at least there was a place of refuge. Even after their convictions, the church continued to demonstrate its faith in the Chamberlains by advancing hundreds of thousands of dollars for legal fees and other expenses. The church had borne some of their ignominy, but remained willing to bear some of their burdens.

The Chamberlains were also fortunate in having so many people from varying walks of life prepared to champion their cause. Professor Boettcher, who had been much maligned by the Crown not only at the trial but before the Commission of Inquiry, had been prepared to sacrifice much of his academic career to a cause he believed to be just. Even now, when his views have been vindicated, it is doubtful that he will be able to recover the ground lost during the past few years.

Bob Collins had been prepared to speak out on their behalf in the face of a mounting storm of criticism not only from his political opponents but from his own party. Ultimately he was asked to resign as Leader of the Opposition because the Northern Territory Labor Party perceived that his decision to champion the cause of the Chamberlains had been 'electorally damaging'. In all honesty he was obliged to admit that his colleagues were right. The hostility towards the Chamberlains was so great that no-one who constantly defended them could expect to be elected as Chief Minister of the Northern Territory.

Smith and Chapman, the Sanitarium health food scientists who demonstrated that the under-dash spray was made of sound-deadening material and that dingoes' teeth could produce tufts, decided to 'take on' the scientific establishment only because of their faith in the Chamberlains.

Betty Hocking, Guy Boyd, Sir Reginald Sholl and others who campaigned so vigorously on their behalf became involved because there was something about the Chamberlains or the surrounding circumstances of the case which convinced them of their innocence.

What if all this support had not been available to them? What if they had merely been a normal couple, unable to point to anything in the evidence which might capture the public imagination and unable to find any financial support for the immense legal battles to come? Even with all these advantages, the normal processes of our law simply failed the Chamberlains. It was only by the exertion of immense public pressure that they were able to obtain a judicial inquiry and, ultimately, some measure of public exoneration.

Without this support, the overwhelming likelihood is that the scientific evidence led by the Crown would have been inadequately challenged, and the Chamberlains would have been convicted after a trial which left little doubt of their guilt and which could have sparked little of the public controversy that raged after the trial in 1982. Thereafter, any appeal would have been doomed to failure and there would have been none of the scientific investigation or public pressure which led to the decision to appoint a commission of inquiry. In short, Lindy would have been left to languish in prison for the balance of her life sentence and the pall of guilt would have remained over this young family.

Few people accused of serious crime are able to marshall the support which built up for the Chamberlains. The fact that they were able to obtain a judicial inquiry and, ultimately, full pardons no doubt offered some consolation to them, but did nothing to suggest that others might not have been less fortunate. The first issue raised, then, is the disquieting thought that at times justice only comes by the expenditure of large amounts of money and with the support of many friends.

The second issue concerns the rights of the individual. In Australia and in other countries which have inherited the British system of justice there has been a traditional emphasis upon the rights of the individual. All of us enjoy the protection of the right to silence, the presumption of innocence unless and until our guilt is established beyond reasonable doubt and, in serious cases, trial by jury. Perhaps the best known of all legal maxims is the one that holds that it is better that ten guilty men should go free than that one innocent one should be unjustly punished. Those who know little of the law feel completely secure in its protection.

But in recent years, changes have taken place in society which have the potential of undermining our safeguards unless built-in protections are created. Law reform has been increasingly concerned with combatting crime and, in particular, organised crime. The underlying concern has been fully justified. Even in Australia, traditionally the lucky country where crime has been concerned, organised crime has made frightening incursions into the community. The emergence of a massive worldwide trade in drugs has created criminal profits running to many millions of dollars annually. Such vast wealth would have attracted the unscrupulous in any age and any setting.

It has proved particularly difficult to offer any effective counter to the drug trade. The victims are dependent upon the guilty for the supply of drugs. There is an extensive and efficiently organised hierarchy. If someone does 'dob in' his supplier, charges may be laid, but the supplier is likely to be another addict simply seeking to support his habit and even he may escape conviction. It is virtually inevitable for heroin addicts to turn to crime to provide the vast sums of money necessary to support an addiction and they tend to make unreliable witnesses.

Large-scale operations are undertaken with individual teams of workmen being recruited for each major task. They are told nothing more than they need to know and usually refer to their only contact as 'Fred', 'Joe' or some equally monosyllabic alias. If, through some fluke, Fred is apprehended, the police are likely to find that he knows little more than the 'hewers of wood and drawers of water' that he has hired. It is difficult to combat a series of unknown adversaries who organise their operations with almost military precision and who enforce secrecy through a ruthless campaign of fear.

It is understandable that the police have sought to go beyond normal investigative measures and to use phone taps and other electronic eavesdropping equipment. It is also understandable that concerned governments struck by their own impotence would try to make convictions easier to obtain by changing the law. Consequently, most jurisdictions have passed laws providing that anyone who possesses more than the prescribed quantity of a particular drug shall be deemed to have it for the purpose of supply to others. In effect, these provisions reverse the normal onus of proof by assuming the guilt of the accused unless, and until, he establishes that he had the drug for his own use. There have been other changes. More, including restriction of the right to silence, are constantly under discussion. The broader interests of the community may demand that drastic measures be taken, but the overall effect has been to whittle down rather than enlarge the rights of the individual.

A third issue concerns increasing pressure on juries. These come from two quarters: the media and the world of the scientist. The development of television, introduced into Australia in 1956, brought a new dimension to the risk of trial by media. At the same time, forensic science moved beyond the more readily understood disciplines, such as fingerprint and handwriting identification and perhaps ballistics, into new realms of unbelievable complexity.

Science became the new god in the courtroom as well as in the community. Juries seemed willing to accord even its most humble disciples the mantle of infallibility. Defendants were frequently in no position to challenge the scientific findings put forward by the prosecution. They lacked the necessary understanding and could not afford to engage scientists willing to mount such a challenge for them. Scientists, for their part, were accustomed to explaining things to other scientists rather than to juries of laymen. If a jury did not understand the factual basis for a conclusion, that would usually be unimportant because the conclusion was nonetheless sound. But if it proved to be unsound, their lack of understanding may have blinded them to flaws in the chain of reasoning and they may have been beguiled into accepting a plausible but improbable explanation as scientific proof.

In the last two or three decades there have been a number of cases in Australia and New Zealand which have generated considerable disquiet. All of them have involved either enormous publicity or a substantial reliance upon scientific evidence and most have involved both. Our criminal procedure was, in the main, formulated in ages gone by when neither scientists nor journalists had much of an effect on the jury system.

Earlier generations were not confronted by batteries of scientists describing procedures of bewildering complexity in polysyllabic words as unintelligible to the average juror as the incantations of some bizarre religion. Breadth of experience and commonsense may offer little guidance when the whole area of expertise is completely alien. Equally, they were not confronted with the barrage of publicity generated by an electronic media capable of intruding into the homes of potential jurors and their associates in a manner which may create a climate of incredible prejudice. The extent to which confusion and prejudice may contribute to a person's conviction is frequently unknown and unknowable.

Some of the things said by judges of appeal would almost lead one to assume that when twelve ordinary men and women are sworn in as jurors they experience some kind of metaphysical transformation which makes them immune to prejudice and impervious to error. That is a false impression. Appellate judges are reluctant to intervene not because of some misguided notion of infallibility, but for far more pragmatic reasons.

The dominant concern is often the desire to maintain public confidence in the jury system. This is undeniably important. Sir Richard Blackburn, the first Chief Justice of the Supreme Court of the Australian Capital Territory, described the jury system as 'the bulwark of liberty' in our community. Those spendidly descriptive words should be emblazoned in the mind of every would-be reformer.They remind us of the great safeguard to our liberty which each of us enjoys as we go about our affairs. For none of us are liable to be condemned for some serious offence upon the whim of a government appointee. A jury of twelve people selected from a panel chosen at random offers a significant measure of protection against the risk of corruption or individual prejudice on the part of a sole judicial officer.

They also bring to criminal trials a breadth of human understanding which no single judge could contribute. Whilst it is impolitic for a barrister to say so, a judge lives within the most conservative environment our society offers. He wears the wigs and gowns of a bygone era and dispenses justice peering down from a bench on a raised dais in a courtroom designed to reflect the solemnity of the occasion. His appearance is heralded by a sheriff's officer issuing a peremptory command such as 'Silence! All rise!' When he has been seated, after the customary bows by members of the legal profession, the court crier or tipstaff is likely to thump his medieval staff on the ground and proclaim loudly, 'Hear ye, hear ye,all having business before this honourable court draw nigh and ye shall be heard! God save the Queen!' He may fine or even send to prison anyone who disobeys his orders or whose conduct becomes sufficiently insulting or offensive to constitute contempt of court.

Yet, although this measure of power over the individual seems more redolent of medieval barons than public servants appointed to assist in the resolution of disputes, he is in fact bound by a law and practice forged from centuries of legal tradition. Custom decrees that even the most radical of barristers must become circumspect in his public statements when he is appointed to the bench. Even his private life must be approached with considerable caution lest he be seen to have become 'compromised' or to have identified himself too closely with particular groups or issues. Some day a progressive government may take the matter to its logical conclusion by building a series of Edwardian bungalows in some convenient forest where judges could live in a judicial sanctuary or game park. A lodge could, perhaps, be provided to accommodate the odd budding David Attenborough dropping in for some research on his Ph.D. thesis in anthropology.

Of course, it is important for judges to maintain some degree of caution in their social contacts. There can be little doubt that the majority of judges are, by virtue of their background training and experience, ideally equipped to carry out their allotted tasks. The same backgrounds and experience, however, make it virtually inevitable that they will share little in common with many sections of the community. This lack of empathy or rapport may be unavoidable, but it may nonetheless put a judge at a considerable disadvantage compared to a jury of twelve people with widely divergent backgrounds. There is also much in the often-repeated observation that two heads are better than one and, presumably, twelve heads are better than two.

Further, the alternative of trial by a single judge suffers from the problem that judges constantly dealing with criminals are likely to acquire an inordinate degree of cynicism. This is a trend sometimes evident among the ranks of magistrates who try the minor criminal offences without the aid of a jury. This comment might enrage hordes of magistrates but, in reality, it reflects nothing more than the fact that we are all creatures of our background and experience. Someone who derives most of his experience from dealing with the devious and the dishonest is likely to be more sceptical than people drawn from the people at large. This can produce a tendency to dismiss anything that smacks of the improbable but, in real life, improbable things happen every day of the week.

It is important to keep these things in mind, for our

community seems to be afflicted by a smattering of academics willing to seize upon any suggestion of the jury system's inadequacy as a reason for abandoning it altogether. In this context, it is understandable for those who appreciate its strengths and virtues to seek to protect it from adverse criticism.

Furthermore, many proposals for reform have been ill-considered and are likely to cause more difficulties than they would have solved. One such creature of misguided trendiness was the proposal to reform the sexual offences laws in one Australian jurisdiction by defining sexual intercourse as the penetration of any part of a woman's body by any part of a man's body. This splendidly impractical proposal would have meant that a dentist who allowed the tip of his finger to stray into a female patient's mouth would have been taken to have had sexual intercourse with her. A doctor who sought to clear the tongue from the blocked airway of a woman who had suffered an epileptic seizure would have been guilty of rape unless he had been able to first revive her and obtain her consent.

Such gaffes have not only left lawyers aghast, but ensured that subsequent proposals would be treated with considerable caution. Law reform bodies are, in the main, staffed by academics whom experienced 'practitioners' may deride as mere theorists. This undoubtedly adds weight to the resistance to reform.

Many simply feel that we have a very good system and should be content with it. It offers all the protection an innocent person could want, they suggest. The existing law does, in fact, offer considerable protection for an accused person, but that protection is available only because reformers of bygone generations were zealous to meet any new threat to the 'liberty of the subject'. Those who see themselves as traditionalists sometimes fail to perceive that constant reform has been an indispensable part of the law's tradition. Every age has brought new threats that have demanded new responses. This age has been no exception.

The Chamberlain saga has shown that there are cases in which the traditional protections prove inadequate to deal with the relatively new perils of forensic science and the media. It now falls to us to take up the mantle of reform and find some means of minimising these threats.

The German judge in the film 'Judgement at Nuremburg' sought to excuse himself with the comment that he had 'never thought it would come to this'. The judge who had sentenced him replied that it had 'come to this' the first time he had been prepared to condemn the innocent. In our society, the main threat to the innocent comes not from judicial corruption but from error and prejudice. Yet to sit by in complacency or conservatism and permit the innocent to be condemned is equally abhorrent.

Many greeted the decision to hold an inquiry into the Chamberlains' convictions with comments such as, 'It's too expensive' or, 'She's had a trial and two appeals — you've got to stop somewhere'. Even now when it is plain that they should not have been convicted, some suggest that we may have paid too high a price for justice. It is not merely a matter of money but of loss of confidence in the system. There seems to be a feeling that the myth of infallibility must be maintained at all costs. If that means occasionally convicting the innocent then they should presumably be content with the knowledge that they have been martyrs in a good cause.

Yet, in the long run, public confidence will only be maintained by ensuring that the system is as reliable as humanly possible. When the individual's chances of receiving justice may be dependent upon immense sums of money or the ability to capture the public imagination, then it is apparent that lawyers need to seek reform rather than retreat into defensiveness.

33

The need for change

THE CASE OF THE CROWN VERSUS CHAMBERLAIN provides a timely opportunity for a constructive response to weaknesses and tensions within our legal system. A number of areas would appear to need further examination if the law is to justify the confidence of those it is meant to serve.

The role of the press

The problem of trial by media is seemingly insoluble. It is not a problem only in countries which exercise considerable press censorship and few, if any, of such countries boast a jury system. The dilemma lies in seeking to balance the interests of the individual being tried against the interests of the wider community to be kept informed.

This latter consideration is not merely a matter of pandering to the nosiness of those who turn on their television sets looking for something sensational. It is a matter of exposing the administration of justice to public scrutiny, of justice 'being seen to be done'. Furthermore, to prevent publicity might hinder public debate especially since neither lawyers nor judges normally feel free to make comments concerning cases in which they have been involved.

This dilemma was, perhaps, exemplified by a recent Victorian case involving a journalist who had reported that an accused person charged with molesting a child had been allowed to keep his job, which involved having children in his care, despite earlier allegations of molestation. Viewed from the accused's point of view, this publicity was grossly unfair. He was entitled to have a jury decide his guilt or innocence on the basis of the evidence relating to the particular offence charged, without the risk of prejudice arising from allegations of earlier misconduct which may have been unsubstantiated. Cliches such as 'where there's smoke there's fire' have no place in the administration of justice.

From the journalist's point of view, however, there was a wider issue at stake. Whilst the law might properly give an accused person the benefit of any reasonable doubt in determining whether he should be convicted of a crime, parents were entitled to approach the matter somewhat differently. They were entitled to expect that the authorities would regard the welfare of their children as paramount and to protect them from the risk of molestation whether that risk was established beyond reasonable doubt, on the balance of probabilities or merely as a not insignificant chance. Ultimately, of course, some compromise has to be found between the competing demands.

In some areas, the law has tried to provide for such a compromise by permitting the bulk of judicial proceedings to be reported, but providing judges with a discretion to prohibit publication of parts of the evidence in particular circumstances. For example, a judge may decide to embark upon a *voir dire*, in which he hears evidence in the absence of the jury with a view to determining whether it is properly admissible. If he decides to exclude it, then the jury should not be informed of it by a press eager to make up for the judge's perceived deficiencies. Equally, if a judge takes the view that the publication of a witness's name might endanger his or her life, it would be unthinkable to permit some journalist to publish the name even if the resultant murder helped boost his paper's circulation.

The real difficulty stems from a seeming reluctance to entrust judges and magistrates with a sufficiently wide discretion to minimise the likely prejudice caused by adverse publicity. No magistrate, or judge for that matter, should be constrained to insist that a witness choose between condemning himself in the eyes of the media by a public claim of privilege against self-incrimination or abandon his rights and wander unawares into an uncharted minefield carefully laid by prosecuting authorities seeking to exploit his ignorance. A magistrate faced with such a situation should have the power to hear any claim of privilege 'in camera', that is,in a procedure akin to a *voir dire* which could not be publicly reported. No-one should be forced to fall prey to 'trial by ambush'.

In other circumstances, of course, it may be appropriate for any claim of privilege to be made in open court. Whilst the law permits evidence relating to the prior conduct of an accused person to be disclosed only in certain stipulated circumstances, witnesses may generally be asked questions about their prior conduct because it is relevant to their credit; that is,the weight to be attached to their credibility and reliability. If a witness is to be relieved of the obligation of answering questions which may have shown that he has behaved dishonestly in the past, it seems not unreasonable to suggest that the jury should know that he has made such a claim. If that were not the case, they may infer from the fact that he has escaped without any attack on his prior conduct, that he is a person whose character has been exemplary. One does not have to choose between two extremes. It is possible to provide a judge with a discretion to provide protection where necessary. No doubt there would be cases in which the competing considerations were evenly balanced and it may be necessary not only to delineate the ambit of such a discretion but to provide some guidelines for its exercise.

Coroners should also be empowered to exercise some jurisdiction over those appointed to 'assist' them. If it seems likely or even possible that a case will be made out against a particular person likely to be called as a witness in the proceedings before him, the magistrate should be entitled to insist that that witness be called last and that he be given sufficient information to enable him to understand the nature of the case likely to be brought against him. If by then it is apparent that charges will be laid, the magistrate should be entitled to treat the inquest as being at an end and to offer the person likely to be charged the same rights as those enjoyed by a defendant in committal proceedings. Inquests are intended to be inquiries held to determine the cause of death and the surrounding circumstances. They are not intended to be some kind of forensic chess game in which the prosecuting authorities and the defence engage in a battle of tactical manoeuvres against a backdrop of publicity, with public prejudice or sympathy available as a prize for the most skilful.

The problem of scientific evidence

Mr Justice Morling expressed considerable concern at the lack of safeguards and the practices of forensic science laboratories:

> In criminal cases, where the standard of proof is proof beyond reasonable doubt, it is highly desirable that complex scientific evidence called by the prosecution should be so carefully prepared and expressed that the necessity for the defence to challenge it is reduced as much as possible. This was especially the case at the Chamberlain trial because of the complexity and novelty of so many scientific questions which arose for the jury's consideration.
>
> At the time of the Chamberlain case, it was the practice of the New South Wales Health Commission not to prepare plates on which blood tests had been done or photographs of them or samples of blood for testing by experts on behalf of the accused. The undesirable consequences of this practice, which has since been changed, are obvious.
>
> Mrs Kuhl was called upon to perform an extremely difficult task in a scientific area where controversy between experts was, to say the least, likely. Yet it appears that her laboratory had not laid down any criteria for determining whether a particular result was sufficiently certain to be used as a basis for giving evidence. At the Commission Mr Martin, who was called at the request of the Crown, said that some of the test results, especially in respect of the scissors found in the car, were so uncertain that they should not have been relied upon.
>
> Mr Martin thought that in the field of immuno-chemical reaction testing certain criteria had to be adopted to ensure that only reasonably certain results were relied upon in a criminal case. The absence of such criteria in the Chamberlain investigation produced a risk of injustice to the accused and aggravated the difficulty of the task which confronted Mrs Kuhl.
>
> It will often be the case that experts will disagree on matters concerning which there is little prior experience. However, in the present case a number of opinions given in evidence at the trial have been shown to be plainly erroneous. Some of them were extremely adverse to the Chamberlains and it is unfortunate that they should have been given in evidence in a murder trial.

He expressed the hope that 'lessons may be learned which may prevent similar errors being made in the future'.

He then proposed the establishment of a national forensic science institute. Similar proposals had been made in 1973, 1974 and by a task force which reported to the Australian Police Ministers' Council in March 1982. He commented:

> [It] is essential that the forensic scientist be free from pressure to produce results, except after adequate testing procedures have been observed. Dr Baxter expressed the firm opinion that a forensic science centre should be autonomous and so structured that it is not subject to external pressure. He is obviously correct in his opinion.
>
> Professors Schreiber and Nairn suggested that there should be closer links between forensic science centres and universities and other appropriate institutions so as to ensure that the former have the advantage of the research conducted by the latter. I agree with this suggestion, but how close the links should be was not explored in evidence before the Commission. . .
>
> The laying down of appropriate standards in matters of forensic science would not be easy. The evidence I have heard discloses differences of opinion between various experts as to what standards should be adopted. For example, in the testing of blood, scientists have disagreed as to the merits and reliability of the crossover electrophoresis test as compared with the Ouchterlony test. If the former is unreliable, as some witnesses suggested, it is unfortunate that it is the standard final test in some laboratories, when others regard it as a preliminary test only. This is the type of problem which the suggested national forensic science institute could address and, it is hoped, resolve, so as to establish a uniform and reliable practice throughout Australia.
>
> Such an institute might also be a centre for the exchange of information, and the location of reliable experts in unusual fields of expertise. Thus Dr Harding could have been informed about Mr Brunner's work if such an institute had kept an up-to-date register of relevant research work done in Australia and overseas.
>
> . . . Furthermore, the existence of such an institute would hopefully reduce the need to obtain experts from overseas. The fact that some of the Crown's experts who gave evidence at the trial resided overseas may have contributed to the lack of consultation between them and other experts in the matter of the alleged hand

> prints on the jumpsuit and also in the matter of the alleged under-dash arterial spray. . .
>
> Juries may attach great weight to the opinions of experts on matters outside the competence of the layman to understand. It is essential that everything possible be done to ensure that opinions expressed by experts, especially Crown experts, be soundly based and correct. In many cases, the opinions expressed by the Crown's experts are accepted by the defence. If they are not accepted, the resources of an accused person may well not suffice to enable him to challenge them. The risk of an injustice occurring would be diminished if an accused person, in common with the Crown, had access to a national forensic science institute and its staff of experts.

The Northern Territory Attorney-General, in tabling his report, announced that 'it is our intention to take up with the Commonwealth and the States, the question of creating a national forensic science institute'. It is to be hoped that the Commonwealth and the States will support this initiative. Similar suggestions have been made in the past, but they have fallen on the deaf ears of governments who could see no vote-winning potential in reforms of that nature. Yet it remains a matter of critical importance.

To suggest the formation of such an institute is, of course, merely the first step. There will, no doubt, be considerable debate over its structure and objectives. It is to be hoped that the relevant governments will seek advice from an advisory committee of forensic scientists and, perhaps, the odd lawyer before embarking on this ambitious project.

One task which might be undertaken by such an institute lies in determining just what a jury should be told as the result of a particular test. During the proceedings before Mr Justice Morling, a number of biologists agreed that the application of orthotolidine to a suspected bloodstain was merely a screening test and that it would be 'quite wrong' to regard it as even prima facie evidence of the presence of blood. At the trial, the jury had been told that there was practically nothing but blood which would react with the chemical and were encouraged to treat a positive result as indicating, if not the certainty, at least a high likelihood that blood was present. But if manuals can be produced setting out standard methods for conducting particular tests, then it should not be impossible to lay down guidelines for their interpretation and for the manner in which the results should be explained to the jury.

This proposition is not completely novel. Handwriting experts, for example, have reached agreement that a particular number of points of similarity must be evident before any conclusions can be drawn as to the identity of the handwriting in question. If there is one less, the jury is told nothing except, perhaps, that the identity of the handwriting could not be established. No doubt there are many tests in other disciplines which are not amenable to a rigid delineation, but it should be possible to find some means of conveying to the jury an agreed explanation of their significance. Where even that degree of standardisation is not possible because of the subjective nature of the assessment then the jury could, at least, be told that. It is simply not good enough to leave it to a jury to deduce for itself the significance of results which might have a crucial bearing on the outcome of the case simply by considering the answers to particular questions asked by opposing counsel.

The institute should also give considerable priority to retaining sufficient quantities of any samples tested to facilitate further examination by experts retained on behalf of the defence. If there are insufficient quantities to permit the retention of any for subsequent testing, then the solicitors for the accused should be informed of the problem and given the opportunity to nominate an observer to be present when the test is carried out. Equally, if the sample to be tested is some biological material likely to deteriorate with the passage of time, then the defence should be informed immediately so that they may have an observer present during the tests or may have their own tests arranged as a matter of urgency. In some cases this may deprive the Crown of the element of surprise, but the loss of this questionable advantage is a small price to pay for confidence that the scientific evidence put before the jury is accurate.

It may also be necessary to consider how much information should be made available to a scientist trying to resolve a particular question. Before the Commission of Inquiry, Professor Cameron conceded that he had taken into account various things he was told about the other evidence which subsequently were proved incorrect. Accordingly, his opinion was based, at least in part, upon a series of misconceptions. His report was, in turn, taken into account by Mr Kuchel, the botanist. No doubt there have been many other cases in which an initial error or series of errors has infected the reports of subsequent experts who have added the weight of their own opinions, producing a snowballing effect and, ultimately, a strong but quite misleading circumstantial case.

Dr Baxter was adamant that police should not be permitted to bring exhibits into a forensic science laboratory and to discuss them with the scientist charged with carrying out the testing programme. That is sound commonsense. Any accused person is entitled to expect that a scientist will not be swayed in his interpretation of results, many of which do involve a subjective element, by presuppositions or a desire to fulfil the expectations of the police. Yet it is equally important that a scientist remain unswayed by the opinions of his colleagues in other disciplines who may have carried out tests in relation to the same case. A scientist, whether pathologist, biologist or ballistics expert, is asked to give conclusions based on his own expertise, not on the basis of an overview of that part of the case which has been recounted to him. It is for the judge or jury to become concerned about the manner in which the opinions of experts in different disciplines are to be reconciled.

Scientists have most frequently been misled when they have carried out experiments with a view to validating presuppositions rather than with an open mind. As the diary of one Nobel prize winner demonstrates, even the most eminent are not immune from the risk of being misled in this manner. Perhaps one way of guarding against this risk would be to ensure the anonymity of samples. Just as examination papers are marked by examiners who know only the number of a particular candidate, so samples to be tested in a forensic science laboratory could be rendered annonymous. Of course, it is possible to be misled by not having sufficient information and it may be necessary for a scientist to take a multi-disciplinary approach to the whole exercise when all of the results have been obtained.

It was central to Mr Justice Morling's proposal that the institute be available to assist defendants as well as prosecuting authorities. This is an admirable suggestion, but it would need to be implemented with considerable care. Is it contemplated, for example, that two scientists working side by side in the same laboratory would test the same samples, one on behalf of the prosecution and one on behalf of the defence? What if they disagreed? Would they be happy to go to Court 'against' each other? Would there be some risk that one or the other might be tempted to give way in order to preserve a cordial relationship or that they might be tempted to compromise for similar reasons?

Furthermore, forensic science laboratories are presumably as prone to internal politics as any other hierarchical structure. What kind of emotional pressure might be exerted upon a junior scientist if he found himself in complete disagreement with his superiors? At present, solicitors for an accused person can approach a forensic science laboratory in a different State and obtain opinions which are completely independent of those upon which the Crown intends to rely. If it were intended that those individual forensic science laboratories would gradually be phased out, then considerable care would need to be taken to ensure that the institute was organised in a manner that would facilitate completely independent testing by capable and experienced scientists, free from any extraneous influences. If that were not done, then the avenues for independent testing would have been diminished rather than increased.

There are also strong grounds for suggesting some changes to the law governing the admissibility of scientific evidence in jury trials. The High Court of Australia has now held that, at least in a circumstantial evidence case, no inference can be drawn from primary facts unless those facts have been established to the requisite standard of proof beyond reasonable doubt. The Court also suggested that where there are two conflicting bodies of scientific opinion, and there is no question of bias, dishonesty or any other factors which might impugn the validity of the views expounded on one side, then it would not be open to a jury to be satisfied beyond reasonable doubt that one group of experts was right and the other wrong. Despite that, the Court held that the disputed evidence concerning the foetal haemoglobin content of 'blood' found in the Chamberlains' car had been rightly admitted.

Whilst that undoubtedly reflects the law as it presently stands, it is obviously unfortunate. If the jury cannot be satisfied beyond reasonable doubt that one contention is correct, and cannot draw inferences based upon anything not proven beyond reasonable doubt, then it follows that it is not open to the jury to draw inferences from the disputed evidence. If it is not open to the jury to rely upon the evidence then, clearly, it should not be admitted in the first place.

To admit evidence which could not properly assist the jury is to simply invite some improper use of the material. At best, it constitutes a waste of time and an unnecessary risk. At worst, it is likely to result in a person's wrongful conviction. Where the dispute has been anticipated, it would seem appropriate to deal with the matter by way of a *voir dire* or even a preliminary hearing before a single judge some time before the trial commences. If a bona fide dispute of the kind envisaged by the High Court in fact emerges, then the evidence should be excluded. If, on the other hand, such a dispute emerges only during the course of the trial, then the jury should be directed by the trial judge to ignore the evidence so disputed. The limitations of the present appellate procedure also need to be addressed.

The judge's power to intervene

There would seem to be strong grounds for suggesting that the trial judge should be empowered to direct an acquittal if the prosecution case is obviously unsatisfactory in some respect. In New South Wales, judges regularly exercised such a power for many years before the Court of Criminal Appeal ruled that they were not entitled to do so. Despite the criticisms of purists who saw this practice as usurping the jury's role, there were no reports of judges seizing the opportunity to let hordes of obviously guilty felons loose on the community. It was the experience of most barristers that judges intervened only when the Crown case was clearly inadequate and, even then, some would only intervene if they felt that the jury might be tempted to convict for quite improper reasons. The real value of the practice lay in its potential to protect an accused person against whom there was little evidence of real probative value from a climate of prejudice.

Even in cases in which there is no question of any attitude of prejudice towards the accused, there would appear to be little point in continuing to go through the motions of a trial once it has become clear that there is insufficient evidence to warrant a conviction. In one trial conducted in Sydney some years ago, the Crown conceded that the accused had an iron-clad alibi: he had been an inmate of an interstate prison on the date of the offence. Why should the public purse be drained by the expense of the balance of the trial when the outcome was a foregone conclusion? The answer usually given is that a jury might take a different view of the evidence, but if judges exercised the power to intervene sparingly as, indeed, they did in the past, then this should present few practical difficulties. It is, after all, scarcely in the public interest to persevere in the hope that a jury might act perversely by, for example, deciding that a man broke into a Sydney apartment whilst confined in a cell one thousand kilometres away.

Providing more effective appeals

The technology now exists to record the evidence of witnesses by video tape. It is no longer true that appellate judges need to be deprived of the opportunity to observe the demeanour of the witnesses. Audio tapes are already widely used and, in the course of a trial, may be replayed so that a jury can hear part of the evidence again. There is no real reason why they should be denied the benefit of a video tape in these circumstances. No doubt there would need to be safeguards to avoid tampering with the tapes, but such safeguards have been incorporated to preserve the integrity of audio tapes and there is no reason to imagine why similar safeguards could not be incorporated to ensure the integrity of video tapes. Appellate judges would no doubt fear that such a proposal would open the floodgates, but that need not be so. There would be nothing to prevent the legislature from providing that a 'full' appeal with recourse to the actual video tapes be limited to cases in which certain stipulated criteria are met.

In any event, any additional costs must be considered in the light of the other costs already accepted by the community. In many cases it may be quicker to watch the video tape of a particular witness than to embark upon a lengthy and esoteric debate about whether the point at issue really depends upon the credibility of the witness or upon issues drawn from his evidence. The cost of needlessly confining a prisoner for many years is also considerable and regard must be paid to the cost, in a wider sense, of maintaining questionable convictions.

An alternative approach to the use of video tapes might be to clothe appellate courts with the power to direct that a judge be appointed to conduct a judicial inquiry into the conviction appealed from. At present, one usually has to approach the government of the day although, in New South Wales, a judge of the Supreme Court may initiate such an inquiry of his own motion. Ironically enough, although a New South Wales judge has that power, it has been held that he should not entertain an application from the person concerned who might be in a position to provide him with full details of the reasons for which he considers such an inquiry to be necessary. The consequence of the present system is that decisions are made usually by the State cabinet for considerations which may be purely political.

No doubt, the majority of parliamentarians placed in that situation seek to make their decision on the basis of their understanding of the justice of the cause, but they are necessarily dependent upon what others tell them and it would require a boundless optimist to imagine that a leading member of a major political party convicted of a crime would have as good a chance of obtaining a judicial inquiry from the opposition party as he would from his own. Politics should play no part in the administration of justice.

The transference of this function to the relevant State Court of Criminal Appeal could be accompanied by an amendment to the relevant statute to provide a series of criteria for the granting of such an order. It would clearly be undesirable to open the floodgates and permit every trial to be relitigated before a single judge, but there are cases in which the verdict has been clouded by considerations of a kind which simply cannot be raised in the context of a normal appeal. One might have a case, like the Chamberlain trial, in which there has been immense adverse publicity. Alternatively, one might have a case like the first trial of the late Mr Justice Murphy in which correspondence from jurors raised the possibility that the accused may have been convicted for improper reasons or upon an inadequate basis.

It may also be prudent to provide a general ground enabling an appellate court to grant such an inquiry whenever justice appears to demand it. People seem to become very nervous about enlarging the powers of our courts, but one could safely assume that an appellate court would not act capriciously in this matter and would direct that inquiries be conducted only when there were strong grounds for suspecting that the applicant had been wrongly convicted. Had such a procedure been available, Lindy Chamberlain would probably have been released some two years earlier.

Prosecutors or persecutors?

The reputation for justice which our courts have justly enjoyed has been due, in large measure, to the fairness of our Crown prosecutors. As Mr Justice Deane said recently in Whitehorn v The Queen:

> Prosecuting counsel in a criminal trial represents the State. The accused, the Court and the community are entitled to expect that, in performing his function of presenting the case against an accused, he will act with fairness and detachment and always with the objectives of establishing the whole truth in accordance with the procedures and standards which the law requires to be observed and of helping to ensure that the accused's trial is a fair one.

This role is in stark contrast to the normal role of a barrister who is briefed as an advocate to do his utmost to win a case for a particular client subject only to the rules of ethics which govern his profession. As Michael Adams rightly said in his opening address to the Commission of Inquiry, 'The Crown neither wins nor loses cases.' A prosecutor's 'client' is the State and its interests lie in ensuring that justice is done. It is not his task to 'win' by obtaining a conviction even if the accused was innocent.

Most prosecutors are acutely aware of this distinction and temper their natural desire to present the Crown case effectively with conspicuous fairness. For example, prosecutors normally call

all relevant and credible witnesses available, even if the evidence of some favours the accused rather than the prosecution. However, whilst there are some guidelines, much is left to the discretion of the individual prosecutor.

One recent survey of Crown prosecutors in New South Wales revealed that one-third would always disclose to the defence counsel the criminal record of any Crown witness, one-third would sometimes do so whilst one-third would never make such a disclosure. In other words, despite the duty of fairness, one-third of all Crown prosecutors would have been willing to put someone forward as an apparently credible witness even if he had an extensive record of dishonesty or had previously committed perjury. The very fact that the views of prosecutors could be so divided suggests the need for far more definite rules of conduct.

In many respects, prosecutors enjoy far greater discretion than judges. If a prosecutor decides not to call a witness, then there is no effective means of challenging his decision, but if a judge decided to exclude the evidence of that witness his decision could be reviewed in an appellate court. Equally, a prosecutor is entitled to simply withdraw a case in circumstances in which a judge would have no power to direct that such a step be taken.

In the circumstances, it seems not unreasonable to suggest that a series of rules be drawn up which would offer at least more detailed guidelines for prosecutors. Clearly, these would need to be hammered out in consultation with prosecutors, judges and those who regularly appear for the defence.

It seems equally reasonable to suggest that there should be some means of redress available to people who wish to challenge decisions made by prosecutors. Some may protest that an accused can always appeal but, in recent years, appellate courts have displayed a marked reluctance to interfere with the discretion of prosecutors.

That is understandable to a degree, because it is important to ensure that prosecutors maintain a degree of independence. It is not every decision which should adequately be explained. For example, to explain that a case was dropped because the accused was working as a police informer who had infiltrated a heroin ring might result in his being found floating face down in the harbour.

Yet there is no reason why the relevant legislation should not be amended to provide some right of appeal when a prosecutor has breached the guidelines in some important respect.

There should be no more cases in which important evidence is not heard simply because there is no obligation on the prosecution to call the witnesses.

Mr Justice Watson has also raised the important question of pre-trial disclosure. In his preliminary report to the Commonwealth Attorney-General, entitled *Review of the Criminal Law of the Commonwealth*, he has prepared a code which would require prosecutors to provide the defence with copies of statements made by potential prosecution witnesses and to provide copies of, or access to, items likely to become exhibits. His draft code would also enable the defence to apply for orders requiring the prosecution to disclose other information or evidentiary material. A court, hearing such an application, would be empowered to give directions of various kinds, including directions referring any conflict of scientific opinion, to a panel of experts agreed upon by the prosecution and the defence. These proposals warrant serious consideration.

Forgiving the innocent

The law also should be amended to prevent this anomalous situation in which a person granted a full pardon on the basis that a properly constituted judicial inquiry has found that his conviction could not be sustained may nonetheless remain convicted. It is unjust and absurd. Appellate courts should be clothed with the power to act upon the reports of such inquiries and to quash the relevant convictions where appropriate. If future inquiries were to be appointed by the appellate courts rather than the legislature, it would be a natural progression to require the commissioner to report back to the court which appointed him. Any appropriate orders could then be made in the light of the commissioner's findings.

This type of procedure is by no means novel. Appellate courts frequently remit matters to a single judge. Even single judges frequently remit particular questions to a master or registrar for determination. Ultimately, of course, it is not the choice of procedure that matters, but the fact that there is some real means of redress available to a person who is not willing to accept that a pardon is an adequate response to a finding that his conviction is unjustified. As Lindy Chamberlain put it, 'Would you be happy to be pardoned for something you had never done?'

Compensation and costs

In Australia there is no right to compensation due to wrongful conviction. One is expected to accept that with equanimity. It is merely the 'luck of the draw'. In some cases a person spends months in prison awaiting trial only to be found 'not guilty'. For this enforced stay as a guest of Her Majesty there is also no redress. A person may lose his job, spend his savings on legal fees, have his car repossessed, his house sold by his mortgagee and his wife leave him in despair, only to be told that he was lucky. After all, he was acquitted. If, like Lindy Chamberlain, he is convicted and spends some years in prison before the authorities are constrained to admit that a mistake had been made, he will still be bereft of any legal remedy.

Of course, compensation is paid in some cases, but one must go cap-in-hand to the government which initiated the prosecution and ask for an ex gratia payment. There is no logical reason why this should be so. If the government resumes my land, I may claim compensation and if I don't like what I am offered I may challenge it before an appropriate tribunal. However, if the government takes my body rather than my property, I am powerless. It matters not one whit that my prosecution was due to error, negligence or even the perjury of a police officer or government official. I cannot even claim an order requiring the prosecuting authority to repay what I have spent on legal costs at my trial.

This situation cries out for redress. It is high time the law was amended to permit an application for compensation to be assessed by a judge and for the necesary criteria for its award to be specified.

It is also high time that a successful defendant could depend upon the law to ensure that he would be reimbursed for his legal expenses. The present situation in which a person who successfully defends a lengthy fraud trial may find that his innocence has not staved off bankruptcy is morally indefensible.

For whom the bell tolls

At the end of the day, let us remember that we are all equal before the law. Legislative reform which protects the individual from the risk of wrongful conviction is not merely a matter of pandering to the criminals. It is a matter of enlarging our own rights, of protecting the liberty of our husbands, our wives, our children, our friends and our neighbours. The problem with the head-in-the-sand approach, urged upon us by those who wish to maintain the status quo at all costs, is that we never know which of us might become the next Lindy Chamberlain to be sacrificed upon the altar of conservatism. Some time ago someone posed the question: Surely you can't complain if the system produces the right result in ninety-nine cases out of a hundred? The answer to that question is simple: It all depends on whether you are one of the ninety-nine or whether you are the one left to sit in a small concrete cell and wonder whether your sentence or your sanity will expire first.

Epilogue

ON FRIDAY 22 MAY 1987, Mr Justice Morling called upon the Governor General Sir Ninian Stephen to present him with a copy of his report. Over the weekend he flew to Darwin and on Monday 25 May 1987 made a similar presentation to Commodore Johnston, the Administrator of the Northern Territory.

A few days later it was announced that the Commonwealth had agreed to withhold the report until it had been tabled in the Northern Territory parliament. The media reported that it would be tabled on 11 June, but the view was apparently taken that Azaria's birthday might not be an appropriate occasion. The Attorney-General finally announced that that would occur on Tuesday 9 June 1987. Inquiries about the necessity for a delay of more than a fortnight brought the response that it had to be printed and the government printer could not accomplish such a feat any earlier.

One might have thought that both justice and compassion would have demanded that Lindy and Michael be informed of the results at the earliest possible opportunity. Not only Lindy and Michael, but their sons Aidan and Reagan had lived out a nightmare for the past seven years. They had been reviled and ostracised. Another family in a similar predicament might have been able to simply change cities and start again, but the Chamberlains' names and faces were known throughout Australia. There was no escape. It was as though each one of them bore the mark of Cain on his forehead.

The inquiry had been an added source of strain. The public spotlight had been refocussed and the gauntlet of reporters reassembled. They had sat in court day after day whilst dispassionately objective scientists clinically discussed the manner in which a dingo might have devoured their baby and what telltale signs of blood, tissue and other human debris should have been left on the jumpsuit if it had chosen to eat the head first. From time to time the ordeal proved too much and either Michael or Lindy would leave the court ashen-faced to return when they had regained their composure.

There was also an all-pervading uncertainty. Would the truth again be shrouded in the swirling mists of scientific opinion? Common decency demanded that they be liberated from the agony of suspense at the earliest possible opportunity, especially when it became apparent that virtually the whole of the case which led to their conviction had been misconceived.

Representations were made to the Northern Territory government with the view to obtaining an advance copy of the report. The response could scarcely have been described as magnanimous. The Chamberlains could come to Sydney and be 'locked up' with the report two hours before it was tabled. Once they commenced to read it they would not be allowed to leave the room until it had been tabled in the Northern Territory parliament. They could then expect to be besieged by reporters, but would at least have some idea of the report's contents before they were asked to comment on it. Even for that privilege, they would have to wait a fortnight.

The Chamberlains were not favoured with an excuse for this apparent callousness. If there was one, it probably lay in the need to maintain parliamentary privilege. However, parliamentary privilege is rarely maintained to the point of absolute secrecy, especially if reports have to be printed. There are always secretaries, administrative officers and personnel involved in the actual task of printing who have access to the information. It was difficult to imagine that the fabric of parliamentary democracy would be rent beyond repair by informing the Chamberlains, albeit on a confidential basis, of the judge's ultimate conclusion. Even if the thought that such an elementary act of compassion might constitute some trivial irregularity was anathema to the government, then there was nothing to stop the report being formally tabled on the first available sitting day. No doubt it added a nice professional touch to have copies of the report printed, but the Chamberlains would have been just as happy with a photocopy. Some might also have been radical enough to suggest that if the press had had to wait a few extra days for their copies, it would not have struck a fatal blow to any of the liberties we hold dear. As it was, the delay seemed strangely incongruous, given that Mr Justice Morling and those who assisted him must have laboured long hours to produce the report quickly.

It was also unrealistic to expect to maintain secrecy for such a period. Within a week the overall effect of the report had been leaked to a Sydney journalist, Paul White, who announced it on Channel 9 television.

His announcement produced outraged denunciations and threats that any further publication would result in prosecution. However, there were no denials and the threats amounted to little more than an unseemly rush to shut the barn door after the horse had bolted. Bob Collins called for the report to be tabled on the first day of the next session of parliament rather than a week later and the stimulus of publicity proved able to achieve that which had been impossible when only questions of simple compassion were involved.

The reports were printed in time to be tabled on 2 June 1987. The report was due to be tabled at 11.00 a.m. At 9.00 a.m. Stuart Tipple was permitted to read the report in a lock-up situation in the offices of the Commission's solicitors, Dawson Waldron, in Sydney. A similar lock-up was organised in Darwin but, in accordance with what seemed to be a Northern Territory practice of informing the press before the Chamberlains, journalists were allowed in at 8.00 a.m.

In tabling the report, the Attorney-General referred to Mr Justice Morling's conclusion and commented: 'Mr Speaker, the finding is that the Chamberlains would not be convicted beyond reasonable doubt on the basis of the evidence which is now available. Accordingly, the government has advised the Administrator that each should be pardoned, and he signed orders to that effect this morning.'

The report was received in many quarters with sympathy. At

last, it seemed, the Chamberlains might be given a fair go. Around Australia, many people were fairminded enough to admit that they must have been wrong. Unhappily, this response was by no means universal and television stations reporting the Northern Territory's decision to pardon the Chamberlains received a succession of phone calls from people determined to maintain their belief in Lindy's guilt no matter what Mr Justice Morling's report might have disclosed.

The effect of the report was misunderstood by many. Some stressed that there had been no actual finding that a dingo had taken the child. That was perfectly correct. Mr Justice Morling had been appointed to inquire into doubts as to the Chamberlains' guilt and had maintained that he would confine his inquiry to that issue. The likelihood of dingo involvement was obviously relevant, but he took the view that to even consider whether such a finding should be made would be to reverse the onus of proof.

Some also stressed the fact that he had merely found there was a reasonable doubt as to the Chamberlains' guilt. However, the report made it plain that of the many disputed allegations the Crown had been unable to prove even one beyond reasonable doubt and the vast bulk of them were improbable. But the report went much further than the mere finding that the Crown case had not been proved. It pointed out that in the circumstances now established by the evidence, the Crown case involved a whole series of allegations which were inherently implausible. It also pointed out that there was an extensive body of evidence to support the Chamberlains' claim that a dingo had taken Azaria.

At the end of the day, it was clear that Lindy, Michael, Aidan, Sally Lowe and Greg Lowe had all given evidence of facts fatal to the Crown case. Consequently, if one believed any one of the five, the Chamberlains must be innocent. Equally, if one accepted the views of Derek Roff, Nui Minyinteri and the Winmattis that the tracks which they had seen did display the telltale marks of a dingo with the baby then, again, the Chamberlains must be innocent. If one accepted, as Mr Justice Morling did, that there was little, if any, blood in the car and that the tent contained significant quantities of direct flow blood then, although that fact alone did not prove the matter with absolute certainty, it was overwhelmingly likely that a dingo had taken the child from the tent and that the Chamberlains were innocent. The fact that the scientific evidence relied upon by the Crown had been so thoroughly discredited meant that there was no reason why the strong body of evidence in the Chamberlains' favour should not be accepted.

Lindy and Michael were relieved that the truth had at last emerged, but eager to fight on until their convictions were quashed. Strangely enough, this seemed to cost them a lot of sympathy. People felt that they should have been more gracious and accepted that their pardons were adequate. Yet few might have adhered to such tolerant views if they were asked to remain convicted murderers.

There was also widespread opposition to the payment of any compensation. Paul Everingham suggested that the Chamberlains had been partly responsible for their own plight. They had failed to call relevant evidence at the trial. Mr Justice Morling had expressed surprise that some witnesses had not been called, but he had not suggested that their evidence would have been decisive. In any event, it was plain that the decision to call witnesses had been a matter for the Chamberlains' legal advisers and that their convictions had really been attributable to an extraordinary series of scientific errors and misconceptions. It was difficult to see how even the Northern Territory government could have blamed Lindy and Michael Chamberlain for that. They had cooperated with the authorities in every way possible. Paul Everingham was also to suggest that compensation was unnecessary because they had 'commercialised' the matter. That was presumably a reference to an amount which had been paid by a section of the media for their story. The money was not, however, paid to the Chamberlains, but to the Seventh Day Adventist Church which had advanced massive sums for legal fees. No final accounting has yet been completed, but at the time of writing the Chamberlains' debts are approaching two million dollars. The notoriety has left them in a situation in which it is almost impossible to find some acceptable form of employment. The emotional toll on their sons has been enormous. Aidan, in particular, has repeatedly been described as the murderer for whom Lindy covered up. Mr Justice Morling expressly rejected any such suggestion, but Aidan has had to live with these devastating accusations for half of his lifetime. Kahlia has settled down and formed a close bond with Lindy, but only time will tell what impact the deprivation of a mother during those early years may have had.

Mr Everingham was also moved to offer the comment that if the Chamberlains had never taken their baby to Ayers Rock, the Northern Territory would be ten million dollars better off. The Chamberlains, for their part, have even greater reason to regret their visit to Ayers Rock. But it must not be forgotten that it was the Northern Territory authorities who permitted the dingo attacks in the Ayers Rock camping areas to go unchecked and who failed to warn people like the Chamberlains of the dangers. It was also the Northern Territory government which initiated the prosecution — a prosecution, as it turned out, completely misconceived.

The government is entitled to point out that it was not to know how badly it had been misled by the experts but, even in a civil case where an unsuccessful defendant suffers nothing more grievous than an order to pay money, the law takes the view that a person who brings an unsuccessful action should pay the costs the defendant has incurred in meeting it. It can scarcely be doubted that the Chamberlains should be entitled to at least the same degree of protection as that which the law offers someone unsuccessfully sued for a civil debt.

But this was not merely a case in which someone was ordered to pay money. It was a case which shattered the lives of the Chamberlains, both parents and children alike. No sum of money could adequately compensate them for what they have endured, but simple justice surely demands that they be given enough money to pay the debts which they incurred in defending themselves, to provide a fresh start uninhibited by lifetime insolvency and to tide them over for the first two or three years until they can find a means of earning a normal living again.

This had proven to be a case of strange coincidences. One further coincidence was to be mentioned by Paul Heinrich, a Ph.D. student studying communications in Chicago. The Book of Daniel in the Old Testament recounts the story of three faithful Hebrews,

Shadrach, Meshach and Abednego, who were thrown into a fiery furnace because they refused to worship anyone but the God whom they acknowledged. The furnace was heated seven times hotter than usual and those who threw them into the fire were themselves consumed. Yet the king who had ordered their execution saw that they were unharmed and that a fourth man stood in the fire with them. Not surprisingly, this impressed the king who ordered them brought out and promoted them to positions of authority.

The three men had been given Babylonian names. Intriguingly, Azaria is the feminine form of Azariah, the Hebrew equivalent of Abednego, Michael is the anglicized version of Mishael the Hebrew equivalent of Meshach, and Alice, Lindy's first name, has the same meaning as Shadrach. But perhaps the strangest feature was the occupation of these three men. They were chamberlains to the king.

Unlike Shadrach, Meshach and Abednego of old, the Chamberlains have not emerged from the furnace of hate, prejudice and tragedy unscathed. Michael and Lindy have suffered much and they will not be reunited with Azaria in this life. Yet they, too, sense that there has been a fourth man in the fire with them. Their faith in Christ remains strong and they are certain that he has sustained them through these bleak years and, even now, is leading them out of the fire to reinstate them into the community. There are times when they have been crushed and times when their faith has been overwhelmed by despair. These are flesh-and-blood people, not storybook saints. Yet they have endured, maintained their trust in each other and clung together as a family. Now they are taking their first faltering steps to forge a new life. They are confident that their faith has been vindicated.

In our community, of course, there is no king who can order these things on pain of death. There are governments who will, ultimately, make decisions about such practical matters as compensation, but no government can order a community to give a family 'a fair go'. It would be a shame if they were not, for there is something special about the Chamberlains. There is a faith, not only in God but in their fellow man, which is remarkable, given the experiences of the last few years. One gets the impression that even now Lindy would be prepared to affirm that if one person turned to God as a result of Azaria's death and the personal tragedy which followed, it would all be worth it. Like Shadrach, Meshach and Abednego, they have been worthy witnesses to the God whom they so obviously trust.

It now falls to the Australian community to decide how it will treat these people: whether it will welcome them back with warmth, sympathy and even admiration or whether it will continue to provide a climate of suspicion and hostility. We have the capacity to drive these people from our midst, to force them to live overseas as virtual refugees. Yet the Chamberlains have faith in us. They still believe that there is sufficient fairness and decency in the community to permit them to re-establish a normal and productive life among us. Only time will tell whether we are worthy of that faith.

They are also anxious for the plight of others who may have been unjustly convicted. One of the discomforting things about a case such as this is that it reveals inadequacies in the system, inadequacies which may have led to the wrongful conviction of others. It is a prospect which we would rather ignore. Yet it is undeniable that mistakes are made and that, even now, there may be innocent men and women locked away in Australian prisons. It is essential that any material which points to a possible miscarriage of justice be adequately investigated and that the predictable reluctance to permit a full review of such cases, due to fear of opening the floodgates or incurring further public expense, be resolutely rejected.

It is also imperative that some of the flaws in our system which have been exposed by this case be examined. No risk of injustice should be tolerated if there is any practicable means of eliminating it. These issues provide a considerable challenge to lawyers, scientists, police and, ultimately, to the community at large. One must learn from the lessons of the past. We are all entitled to expect that the community will do everything possible to ensure that we are never placed in the position of Lindy or Michael Chamberlain. This will not be quick or easy.

As Lindy put it when she came home, 'The battle has just begun.'

Glossary

A list of some of the key participants

Adams, Michael
Counsel for Crown at the Morling Inquiry

Barker, Ian QC
Senior prosecuting counsel

Barritt, Dennis
Coroner at the first inquest

Baudner, Dr Siegried
Director of Behringwerke, West Germany

Baxter, Dr Simon
Senior forensic biologist, NSW

Boettcher, Prof. Barry
Professor of Biological Science, University of Newcastle, NSW

Bradley, Prof. Keith
Professor of Anatomy, University of Melbourne

Brechwoldt, Roland
Dingo expert, NSW

Bresee, Prof. Randolph
Textile expert, Kansas, USA

Brown, Sgt Irvine Gregory
Queensland Police, Mount Isa

Brown, Dr Kenneth
Dentist, University of Adelaide

Caldwell, William (now QC)
Counsel assisting at the Morling Inquiry

Cameron, Prof. James
Forensic pathologist, London

Cawood, Ian
Deputy Chief Ranger, Uluru National Park

Chaikin, Prof. Malcolm
Textile expert, University of New South Wales

Chapman, Ken
Scientist, Cooranbong, NSW

Charlwood, Det. Sgt Graeme
(later Det. Inspector)
Northern Territory Police

Cocks, Sgt Frank
South Australian Police

Corbett, Dr Lawrence
Dingo expert, CSIRO

Cornell, Dr Findlay
Biologist, NSW

Cozens, Pastor Bert
Seventh Day Adventist minister from Alice Springs

Crispin, Ken
Counsel for Chamberlains at the Morling Inquiry

Culliford, Dr Bryan
Forensic biologist, Metropolitan Police Laboratory, London

Dean, Peter
Solicitor for the Chamberlains at the inquests

Downs, Bobbie (now Mrs Roberta Elston)
Nurse at Ayers Rock

Everingham, Paul
Former Chief Minister and Attorney-General of the Northern Territory

Fernhead, Prof. Ron
Odontologist, Japan

Ferris, Prof.
Forensic pathologist, Canada

Fowler, Dr Craig
Forensic biologist, SA

Fullerton, Elizabeth
Counsel for the Crown at the Morling Inquiry

Galvin, Jerry
Coroner at the second inquest

Gilroy, Inspector Michael
Northern Territory Police, Alice Springs

Goodwin, Wally
Tourist who found Azaria6s jumpsuit

Griffiths, Dr Ross
Textile expert, University of New South Wales

Gufstafson, Prof. Gosta
Odontologist, Sweden

Haby, Edwin Murray
Tourist who found imprint in the sand

Hansell, Mrs Joan
Drycleaner at Mount Isa

Harris, Les
President of the Dingo Foundation

Hart, Floyd
Person who installed radio-cassette unit in Michael Chamberlain's car

Jones, Dr Anthony
Forensic pathologist, Northern Territory

Kirkham, Andrew (now QC)
Defence counsel at second inquest and trial

Kuchel, Rex
Botanist, SA

Kuhl, Mrs Joy
Forensic biologist, NSW (now forensic biologist, NT)

Leach, Prof. Simon
Professor of Immunology, Victoria

Flenehan, Keyth
The bleeding accident victim driven to hospital by the Chamberlains

Lincoln, Dr Patrick
Forensic biologist, London
Lincoln, Sgt John
Northern Territory Police, Alice Springs
Lowe, Greg
Tourist at BBQ area whilst Lindy took Azaria to the tent
Lowe, Sally
Tourist at BBQ area who heard 'dead' baby cry
McAulay, Peter
Commissioner, Northern Territory Police
McCombe, James
Tourist involved in search
McNay, Ashley
Counsel assisting the coroner at the first inquest
Martin, Brian
Solicitor General, NT
Martin, Dr Peter
Forensic biologist, London
Metcalfe, Sen. Constable James
Northern Territory Police
Milne, Dr Irene
Mount Isa medical practitioner who delivered Azaria
Morling, Mr Justice Trevor
Judge at the Morling Inquiry
Morris, Sen. Constable Frank
Northern Territory policeman at Ayers Rock
Muirhead, Mr Justice James
Judge at trial
Murchison, Pastor Cliff and Mrs Avis
Lindy's parents
Nairn, Prof. Richard
Pathologist, Victoria
Newsome, Dr Alan
Dingo expert, CSIRO
Noble, Constable James
Northern Territory policeman at Ayers Rock
Ouchterlony, Dr Orjan
Biologist, inventor of radial immunodiffusion or 'Ouchterlony' technique, Sweden
Pauling, Thomas (now QC)
Prosecuting counsel at trial
Pelton, Dr William
Textile expert, NSW
Phillips, John QC
Senior defence counsel at trial
Pleuckhahn, Prof. Vernon
Forensic pathologist, Victoria
Porter, Chester QC
Senior counsel assisting Morling Inquiry
Ransom, Jenny (nee Richards)
Lindy's friend at Mount Isa
Rice, Phillip QC
Senior counsel for the Chamberlains at the inquests
Robinson, Dr Vivien
Microscopist, NSW
Roff, Derek
Chief Ranger, Uluru National Park, NT

Sanson, Dr Graham
Zoologist, Melbourne
Scott, Dr Andrew
Senior forensic biologist, SA
Scott, Constable Maxwell
Police biologist, NT
Sims, Bernard
Odontologist, London
Smith, Les
Scientist, Cooranbong, NSW
Sturgess, Desmond QC
Counsel assisting coroner at second inquest and prosecuting counsel at trial
Tew, Rohan
Person who assisted Hart in installing radio-cassette unit in Michael Chamberlain's car
Tipple, Stuart
Solicitor for the Chamberlains throughout all proceedings
Torlach, Mr D.M.
Soil expert, NT
West, Judith, William and Catherine
Family in nearby tent at time of Azaria's disappearance
Whittaker, Amy (social worker), *Vernon and Rosalie*
Family in camping area at time of Azaria's disappearance
Winmatti, Nipper
Aboriginal tracker
Winmatti, Barbara (also known as Barbara Tjikadu)
Aboriginal tracker
Winneke, John QC
Senior counsel for the Chamberlains at the Morling Inquiry
Zichy-Woinarski, Brind
Counsel for the Chamberlains at the Morling Inquiry

Judges and counsel involved in the appeals, members of parliament, journalists and others who made public statements are identified in the relevant chapters.